PATRIOTS ACT

PATRIOTS ACT

VOICES OF DISSENT AND
THE RISK OF SPEAKING OUT

Bill Katovsky

THE LYONS PRESS
Guilford, Connecticut
An imprint of The Globe Pequot Press

The Lyons Press is an imprint of The Globe Pequot Press

10 9 8 7 6 5 4 3 2 1

Printed in the United States of America

ISBN-13: 978-1-59228-816-8
ISBN-10: 1-59228-816-2

Library of Congress Cataloging-in-Publication data is available on file.

In loving memory of my father,
Edward Katovsky, who showed me
the path to integrity and honesty.

"We must not confuse dissent with disloyalty. When the loyal opposition dies, I think the soul of America dies with it."

—Edward R. Murrow

"A patriot must always be ready to defend his country against his government."

—Edward Abbey

"It is dangerous to be right when the government is wrong."

—Voltaire

CONTENTS

INTRODUCTION

What is the relationship between patriotism and dissent? Is it defined by an uneasy truce? Or is it an inseparable bond, like blood brothers? Because if dissent is part of our nation's historical DNA, why is political protest often maligned as disloyal and un-American? What must citizens do to reclaim their natural birthright and liberate it from the impoverished language of bumper sticker sentimentality and partisan rancor? What is the price for speaking out and taking a principled stand?

These questions form the backbone of *Patriots Act*. The book's purpose is to honor the defenders of our country's freedoms and civil liberties. Here are interviews with federal whistle-blowers, peace activists, military veterans, members of the media, practitioners of nonviolent civil disobedience, and former high-ranking government officials. They represent the many types of protest found in America. These individuals have exercised their rights, resisting censorship and the restriction of free expression—often with surprising results. Some were publicly vilified as a result of their defiance and outspokenness. Others jeopardized their careers. Several went to jail. They have diverse backgrounds and political views—liberal and conservative, young and old, secular and religious—but they all share a common commitment to speaking the truth, regardless of the consequences. The cumulative effect of their oral histories embodies what is very best about our national character. They also show why it's important to stand vigilant against those who wrap themselves so tightly in our nation's flag that they can neither see nor hear what others are actually saying.

Little good emerges when citizens are asked to submit to the "you-are-either-for-us-or-against-us" standard that the White House has wielded as a jingoistic slogan ever since September 11. This loyalty litmus test, while initially lauded for its moral clarity, devolved into a hollow exercise in fear-based consent and phony, grandstanding patriotism. It intimidated the mainstream news media, which failed to ask tough, skeptical questions when the administration ramped up its military plans to invade Iraq. It poisoned the talk show airwaves with sulfurous, hate-filled content. It weakened the resolve on Capitol Hill to conduct a real war-on-terror debate without fear of reprisal at the voting booth. And it gave rise to the politics of personal destruction, which has significantly impacted the electoral landscape.

Consider the fate of Max Cleland, a dedicated public servant who served one term in the U.S. Senate as a Democrat from Georgia. He is a Vietnam War veteran, triple-amputee, and former head of the Veterans Administration. In 2002, Senator Cleland was defeated by his Republican opponent who ran a television commercial linking him to Osama bin Laden and Saddam Hussein because he had voted against a homeland security amendment still being debated in committee. "Today, there are no manners in politics," says Cleland in *Patriots Act*. "We've seen the viciousness with which the Republican crowd goes after people. With the impact of 9/11, they began trashing everybody as if they were un-American."

Jeff and Nicole Rank are a young Texan couple who were interviewed for *Patriots Act* because they had been arrested for wearing anti-Bush T-shirts during the president's visit to Charleston, West Virginia, on the Fourth of July in 2004. "It takes a lot of guts to stand up, especially when there's a mob mentality about," says Jeff. "Large numbers of the crowd began chanting against us. It became surreal. "America the Beautiful" was playing on the loudspeakers while we were being walked out in handcuffs by the cops. Post-9/11, a lot of people got caught up behind the flags they were waving and didn't stop to think about what those flags really stood for. It certainly has cost us, both on a personal and financial level, but unless people exercise their constitutional rights, those rights will erode."

California Army National Guard Staff Sergeant Lorenzo Dominguez, forty-five, was selected for *Patriots Act* because he had put himself at risk by speaking on the record with a *Los Angeles Times* reporter investigating training and equipment problems with his battalion unit about to deploy to Iraq. After the story appeared, Dominguez's military superiors stripped him of his command and weapon. "The base's upper command accused me of endangering the military and possibly aiding the enemy," says Dominguez. "I was told by the public affairs officer that the *L.A. Times* article would probably be grabbed onto by Al Qaeda and Al Jazeera, and that we would be shown to be unmotivated and unwilling to fight. That's so untrue. I loved my men and I didn't want anything to happen them. I had to lead by example. How could I not put my name to my objections? I was responsible for nine men in my squad as their squad leader. I made commitments to them and to most of their mothers and fathers that I would bring them back home from Iraq in one piece."

Neither Dominguez nor the Ranks belong to fringe extremist groups. In civilian life, Dominguez is vice president at a mortgage bank in Southern California. He's always voted Republican and has a daughter and young son, Reagan, named after the fortieth president. Jeff Rank is a first-year law student, and Nicole works for the Federal Emergency Management Agency, which attempted to fire her after the Charleston incident.

Daniel Ellsberg was one of the book's final interviews. In 1971, he leaked the Pentagon Papers to the *New York Times* because he wanted to help stop the Vietnam War. By releasing those top-secret documents, which detailed how the U.S. government had deliberately lied to the public about Vietnam, Ellsberg knew that he was crossing a line that could lead to life imprisonment. Yet he was prepared to take that step because to do otherwise was to abandon his conscience. Now nearly four decades later, the seventy-four-year-old peace activist is seeing the same tragic war movie unfold with only minor differences. "In Iraq, it's desert, not jungles, and the insurgents are fighting in the cities, not the countryside," he says. In the current political climate, he encourages others in government and in society to come forward and tell the truth. Ellsberg's request is not always the easiest thing to heed, because in times of war there's a trigger-happy tendency to single out dissenters by labeling them "enemies" or "traitors," which only amplifies the personal risks for whistle-blowers, activists, and protesters.

The nation grows weaker, not stronger, when dissident voices are silenced and civil liberties stripped away. Benjamin Franklin said it best: "Any society that would give up a little liberty to gain a little security will deserve neither and lose both." In the weeks and months following 9/11, the U.S. government detained thousands of foreign nationals from Arab-speaking countries because of suspected ties to terrorism. America has weathered similar government abuse in the past. During the Second World War, 100,000 Japanese-Americans were shipped off to internment camps. In the 1950s, the House Un-American Activities Committee began to aggressively target alleged communist sympathizers. Against the backdrop of the Cold War, careers and lives were ruined by highly politicized witch hunts. President Harry S. Truman remarked, "I think the Un-American Activities Committee in the House of Representatives was the most un-American thing in America!" The McCarthy era was characterized by paranoia and suspicion. Some see disturbing parallels with that dark period occurring in our own time.

It remains vital for each generation to renew its commitment to our nation's democratic values. The long-term health of America's political institutions suffers when that democratic spirit calcifies, hardening into something exclusionary, divisive, and rigid. Those who challenge the status quo in meaningful and constructive ways are integral to our democratic tradition. It is our moral and civic duty to acknowledge what these patriots stand for and what they have sacrificed in the process. I hope this book calls attention to their courage under fire.

Bill Katovsky
Northern California
January 2006

1

MR. RUCKUS SOCIETY

John Sellers is an impresario of the bold, nonviolent
political statement.

> "Nonviolent civil disobedience has really been
> maligned. Oftentimes the violence done to people
> of nonviolent means is then turned around and
> projected back onto them, so it looks like they
> deserve what they got. Then it's easier for protests
> to be dismissed or marginalized by the media."

John Sellers has perfected the art of creating bold political statements. Here are
three attention-getting examples from his direct-action past: In the dead of winter, he climbed the Sears Tower with three fellow anti-nuke activists and unfurled
a massive banner; to raise awareness of the dwindling ancient redwood groves
in Northern California, he was part of a small crew of stealth protesters—actor
Woody Harrelson was among them—who erected an anti-logging message over
the Golden Gate Bridge; and in Washington, D.C., he sneaked onto the roof of the
World Bank building with a female partner before unveiling a "Bankenstein" banner. Each of these well-planned actions netted a publicity jackpot of international
press coverage.

Sellers, thirty-nine, is the executive director of the Ruckus Society, which the
San Francisco Chronicle calls "the graduate school for the protest movement."
Ruckus holds action camps where participants learn skills like radio communication, logistics, blockading, passive resistance while being arrested, urban-building
climbing, media relations, and advanced direct-action role playing. Like Sellers,
many of Ruckus's trainers have backgrounds in Greenpeace, Rainforest Action
Network, and Earth First!. They have street and forest cred.

Sellers is inspired by the lofty idealism of peaceful civil disobedience. His heroes are Gandhi, Dr. Martin Luther King, Jr., and Rosa Parks. When he stages a
direct action, his *modus operandi* is to maintain message discipline and safety for

1

all participants. Sellers's goal is to control the media spin before reporters arrive on the scene.

In 1999, Ruckus achieved international notoriety as one of the key organizers behind the anti-World Trade Organization demonstration in Seattle where 50,000 activists surrounded the WTO meeting site. The police employed unnecessary and excessive force to break apart the human wall. "Seattle was really a cop riot," says Sellers. "The cops lost their cool. The feds wanted the WTO meeting opened at all costs."

To many young Americans coming up in the activist movement, Sellers is admired as a kind of postmodern archdruid, a media-savvy champion of the fight against corporate greed. *Mother Jones* magazine named him "Hellraiser of the Month." Sellers certainly has spent many Thoreauvian nights in jail. He's lost exact count of the times he's been arrested for his daring acts of civil disobedience. It's between thirty and forty, he estimates.

Although he's never been convicted of a felony charge, he's constantly red-flagged on law-enforcement computers. A Philadelphia judge once set his bail at one million dollars during the 2000 Republican National Convention. The mainstream media play right along with this exaggerated characterization of Sellers as an anarchist mastermind. During the 2004 Republican National Convention in New York, *ABC Nightline* named him "one of the twenty most dangerous anarchists in the country." The NYPD assigned an undercover detail to follow him around town.

But cops often find themselves enjoying the company of the smooth-talking Sellers. On the last night of the 2004 convention, the NYPD undercover detective squad hung out with Sellers as they cheerfully swapped notes with one another. Sellers encourages an open dialogue with police officers. When he's coordinating a banner-hanging on a building or structure, he will tell cops that the climbers will eventually come down and that everyone would be safer if they waited until then before making arrests. Even SWAT teams called to the site often express professional admiration for a well-executed Ruckus action.

Ruckus is less than ten years old and was co-founded by Mike Roselle, a prominent and legendary eco-warrior. With its six full-time staff members and annual budget of $700,000, Ruckus is run from a downtown Oakland office. Sellers does the majority of fund-raising himself. The non-profit organization remains a darling of socially progressive companies like Patagonia and Working Assets. Despite its small size, Ruckus wields considerable influence since its methods and practices are widely imitated by many grassroots and environmental groups.

Sellers' wife, Genevieve, is also a committed activist. The couple's first arrest together was in Houston following a protest against big oil. "When she entered the courtroom, she just looked so beautiful in her orange jumpsuit," Sellers recalls wistfully. They have one-year-old twins, Hazel and Sam, who were born on election day, 2004.

■   ■   ■

I grew up in a little town in Pennsylvania called Phoenixville—old steel town, probably one of the first. Made the steel for the Brooklyn Bridge. The steel mill closed when I was a little kid. Phoenixville is right next to Valley Forge, so it's kind of in the suburbs of Philadelphia now.

Both my parents were in unions. My mom was a fourth-grade teacher, and my pop made tires in a rubber mill for Goodrich Tires. Every couple of years they would walk the picket line. We would get nasty calls sometimes from parents when my mom was out on strike. They'd say, "How dare you! You have a responsibility to the school kids!" My father had a teaching degree but he thought he could make more money in the factory. He wasn't around a lot because he often worked the midnight-to-eight shift. I have a sister, Elizabeth, who is three and a half years younger than me.

I remember this one big family road trip we took to the Everglades. I had an environmental epiphany there. I was eight or nine years old. This beautiful park ranger was giving us an ecology tour. She took us out in this marsh and had us all take our shoes off and walk into this marsh. The mud was squeezing between our toes as she talked about how this ecosystem was dependent on the water that flowed. The Everglades was this giant, wide, slow-moving river. This marsh supported the darter snail, which was the staple food for the whooping cranes, these unapologetic, uncompromising birds that wouldn't eat anything else. They flew across the planet when they migrated, and this was an important stop for them. Because industry was carving up the Everglades, the darter snails were getting fewer and farther between, and that was impacting these whooping cranes. I guess a light bulb went off in my head. My sister was also inspired by what she was hearing. When we got home she totally shamed me by writing to our senator. A couple years afterward, I was lying on the floor of the den and watching 60 *Minutes* and there was this piece on Greenpeace. I watched these crazy hippie commandos put themselves in front of grenade-tipped whale harpoons in their little boats and hang from oil rigs and sail in nuclear-test zones. I could feel the hair standing up on my arms and the back of my head. And that is when I decided what I wanted to do when I grew up.

I got my mom to buy me Save the Seals and Save the Whales T-shirts. I was kind of a misfit in junior high. I had one really close friend. We were smoking dope from a pretty early age, and were left of center—but didn't know it. During the last couple years of high school, we fell into a group of other misfits. We practiced random acts of sabotage. We went to rich people's neighborhoods and played mailbox baseball with bats. We made our own little firecrackers. I played soccer and tennis in school. Our tennis team went undefeated all four years. You could be a misfit and play tennis in my school. It was not a glory sport. It was like being in the band.

I couldn't wait to get out of Phoenixville. I went to college in upstate Pennsylvania out by Pittsburgh. It was Indiana University of Pennsylvania, in a town called Indiana. Jimmy Stewart is from there. The college was just cheap enough for my family to afford, about $4,000 a year for room and board. I didn't realize until I got out there that western Pennsylvania is like the Deep South: a super redneck, racist place. But fortunately, I somehow landed in the international student hall. I was in a dormitory with African kids and Asian kids and European kids and South American kids. I had a friend next door; he was from Cameroon. He was in his thirties. The guy had moved mountains to get himself an education. It was incredible. He got to school with only the clothes on his back from Africa.

I fell in with the punk rock crowd my freshman year and started cutting my hair shorter and shorter. I shaved stripes into my head, started to wear the trench coats and Converse Chuck Taylor sneakers. One of my best friends was Newt Gingrich's younger sister, Candace. She is now the national spokesperson for the Human Rights Campaign. We took a class on the sociology of human sexuality, and she came out during that class. It was her sophomore year. Newt was in Congress. She was so proud when *Hustler* named him "Asshole of the Month." Candace was a hard-core jock and rugby player, and we had some great parties in her room.

I got really political. I was inspired by economic, social, and racial justice. I loved Marx and Engels' critique of capitalism. I read Max Weber. I thought he had an interesting analysis of how the human desire for power will almost always lead to exploitation of some kind. I was into Toni Morrison, Kurt Vonnegut, and Tom Robbins. Robbins actually lives across the street from my wife's family in La Conner, Washington. I got to hang out with him in the room where he wrote *Even Cowgirls Get the Blues*. That book was *huge* for me.

During my first couple of years in college, I had the zeal of the recently converted. I was such a self-righteous shit. My dad once took me out for a nice prime rib dinner, and I was such a little smartass as I tried to break down capitalism for him. I wanted to make him understand how he was a puppet of the system by working in the tire factory. Yet here was my dad working twelve-hour days from midnight until the afternoon and busting his ass to get me to college, and I gotta tell him that he was part of the exploited proletariat. We definitely had some awkward years there for a while.

The school was mostly white kids, but there were a number of African-American kids from Pittsburgh. It was a pretty intense racial divide, so we started a group called Students Organized Against Racism, or SOAR. We started a sociology club and political coffeehouse called the Free Zone. I got to be a fairly well-known person on campus from the sociology club.

During summers, I worked in a factory that made big fake marble bathroom sinks. It was super-toxic. Limestone and liquid polyester were mixed with different color dyes. It cooks through a chemical process. It would stick to your skin so you were constantly washing your hands in acetone up to your elbows to get this shit off you. Most everybody else were African-American folks from the poor side of Phoenixville. I got to waltz off back to school at the end of the summer. Everybody else was stuck there.

After I graduated with a sociology and anthropology degree in four and a half years, I moved back home. I started looking for a job with these pretty lackluster credentials. I wanted to go teach English in Egypt. I wanted to travel. My dad's oldest brother was a petrochemical engineer in Australia. He worked for big oil. He lived all over the world. My cousins would regale me with stories of safaris in Africa. And so, when I saved enough money doing landscaping, I flew down to Sydney. My mom helped buy a ticket as a graduation present because it cost $1,700.

My uncle is this incredible self-made man who's got several homes and is worth millions and has his own engineering company. He is a Scientologist. It is just a really interesting family sociology. He's still like my dad. He has junker cars sitting around his yard just like they did when they were growing up, so they could cannibalize two cars to make one car go. I stayed at his house when I first got there, in the suburbs of Sydney. He was then managing the largest oil refinery in the Southern Hemisphere which is at Cronulla Bay. Greenpeace was actually doing actions there, plugging the company's outfall pipes to stop its wastewater from going into the ocean. Greenpeace is huge in Australia and gets incredible news coverage that it doesn't get here. So every day I'd be watching the news and my uncle would come home and throw stuff around, yelling, "Those Greenie bastards were out there again!"

I lived in Australia for six months. I learned to scuba dive on the Great Barrier Reef in Cairns. I picked grapes for a while just above Melbourne and just got killed by the sun. It was 130 degrees during the day. I saw incredible beauty and incredible environmental devastation. I then spent a couple months in New Zealand and Fiji. In New Zealand, I actually rode around in a bus that Greenpeace operates for backpackers. I dove to the wreck of the *Rainbow Warrior*.

When I came back to America, I was twenty-four years old and deep in debt. I got a job as a foreman for a company that was building decks and retaining walls. The owner ended up being a shyster jerk. And so, I went down to the Greenpeace office in Philadelphia for an interview. They gave me a job right away. I didn't realize at the time that they pretty much would hire any warm body. The job was canvassing, which was based on a percentage. There was no risk in hiring somebody, because if you didn't raise any money, then you didn't get paid.

We canvassed in the Philadelphia suburbs of New Jersey and Pennsylvania. The first night I got dropped off in Cherry Hill, New Jersey. Probably about every third home had a white marble entryway and plastic slipcovers all over the furniture in the living room. I thought I was in hell. It was tough going. I'd knock on doors from five until nine in the evening. But I ended up being a pretty good canvasser. I felt very strongly about the issues that I was talking about. I was comfortable asking middle-class people for $50 to $100, which is interesting. Because when I came out to the West Coast and started running Ruckus, I had to ask rich people for $5,000 or $10,000, and then a lot of class issues came out for me. I felt like a squirrel looking for a nut.

After about two or three months in the Philadelphia office, I got fast-tracked and became a field manager. I was now driving a van full of canvassers. They were mostly white kids. One of the women in the office was an Amish girl who had defected from Pennsylvania Dutch culture. There was a Quaker girl who practiced witchcraft. There was a lot of turnover in this canvassing world. Lots of drinking and partying. The whole reason that I was willing to canvass was that I wanted to do direct actions for Greenpeace. I wanted to sail with their ships. At that time, there were seven or eight ships. Today, there's about four ships. Its maritime division is based in Amsterdam. That is where Greenpeace International made some decisions about the kind of ships that they wanted to operate because of budget cuts. Greenpeace in the U.S. is probably about half the size it was back in its heyday. Greenpeace just doesn't have the public notoriety that it had when it was literally changing the world. Back then, when I was involved with Greenpeace, you were really proud of Greenpeace and how radical it was. How it pressured the system from the outside. But Greenpeace has become much more institutional, and its ranks have swelled with career activists and bureaucrats. It makes people more cautious.

Anyway, Greenpeace at that time had a nonviolent action team. Still does. There was this cement kiln facility in Bath, Pennsylvania, which was not too far from Philly. They were using toxic flammable waste to fire the kiln. They had actually received a commendation from the U.S. government for creatively disposing toxic waste. They had expanded their permit so they could burn chlorinated compounds. Our toxics campaign targeted this place, but in order to scout the facility, Greenpeace asked me and another guy to drive out there and pose as documentary filmmakers from Temple University. We told the company that we were making a documentary on the re-emergence of industrialism on the East Coast. We actually got the company president on film. He took us inside, bragged about his government award. The guy was just totally delighted and honored to be in the film. We mapped out the whole facility, drove around it, filmed it, looked at all the entrances where the actual waste trucks were coming in. Really dialed it in. I think we did a real thorough job. Greenpeace's East Coast action coordinator was so impressed with our scouting job that I was invited to be in the actual action itself. So that became my first action.

We went to a farm in upstate Pennsylvania and trained for three or four days. Our plan was that we would deploy a cargo truck at the most important entrance where the toxic waste came into the facility. We'd block that entrance and jump out of the truck and cover it with banners explaining the toxic-waste issue. We'd then chain ourselves up under the truck. I was working with another woman who was a toxics campaign intern from New York. She was going to be my partner. It was late fall and we wore big padded union suits. We cut sleeping bag pads to fit inside our suits so that we could lay on the cold ground for hours. We were wearing diapers. We also had a long steel tube to lock our arms in. It was cut at a right angle and welded together so that it could go over the axle, and we would each place one of our arms inside the tube from opposite directions.

We ended up pulling off the action and chaining ourselves under the truck. Because we each had an arm up over the rear axle of the truck, we were on both sides of the tire; they couldn't move the truck without running one of us over. It took them about eight hours to cut us out. They had to remove the floorboards from inside the truck. The president came out and recognized me. He was so pissed off. The state troopers were playing good cop and bad cop. At the end of the day we got arrested. It was amazing and inspiring to have crossed that line, to do something where you are heeding a higher moral calling. The U.S. toxics campaign at that time was just really kicking butt. And they actually got a full-blown moratorium on the construction of any new incinerators. That particular cement kiln was later declined a permit to burn even more dangerous compounds.

We spent maybe twenty-four to thirty-six hours in jail. Greenpeace has great lawyers. They almost always pay the bail amount, which was $5,000 that time. I didn't start getting tremendous bail amounts until much later. I was really naive in that arrest. I didn't know that much about the legal system then, or the difference between different levels of misdemeanor. I pleaded guilty to one of the highest levels of charges. No contest, *nolo contendere*, to a criminal mischief charge. That is a high-level misdemeanor. It is one of the things that comes up on computers. In fact, I have been permanently requested to never visit Canada again by the Canadian authorities. In 2004, I had flown to Vancouver. I was on my way up to the Canadian Arctic to support the work of indigenous youth who are fighting a giant oil pipeline coming out of the Beaufort Sea through the McKenzie River Valley. Instead, I got arrested for the day. They locked me up at the bottom of the airport and then sent me back on another plane. The Canadian government has these incredible computers, because it finds more of my arrests than just about anybody when it runs me through its system. What's interesting with folks who practice nonviolent civil disobedience is that what often remains in the computer system is what you get charged with, rather than what you get convicted of. Because Canada has a two-tier system—civil and criminal—a lot of my high-level misdemeanors fall into the criminal category. Therefore, they can refuse my entry on those grounds. Canada looks for activism coming up. The U.S. looks for pot coming down. Best pot in the world is grown in Canada.

Anyway, after we did this action at the kiln, Greenpeace fast-tracked me toward more responsibility and more action training. I got invited to what turned out to be the last action camp that Greenpeace ever did. It became the model that Ruckus stole or borrowed. It was held outside of Silver Springs, Florida, at a children's camp. The action camp was just remarkable. There were 150 people from all over the world. We practiced urban-climbing techniques and banner-hanging on scaffolding four or five stories high. There was a lake where we practiced boat-driving skills with inflatable Zodiacs. Some of the old dogs were there, the people who had inspired me when I was ten years old. I met Mike Roselle, who is the main founder of Ruckus. He was my nonviolence trainer. He talked about mass civil disobedience in which they would get hundreds or even thousands of people arrested, and then the action would continue into the jails and clog up the system itself. It was an awe-inspiring nine days.

After Tampa, I got hired as the assistant director of the Greenpeace office in Washington, D.C. Both the local office and the national headquarters were right in the same building. I was in charge of the local office for about five years. We were the largest and most effective local office in the country. We raised over a million dollars a year. I worked on several local campaigns. One dealt with the toxic Anacostia River, which runs through the poorest neighborhoods in Washington. Predominantly African-American communities. The river is superpolluted. A lot of people say, "Oh, those poor, black neighborhoods don't take care of their river." If you really look at it, however, most of the sewage and waste is coming out of some of the wealthiest suburbs in Maryland where the headwaters of the river are. It's actually rich white people shitting in the river and poor black people getting blamed for it. The older folks in the neighborhood remember swimming in the Anacostia when they were young. Now, no one can think of anything more dangerous than swimming in that river. And all that has happened within five or six decades. If that had happened overnight, you'd think people would be up in arms about it. But because it happened just slow enough within a few generations we were able to rationalize it. We have antiquated sewage systems all over the United States. Lots of people in Los Angeles, for example, are finding that out now. There are a bunch of beaches that aren't safe to swim in due to sewage pollution. One of my favorite movie lines is from *Moonstruck*. Olympia Dukakis says, "Don't shit where you eat!" It's so commonsensical. Almost any animal understands this, but human beings do it all the time.

Waste incineration is an another example of shitting where we eat. Our office helped a group from East Liverpool, Ohio, build a mock toxic incinerator out of a big truck that Greenpeace called Big Bird. We covered the truck with messages about incineration. We stopped Big Bird in the middle of Pennsylvania Avenue right in front of the White House. We had maybe eighty to a hundred people chained all around this truck in concentric circles. Martin Sheen came out and handcuffed himself in one of those loops. We had a smokestack on top of the truck billowing fake smoke. Can you imagine doing this now on Pennsylvania Avenue? The head of the White House Secret Service later said to me, "So, John, nice deployment." I was like, "Huh! They know who I am?" This was an honor. But what a dubious distinction to have been given.

I did other D.C. actions, including one against the World Bank. I did this with my friend, Sebia Hawkins, who is a Greenpeace legend in the South Pacific. It was on the fiftieth anniversary of the World Bank. The World Bank is such a mysterious thing. It is in downtown Washington. I once overheard some tourists walk by the World Bank building and say, "Hmm. I've never seen ATM machines for that one around." On the day of our action, we dressed up looking corporate. We went into the office building right next door to the World Bank.

I was carrying a big squash bag with some racquets sticking out, but the bag was also full of climbing anchors and all this really heavy climbing gear. Sebia is this beautiful Greenpeace hippie chick. She's got hairy legs and her leg hairs are poking through her stockings. We opened the door to the delivery entrance and brought in the climbing team and this big banner. We took the elevator to the roof of the building and waited till some smokers left, and then we traversed the roofline over to the World Bank. We used their window-washing anchors and set up a bunch of our ropes. We then hung a giant banner on the side of the building. It was Frankenstein with a giant chainsaw. It said: "World Bankenstein. 50 Years is Enough." We got really good media coverage for that action.

One of my biggest climbing actions was the Sears Tower in 1992. A friend of mine, Claire Greensfelder, who worked in the No Nukes campaign for Greenpeace, started thinking about the fiftieth anniversary of the first sustained nuclear reaction, which happened on December 2, 1942, at the University of Chicago underneath the squash court. We knew that the Nuclear Regulatory Commission and nuke advocates from around the world would be in Chicago to celebrate fifty years of nuclear energy. There was no way we were going to let their pro-nuke pep rally go off unchallenged. We wanted to metaphorically piss on their atomic bonfire. Because Chicago's symbol to the world is the Sears Tower, we decided that we would climb it and hang a banner.

We started training one month out. In most building-climbing situations, you try to sneak up to the roof and then rappel down. But in this climb we decided to work with these crazy engineers. The coordinator of this climb was Dave Hollister, who designed some aluminum devices that we would use as cams inside the window-washing tracks. This would allow us to start at the base of the Sears Tower and climb up the outside of the building. It is 110 stories. We had no illusions that we were going to climb up the whole side of the building, although you could with these devices. If we climbed the whole building and hung the banner at the top, nobody would have been able to see it. So our strategy was to climb about thirty floors up, or about 400 feet off the ground.

There were four of us. We actually built a piece of window-washing track in Washington at the Greenpeace equipment center where we practiced climbing. Because we were going to be climbing the side of the Sears Tower in one of the windiest cities in the United States in December, and in the freezing cold, we bought $3,000 worth of cold-weather gear at REI. Once in Chicago, we got a big team to help us with deployment. We got to the side of the building about 5 A.M. It was pitch dark. We looked like spacemen in all our gear. We brought along these big stoppers to stop the window-washing carts from coming down—

because this French climber guy nicknamed Spider Dan had gone up the Hancock Building, and the police came down on the window-washing cart and used high-powered hoses to try to blast him while he was free-climbing the building. The mayor of Chicago had to come out and basically save this guy's life by telling these cops not to blast him off the side of the building. We were painfully aware that we did not want any kind of dynamic confrontation while we were on the side of the Sears Tower.

We put our devices in the window-washing track and started to climb. Right around the first or second floor—we are just twelve feet above the ground—all of us start getting stuck in the track, because it was a slightly different design than the track we had been using. We had to take these screws out of our devices. Three of us got unstuck. I am lifelined to the woman next to me. Her name is Nadine Bloch. We have a rope between us in case one of us falls. Bill Richardson is our pack horse. He is carrying a seventy-pound pack up with the banner, a 2,500-square-foot banner. It's massive. He starts climbing. Diana Wilson is the fourth climber. She literally got stuck for the entire day. She could not get her device free. So she spent the day outside the second floor.

Right around the sixth floor, I get stuck again because the track is a little too narrow. The pins are stopping me from ascending. Just then the firemen roll up in a big ladder engine. I needed to get up around the eighth or ninth floor before the ladder gets there. I am wailing with one device on the side of the building. I took an industrial suction cup, which we all carried as a third point of protection, and placed the cup on the glass. I set it and then tied myself off to it so that I could safely take my cams out of the track. I finally got the damn pins out and I start moving. The ladder is coming up the building. I'm just humping it up the side of the building to get out of harm's way. I end up getting away. I tied back on to Nadine so we would be lifelined to one another. We went up to the thirtieth floor and began deploying the banner. We now are working with three different ropes to hold the banner down and secure it to the side of the building. It's about twenty below zero with the wind-chill factor. It starts to snow and it's blowing a gale. Snow is flying up the side, kinda going up into your nose. We have been up there for several hours now. We are trying to pull the banner down and deploy it on the side of the building. All the different ropes are just spinning around below me in the wind; they were all going through one carabiner on my harness. This gust of wind blows up the side of the building and catches the banner like a giant sail. Kind of like parasailing. As the banner fills with wind, it blows the ropes up and they all get stuck in this carabiner, and I literally start to sail off the building. My climbing devices were designed to keep me safe by my weight pressing them down in the track. All of a sudden my weight is coming off the devices and I am going in reverse, up the building. That was the scariest moment in my life. I could have been pulled right off the building. I didn't know what was going to happen. A 2,500-square-foot sail pushes a really big boat through the water. It was probably catching a thirty-knot wind in it. I was paralyzed with fear. Nadine was screaming, "Get that goddamn carabiner off your harness!" For a split second the wind died down and I was able to take the carabiner, unclip it, and untangle myself from the whole rats' nest of ropes and carabiner. Ten minutes later, we were deploying the banner. Pulling it down nice and taut and tying it onto the building. It was an incredible moment.

The story went global. It made the front pages of newspapers in Japan and China and Australia, with the image of our huge banner. It was a giant, ominous-looking mushroom cloud with a skull peering out of it. Below the mushroom cloud were missiles and radioactive casks of waste. It said: "End the 50 Year Nuclear Nightmare. Nuclear Free Future Now!"

There were a thousand people gathered underneath us. This was spontaneous. We hadn't called for a rally. People were chanting, "Go Greenpeace! Go Greenpeace!" We did a bunch of phone interviews with TV and radio stations while still hanging off the side of the tower. I talked to people inside the building. The windows weren't open. We were just yelling to one another. One of the women called my fiancée at the time and said, "Hey! Your fiancée is right outside the window of my office. I happen to work on the twenty-fourth floor."

Throughout the day, we had been communicating with the police by radio. We had a coordinator on the ground who allowed the cops to use our radio system to communicate with us. They had told us that we'd be arrested. We said we understood that. We were willing to take that responsibility. We had done everything possible to ensure both our own safety and the safety of everyone else. We had lanyards on everything so we wouldn't drop anything. We told the cops that we would be down by the end of the day, that they could arrest us then. We asked them not to endanger firefighters by sending them after us. By the end of the day, the banner had been shredded by the high wind. We stuffed it into different packs and climbed down. Oh man, I was exhausted when my feet touched the sidewalk after hanging out in the freezing cold for eight hours.

The arresting officers were cool with us. They'd been on TV all day. They were very impressed with the action and the skills we had displayed. They kept us in their offices at the station longer than they could have or should have. They were telling us these stories of people who had jumped from buildings. Crazy jumper stories like a woman who jumped off a sixty-story building and whose brains shot out the top of her head and hit some people. It sent them into shock. But when it was time for a shift change, all these grumpy cops came in who didn't know who we were and hadn't spent the day with us. They threw us in the dankest, dirtiest cell that I had been in so far. I got body lice in there. Took that home and gave it to my fiancée. We were in that cell for half a day until Greenpeace bailed us out. We then met all our friends who were there waiting for us. They brought our favorite foods. The media was there. The next day, we were all sitting around the conference table of the Greenpeace office in Chicago. We were debriefing when we got a call from Daniel Ellsberg on the speakerphone. He said, "Good action."

After Chicago, I had a pretty good reputation at Greenpeace. In '95, I was given the opportunity to sail with the *Rainbow Warrior*. I met the ship in northern Spain, in Galicia. I was with that boat just six weeks. We had the BBC and international press on the ship. We sailed out into the Bay of Biscay, just below Ireland, where we got into a crazy confrontation with the French Navy. We were working on drift net fishing. The nets can be ninety miles long. They go from the surface to about one hundred feet down. We call them "curtains of death." They indiscriminately kill everything that gets caught. They catch large and small fish. We saw a baby sperm whale caught up and killed in one of those nets. It was horrible to see. The nets were being used by the French fishing fleet for yellowfin tuna. Greenpeace had been instrumental in bringing the international limit on drift nets to 2.5 kilometers. France was pushing the United Nations to raise the limit to five kilometers. Each country was supposed to police its own vessels. But the French Navy and Greenpeace have fought a lot of battles and go way back. There's a lot of bad blood since they sank the first *Rainbow Warrior* in Auckland Harbor in New Zealand and a photographer was killed.

There were big swells in the bay. I thought I was gonna die for about three days. Greenpeace's campaign director in the Mediterranean told me, "What the hell did the U.S. send you for? You're worthless!" There were about twenty-five or thirty of us on the *Warrior*. The *Warrior* is probably 150 feet long. It's an old trawler that they had fitted with these giant downwind sails. She doesn't have a keel like a sailboat keel. They just poured hundreds of tons of cement into the bottom of her, so she only sails downwind really well. I think she has the largest spinnaker in the world—and what a beautiful and potent symbol of ecology.

We drove these hard-shell inflatables around the North Atlantic looking at the different French drift nets. We used a radar reflector. We would fix a position at one end of the net and use the radar reflector again to measure how long the nets were. We confirmed they were using illegal nets. One day, as this brilliantly insane British guy named Dave Roberts and I were out measuring a French drift net, the *Rainbow Warrior* radioed us and said that she was under attack from a French Navy destroyer and an ocean-going tugboat. The tugboat was much taller than the *Warrior*, and it was using its high-powered water cannons against the ship's bridge. If one of the windows had given way on the bridge, it would have taken away all of our navigation equipment. So Dave drove the inflatable back to the *Warrior* and masterfully started to manipulate the situation to create sensational images to go around the world. At first, Dave drove between the two French warships, charging through a gauntlet of water cannons, trying to drive their fire away from the *Warrior*. The French sailors couldn't reach us. Then, with the BBC cameras rolling, Dave drove straight into their water fire while I stood in the Zodiac's bow and held up a banner which read "Ban Drift Nets Now!" The images of us being deluged by the water cannons were exactly the dramatic confrontation we wanted.

We had so pissed off the guys in the tugboat that one of them threw this black metal pineapple into our little inflatable. This thing came whizzing down and it hit our floorboard. And then *bloosh*! It went off. It was a stun grenade. It knocked us out for several seconds. There was no shrapnel. We weren't injured. The boat wasn't damaged. But it was a pretty sensational thing to have happen to you. And fortunately, the explosion and the plume of smoke were caught on film. The footage went around the world, and the French were accused of blowing up a little Greenpeace inflatable and beating up a bunch of hippies in a sailboat in the middle of the Atlantic and getting caught red-handed. It just proved they weren't even enforcing the drift net limits. International pressure mounted, and the 2.5 kilometer limit stood.

That was my last really big campaign for Greenpeace. When I returned to the U.S., I felt like I needed to challenge myself in other ways. I had been with the organization for six years. I had become a workaholic. I lost my first marriage to the crazy kind of political world I was in. Probably, in hindsight, I should never have gotten married. She also worked for Greenpeace. When we first separated, I was on the *Rainbow Warrior* in the Atlantic, and she was on the *MV Greenpeace* down in the Amazon. We went to different corners of the planet. When we finally broke up, it was a pretty intense time for me. I started to find myself again. Greenpeace had been my only experience in the environmental movement. Because Greenpeace is so large, it is pretty insular. You don't really have to work with a lot of other organizations. You have all these resources. I really wanted to see what the rest of the movement was like. And so, in 1996, I decided to cast myself away from Greenpeace.

But before I left Greenpeace, The Ruckus Society had asked me to be its program director. Ruckus was then based in Missoula, Montana, and its founders were Mike Roselle, who was one of the founders of Earth First! and the Rainforest Action Network, a guy named Twilly Cannon, who was the longtime director of the Greenpeace Action Team, and James "JR" Roof, another Greenpeace Action stud. They saw a real opportunity within the forest movement in the United States to move that campaign forward. And while I turned down their job offer, I still did a bunch of work for them. I was the lead climb trainer at that first camp in Georgia where we had forty folks. I helped organize their second big national camp in North Carolina.

I spent most of the next two years backpacking and hitchhiking around. I bought a pickup truck. I was doing Earth First! stuff. I worked up in the British Columbia forests and redwood groves in Humboldt County, California. I got arrested a couple times. That was the first time I spent more than two days in jail. I went from Greenpeace, where you have the best lawyers, to using public defenders and getting arrested in the middle of a forest far away from the eyes of the media or any kind of witnesses. The first time I got arrested in Humboldt, I spent about four or five days in jail with about twenty other folks. We had locked ourselves to a whole bunch of logging equipment. The loggers certainly didn't care for us. And that's one of the things that I found really unsatisfying with the forest movement. I felt that they were focusing a lot of their anger at working-class folks who were really pawns of a much larger system. Instead, they should be focusing on the guys in the corporate boardrooms—like Charles Hurwitz, the head of Maxxam Corporation—who were calling the shots and really moving the big pieces around on the board and liquidating forests across the planet.

In November '96, my friend Celia Alario, who knew Woody Harrelson through the grapevine, got him to come up to the redwoods specifically to do an action with a bunch of Earth First! activists. We had just spent three months defending these magical groves of ancient redwood trees from the cutthroat Maxxam. With Woody there, we planned on doing a high-profile action using his celebrity to get a lot of media. We were going to climb between ancient redwoods on both sides of Highway 101 and set up traverse lines from one tree to the other and then hang a banner out over the highway. This was toward the end of the logging season when torrential rains stop logging because of the threat of landslides.

We were camped out in the forest when Woody came in the middle of the night. We were hanging out and smoking dope and brainstorming about what we should say in the action. Somebody said, "We could do the action naked." Another said, "We could do it on the Golden Gate Bridge." Woody kinda thought about it for a second, then said, "Yeah. Let's do it on the Golden Gate Bridge, but I gotta do it in the next four days." My mind started reeling because I knew that Greenpeace and Earth First! had each tried unsuccessfully to hang banners on the Golden Gate Bridge. It was this Holy Grail of action targets. We would be up against the most zealous bridge security in the world. These bridge guys really take their jobs seriously. They stop jumpers all the time. They are really aggressive. They love their bridge. They don't ever want it to be used in a disrespectful way.

The next day we thrashed down out of the redwoods in a car to get to San Francisco and to scout the bridge. I started calling my favorite gear companies like Patagonia. Mountain Hardwear agreed to sew this giant banner for us. I called every action jock that I knew. It was incredible, because about thirty-five people came together within just a couple days. Greenpeace, through my old connections, let us use their action warehouse in San Francisco, and they sent one of their radio geniuses. So we got everybody together and trained for a while up in Marin at this crazy German chalet resort that was closed. It had a working bar that we had to ourselves. We decided that we would need at least two diversion actions, on each side of the bridge, so when the cops rolled onto the bridge, they would be diverted to the smaller actions and give us more time to deploy for the large action. We had two or three climbers on each of those diversionary actions. Then we had five climbers on the giant banner itself. We decided to ascend the cables from the deck of the bridge. We had to figure out how to safely stop all the traffic on the Golden Gate Bridge and deploy this five-person team with ropes across the deck of the bridge. This couldn't take more than a minute or two so we could get traffic flowing again.

It all went like clockwork. There was an amazing confluence of elements and ingredients. We had two pairs of cars driving in opposite directions across the deck of the bridge. They timed themselves to connect with one another right where we were going to unfurl the banner. The cars stopped in perfect synchronicity, blocking six lanes of traffic. With the traffic stopped, there was complete pandemonium. Woody and most of the climbers were already out on the bridge. Bill Hebert, who was our packhorse climber, carried the giant pack with the banner that weighed 120 pounds.

It just so happened that there were two female plainclothes detectives about two or three cars back, in the northbound lane. And there was this total wild card. A huge guy jumped out of his car and he snapped. He went a little berserk. He was our immediate concern. He started assaulting people. He was a big guy. He took a swipe at me and knocked my cap off my head. He stood on the ropes that we were bringing across the deck of the bridge to pull the banner across and rig it on the bridge. We were going nowhere with him there. And so, Mike Roselle, who looked like a school crossing guard gone wrong in his giant yellow jacket and red stop sign standing in the middle of the bridge, went over to this guy and pretended to trip and bounced this guy off our ropes. All of a sudden, the climbers who had already been ascending the cables, were able to pull the lines taut and got them out of the way of traffic.

Then we had to deal with the two detectives. "What the hell is going on?" they asked. I pointed to Woody Harrelson and said, "Look, there's Woody Harrelson! We're shooting a movie." That diverted them to give Woody and the climbers enough time to get out of harm's way and far enough off the deck of the bridge. We had trained Woody in rope ascending techniques and how to rappel and how to climb and how to do it safely with two points of protection at all times. We put one climber, Hillary Hosta, as Woody's personal safety coordinator. He was great. He was critical in getting those ropes out of the way. He grabbed the ropes and just went hell for leather up the cable of the bridge. He went up about 150 feet off the deck of the bridge. They stretched the banner across the road. It read: "Hurwitz, Aren't Ancient Redwoods More Precious Than Gold?"—which, I must confess, was one of the most lamely worded banners I've ever hung in my life.

We had alerted the media right as it was going on. It was a feeding frenzy. It dominated the local news. It bounced nationally immediately. It went international. The *Today Show* was looking for Woody. Letterman later had him on. It's kind of interesting when you're doing actions with celebrities because they get so much media on their own. But it was clearly great for Woody as well. I am sure he got millions of dollars of free PR in this action. We wanted to create a personal confrontation between Woody Harrelson and Charles Hurwitz.

Other interesting things happened that day. First of all, the angry-motorist wild-card guy went over to one of our cars that we had stopped on the bridge. He reached inside and grabbed this stack of stuff off the dashboard that had the driver's passport and all of his important stuff, in case he got arrested. It was bound together with a rubber band. This guy grabbed the packet and threw it as hard as he possibly could into the San Francisco Bay. But the packet hit a cable, and it fell back down on the deck of the bridge. It was one of those signs that the universe was with us.

Both of the diversionary climbs had worked. So we had three successful climbs on the bridge. I was the action coordinator to ensure the safety of the climbers and negotiate with the cops. The cops stopped all the traffic on the bridge. And, of course, we later got blamed for it. But they finally got the traffic flowing again in each direction. It was incredible because people would let you know how they felt about our action. The mood was running at least 70 percent in our favor. People were thrilled about the action. The headwaters forest had been in the news all that year. The State of California and the redwoods were being held hostage by Hurwitz, who was negotiating for billions of dollars. It was just really insulting. The other 30 percent of the people hated our action. They were pissed off that they were stopped in traffic. This one Cadillac pulled up and the electric window came down. There was this sweet-looking, little old lady with her hands way up on the steering wheel. She was really short. She looked at the cop and said, "Shoot them! Shoot them down!" Then the window rolled back up and she drove on.

The same cop whom I had been dealing with all day asked me to give him a forest name because everybody had these critter names. Most Earth First! people called me Goat. He said, "I want a forest name. What am I gonna be called?" The bridge security guys loved the way we hung the banner. I had gone through all the systems and stuff with them and talked about what we were doing. The head of bridge security looked at the cop and said, "This is the exact way I would hang a banner on the Golden Gate Bridge if I were gonna do it." That cop also had a fight with his superiors at the end of the day about whether to arrest me. He said to them, "I told this guy he was not gonna get arrested. He's been straight with me all day. And nobody is arresting this guy." And he won. I wasn't arrested for the Golden Gate Bridge action.

Best of all, I met my future wife Genevieve that day on the Golden Gate Bridge. She was part of our crew. At the time, she was an intern at Rainforest Action Network. I had a crush on her for the next two years. I didn't think she really liked me very much. Then we started hanging out and seeing each other and fell in love.

In 1998, Genevieve and I went to Houston for a Rainforest Action Network protest against the World Petroleum Congress. It's this global petroleum cartel. The Royal Saud family was there. Everyone who is oily and dirty around the planet was there. Cheney and Bush Senior and Junior. It was at the Houston Convention Center. Right next to it, the new Enron Stadium was going up. They had these giant construction cranes. I coordinated a team of climbers, including Genevieve, to go into the construction site, climb the 300-foot crane, and put up a giant banner which read: "Houston, We Have a Problem. No New Oil Exploration."

We just got our butts kicked by the power elite of Houston, by the oil gentry. That was my first $1 million bail. We had these serious felony charges. They said that we had done significant damage to their crane, by hanging four hippies on it with a banner. These cranes pick up cement mixers. In the process of hanging the banner, we surfed the crane, which meant hanging a sail on a rotating arm. The banner catches the wind and the arm moves. We sailed it around, probably 180 degrees in its arc. And so these guys said that they were going to have to recalibrate the crane. We had a lawyer with us in Texas, but he didn't find out that there were new felonies on the books for criminal mischief.

Houston has one of the most mechanized, twisted, dehumanizing, and fucked-up prison systems. Its incarceration system is incredible. The jailers wake you up at four o'clock in the morning for breakfast. They get right in and disturb your REM cycles; keeps you off balance. They keep the temperature in the fifties, to keep you cold so you use all your energy trying to stay warm. The guards won't let you use blankets during the day. You can only use your blanket at night. They had separated us in these cell blocks called pods.

You don't want to mess with Texas because it is a zero-tolerance state. It has a huge prison population. It is mostly young kids from poor and working-class backgrounds — mostly black and brown, kids who are there for mostly consensual nonviolent crimes. I met a bunch of cool young guys who were doing a second felony in a three-strikes-you're-out system. This felony was maybe smoking a joint while they were on probation. Their first felony was maybe having a bag of dope. They are twenty-three years old and doing three years for smoking a joint on probation. If they get caught one more time, they are going away forever. If that's not throwing away human potential and dignity, I don't know what is.

We were in jail for five days. I hadn't seen Genevieve the entire time. We were totally falling in love down there together on this action. I was really worried about her. This was our first big arrest together. She came out in the courtroom, and we were all in our orange jumpsuits. She was just so beautiful in her orange jumpsuit, I couldn't believe it. She was the only one who didn't look like a serial killer.

They completely overplayed their hand with us. They could have carried the day in the PR wars with us by charging us with some reasonable offense. But they got greedy. They went after us to make an example of us. What it did was increase the media's interest in the whole thing. The press asked, "Why did these nonviolent people get second-degree felonies? Who's calling the shots in this town? What's going on?" By the third day, the reporters were showing up at the jail demanding to do interviews with me and this other guy named Danny Kennedy. They scheduled this press conference in the prison. But first they had to move me to the area where the press conference was.

First I have to explain something significant about the jail. It's a skyscraper in downtown Houston, but you can't tell it's a jail from the outside. It looks like it has windows, but then you realize that this giant, tall building does not have windows. It's just full of mostly young human beings in cell blocks. This building is connected to other buildings through underground passageways. And so, when the day came for my press conference, this booming voice comes out over the speaker: "Sellers, come to the door!" Then you go through this door lock and into another chamber. Another door opens. No one's with you. And then the voice says, "Sellers, go through that next door and move into the elevator. Face the wall." You are still alone. They are watching you on closed-circuit television. I went through this weird maze with these different locking chambers. I walked maybe three-quarters of a mile underground to another place. I am unescorted the entire time. At one point, the strap on one of my flip-flops broke. I bent down to fix it. This giant metallic voice booms out of the walls: "Sellers, what are you doing?" "I am fixing my flip-flop," I answered. The voice said, "Stop doing that! Move on!" It was so weird, man. It was like a crazy science-fiction movie.

Based on their psycho accusations that we had done all this damage to the crane, their case later fell apart in court. They couldn't do a thing. We had this dream team of lawyers including the stud of Texas law, Mike DeGuerin, who jumped into our case because he was so outraged. Some rich do-gooder put up the money to a bail bondsman. The bondsman gave us a great break too. He did it for 5 percent, instead of 10 percent—because he lost his office to the new stadium.

Around this time, I helped Ruckus with a human rights action camp in Virginia. Roselle saw that I had the skill set to keep Ruckus afloat and raise the money and become the director of the organization. We were friends at the time, and it was no big deal. Roselle is one of the smartest people I know, but he also has a dark side. I had seen him fire executive directors of other organizations that he had founded. When it came time for us to create the board of directors at Ruckus, I made it my main priority to bring people onto the board who Roselle would be okay with, but who wouldn't kill me when he said it was time for me to go. And of course, Roselle and I later had a real parting of the ways. It was sort of a slow-motion train wreck. He wanted to solely work in support of the forest movement; I wanted to move past pure environmentalism and work on human rights and social justice issues. That was the cause of our big split. He left in early 2002. He actually has a brilliant blog now called LowBagger.org. A lowbagger is a Ruckus tradition. It is a journeyman or journeywoman activist who lives out of his or her backpack with a sleeping bag. You're constantly sleeping on other people's couches. Then the last person who arrives has to put his or her sleeping bag on the floor, because all the couches are taken. So, that's what a lowbagger is—the person with the lowest bag in the room. Roselle is a great writer. He likes to model himself after Hunter S. Thompson.

Ruckus had its first big national camp in Montana in the Bitterroots. We had *Outside* magazine there, and they did a really big story. Every successful social movement has used nonviolent direct action. The civil rights movement invested incredible resources in training and strategy around direct action. Before Rosa Parks got on that bus in Montgomery, she had been trained for two weeks at the Highlander Institute in Tennessee. The students who broke the back of Jim Crow laws in the Deep South by sitting at lunch counters were also trained for months in advance by Rev. James Lawson. There was this real recognition that nonviolent direct action and civil disobedience took training, discipline, and coordination. The anti-nukes movement did a lot of training as well, like the Clamshell Alliance and the Abalone Alliance. Ruckus has always tried to follow in their footsteps.

Our Action Camps are free to participants. We set up the ultimate field kitchen and feed everyone. We provide some pretty outrageous gourmet food for folks in the wild. Our volunteer kitchen staff really takes pride in its cuisine. We have some of the most skilled climbers, blockaders, and accomplished forest defenders. Because of our emphasis on safety, Ruckus sometimes gets into trouble inside the movement. We are thought of as uptight safety fascists. But we don't want people climbing on cheap ropes or using equipment that could possibly hurt them.

Ruckus was started out of the wallet of one incredibly generous guy who was giving $10,000 a month for the first couple years in order to get us on our feet. Patagonia has supported us from the very beginning. It is one of our longest standing sponsors. It will actually pay bail for its employees who practice nonviolent direct action and get arrested, as long as they have had nonviolence training from Ruckus. Ted Turner was very supportive of Ruckus when we were just working on preserving wilderness areas. But when we started questioning global trade, he cut us off pretty quickly. Anita Roddick from The Body Shop used to be on our board of directors. Ben & Jerry's was quite generous when they were giving money to us. The money they gave us was Unilever money. Unilever was not psyched about it at first. It had bought the ice cream company against the wishes of Ben and Jerry who were trying to have a bunch of their friends—socially responsible businesspeople—buy it. But they were sued by their own shareholders for failure to maximize profits. So they ended up being sold to Unilever against their will. But during the takeover and buyout, they were able to leverage $5 million of Unilever money directly to their foundation. They've given that money away in pretty healthy chunks to support anti-corporate globalization work. While Ben and Jerry have cycled out of us, they are giving to some other good groups now. Ben continues to be a good friend, and we work on stuff together.

We have six full-time staff at our Oakland office. Our budget is around $700,000 a year. It's probably 30 to 40 percent from individual donors, 30 to 40 percent from foundations, and 20 percent from other non-profit groups who are paying us to help them do creative actions. We try to target as much of our money as we possibly can for actual training—to the grassroots, investing in folks who are on the front lines. We feel that makes the money go a really long way. When you can inject $2,000 into a truly hungry grassroots group, it makes a huge difference.

By 1999, Ruckus had been doing work straddling the line between the environment and human rights for about two years. That summer, Ruckus did a camp just outside of Washington, D.C. It was our second human rights action camp where a bunch of people were talking about this upcoming ministerial meeting of the World Trade Organization in Seattle. There was a real buzz. Environmentalists were real hopped-up about the trade rules because there were no real environmental standards. The labor activists at this camp were very motivated to confront the WTO. The same with human rights folks. It became clear to us that this unifying villain was unaccountable to civil society at large. We made a gut, spur-of-the-moment decision to make the WTO a concrete target and offer our resources and skills to a nonviolent opposition of its meeting.

We realized that the WTO picked just about the dumbest place you could possibly choose in North America because Seattle is the epicenter of the direct action community. Seattle was a one-day drive from thousands and thousands of the most serious, skilled, experienced nonviolent direct action practitioners in North America. You had the forest movement all over that area, from Vancouver and above on the coast of British Columbia. From west of Minneapolis, you had all kinds of Earth First! activists and folks defending the largest roadless areas in the Lower 48 States. You had San Francisco and the activist circles there, and cities in Oregon—Portland and Eugene.

We decided to sponsor an advanced action camp. We called it Globalize This! Action Camp. In our announcement, we said that we weren't interested in a cannibal-fest of lefties chewing up their own and fighting among each other. Only people with a sense of humor and a sense of rhythm could come to this camp. You had to have two years of demonstrated applied direct action experience in the field to come to it. We just wanted to get the best and brightest together. We ended up drawing about 200 people. This camp was held two months before the WTO. One of the requirements we asked of attendees was that if they were accepted to this camp, they had to commit to organizing action teams in their cities and bringing these teams to Seattle. This request ended up being really effective. We stayed away from tree climbing and just trained people in urban-climbing techniques. We taught things like holding a space and blockading buildings, bridges, or roads. We had some incredible political theater workshops. We did action planning and strategy. We did a lot of role-playing. For example, doing a kind of modern-day sit-in with devices to help you sustain that sit-in and make it more difficult for law enforcement to remove you—but you are not resisting arrest because you are locked into the positions. We do not teach resisting arrest because resisting arrest is going to get you beaten up. And it's only going to increase your arrest charges. It was an incredible camp. We had some of the best Earth First! musicians like Dana Lyons and Danny Dollinger. For our final night party, a lot of the Ruckus men and women got dressed up in festive gowns and prom dresses.

The camp itself made the front page of the *Wall Street Journal* and the *Financial Times* in Europe. It was all over the Seattle papers. It really created a lot of buzz. You could just feel in the movement that people were going to really turn out and work together to intervene against this faceless organization that represented multinational corporations taking over the planet.

Afterward, we rented a warehouse near Seattle. We began to move our volunteers and trainers into that warehouse. We had a kitchen crew feed everyone. We began producing plastic tubes that we call lock boxes for people to lock their arms together. We built 500 of them. We coated them with tar and chicken wire and duct tape so that if the police did try to saw through them, it would gum up their saws pretty quickly.

As the WTO meeting got closer and more of our trainers began rolling into Seattle, our program director, Han Shan, and myself started to meet and negotiate with the Seattle Police Department. There were two officers, a captain and a lieutenant, who were in charge of the protest response. We met them at an action outside an Old Navy clothing store. Much of the clothing in Old Navy and The Gap is made in sweatshops in China. I felt this was a great opportunity to meet someone with power within the police department and talk to them about what was going to happen, and assure them that Ruckus was a nonviolent organization. We had started to hear things from friends in town that the Seattle Police Department had these war games where one of the cops who was playing a protester had his arm broken. We realized that they had a lot of misinterpretations about us. They were getting ready for these violent anarchists coming to the city. So we reached out to them. We challenged them to a bowling night. They refused to bowl with us, but we ended up having dinner in Chinatown with two cops in charge of the downtown area. They had no clue how many people were going to show up to shut down the WTO meeting, or how strong our resolve would be. They were asking us questions like, "Do you think more than two hundred people are gonna want to get arrested? Should we have buses to take them to jail?" We were kicking ourselves under the table. We couldn't believe how unprepared they ended up being.

The day before the giant showdown on November 30, I jumped into one of our actions because one of the climbers had dropped out. We hung a huge banner on a giant crane that was being used for construction near the Space Needle. The banner was of two one-way street signs pointing in opposite directions. One sign said "WTO" and the other said "Democracy." It went global. I was let out of jail that night because Ruckus had cut a deal with a bail bondswoman in Seattle to have a running tab.

After I got out of jail, I didn't have any responsibilities to speak of on the giant day of action. I got to walk around the city and see the most inspiring, amazing actions that I've ever witnessed. At the heart of the blockade around the WTO were around 5,000 people. These people came in affinity groups. Each group made consensus decisions. They sent spokespeople to a cluster who also made consensus decisions, and then the cluster sent a spokesperson to the spokescouncil. There were thirteen clusters of hundreds of affinity groups that divided up the entire city in a giant pie. At the center of the pie was the convention center where the WTO meeting was scheduled. Our strategy was that no matter how far out the cops and security pushed their perimeter to defend the WTO, each cluster had its own responsibility to be part of the blockade that stopped delegates from going into the meeting.

It was shocking to see that the perimeter that the Seattle Police Department had set up was so tight. It was so small. It was just a ring right around the convention center itself. They had underestimated our size. And then thousands and thousands of people started to show up and march toward them. Teamsters had these giant trucks with music blaring. It was just an incredible street party.

People were happy and celebrating. There was such a big ring of humanity around the WTO that there was no way that any delegates were getting inside.

For the first couple of hours, the Seattle Police Department was poised and committed to not hurting anyone. The blockade held. The worm turned when Secretary of State Madeleine Albright freaked out. Here was the most powerful business meeting that had ever occurred on the planet, and it was being stopped on U.S. soil. It was being shut down. The feds themselves completely freaked out and pulled the cord of the Seattle Police Department. They gave it an ultimatum to open the meeting up, by any means necessary. The police did an about-face and became a brutal, marauding presence. They looked like Darth Vader. They had the full black riot gear—black face masks, black gas masks, and all this black padded Nike gear. They gave some warnings first. "You must disperse! You gotta let this meeting happen! You gotta get out of the way!" People were fearless and just stood their ground. It was incredible to witness thousands of people with their will set to stop this meeting from happening and to hold this global corporate governance board accountable. And for their troubles, they were teargassed and pepper-sprayed and beaten. It was just a melee. So when people talk about the riots in Seattle, it was the cops who had the riot. It was a full-on cop riot. They just completely lost their shit.

If you look at it today, they talk about the riots in Seattle. But if you go back and look at the *New York Times* and the *Wall Street Journal*, they talk about the violent reaction of the Seattle Police Department to a nonviolent action. History is rewritten all over the world. History is written by the conquerors. The elite status quo has a vested interest in reframing Seattle as a violent protest. Ruckus got labeled with having fomented the riots in Seattle. There were no riots in Seattle. There was a small group of young, mostly skinny vegan anarchist kids from Oregon who were hell-bent on beating up on Starbucks and McDonald's. I remember doing the *Hannity & Colmes* show on Fox. I was just having it out with Sean Hannity on the show. I was standing in a studio in Seattle against a blue screen, and every time I would talk about how principled and nonviolent we were being, they would just show the same tape loop of young kids looting Starbucks. There was only one group that was doing violence against people in Seattle: that was the Seattle Police Department. They were just letting loose on people for hours. People in the nonviolent protest center at the WTO site finally started to tire and buckle from the police onslaught.

At the end of the day, the police began using stun grenades. It was like a war zone. They were marching in phalanx in their black uniforms, while beating their shin guards with these giant billy clubs. They used shotgun shells full of little pellets of pepper gas. They actually ran out of chemical weapons after that first day, so they went and grabbed stuff from Army Navy surpluses and National Guard units.

I got pepper-sprayed and gassed a bunch of times. I was trying to help with different blockades that were weakening under the police onslaught. That first day, I don't think there were many arrests. They were more interested in punishing people. It was totally unsafe to be around. The Seattle Police Department was a police force gone completely awry. They were just marching around the city hurting people, using all kinds of crazy force indiscriminately. By sundown, people were evacuating the downtown area.

The next day, the mayor declared hundreds of square blocks in downtown Seattle completely off limits to anyone criticizing the WTO. It was a No Protest Zone. The First Amendment did not apply. And that became the focus of the action that second day. Even though it was unsafe to be downtown in Seattle, thousands of people did attempt to march into the No Protest Zone. I was singled out and tackled by three or four riot cops. Not arrested, just tackled! I was trying to help a large group of people. The cops grabbed my Nextel radio, which I had been using to coordinate communications. All this was captured on CNN. Genevieve was arrested a couple hours later.

Hundreds of people were being arrested. Thousands of people marched on the jail and demanded the release of our comrades. By then, the WTO meetings had collapsed. They didn't get the new round of negotiations they had originally wanted. The delegates from the Global South were saying that the protesters were right. Third World countries felt that they were being railroaded by the delegates from Europe and the United States. They were strengthened in their conviction that the WTO doesn't operate on consensus. It operates on coercion in which powerful industrialized countries coerce the less industrialized and poor countries to eat a bitter pill just to sit at the table. We received reports from people who were accredited to be inside that Global South delegates staged a demonstration and protest of their own inside the meeting. Overall, the meeting was a dismal failure for the WTO.

It was a crazy whirlwind after the WTO and Seattle. Because following right on its heels was this giant meeting in Washington, D.C., of the World Bank and the International Monetary Fund—the other two legs of the unholy trinity. We brought along this powerful portable public address system because we were really sick of seeing these black-clad storm trooper cops. We waited until there were hundreds and hundreds of them gathered, looming like Darth Vader, and then we let loose with the Death Star theme from *Star Wars* coming out of this powerful sound system. The television crews ate up our little theater piece and many of the cops were forced to take off their silly masks.

In 2000, Ruckus focused on preparing for the Democratic National Convention in Los Angeles. We coordinated a national camp to prepare young people from California who had important issues to bring to the table during the convention—especially how the government has been bought and bankrupted by the influence of corporate money. We spent a lot of time gearing up. My wife was on another Ruckus climbing team. It was preparing to hang a giant American flag banner with the stars replaced by corporate logos. "Sold" was stamped across the body of the flag.

Around that time, I went home to Philly to visit my family. I planned my trip to be around the same time as the Republican National Convention. I wanted to check out the convention, though I really didn't have any illusions that the Republicans were going to do anything for ordinary people. They weren't going to address any of our concerns. It seemed that our time and resources and creativity were better spent on moving the Democrats in some subtle ways. I knew the people who were at the heart of the big actions in Philly, so I decided to pitch in and help out. I was planning on using some of my notoriety and connections with the press to help steer media people around to the most strategic actions.

As my friends and colleagues were organizing for the convention, the Philadelphia police preemptively raided the warehouse where they were preparing all their props, costumes, puppets, banners, and political messages. They arrested a bunch of people preemptively and illegally. They seized all their political materials. The messages of the nonviolent action were seized and silenced before they even happened. The folks were planning on doing a day of action against the criminal justice system. The Philadelphia Police Department, just a couple months before, shot and killed a black man who had been driving on a bridge.

After the raid, people were angry. They lost their discipline. And the Philadelphia Police Department was just brutal. It's interesting because at both conventions—in Los Angeles and Philadelphia—the police departments completely lost their shit. In Philadelphia, it was much more of an East Coast tough-guy, up-close-and-personal kind of brutality. They'd beat you with a baton and throw you down. Bicycle cops were hitting people with their bicycles. In Los Angeles, it was much more of a West Coast offense. It was much more Hollywood pyrotechnics with stun grenades and tear gas.

The next day, I walked down to City Hall because I had heard there was going to be a press conference by some anarchists. I was pissed at some of their tactics. These anarchists had endangered people who had shown up to do actions that didn't involve property destruction or getting their asses kicked by Philadelphia cops who were incited by seeing property destruction. I went to the press conference because I wanted to have a debate—because it just really pisses me off when thousands of people decide to do something really creative and constructive and nonviolent that exposes the injustices of the system, and then five or ten opportunistic people come in with some kind of provocative tactic that really endangers everybody else. It scares people away from us. Of course, these anarchists didn't even show up. No press conference ever unfolded. I did notice a cop out there with his video camera. I stood around for a while. I talked to a couple of reporters I knew. I then left and was walking up Market Street. I was going to take the train up to New York to do some fund-raising for Ruckus before flying out to Los Angeles. About two blocks from City Hall, I kind of felt it rather than heard it: a big guy came running up behind me. It was a cop. He grabbed me by the shoulder and said, "Would you step out in the street, sir?" I said, "Yeah, sure." We stepped off the sidewalk out into the street. And he said, "I'm placing you under arrest." I asked, "What am I being arrested for?" He kept repeating, "I'm placing you under arrest." I kept questioning him. I was standing my ground. I wasn't kowtowing to him. As we continued this verbal back and forth, more cops started showing up in their cruisers. A lot of brass was out there. There were a couple of captains, plainclothes guys. I was by myself. Some independent media folks started filming what was going on. A reporter from the *Los Angeles Times*, who had been at one of our action camps, started asking the cops what I was being arrested for. The deputy commissioner of the Philadelphia Police Department was now on the scene. I had never seen this kind of cop mobilization before. And what the hell is the deputy commissioner out there for little old me? He just nodded to everybody and said, "Okay, we're out of here." They then threw me in the back of a police cruiser and we high-tailed it through the streets of Philadelphia. We are doing sixty or seventy miles an hour. Motorcycle cops are weaving in and out as they shut down traffic up this one-way avenue so we can zip up the wrong direction. To this day, I don't know whether they thought some crack team of hippies in a van was going to try to spring me while they were arresting me. I don't know why they always seem to overplay their hand.

We ended up four or five blocks away as the crow flies, at the homicide headquarters of the Philadelphia Police Department. We went in an underground entrance, and they took me up in an elevator. I was taken into one of those interrogation rooms that you see in the movies. They handcuffed me to this metal stool in the corner. They left me alone in the room. They never frisked me. I still had my cell phone, so I start making calls. They came in and took the phone from me. They began sending in different people to interrogate me. They literally have the stereotypical Hollywood good cop and bad cop thing going on. There's the one-way mirror on the wall—and you know that police are looking at you from the other side. For the first few hours I was totally cooperative with them. I gave them Ruckus's Website, and I told them how to find out about our curriculum. I answered any questions that they had. I told them what it is that we do. I tried to clear up some misunderstandings that they had. They kept asking me, "What are these sleeping dragons you are bringing into the city?" I said, "There are no sleeping dragons coming into the city for the Republican convention. They are cement anchors used in forest actions. They are used to block logging roads."

These local police forces are totally manipulated by the feds. In Seattle, I was talking to this young captain, Jim Pugel, who is going to be chief one day—he was such a diplomat and such a politician—and he told me that the Seattle Police Department had gotten information from the feds that they would probably lose three to five officers during the WTO protests. I asked Jim, "What do you mean, you're gonna *lose* three to five officers during the WTO protests? What is that supposed to mean? That they are going to drive to Tacoma and take a wrong turn?"

After about six hours, one of the Philly cops said, "We are going to charge you with aggravated assault on a police officer"—which is a felony. I was like, "What? How and where does this come from?" I replied, "Okay, that is it. I am not cooperating with you guys any more. I'm not answering a goddamn question. I want to see my lawyer right now." The guy left. He was obviously sent in to play bad cop. It definitely got under my skin. If there is one thing that I will never be charged with it's a violent act. And so, a couple hours later he comes back and says, "Captain told me to pull that charge and dump a bunch of shit on you." I asked, "What do you mean?" He said, "Just what it sounds like. I'm gonna charge you with everything in the book I can think of. Conspiracy to blockade a road and conspiracy to light dumpsters on fire." It ended up being thirteen misdemeanors, all of which were completely and patently untrue. And they set an unprecedented $1,000,000 bail for these thirteen misdemeanors— you know, in a city where murderers get away with $10,000 bail. Because they had removed all of the actual judges from the benches during convention week, they had these political appointees acting as bail commissioners setting bail.

They were people who could be easily pushed around. I only later heard about my $1,000,000 bail after they moved me from homicide to this dirty, dark dungeon in an old police station in west Philly. I was asleep in my cell, using a roll of toilet paper as a pillow, when I met one of my heroes. Larry Krasner was my lawyer in Philadelphia. He's a Quaker, awesome do-gooder, First Amendment champion, guy who does way more than his share of pro bono work. The legal support collective for the convention, known as R2K, had called him. He told me, "I'm willing to defend you for free."

We did the bail hearing in this closet-like room with closed-circuit television. We didn't have a chance from the get-go. Larry made some strong arguments about reducing the bail, but the bail commissioner shot all of them down. The district attorney was really candid about the unconstitutional reason that she wanted to set the bail amount at $1,000,000. This was an all-Democratic city administration that was protecting the Republican convention. She believed that I was going to go to L.A. and speak out at the Democratic National Convention. Of course, that is not what bail is meant to do. Bail is meant to insure that you are not a flight risk, that you are going to come back for your court date. Larry argued that I had thirty political arrests and that I had never missed a single hearing in any of them, that I have always dealt with my legal obligations, that my family lived outside of Philadelphia, and that I represented no flight risk. None of those arguments worked, and so they set my bail at $1,000,000.

Well, after the Republicans left town, they dropped my bail to $100,000. This businesswoman hero of mine in west Philly who owns the White Dog Café bailed me out after eight days. Her name is Judy Wicks. We have since become good friends.

When it was time to appear in court, the DA went up in front of the judge and said, "We have no evidence. We can't make any arguments. We can't back up any of the charges." So they legally settled with us for violating my rights. It wasn't a lot of money. Of course, they would never give it to me. So I had the money go to a prison support group that gives books to prisoners. It's called Books Through Bars.

Throughout all this ordeal, the Philly media called me "the ringleader of mayhem and destruction." My parents had to sit at home and see all this bullshit in newspapers and on their local TV stations. I was in jail and couldn't defend myself. My dad was frustrated. He was practically in tears. It was interesting. He is a Reagan Republican, but when this went down, my dad was radicalized. He just couldn't believe what America had come to. It was really shocking for him.

In the last several years, Ruckus has worked hard to actively blur the lines between the environmental, social justice, labor, and human rights movements. Since the uprising against the WTO, we have made a commitment to become a multiracial multi-issue network of trainers that is truly representative of the rainbow of just struggles. We have hosted several Global Justice Action Camps that brought middle-aged trade unionists together with crusty tree huggers, gender queer warriors, and urban youth struggling for economic justice. There are a lot of social and racial barriers that still divide folks who are fighting the good fight. I'd be lying if I said that all the camps have gone off smoothly. We've learned a bunch of our lessons the hard way.

We now have thousands of graduates from our Action Camp Programs out there in the world today. The camps run five to seven days and usually bring together about 150 people. They have taken place all over the U.S. and Canada. Folks get lit up by a Ruckus camp, and the glow can last for a long time. Days are split between theoretical workshops in subjects like organizing, campaign strategy, media, action planning, and hands-on instruction in climbing, blockades, and political theater. After dinner there are slide-shows, movies, and presentations. The last day is spent in a direct action role-playing. Ruckus trainers are all transformed into cops, executives, media, and corporate security; and the student protesters have their way with us.

But the real magic happens at night around the Ruckus campfire. There's nothing like plotting and scheming to save the world under the full moon with your friends. Many creative actions have been hatched this way. Ruckus has quite an array of musicians, singers, bards, spoken-word poets, and fire dancers. Because many lefty activist types have a well-deserved reputation for taking themselves *way* too seriously, we've made it a priority to liberate these folks from their workaholic office-heads. Who's gonna want to join a movement of shrill, self-righteous gloom and doomers who don't know how to let their hair down? Plus, Ruckus has a deep belief in the political importance of having more fun than our right-wing adversaries. Our skinny-dipping sessions and final night parties are legendary throughout the movement.

In 2003, Ruckus did a lot of logistical support for different anti-war marches, both on the West Coast and East Coast. We took an art installation and a giant flying banner with these weather balloons to the first big one in Washington, D.C. We had our balloons grounded by the U.S. Park Police and Secret Service, who said that we couldn't fly them because we might harm migrating birds in the area. In New York, we were out on the East River when Bush addressed the United Nations to justify going to war with Iraq. We flew a giant fishing net, which had huge letters stitched into it that said, "Earth To Bush: No Iraq War." Our boat got boarded by Navy SEALs who made us prove that we had gotten permission from the harbormaster to be in the water.

We did a really fun deck of playing cards called War Profiteers. It was our response to the Pentagon's card deck of Iraq's most wanted war criminals. We picked the fifty-two people who we thought were benefiting the most from United States militarism and its new permanent war footing. We sold about 25,000 decks. We got quite a lot of press coverage.

In 2004, we targeted Diebold, which makes electronic voting machines. We went to their shareholders meeting in Columbus, Ohio, and built a giant carnivorous voting machine that looked like one of their voting machines. It constantly gave error messages and would spew clouds of smoke whenever a voting card was inserted. Diebold officials didn't even come out to debate us. Diebold's CEO is one of President Bush's fund-raising rangers. He made some boast about doing everything in his power to deliver the election to Bush, and then later said there was no conflict of interest.

For the 2004 Republican National Convention in New York, we worked with a super-cool local businessperson who allowed us to take over his office live/loft space in Chinatown. We brought along our state-of-the-art communications infrastructure. We had all kinds of scanners for scanning tactical police frequencies. We had this amazing network of cell phones using text messaging. We had a network of 900 cell phones that was coordinated with groups that had another 7,000 cell phones in networked loops, so that we could instantaneously communicate with all these people on the street and receive intelligence from those 7,000 people. We had encrypted chat rooms on-line. We had just an incredible communications hub—helping people stay safe and be strategic and know where Republicans were having their corporate pep rallies at any time. We went there mainly to test-drive a bunch of technology we were working on. These emerging cell phone technologies are being used by citizen activists all over the world. Folks used text messaging in Spain after the 2004 train bombing to organize opposition overnight to the pro-war ruling Spanish party. It's the preferred method of communications for Chinese dissidents. There are billions of text messages being sent in China. It is really a hyper-democratic form of communications. Unlike computers, cell phones cross the digital divide because they are cheaper than landlines.

While we helped provide communications assistance to a lot of the folks who were doing different actions in New York, I was mostly staying off the streets. During the convention, my photo was flashed on ABC's *Nightline* by

Ted Koppel as "one of the twenty most dangerous anarchists in the country." I ended up going on an unpermitted People's March from the United Nations on the East River over to the Republican convention at Madison Square Garden that was sponsored by Kensington Welfare Rights Union of Philadelphia. We helped do some of their communications. The march started out with probably about 2,000 people. By the time it went around the city to the Garden itself, it was probably only about 1,000 people. It was getting pretty crazy, and the cops were getting more and more provocative and aggressive. It was not a good scene. The cops didn't play fair. They would pen people inside these plastic mesh barriers, and then you had to defend yourself later in court. Hundreds of people were arrested just for being in the wrong place at the wrong time. I remember walking away when I overheard two plainclothes cops talking. One said, "Who is that long-haired guy with John Sellers?" I realized we were under surveillance. And so we ended up putting a team in place to do counter-surveillance.

The cops saw that we were watching them. The streets were just crawling with different people. The feds were watching us. It was crazy—snipers on roofs, pointing. We were waving to the snipers on the roofs. On the last night, I had taken a cab back to Chinatown and I was about to walk into the place where I was staying when some of our own counter-surveillance folks who were coming in behind me waved to the undercover cops in a van parked nearby. To their surprise, the cops rolled down the windows and said, "Hey, we want to meet Sellers. Come on, it's all over." So my friends came up to me and said that the undercover team of New York's finest who were watching me all week wanted to meet. The guys started yelling out of the van, "Yo, Sellers! C'mon, ya chickenshit!" I was like, all right. So I walked down there. I got in their van and we ended up having a great conversation. The guy in charge of the team was this really scrappy, funny Italian guy. He said, "Yo, John, I had a lot of money riding on you, dude. You were supposed to destroy this whole city." I asked, "What are you talking about, dude? I am a nonviolent guy." He said, "C'mon. You were supposed to destroy the whole town." I was like, "I dunno what you are talking about." It was pretty clear that they didn't know anything about me or Ruckus at all. I think they just got handed a file by the feds. They realized by the end of the convention that they had been given a bunch of bullshit by the feds. I've been convicted of a bunch of stuff. But it's all stuff I've been proud of. I have never been convicted of a felony. I've been charged with a bunch of felonies. A lot of times that is what they see when they get your record. They can say, "You've been charged with seventeen felonies." It doesn't mean you've been convicted of them. They try to make it sound as bad as they can. And so, these undercover cops wanted to know who we really were. We ended up hanging out for several hours.

In recent years, Ruckus has been requested to get involved with campaigns all over the world. But our focus at Ruckus is North America, not global. We live in the belly of the beast. We resist the urge to take our show internationally, because we have a responsibility living in America to work on the handles of power right here in this country. We feel that the rest of the world will benefit by making the United States a more democratic and just place, because America imposes its will on the world. We are certainly willing to share our stuff internationally. We've made our training manuals available online and open source so people can grab the information and use it.

Today, at Ruckus, we have an active volunteer network of trainers and logistics coordinators. One of our big campaign pushes for the next couple years is our Indigenous People's Power Program — or IP3, as we call it. IP3 supports native youth who are struggling for environmental justice. Young indigenous leaders from the Arctic, the Southwest, and the Great Plains are stepping forward to build a powerful native youth movement. We have a real special partnership with the Lakota Action Network. We've recently put on an action camp in the Black Hills of South Dakota for about sixty organizers from different nations. The U.S. took the most sacred holy place for the Lakotas and carved the faces of the white conquerors in the Black Hills. Mining, logging, and liquor companies continue to wage war against the Lakota today. Young Lakota warriors are demanding sovereignty and environmental justice on their own lands, and Ruckus will stand with them in this nonviolent fight.

Ruckus is also working on a campaign called Not Your Soldier. It supports young people who are resisting military recruiters and their underhanded tactics in our schools. America is starting to act like Sparta, breeding soldiers from an early age. The United States Army has designed one of the most popular computer-video games out there today. It's called Overmatch. It's a very realistic mockup of desert warfare. The game is free for young people to download. Go to USArmy.com. There are five million people playing it. Military recruiters can sign in and host gaming sessions. We are working with partners to expose the No Child Left Behind Act, which has a loophole allowing military recruiters to access the private information of kids unless they specifically decide to opt out. So we're helping to mobilize action to counter military recruitment in high schools.

Ruckus's third major campaign is Jumpstart Ford. This is a campaign to get Ford Motor Company to build a fleet of cars by 2010 that average fifty miles per gallon. Ford has had the worst mileage of any fleet of U.S. automakers, five years running. They have made the most promises about doing the right thing and becoming responsible with their vehicles. They have a rich tradition of innovation. They are an American institution. Because we don't have the political capital to really go after big oil, this is an intermediate campaign to drive a wedge between Detroit and Texas. We want to get automakers to break ranks and make hybrid cars that are much less dependent on fossil fuels.

Now that I am a family man with twins, I have an even greater stake in the future of our planet. Hazel and Sam have totally changed my perspective on things. I have optimism for the world that I want them to live in. Hopefully, they are going to be around far longer than me and Genevieve, and then have kids of their own. Native Americans talk about the seven generations. It forces you to consider the impact of your own actions on the next seven generations rather than thinking just about yourself.

I am thirty-nine years old, getting a belly. My sympathetic pregnancy weight hasn't left yet. I'm not going to get drafted. I'm not going to have to fight in wars of U.S. domination and imperialism and for oil or whatever else we are going to be fighting for in ten or fifteen years. It will probably be water by then. But Sam and Hazel might have to fight unless we stop this crazy fascination we have with violence as a culture. I want us to evolve.

My wife is still a great activist. Genevieve is one of the cofounders of this group called MOMS—Making Our Milk Safe. They are going after different toxins in women's breast milk. If American women's breast milk were introduced in the marketplace as a product right now, it wouldn't pass FDA standards because it is so heavily contaminated with carcinogens which are coming from the food chain. It is coming from dust and particulates and building materials that are in our houses. There is this crazy perchlorate stuff that is in rocket and aerospace fuel that is making its way into women's breast milk. I am real excited about helping Genevieve and her friends who have had babies. Women's breast milk is still the very best thing you can give your baby. It has all these antibodies in it. It has all these important nurturing aspects. It's the first food. It should be the purest food that babies get, and it's becoming more and more polluted.

In the short term, I am stepping back from the edge as far as risk-taking and jeopardizing my personal freedom. I've been in jail for decent stretches of time. I can imagine what it would be like to spend six months or a year or two in jail. I am not scared of that. But I am scared of not being with my children, especially right now. It is just so amazing to see them develop their little brains and watch their consciousness grow. I want to be around for that. I have a responsibility to them now.

Meanwhile, I think nonviolent civil disobedience has really been maligned. Even during the civil rights movement, profound violence was being done to nonviolent protesters. Oftentimes the violence done to people of nonviolent means is then turned around and projected back onto them, so it looks like they deserve what they got. That is certainly happening with the global justice movement. Then it's easier for protests to be dismissed or marginalized by the media, making it look like we are the ones who are unreasonable or criminal or violent in our tactics and purposes.

The people who leave the United States to go fight in our wars are often seen as patriots and heroes. While this is certainly true, I've felt for a long time that you don't have to kill to fight for your country. You don't have to leave the borders of your country to fight for your country. In fact, the people I have the greatest respect for are people who nonviolently fight for the heart and soul of this country from within its borders. They stay here and fight for democracy in the United States, because we now live in a country that is ruled by unaccountable corporations that are buying up our elected officials and are literally buying up election day itself. All of this corruption to our democracy is going on unfettered. There is a tremendous amount to lose if we allow our democracy to continue being undermined and corrupted. And so, I think the true patriots are here within our borders fighting for the promise of America. They are doing it creatively and nonviolently, exposing themselves to incredible repression and violence to fight for the true ideals of democracy that can and should exist in this country—but don't.

If I can help in that struggle and do my small part, I love it. It's what I'm called to do. It's what I enjoy doing. It's incredibly satisfying and rewarding. I can't imagine myself doing anything else. I guess I'm a lifer. I am addicted to struggling with my friends for what we believe in and the values that we hold dear. I hate being framed as a protester by the corporate media which likes to really confuse things. I'm not just against things. I like to be talked about in the context of what I am for. I want a more democratic, more responsive government. A cleaner, healthier, more nurturing environment. A real sense of respect and justice from our legal system for everyone. Those are things that are worth fighting for.

2

AN AMERICAN HERO

Max Cleland frames the current war in Iraq in
the context of his painful past as a veteran of the
Vietnam War.

"Iraq is Vietnam on steroids."

Max Cleland is a highly decorated, triple-amputee Vietnam War veteran with a
long and distinguished record of public service. Senator John McCain calls him
the greatest hero he's ever known. Reaching far beyond what able-bodied individuals physically take for granted, Cleland is that rare statesman: a courageous
everyman defender of what is true and decent in American politics.

Modest and unpretentious, he prefers being called just Max. So let's begin
there. Max grew up in the small town of Lithonia, Georgia, where he was named
his high school's outstanding senior. He played the trumpet and French horn in the
school band, lettered in varsity baseball all four years, and placed second in a
statewide tennis tournament. At Stetson University in Florida, he joined the ROTC.
A college internship in Washington, D.C., stoked an interest in politics. He entered
the Army as a signal officer and became an assistant to a stateside brigadier general, but requested a transfer to Vietnam. "I could no longer hide behind a ma-
hogany desk," writes Max in his autobiography *Strong at the Broken Places*, "while
men less trained, less motivated and younger than I, were being drafted."

When Max returned to the United States, it was aboard a C-141 Air Force
hospital ship—strapped into a stretcher, naked under a sheet, and missing both
legs and his lower right arm. He spent the next eight months at Walter Reed
Hospital in Washington, D.C., where he underwent extensive physical rehabili-
tation. The staff was thoughtful and compassionate; the treatment exceptional.
Only after being transferred to the local VA hospital did Max begin to lose hope.
As he says in his book, he felt like a "discarded warrior" who had been "ware-
housed" as a long-term patient. The futility and folly of Vietnam crashed down

upon him. The VA staff was simply unable to cope with all the young wounded men coming home from the war. Veterans were identified not by name but by a claim number.

He reached rock-bottom on Easter Sunday 1969. While other men in his ward were out visiting friends or families, Max stayed behind, miserable and alone. "I wasn't living," he confesses in *Strong at the Broken Places*. "I was existing. I lay in bed, convulsed with gut-wracking sobs. I was bitter over the past. I was afraid of the future. And the tortuous present seemed unbearable. I wanted to die." Yet from the depths of that dark day, a new kind of warrior emerged, determined to regain control of his life. He battled back in small increments. Max moved into his own apartment. He went on dates, awkward as they invariably became. Striving for the appearance of normalcy, he began using artificial wooden limbs for walking even though they made his body ache with pain and were cumbersome to use. Ultimately he switched to a wheelchair. He started to swim and learned to operate a car with a specially equipped steering wheel.

Max then moved back to Lithonia. But jobless and aimless, he began drinking and going to bars. What rescued him from this self-destructive path was the allure of politics. He ran for the Georgia State Senate and won on his first try. At the age of twenty-eight, he became its youngest member. When Georgia governor Jimmy Carter was elected to the White House, he appointed Max to run the Veterans Administration. In this cabinet-level post, Max oversaw a sprawling bureaucracy of several hundred thousand government employees. He expanded veterans' rights and care, while creating veteran centers across the country that offered psychological counseling for the first time. After Ronald Reagan became president, Max returned to Georgia and won election as secretary of state. He served at that post for twelve years, then won election to the U.S. Senate in 1996.

During his 2002 re-election campaign, Max faced a new kind of adversary. Democrats like himself were fast becoming an endangered species in the New South. Even so, his Republican challenger played dirty. Four-term Congressman Saxby Chambliss, who sat out Vietnam with a bum knee, sought to discredit Max's integrity. One particularly odious television commercial displayed images of Osama bin Laden and Saddam Hussein which then morphed into an image of Max, while the narrator criticized him for voting against Bush's homeland security bill. What the ad intentionally left out was that Max had supported Democratic legislation that was fairly identical to the president's (the White House initially opposed the creation of the Homeland Security Department). "That was the biggest lie in America," an angry Max later told the *Washington Post*. "To put me up there with Osama bin Laden and Saddam Hussein and say I voted against homeland security!"

Because Max wanted to spend the rest of his political career in the U.S. Senate, he took the electoral loss hard. He grew increasingly depressed. "It was the second big grenade in my life," he told the *Post*. "It blew me up. It happened very quickly and very intensely, and I was left with virtually nothing but my life." But Max was lured back to politics by John Kerry's decision to run for president. A band-of-brothers kinship bonded these two war veterans and Senate colleagues. Max went on the road, and campaigned for Kerry before large, appreciative crowds.

Bush's victory, however, rekindled Max's anger and disappointment. It further aggravated the pain of losing his Senate seat. As for that *first* big grenade in his life, it took place in Vietnam on April 8, 1968, during the siege of Khe Sanh. Max had recently been promoted to captain. He volunteered to help the First Cavalry's infantry battalion as one of its communications officers, which meant leaving the relative safety of a rear base and being choppered into a combat zone. After five days of point-blank rocket attacks on their hillside position (four men were killed and many were seriously wounded) a Chinook helicopter scooped up Max and flew him to another location so that he could set up a new communications post. Upon leaving the aircraft, he saw a grenade at his feet. Thinking that it was his, he reached down to pick up the grenade. It exploded.

In the first of three interviews for *Patriots Act*, Max recalls what happened next: "When that grenade went off, I was totally conscious. Totally. Saw the bone sticking out from my right arm. Body was on fire, filled with hot shrapnel. The flash burns seared my flesh and was the only reason I didn't burn to death right there. I was bleeding to death. Three men ran to me after the smoke cleared. I was burning. I was literally smoking, dying, and bleeding to death. They staunched the bleeding. Called in a chopper. Put me on the chopper and medevac'd me fifty miles to a hospital. A Quonset hut. I was just about to pass out by then. I said, 'Do what you can to save my leg.'"

"Every time I think about the incident," he writes in *Strong at the Broken Places*, "I blamed myself for getting wounded, for not coming back from the war whole, for somehow 'screwing up.' For thirty-two years, I had carried around the weight of that uncertainty. When I was having a bad night, the lingering self-doubt could keep me awake for hours."

Emotional release from guilt's paralyzing hold unexpectedly arrived in the form of a phone call in 1999. The caller had just watched a History Channel show on combat medics in which Max was interviewed. He was a former Marine named David Lloyd who had been in the helicopter with Max. He was also the first to come to his aid, tying off the bleeding on one of his legs with a tourniquet fashioned from strips from Max's uniform and web belt. Lloyd then attended to a young soldier who was wounded by the blast. The soldier kept crying, "It's all my fault!" Fresh out of basic training and only in-country for several days, he had foolishly straightened out the pins of his grenades for quick access. That made them live grenades. When one fell loose from his pack, it exploded.

With that day's mystery finally revealed after all those years, Max felt reborn. "David had given me an invaluable gift, the gift of peace of mind. Finally, I can say, 'It was not my fault.' That is a great burden off my shoulders. It makes all the other burdens in my life seem less significant and more manageable."

■   ■   ■

I find myself today, going on sixty-four, a washed-up, dried-up prune of a military veteran who has been thrown on the scrap heap of time and looking back wistfully and saying, "I wished I'd done more to prevent the current disaster in Iraq that's exactly mocking the first disaster in Vietnam that I was personally a part of."

I go to Walter Reed Hospital now for trauma counseling. For my own self. Because it never ends. I've got post-traumatic stress disorder. Didn't know I had it. Anxiety and fear and all that crap. And it never goes away. But you can submerge it into a higher cause like politics.

So here I am, back at Walter Reed, thirty-seven years later, dealing with the trauma of Vietnam. I never got the counseling back then. But I look down the hall, and it's still 1968. Seeing all these young Iraq War veterans blown up, missing arms and legs and eyes, I just can't stand it. It triggers all of my stuff from Vietnam. And these young men had the same grit and courage that we had going off to war. You go up to 'em, and say, "How ya doing, son?" "Fine, sir!" they answer. But years later, it will take its toll. They just don't know yet.

I'm seeing the full circle of the Vietnam experience. What's happening today is that a certain number of young Marines and Army guys are doomed to get killed and blown up and have missing arms and legs and eyes, and maybe they'll be on the phone twenty to thirty years later talking to some guy writing a book about them. I have seen this movie before. I'm terrified that I'm seeing Vietnam all over again in my lifetime.

Iraq is Vietnam on steroids. I recently had a phone call from a friend of mine who was in the same infantry battalion that I later went into. He wrote the history of that battalion in a book called *The Lost Battalion*. His name is Charley Krohn and he teaches at the University of Michigan. He is a hard-core Republican, but he transcends his party. He says, "We have the worst of both worlds in Iraq." Charley knows combat. His squad lost over half its men—over twenty men—in the woods outside Hue during the Tet Offensive.

Anybody who understands Vietnam or went through it, like me and Charley and others, sees this war in Iraq as nothing other than total folly. Its impact on me has been profound. It got me involved in the Kerry presidential campaign. It attracted my fellow Vietnam veterans who understood the arrogance of power and were wounded by it. When I speak with soldiers back from the Iraq, they have the same deep, mixed feelings that we had when we came back from Vietnam. They are proud of having served their country. But then again, they are disgusted and angry with the way they were used and finding themselves in a situation where they get blown up and maimed and worse.

Bush has created a war that didn't have to happen. As Richard Clarke put it, "Invading Iraq after 9/11 was like invading Mexico after Pearl Harbor." Instead of going after bin Laden and all of his terrorists in the mountains, Bush transferred those resources and those men on the ground to Iraq. We now see a new generation of terrorists willing to blow themselves up to take out a bunch of Americans. And you add the Iraqi people. What you have is an absolute disaster.

Bush has gotten young Americans killed and wounded and blown up in a shooting gallery in Iraq. In a way, that is criminal. It is grinding the American military down. People are going back for their third tours. We have in effect thrown in everything we've got. And it ain't working. It's getting worse. There's continued killing. And sooner or later either the people or Congress are gonna ask, "Is it worth it?" And they are gonna answer, "No!" And then where are all these young men and women who have lost legs and arms and eyes going to be? That's called Vietnam.

The main problem is that there is no exit strategy to win in Iraq. What was our exit strategy in World War I and World War II? My answer was to win. Former Army Chief of Staff General Shinseki requested 250,000 to 500,000 troops for Iraq. These additional troops were necessary to secure the population. Bush didn't want to go with that number. So there are not enough troops on the ground to win. We are trapped in the quagmire. And the American people will ultimately reject that. As a matter of fact, the majority of Americans think it is not worth it anymore. I knew it would happen. It took the American people about two years to come to that realization.

Sooner or later, the U.S. will ultimately withdraw from Iraq. What they have created in Iraq is a terror haven, a civil war that has no end. We destabilized Iraq. It had a stable government. We didn't like it. We had Saddam Hussein in a box.

But this president went in and took Saddam Hussein out and thought that was gonna be the end of it. He didn't listen to Secretary of State Colin Powell, who said, "Mr. President, do you understand the consequences?" Of course he did not. Not only didn't he know the consequences of those decisions, Bush wanted to be macho and be better than his daddy.

The people who got us into this war didn't want to learn from history. Of the 550,000 who served in Vietnam, 100,000 were foxhole strength. So Defense Secretary Rumsfeld wanted to go in on the cheap. The original Pentagon Plan for the invasion of Iraq called for 500,000. That's the first plan Bush was shown, because the Army has about 131 indices on a matrix that says: Given the terrain, given the forces, given the population, if you are going to invade the country and do regime change and have to occupy and secure the population and control the terrorists, then take all these factors and you come out with the X factor, which was 500,000 troops. Rumsfeld and Bush wanted to go in and do it on the cheap in a running start—not as Colin Powell did in the first Gulf War and send 500,000 people in there at one time. Your ground war lasts ten hours and it's over. No. Not this crowd. They had no idea what they were doing. So the problem is that another generation of young Americans will come to grief over war. Under Bill Clinton, General Hugh Shelton, chairman of the Joint Chiefs of Staff, used to say, "American military is the great hammer. But every problem in the world is not necessarily a nail."

You have to be willing to give up control of Iraq. Give up the oil fields. Only then will you get the international community to come in and set up an international protectorate. I heard one hard-core Republican say that the best thing we can do is turn over everything to the Shiites and get the hell outta there. But this crowd is stuck with its war policy. It will not give up the oil fields. It will not do what is necessary to call in the international community. And so there will be war for another five or ten years. It will take a Democratic president to come in, make peace, extricate the American forces and replace it with an international coalition. Ultimately the Shiite majority will rule. Now is that in our strategic interest? Well, the Shiite majority in Iran is backing the Shiites in Iraq. So you just made the international balance of power in the Middle East tilt to Iran, which is developing a nuclear program and supports Hezbollah. The whole thing is now totally antithetical to American foreign policy goals. We are screwed, and Tehran comes out the big winner. So that is the endgame. But we re-elected Bush on fear and smear. And so we got several more years of hell.

Back in '66, Walter Lippman, when he was criticizing the Vietnam War, used to say that that the battles we fight we win, but the battles we fight can't win the war. You see, that's the essence of guerrilla warfare. You can send in a highly mechanized operation and kill more of them than they kill of you. But you're creating tremendous political backlash, and you're making more enemies than friends.

Western democracies, particularly America, do not fight guerrilla wars well. If we put in 750,000 troops and keep them in Iraq for ten to fifteen years and make Iraq the fifty-first state, then we can win there. We would need to seal off the borders with Syria and Iran. But we couldn't even seal off the DMZ in Vietnam. The point is, you would have to have the most massive call-up of soldiers. You'd have to call up all the reserves. Institute the draft. The Bush crowd doesn't want to do that. They are not willing to pay the price to do it right militarily. Yet they wanted a military solution. So they are stuck with the tar-baby war.

John Kennedy once described himself as an idealist with no illusions. In conflicts outside the boundaries and waters of the United States, you better be a realist. The history of the world teaches us that no foreign power is going to invade some country without tremendous opposition. We ran up against the Oriental mind-set in Vietnam. In the Middle East, they think in thousands of years: "Though it takes a thousand years for revenge, I'll get ya."

Sooner or later, the impact of the politics of unmitigated war in the Middle East will be felt here in America. But it will take time as the impact of these policies is felt in our pocketbook, in the gut, in the minds and hearts of American people. There is a great line by Benjamin Franklin. Coming out of Constitution Hall in Philadelphia, a lady asked, "Dr. Franklin, what kind of government do we have?" And he said, "We have a Republic—if you can keep it." So this sense of an American experiment is not a given thing.

I've run across people—young people, old people—who want to continue the fight for what they perceive as the defense of democracy in our country. I met this lady who worked for former Senator Tom Daschle. They were clearing out his office on Capitol Hill. She said that she initially wanted to leave the country and move to Costa Rica. She then quoted something from Thomas Jefferson, and I will paraphrase: "Every generation has to decide anew whether it wants to continue this democracy."

One of Kerry's campaign speeches used a quote from President Kennedy. It went: "Every man can make a difference. And all of us should try." That is what inspired me to get involved in politics. I had come to Washington in the fall of 1963. Twenty-one years old. Out of a little school called Stetson University in Florida. I was a senior and signed up for the Washington semester program. The course catalog said: "See government in action." I was not a political animal when I arrived. I was not registered to vote. I didn't even know what a liberal was. I had never taken a course in political science or government. So I found myself at American University taking courses in American politics.

I latched onto the excitement and promise of John Kennedy, our nation's youngest president. I never met him personally. But it was the charm and charisma and talent and optimism and hope that John Kennedy brought to American politics that turned my generation into political activists. He motivated us. Compare that today with what you see on Capitol Hill. We're in combat mode on Capitol Hill where you see all these guards and concrete slabs. Think of that.

I was one of the last people to see Kennedy in an open convertible. They were honoring Haile Selassie, the Emperor of Ethiopia. Selassie was standing up in the car as they came down Pennsylvania Avenue. The crowd was adoringly cheering them on. Kennedy was sitting in the back right seat where he also found himself in Dallas. All I could see of him was a shock of hair. It wasn't as dark as it appeared in black and white photographs. It had a reddish tint to it. I couldn't quite see his face.

At one o'clock on November 22, 1963, I was in my dorm room in Letts Hall on the campus of American University. My roommate was listening to the radio and looked up at me. He was down on the floor listening intently. He said, "Kennedy's been shot." I ran to a television. Saw Cronkite break down. I just ran for a taxi. I wanted to go right down to the White House. I went down Massachusetts Avenue. I don't know what got into me. I stopped off at the British Embassy and went inside to get their reaction. Isn't that silly? By the time I got to the White House, there was black crepe dressed over the door.

His death gripped me completely. I stayed down near the White House. That night, I peered through the gates to the South Lawn to see when Johnson's helicopter landed. So in one day, the earth turned for me, for my generation, for the world. But we forget that there had been an earlier assassination in October. Now we call it regime change. When things were not going well in South Vietnam, the Kennedy administration opted for regime change and a bunch of generals captured Ngo Dinh Diem and assassinated him. And then we went through twenty-six different governments fighting "the insurgents," in this case, the guerrillas. For ten more years, 58,000 soldiers were killed, 350,000 wounded. Of which I was one.

I had volunteered for the Army. We had the draft, so you either were going into the military as an officer or enlistee. If you were in college, you wanted to go in as an officer. That's why I joined the ROTC at Stetson. I remember one day in June of '63, before I moved to Washington, D.C., I was standing there by the highway in my ROTC uniform watching the 102nd Airborne and the 82nd Airborne out of Fort Bragg come down with trucks and head to Miami and the Keys for the jumping-off point for the invasion of Cuba. The previous year, in '62, we were eyeball-to-eyeball with the Russians in what later became the Cuban Missile Crisis. South Florida was almost washed into the ocean with a thermonuclear holocaust. We now know how close we came to that. But Kennedy showed restraint, not taking the bait from the generals. They were all calling for an invasion of the island.

Believe it or not, I volunteered for an extra ROTC night course in counter-insurgency. I was studying counter-insurgency and anvil-and-hammer techniques, in 1962! I went to summer camp at Fort Benning with the 11th Air Assault Test Division that was being formed and which later turned into the First Air Cavalry Division—and which I later volunteered for. I thought that the way to fight guerrilla was to be mobile, hostile, and agile. Not ground-bound like the French were.

I volunteered for Vietnam in the spring of '67. I had just come out of a masters program in history at Emory University. My thesis was about the onset of the Great Depression. I became a big aficionado of the New Deal, which is why I have three pictures up in my office in D.C., only three, Franklin Roosevelt, Winston Churchill, and The Lone Ranger. All three great heroes in history for various reasons.

I look at that period now, and I see that Vietnam was stalking Lyndon Johnson right from the beginning. He just made the wrong call. He didn't want to "lose" Vietnam and go through what Truman went through after Korea. He bought Secretary of Defense McNamara's line: "We've got to go invade." Six months later, McNamara didn't believe it. By that spring, when I volunteered to fight, we now know, according to the Pentagon Papers and McNamara's own book, that he didn't believe the war was winnable. McNamara should have told us before we volunteered. So, me and 550,000 troops were on the ground during the Tet Offensive. And they cleaned our clock. On televisions back here, Walter Cronkite said, "I thought we were winning the war over there."

When I had gone over to Vietnam, I was thinking it would be like South Korea. Finger in the dike. Stop the bad guys from taking over the south. You know, we are the good guys. They are the bad guys. I bought the whole premise. But then each week, each month that went by, I saw that we were more motivated than the South Vietnamese troops. Then I ran across a friend of mine who was an adviser to the Vietnamese. He was an Army captain. He said, "We are on the wrong side." The situation on the ground was completely different than we had been told. The Viet Cong went after us with dynamism, and they did so with such ferocity that they were looked upon as patriots. The Viet Cong swam in the sea of the people. They could not have existed had the public not supported them. So we became the new French. Later, as I read some history about Vietnam, I discovered that the U.S. had air-dropped supplies to Ho Chi Minh when he was fighting the Japanese. But when we started fighting communism, Ho Chi Minh became the enemy.

I wound up being retired from the United States Army the day before Christmas Eve 1969. I was sitting in my mother's living room in my little hometown. No future. No hope. No job. No income. No apartment. No car. So the decade which had dawned with such promise in January 1961 and with such great words—"Ask not what your country can do for you; ask what you can do for your country"—ended up with me biting the whole bait. I went with the whole program.

In Georgia, nobody would give me a job. Nobody was coming around and saying, "Oh, you're a great American hero." I'd have a friend take me to Atlanta and we'd get drunk. I'd come back and think, "What the hell kind of life is this?" So I decided to get back into politics. I really had no other alternative if I wanted to get out of all this pain and sorrow. Running for public office was something that would give me a sense of meaning and purpose and direction. It was something I could do to make a contribution. I had been interested in running for Congress, but I didn't think I could win as a fresh face. I looked at the State Senate, which included my hometown in the district. I thought, "Well maybe if I ran a good campaign, I could win." And so I ran and raised my own money.

After I got elected to the Georgia State Senate in 1970 and Jimmy Carter was elected governor, I put forward a resolution in the State Senate for the withdrawal of our ground forces in exchange for our POWs. Although I had never joined Vietnam Veterans Against the War, what began to sink into my mind, as I saw more and more casualties coming home with arms and legs lost, was, "This has got to stop." The only thing that I thought could get us out of Vietnam was to get our POWs back.

When he became president, Jimmy Carter took a big chance on me to run the Veterans Administration, because I was only thirty-four and I had never run anything bigger than a platoon. He put me in charge of a department larger than eight cabinet departments combined. And it was a glorious experience. Tremendous stress. Tremendous pressure. But we were highly focused. We were highly motivated. Because we had to take care of these Vietnam veterans coming back.

We created a diagnosis for PTSD—post-traumatic stress disorder. The former chairman of the Veterans Affairs Committee in the House of Representatives thought Vietnam veterans were crybabies. World War II guys didn't believe all this stuff. So, PTSD was created as a diagnosis. I created the vet center program with Senator Alan Cranston and Jimmy Carter. The first vet center I dedicated personally. It was in Van Nuys, California. It was me and two guys. No band. No flag. No flair. Nothing. Now there are twenty vet centers in the country. And they are swamped—not only by veterans of the Vietnam era, but also from the Gulf War. Now more and more are from the Iraq War.

In four years, we also were able to create a new vocational-rehabilitation program, which had not been updated since World War II. We were able to do a helluva lot. But after Jimmy Carter lost the election in '80, I only got one phone call the next day. It was from a low-level guy in one of the veterans organizations. That was it. He said that I had the most thankless job in Washington.

I put my stuff back in a truck and hauled it back to Georgia. I moved in with my mother and daddy again for two years. And I then ran for Georgia's secretary of state. Won that. I was secretary of state for twelve years. I probably shoulda stayed there. But U.S. Senator Sam Nunn walked away from his seat. And Clinton was in office. It looked like good things were happening. I figured that the only reason I'd go to Washington would be to take Sam Nunn's place on the Armed Services Committee. So I ran and won. I thought that if I just worked hard and did a good job—I looked after our troops and cared about Georgia—that I would be re-elected and carry on Sam Nunn's legacy.

What I didn't reckon on happening was George Bush winning in 2000 and Karl Rove coming in and teaming up with Ralph Reed. And then in 2002, with the impact of 9/11, the Republican Party began trashing everybody as if they were un-American. I was actually an author of a homeland security bill along with Joe Lieberman. But the Chambliss campaign ran an ad saying that I voted against George Bush and homeland security. Well, I voted against some amendments while the bill was in committee. They just did their normal fear and smear job. And yet, I had voted for Bush's tax cut and I voted for the war, which is the worst vote I ever cast.

Looking back at my six years in the U.S. Senate, I take pride in the accomplishments during the early days. The expansion of NATO in Western Europe, in Poland and the Czech Republic and so on. It was literally the expansion of freedom. The march of justice and freedom expanding through the Western European theater and into some old Soviet-dominated areas.

Then came Clinton's impeachment. The trial in the Senate was the most awful experience you can possibly imagine. I was sick as a dog. Not just politically but personally. I had mononucleosis and didn't even know it. Viral infection in my sinuses. I just thought I was gonna die.

I voted not guilty. While Clinton lied and so forth, it certainly was not an impeachable offense. But it brought down the Democratic progress, and it activated the radical right. It gave them something to beat the Democrats over the head with in the elections of 2000. Which is one reason Bush won.

In the Senate, I also tried to push for families qualifying under the GI Bill to take care of the troops. After 9/11, under the flag that was flown at election time, good works seem to not matter. That is one of the powerful discouraging things about politics today. It's not what you produce or the good works that you do. It's whether or not you're able to withstand a thirty-second negative ad and if you're willing to go out and trash the other guy or gal just as badly. It's all character assassination politics now. It seems to carry the day. That's the sad part about it.

Personally, after my Senate loss on election night 2002, it went downhill from there. I still haven't emerged from that loss. In Robert Caro's book about Lyndon Johnson, LBJ said that he lost the South after the Civil Rights bill. By 1968, Nixon had embarked on the Southern strategy: "Go after the redneck boys on race. It'll bring 'em in every time." You know, it become more subtle over the years. Certainly, it's what Ralph Reed had used against me in my 2002 re-election campaign. The Confederate emblem on the state flag was the incendiary bomb in Georgia politics. And it hit the third rail. Which killed us all. It gave the hatchet to the right wing. They raised the issue that Democrats were trying to take away Georgia's culture. The cultural war included the Confederate flag. That was their symbol. The Republicans were for the whites. The Democrats were for the blacks. They pulled the flag into their cultural issues of abortion, guns, gays, and God. Karl Rove got a lot of money to come down and push nothing but voter registration and turnout for white males. That's what was coming off the charts in anger against all Democrats. There was also George Bush's five visits to Georgia. They buried us with their strategy. It turned out an extra 140,000 angry white males who normally didn't vote. And it turned the mid-term election. Governor Roy Barnes and I lost by approximately the same margin.

When I'm in public office and doing something worthwhile in a cause, I have a mission and a purpose. I can perform and do great things and enjoy it magnificently. When I don't have that, I'm struggling with deep depression and discouragement and a sense of meaninglessness. When John Kerry announced his candidacy, he asked me to introduce him at Charleston, South Carolina.

That's when I really started campaigning for him. I traveled to Iowa for the first time in December 2002. Then I went back in early January in 2004, and Kerry won the Iowa Caucus.

I helped encourage Kerry's focus on war veterans. John asked me to introduce him at the Democratic National Convention. About 40 million people saw that. I think that's what sticks in people's minds—that introduction. Then, on the downside: the campaign did not respond well or quickly to the Swift Boat attack ads. Well, what John had wanted to do was what he did in combat. When they start shooting at you, you turn the boat into the attacker and kill the attacker. That's what you've got to do. John instinctively knew that. Ultimately, that meant overriding his advisers in order to do that. But I was late in coming. So one of the things they did was send me to Crawford, Texas. Well, it was just hell to pay. I had a letter signed by nine Democratic members of the United States Senate, including Medal of Honor winner Dan Inouye. The letter said, "Cease and desist this attack on a distinguished American veteran."

Once I got to Crawford, it was a gaggle of press like I had never seen before. We wound up in this little car going up a two-lane road. There were thirteen vehicles behind us. All press. The Secret Service was waiting for us at the gate to Bush's ranch. They denied us at the gate. Then we turned around and went a few miles down the road to a school yard and got out onto the red dirt. I later realized we were live on CNN. Live on Fox. It was not one of my finer moments. My friends gave me nice rave reviews about my speech at the Democratic convention, but they didn't give me good marks about the trip to Crawford, Texas. They said, "You looked mean and bitter and angry. That's not the Max Cleland we know." My trip there didn't do a damn bit of good. It was a Charge of the Light Brigade. It didn't change anything. It did not reflect well on the campaign or me or anything else.

With John Kerry, it looked like maybe the Vietnam War had produced a leader for the country who could translate that powerful negative into a very powerful positive experience, and with a new positive direction in our foreign policy. But that was not to be.

John and I continue to talk. He said, "You need me, I'm here. You call me. Any time." The other band of brothers have said the same thing. We all reinforce one another because we were all hooked by our Vietnam experience. Trying to give a sense of meaning and purpose and destiny to the Vietnam War, which on its face came out with no meaning and no purpose. You see what I'm saying?

Today, there are no manners in politics. We've seen the viciousness with which the Republican crowd goes after people. They took out Senator John

McCain in South Carolina in 2000; Senator Bob Smith in the New Hampshire primary, again a Vietnam War veteran; Chuck Robb in 2000 in Virginia; myself in 2002 in Georgia; John Kerry and Tom Daschle in 2004. The viciousness of their campaigns of character assassination have reached new levels. It's obvious that they threw out any rules of law. Now it's all about whatever it takes to win and devil take the hindmost. It's getting kids killed in Iraq and our foreign policy is at low ebb. The economy is going down. The dollar is getting weaker. Increasingly we are just the laughingstock of the world.

I'm a Democrat, so I cite Thomas Jefferson. He said there were basically two classes of people: one that tends to leave authority to the select few and the powerful, and the other is one that wants to give the people control. Jacksonian Democracy is really the fulfillment of that. Andrew Jackson. Old Hickory. The hero of New Orleans. He had a great line that I used for John Kerry. "One man with courage is a majority." I've been down to Andrew Jackson's home. The Hermitage outside of Nashville, Tennessee. He ran for president once and didn't make it. But he ran for president a second time and did make it. Ironic that such a man of the South represented Democratic ideals. Now, Democratic ideals are being shunned for the past twenty to twenty-five years in the modern South.

But anyway, the point is that the great history of the United States will ultimately triumph over any radical departure from real authentic American values which go all the way back to Plato and are echoed through Jefferson, Jackson, Benjamin Franklin, and a host of others. And that is the sense of wisdom and justice. And moderation and courage. In fact, with the phrase "equal justice under law," you really don't have an underpinning of law until there is a sense of justice. And what is justice? Life, liberty, and the pursuit of happiness. That one man's life, liberty, and pursuit of happiness is just as valued as another man's life, liberty, and pursuit of happiness. Therein lies your values of the democratic process.

This Republican crowd is a Trojan horse. They say one thing and do another. I don't think you have to be false with people. You have to tell the truth and seriously connect with people. Average citizens thought they were doing the right thing by voting for Bush and this crowd. You need to be honest and straightforward and real with the American people. Ultimately, as Lincoln said, "You can fool some of the people all of the time, and all of the people some of the time, but you cannot fool all of the people all of the time."

I have no more desire to return to politics. I still have tremendous desire for public service. I'm on the Export-Import Bank Board right now, but I want to stay involved in public service in Georgia. But I have no desire to put my name on the ballot. I won't ever run for office again. I can't handle it. Because it did me in. It's too much physically and emotionally. So probably my best venue is out of the limelight. I'm like an old combat commander. I've been in combat too long. I was in combat for nine years, from October 1995 to just recently. I have known both military and political battles. I have been traumatically wounded by both. Winston Churchill said that politics is a lot like war, except in war, you get killed once. In politics you get killed many times.

It's time to get off the old battlefield and into the cheerleader stands. I recently taught some college courses in American politics and history. I've been involved in a series on NPR working with the Veterans History Project called *Experiencing War*. I'm a narrator. Lee Woodman is the independent producer. The Veterans History Project was created in the Library of Congress by me and Senator Chuck Hagel. It deals with the personal histories of servicemen and women, from World War I to the present.

Looking back on my career, I am proud of being the Veterans Administration head and dealing with the aftermath of the Vietnam War, in particular, putting together the program for veterans' centers, which deals with the emotional aftermath of war for veterans and their families. Thank God for that program, because it is being swamped by a new crew of Iraq War veterans. They are dealing with depression, anxiety attacks — stuff like that. We have created a quarter of a million Iraq War veterans. In Vietnam, we had eight and a half million veterans. We are adding to that quarter of a million number every day. Walter Reed is swamped with bona fide casualties. Particularly amputees. The VA is swamped. They don't have enough resources. Senator Craig, a hard-core Republican from Idaho who is on the Senate Armed Forces Committee, admitted that the VA medical program was about a billion dollars short. The private counseling program is where it is most short. That is what ought to be beefed up. With all these Iraq War veterans coming home, their families will also need counseling.

Instead of *American Idol* on TV, we ought to be focusing on the lives of these young kids coming back with injuries that would have killed them in Vietnam, like concussions to the brain, because 85 percent of the casualties in Iraq are due to explosive devices. That's a shock and trauma to the system even if you survive it. It blows up your insides and your brain in a concussion that you won't ever get over. It is just terrifying to come back and have to live with that the rest of your life. But these kids are so brave and so courageous that we ought to be focusing on them. Instead, many people put a sticker on the back of their car that says, "We Support the Troops," and then they put a Bush/Cheney sticker on the other side. And think that that's America.

Meanwhile, the Democrats are trapped in a mixed message. Anytime you have troops at war, you are reluctant to criticize it. Because then you are attacked as un-American and unpatriotic. So it's hard to stand up and speak the truth. Those who do get trashed. They get attacked by the Slime Machine. The price to go up against them is awful. I was on the 9/11 Commission, but I resigned after a year because we would never get access to all of those presidential daily briefs. Ten, twenty years later you'll have another commission and go into this thing in depth. But right now, it's all part of this massive cover-up that somehow we are fighting the war on terrorism in Iraq.

The current political situation is enough to kill everybody's spirits. We are in a deep dark time in American history, but the American character is wonderful. Arthur Schlesinger, Jr. recently told me that the great thing about our democracy is that it is self-correcting.

■ ■ ■

My View of Max

Commercial real estate attorney Stephen Leeds, fifty-nine, has known Max Cleland for several decades. He's a close friend and former chair of his political campaign committee, Friends of Max Cleland. At the present, Leeds is secretary of Georgia's Democratic Party.

I am from the Northeast, and I came to Georgia in 1980. When Max decided to run for secretary of state in Georgia, I contributed a little. He later asked me to chair his political campaign committee. I was the chair of his campaigns from that point forward through 2002. He always referred to me as his alter ego. My temperament is cool when his is hot. I am a behind-the-scenes guy. I tell Max, "If I'm in the newspaper, I'm doing something wrong."

He's definitely emotional, and I'm much more analytical. When he was in the U.S. Senate, my world really changed. He asked me to be honorary chief of staff. That meant I was a government employee, but I never earned a dime off this relationship. I handled his senatorial transition team and went to D.C. a few times. All the press wanted to know were the handicap changes made to the Senate to accommodate him. Max told reporters, "Look, I do not want to be known as the Handicapped Senator. But I also happen to be handicapped."

Max is in a sense a regular guy. He loves to have fun, loves humor. He doesn't drink. You see him sit at the bar, leaning back and just having a great time with the guys and girls. He never married, but is currently engaged. He has not set a date. He's very careful about his privacy. Max is certainly a man of the South. He likes quoting lines from the Confederate Soldier's Prayer.

After he came back from rehab and decided he would devote his life to public service, he was determined to put to use what had happened to him in Vietnam. As Georgia's secretary of state, his office always got calls from folks needing help with the VA and military. Max became a beacon for health and help. He told me this story the other day. He was visiting Walter Reed Hospital where he met a nineteen-year-old of Filipino descent who had come to the U.S., volunteered to go to Iraq, and came back missing, I think, three limbs—just like Max. Max said to me, "Ya know, I looked at him and thought what kind of future does this kid have?" But this kid has the possibility of a better future than Max had when he came back from Vietnam. He shows these guys what one can do.

Max does best when he is helping others. Making money was never a driving force for him. What really drives Max is the opportunity to do good. We talk about that a lot—the chance to do good, the chance to do the right thing for people, to speak for others, and speak for what was right.

He knew that the political process was a difficult calling. That is probably why he took the Senate loss so hard. Because it was at his core—the desire to better other people. Max was as down as I've ever seen him in twenty-five years. He said to me that he took this loss worse than what happened to him in Vietnam. I've always had a hard time believing that. But when he says it, you have to take it at face value because only he can ever equate something with what happened to him in Vietnam.

I tell him all the time his work is not done. I told him that the night he lost the Senate race. We all try and find meaning from loss. Max is a very religious person, and he believes in God. He believes God put himself here. He has no idea what the next thing will be that will call upon him to do something of particular meaning. Some people would like him to consider someday being head of the Democratic Party. To my knowledge, he does not have much interest in that.

A lot of people put Max up on a pedestal and do not think of him in purely human terms. That is probably true with a lot of significant public figures. A friend of Max's said to me, "Just for Max to get up and get dressed is so much greater than most mere mortals must go through." Imagine getting up in the morning, but you can't just get out of bed. Everything takes longer. Just to get across the room. So it takes a helluva long time. Think about getting in and out of a bath? Just imagine setting a table for breakfast if you're in a wheelchair and using only one hand. Think how many things you can put in your lap at a time.

His writing is always dictated. Before dictation he used to have "Maxograms" on yellow paper. He would joke, "To get a card from Max took two hours to decipher." That is because he had to learn to write with his left hand.

FDR went out of the way to shroud the wheelchair. There are very few pictures of him in the wheelchair. Lot of folks, when they come into contact with someone who is in a wheelchair or has some disability—there is a hesitation about how to deal with that person. With Max, it's "Give me a hug" and "How ya doing?" And, "Hey, I'm Max!" Max doesn't know a stranger. That is part of his charm.

Max generates hope and instills a feeling that you can overcome almost anything. Because of that quality he inspires people when he speaks about issues that touch on democracy, reclaiming democracy, defining democracy, fighting for democracy. He is one of the persons most likely to touch someone about democracy's hold on our souls. Many politicians think in terms of succeeding on a particular piece of legislation. With Max, it all ends up in more deeply human terms. All of his political work is a heart-to-heart transaction. He once shared with me a letter he got from a woman, who was either contemplating suicide or was very despondent about life. After hearing Max talk on a show with Rev. Robert Schuller, she felt renewed. She decided things were not as bad as she thought they were. The person who wrote that letter didn't have a catastrophic injury. But it shows the positive effect Max has on another person's life. That is why I say his work is not done, because he has that effect on so many people.

3

"FREE SPEECH" ON THE FOURTH OF JULY

Nicole and Jeff Rank were arrested at the president's
Independence Day speech in Charleston, West Virginia,
because they were wearing anti-Bush T-shirts.

> "Large numbers of the crowd began chanting
> against us. 'America the Beautiful' was playing
> on the loudspeakers while we were being walked
> out in handcuffs."

Nicole and Jeff Rank are a quiet, young couple from Corpus Christi, Texas. They've
been married seven years. They are the type of life partners who politely finish
each other's sentences. There is nothing glitzy, eccentric, or radical about them.
They have very few sharp edges. Well-mannered, serious, and thoughtful would
be an apt description of the pair. About the only unusual thing one can say about
them is that Nicole, at thirty-two, is two years older than Jeff. They met in 1993
on the Galveston campus of Texas A&M.

Jeff grew up as a Navy brat. After obtaining a master's degree in oceanogra-
phy, he worked at the non-profit conservation organization Sea Grant. He held this
job for several years before deciding to change careers, swapping the sea for law.
"When I was in graduate school," explains Jeff, "I was reading a *Physics Today*
issue about the Kansas school board and the evolution debate. This was before intelligent design had been popularized. It was still being called creationism. Several
physicists had written, 'How could this happen? This is ridiculous. We can't believe
we're still arguing over this.' Then the Academy of Sciences responded, 'Hey, look,
the reason it happened is because all the creationists got together and got involved in policy, while the scientists sat cerebrally on the side.' This exchange got
me interested in policy and the application of science to the public sector." In the
fall of 2005, he started his first year at the University of Houston Law School.

With degrees in biological science and marine biology, Nicole landed at the Federal Emergency Management Agency, where she became an environmental liaison

officer in the mid-Atlantic region. She made sure that local governments adhered to specific environmental guidelines before emergency aid checks could be issued. "I dealt mostly with the public entities—city, county, state—and a lot of what we got was roadway damages," says Nicole. "Occasionally, we dealt with things like a threatened or endangered species where they're putting in a new culvert."

In late May 2004, heavy flooding hit the Charleston, West Virginia, region. FEMA was called in. Nicole packed her bags, and Jeff made the trip with her. They took along their cat, Rowr, and cocker spaniel, Feynman (named after the legendary physicist Richard Feynman). FEMA put up the Ranks and their pets at the downtown Embassy Suites Hotel. It seemed like the start of a pleasant, uneventful summer for these two Texans. When they found out that the president was coming to Charleston to give a Fourth of July speech at the Capitol, they decided to attend the holiday event—but as non-supporters wearing anti-Bush T-shirts. This minor act of sartorial defiance led to an unexpected outcome.

■　■　■

Jeff: The only other political event I ever went to in my life was listening to Vice President Al Gore speak in Galveston in the mid-'90s. I just stood in the back of the crowd. While Nicole and I obviously don't agree with Bush on a lot of issues, we thought that here's a great opportunity to see the President of the United States.

Nicole: This was my first political event. But we both wanted to stage a little protest of our own.

Jeff: You have to realize that neither of us had ever protested anything before. This was our first political protest. Ever. All we wanted to do was wear our anti-Bush T-shirts and quietly listen to him speak. His visit to Charleston wasn't a campaign stop, so it would be open to the public. I guess the reason we chose this particular form of protest was because whenever you'd watch television news coverage of Bush speaking at these events there would only be Bush supporters appearing in the background. We wanted to wear something identifying us as non-supporters.

Nicole: The commercials on television said that free event tickets were available to the public. You just had to call in to some telephone number and give them a certain amount of information, and they'd reserve tickets for you. They also made tickets available at the field office at FEMA where I was working—basically, the same tickets they were making available to the public, so I went ahead and signed up to get us tickets through work. They asked for my name, address, Social Security number.

Jeff: When I went to pick up the tickets at the local high school, they never asked anything about party affiliation. Along with the tickets, you got a little piece of paper with some instructions. Number one was: come a couple of hours early to get through security so you are there when the president shows up. Number two was a list of things that you couldn't bring, and on that list were things like coolers, lawn chairs, umbrellas, and signs. But notably, there was nothing on the list that said anything about attire.

Nicole: Jeff went out to buy pro-Kerry or anti-Bush T-shirts, but he wasn't able to find anything on such short notice. So what he did instead was buy plain white T-shirts and magic markers at Target. The morning before the event, we made our homemade T-shirts. Both T-shirts had Bush's name on the front with the international "No" symbol—the big circle with a line through it. The back of my T-shirt said: "Love America, Hate Bush." The back of Jeff's T-shirt said: "Regime Change Starts At Home." And then we had a couple of Kerry and anti-Bush buttons that we were also going to wear. And so, our attire for that day was basically shorts with those T-shirts. We also opted to wear a separate shirt over our T-shirts because we knew that most people going to the event were going to be Bush supporters and we didn't feel like getting heckled while waiting in line at the security checkpoint. So I wore a button-up denim shirt.

Jeff: I wore a Hawaiian shirt that I had bought at Steve and Barry's discount outlet in Charleston for $6.00.

Nicole: Getting through security didn't take quite as long as we had thought. Maybe an hour or so. They were security law enforcement officers and Secret Service people, or those who would appear to be Secret Service. You had to go through a metal detector.

Jeff: I had four little buttons in my wallet that set off the metal detector. Two small Kerry buttons and two anti-Bush buttons—maybe an inch in diameter—that had Bush's face on it with the international "No" symbol through it. One of the uniformed Secret Service officers definitely saw the buttons because he rifled through my wallet. But he didn't confiscate anything. I wasn't nervous. It was just like going through airport security.

Nicole: I wasn't nervous either. There was a lot of excitement going on at the State Capitol grounds; it was almost a festive sort of atmosphere. Bush was going to speak in front of the Capitol building itself. There's this big central garden area surrounded by buildings. It's a big complex. The crowd was standing in that open area. I'd say there were about twelve hundred people or more.

Jeff: By the time we got through the security and through the lines, it was 11:30 A.M., and Bush was not scheduled to speak until 1:00. The event was already in progress. Some of the local dignitaries got to say a couple of words at the podium. We finally got to where we would be standing, which was between the media stand and speaker's podium. All of the local television stations were there, plus members of the Associated Press and local newspapers. We then took off our outer shirts.

Nicole: We received a couple of strange looks when we first removed our outer shirts, but most people ignored us. One woman walked behind Jeff and said, "Don't you think that's tacky?" But we didn't respond. We heard a few other comments, but most people didn't think it was worth bothering us. Most people accepted the fact that we were being quiet—just standing there, not doing anything.

Jeff: We stood there for ten, fifteen minutes. Then these two guys came up. They looked like young Republican volunteers. They were wearing polo shirts. They had little tags around their necks The guy in a blue shirt—the other was in a red shirt—said, "You have to either take those shirts off or leave." We were dumbfounded. We said, "No, why do you think that?" And he replied, "This is not a political event, so you have to take the shirts off." This was just really absurd. There were people standing all around us with pro-Bush things on. Bush hats, pins, shirts. You could buy pro-Bush paraphernalia right there at the event.

Nicole: They were even selling a set of Bush-Cheney playing cards.

Jeff: I told them, "Look all around you and regardless of whether or not you think it's a political event, I can wear any offensive shirt I want as long as it's not vulgar, right? I mean, this is what the First Amendment was made for?" And they kept replying that we could either take our shirts off or leave. Those were the only options they gave us. We each had disposable cameras, so Nicole took a picture of me showing them our tickets while explaining our position. And while we were talking to them, a woman in front of us turned around and said, "Hey, it's their right to wear whatever they want. They may be crazy, but it's their right." Her companions started supporting us. I was really astounded and encouraged. Eventually the two guys walked away. Nicole and I looked at each other, thinking that was easy. I said, "Hey, that's what happens when you stand up to authority."

Nicole: Another thing was that the two guys had never identified themselves. While they had tags around their shirts, they weren't readily visible.

Jeff: We continued standing there. Nothing happened. Then the national anthem played. That's really the only thing we did—sing the national anthem—as far as raising our voices. Otherwise, we only spoke quietly to each other. We didn't talk to anybody else. Then about two or three cops showed up.

Nicole: The first thing the cops said, "Did two gentlemen ask you to remove your shirts or demand you leave?" And we said, "Yes, they did." The cops wanted to know why we weren't complying. We used the same logic we'd given the first two guys: We weren't breaking any laws; we hadn't done anything wrong; we were complying with all of the rules that had been set aside for this particular event; we weren't causing any harm; we weren't booing; we were simply standing there wearing our special T-shirts.

Jeff: I told the cops, "Look, you have seen the sum total of our protest. We're not going to yell, we're not going to heckle, and we're not going to do anything crazy. We're just going to stand here, and you guys are welcome to stand here with us if you feel that we pose a danger or if you're worried about our safety." One of their lines had been, "We are worried about your safety." I added, "If you guys either stand here or leave us alone or whatever, this is going to be the best-kept secret in Charleston, right?" Because they were now threatening to call over the arrest team. That was the term they kept using. Nicole and I were both astounded that it was getting to this level. I finally said, "You guys do what you have to do. We're going to stand here and do what we know that we are allowed to do." And so they called over the arrest team.

Nicole: The arrest team consisted of various members of different state law enforcement agencies. There were probably eight police officers in our immediate vicinity. While there were no uniformed Secret Service men, we noticed a couple of men standing in the background who were watching. They were dressed in the typical men-in-black sort of outfits. It wasn't definitive that they were Secret Service, but they certainly looked like Secret Service. They did not approach us directly. This was all handled with the state law enforcement officials. And then, interestingly enough, some of the people around us started to heckle us once they saw all these police gathered around us. They gained courage all of a sudden. The hecklers even included some of the people who had been previously supportive or who had left us alone. The police officers now said that they needed to protect us from the hecklers. Well, we tried to point out that the people who had started heckling us hadn't been bothering us until they showed up.

The officers then attempted to lead us out voluntarily by taking us by our arms and getting us to walk out. That was their last-ditch attempt at not actually arresting us. They wanted us to voluntarily walk out. But Jeff and I had both decided that we were not going to leave voluntarily, though we certainly were not going to resist arrest. We told the police officers, "If you feel you need to arrest us, go ahead, but we are not leaving voluntarily." At that point, Jeff and I sat down on the ground.

Jeff: After we sat down, they said, "Put your hands behind your backs." We did. They placed handcuffs around our wrists.

Nicole: Throughout this process, the police were pretty friendly to us. They were standing around, smiling. We didn't have any problems except for one particular cop who got in my face when I asked him if I could take a photograph of my husband being handcuffed. He got aggressive and started screaming at me, saying that I was causing trouble.

Jeff: They led us out in our handcuffs. We didn't make them carry us. There were some false news reports that said we had kicked and resisted and spit. That was simply untrue. The officers had no choice but to lead us out directly in front of the media stand. By then, the cameras were already trained on us. Reporters started following us. Then large numbers of the crowd began chanting against us. I don't remember what they were saying. What I do remember was "America the Beautiful" was playing on the loudspeakers while we were being walked out in handcuffs. If you saw it in a movie, you'd go, "Ah, this isn't real." It was one of those very surreal moments.

Nicole: There are news photos of us being walked out and it looks like we have smirks or smug looks on our faces, but it was more an incredulous expression, "Is this really happening?"

Jeff: Some of the reporters, including the local AP reporter, started asking us questions. The police didn't say anything about this, but a couple of golf-shirted young-Republican types started restricting media access to us. They actually pushed the reporters back and prevented them from talking to us any further, which I thought was phenomenal. I couldn't believe that the reporters would stand for that business.

Nicole: We were taken to another building on the Capitol grounds that wasn't in use at the time. We waited in this empty lobby to be turned over to the custody of the city police who came in a prisoner transport van. They wedged Jeff and me inside our own cages in the van. There was mesh all around us. We were still handcuffed so we had to sit on our hands. The van was very hot. I could barely see Jeff through the cage mesh.

Jeff: My mind was just kind of spinning. I was in a tailspin. I couldn't believe that it had gotten this far.

Nicole: We were taken to the basement of this police station. Its detention area basically consisted of two little caged cells with benches inside. You could probably cram five people into each one.

Jeff: There were a bunch of people already in each cage. They were all male.

Nicole: All men! And they were all drunk!

Jeff: They moved all the men into my cage and put Nicole in her own cage. One guy was telling me why he was there. He had been drinking down at the boat ramp. I think he said he was hunting ducks with a BB gun and had a machete with him, and so the police brought him in.

Nicole and I sat there and waited. Meanwhile, the police were processing our paperwork. They called us out, and they did our fingerprints and took our mug shots. They were processing us through fairly quickly. The city charged us with the municipal offense of trespassing, which is hard to imagine because we were on state property with our tickets. The really amazing thing is that somehow if we had removed our shirts, then we wouldn't have been trespassing.

Nicole: So, our shirts were trespassing, apparently. Not us! The idea behind our arrest was to get us away from the event. That was their only goal; whether it was legal or not, they wanted us gone from their property.

Jeff: It doesn't matter if the charge sticks. It doesn't matter if you're charged with jaywalking or littering or trespassing—just get them off the property right now. It'll take two hours to be processed through the system, and that'll be enough time for Bush to give his speech and get out of town. And that's exactly what happened. We were in custody for probably two and a half hours. We didn't have to post a bond. Because it was a Sunday, they said that there was no magistrate available. But I think it was pretty clear to them that we weren't a big danger to society. And so they said, "We're going to release you on your own personal recognizance and give you these tickets for trespassing. These were pink tickets. It's the same ticket they give for offenses like speeding; instead of a check in a box for "speeding," there was a check by "trespassing."

Nicole: After they let us out of the downtown police station, we started walking back to our hotel. It was about five or six blocks away. We were in a bit of a daze. We were still wearing our anti-Bush T-shirts.

Jeff: We started receiving strange looks, first of all, not just for our shirts, but also because Bush's speech had been televised. Apparently, we had made the news—just a little blip on the news—saying that people had been removed from the event. People were pointing at us, saying, "Hi, you're the people who got taken out of the Bush rally!"

Nicole: Back at the hotel, the first thing we did was walk Feynman. Then we had lunch in the hotel restaurant. The television was replaying Bush's speech. It was ironic to hear him talk about the Fourth of July and what it means for freedom.

Jeff: We were choking on our hamburgers, listening to him talk about freedom of expression. He even used that very term. It was another pivotal moment for me.

Nicole: The rest of the day was quiet. On Monday, I went into work at the FEMA field office, but since it was a federal holiday, most people weren't there. On the following day, I got called out of a meeting by our field officer's head secretary. She asked me to come in for a conference with her boss. But he never showed up. He refused to see me, and so I ended up in a conference room with a FEMA legal counsel and the head of our administration department who told me that because of my actions, I had jeopardized FEMA's mission in West Virginia and that they were asking me to leave my assignment. That was crazy. I pointed out, "How many people are going to turn down free checks from the federal government just because of something that I did?" I was not fired at that time—my job was contract work—but they released me with no promise of a future assignment. Several days later, my immediate supervisor took away my FEMA badge.

Jeff: After FEMA kicked us out of the Embassy Hotel, we didn't have anywhere to go. We had kept a bunch of stuff in storage in Philadelphia where the FEMA regional office was, so we figured that we'd go back to Philly, get the stuff, and then head back down to Texas. Well, as we left Philly, we got as far as Roanoke, Virginia, where we stopped off at a Motel 6. I happened to read the back of the trespassing ticket to find out what we needed to do. It said that if you're not charged with one of the following things—and they listed things like domestic violence and driving while intoxicated—then you can just call in and pay your fine over the phone and everything's fine. So I called the clerk at the city office and she asked, "Well, what are you charged with?" I said, "Trespassing." And she said, "Okay, what's your name, hon?" I said, "Jeff Rank." And she said, "Oh, no, you have to come in." I thought, "Oh, shit! Here we go again with West Virginia justice." So instead of heading back to Texas, we returned to Charleston to appear for our court date.

Nicole: But first we called the American Civil Liberties Union. We decided that if they're going to treat us this way, we needed some legal help. This was on a Friday afternoon. I telephoned the West Virginia chapter of the ACLU and spoke to a woman by the name of Terry Barr, who is the attorney for that chapter. Before I mentioned my name, she explained their procedure in taking on a new case. Basically you have to submit a request in writing and then they review it with their board of directors. This process can take a couple of weeks. But she said, "Tell me your story, and I'll see what we can do." And as soon as I mentioned my name and President Bush and Fourth of July, she said, "Oh, we've been trying to find you!" She immediately contacted the board members who were all at a conference in California, and by the following Monday, we had an agreement that they would represent us, which meant that we now had an ACLU cooperating attorney who was a local and knew the judges in Charleston.

Jeff: On the trip back to Charleston, we stopped to get a bite to eat in a place called Tamarack, which is a tourist trap on the interstate coming into Charleston. Nicole was in the restroom and I was casually looking at the newspaper stand, and on the front page of the *Charleston Gazette*, it read, "FEMA worker released for July Fourth protest." We had never told any of the press that she worked for FEMA. We had only told the police, but that information somehow leaked to the press. Once we got to Charleston, we spoke with a lawyer named Harvey Peyton. He tried to put us at ease. He's a great guy. Probably in his early fifties. Kind of a new-fashioned country lawyer. He is very much a man of West Virginia. His family goes back there a couple of generations. He is very much involved in the community. He collects modern art. There's a progressive side to him.

Nicole: When we showed up for our court date on July 15th, there were two or three reporters outside, and five more inside.

Jeff: And that's just the TV people. There were news and radio people. There were supporters as well. The mayor even showed up. A few days earlier, the city council had passed a resolution officially apologizing to us.

Nicole: The entire court proceeding lasted about three minutes. They really wanted to get us out of the way. We were causing quite a commotion. The judge called up Jeff first, spoke with him briefly, and then he called me up and asked me if I understood why I was here and what the charges were. We both answered yes. Then the city attorney said to the judge that they were dropping all charges against us. The judge said, "Okay, you're free to go." And that was about it.

Jeff: You can speculate about the real reasons that the charges were dropped, but the legal reason they gave was that they had improperly charged us with a municipal offense on state property. Basically, they didn't have jurisdiction there. We had been on state grounds; there was no contesting that, but we were being tried for a municipal offense. The legal term they used was "dismissed without prejudice," which meant that we could actually be tried again in state court in a different jurisdiction.

Nicole: Assuming the state was crazy enough to decide to try us again. They could have convicted us of trespassing. We could have been sent to jail for six months, a year. Once we left the courthouse with TV cameras in our face, the media circus really started. We had done some interviews before, but we were a little choosy simply because we didn't know how our case was going to go. So it really picked up afterward, once we were cleared of all charges.

Jeff: Nina Totenberg did a piece on us on NPR. There was CNN, ABC *Nightline*, NBC, Al Franken on Air America Radio. Franken pointed out something: "You know, what if Nicole had taken her shirt off like those two guys had asked, then how would they have *really* reacted?" Nicole and I also considered our next move. We wanted to go ahead and pursue a civil suit against the government. But we didn't have the means or money to do it on our own. Fortunately, the ACLU did agree to represent us. Harvey was still on the legal team, but they brought in some attorneys from New York and Washington, D.C. There was a whole team of attorneys working on our brief. It was filed on September 15, 2004. We held a little press conference on the Capitol steps in Charleston. We handed out a press release naming as defendants the White House Office of Presidential Events and the head of the Secret Service. Then we named a couple of John Does who were the young Republican aides and state law enforcement officials.

Nicole: Once the criminal charges had been dropped, FEMA sent me what it calls a "counseling letter." It was signed by the regional director. It basically said, "Shame on you. You should have known better. We don't behave that way, but if you're good, you can come back to work for us." My return was tainted by that letter. But assignments gradually started trickling back in. At FEMA, one of the things that you forget about as a federal employee is that your e-mail address is pretty easy to figure out. It's generally your name at whatever agency and dot-gov—and so I had people e-mailing me. A lot of it was supportive e-mail. But I had one particular person who e-mailed me and said that if we didn't like it in this country, then we should leave the country and said that my husband and I were lower than whale dung.

Nothing that Jeff and I did was illegal. We hadn't done anything wrong from the beginning. I don't regret anything that we did. I wouldn't go out and look for this kind of trouble—but by the same token, what we did was exercise our right to speak out and participate in the democratic process. I would do it again in an instant.

Jeff: I'd also do it again in a heartbeat. It takes a lot of guts to stand up, especially when there's a mob mentality about. Post-9/11, a lot of people got caught up behind the flags they were waving and didn't stop to think about what was really going on and what those flags really stood for. They didn't stop to think for themselves. And for the vast majority of us, that's pretty easy to do. If your rent's paid, if you're picking up the kids from soccer practice at five o'clock, then get your thirty minutes of news from Fox, everything seems okay. Not to toot our horns, it was not easy what we went through. At each step of the process—when we decided to stand up to the people at the event or when we decided to file the civil suit—we adopted this approach: "I don't really care what other people are going to say, but I know that this is what is right and I know that in the long run, this is what is important." And that was true with Nicole's job. It certainly has cost us, both on personal and financial levels. Yet there's a reluctance for people to stand up and do those things. And I don't think that's unique to our time in history. But unless people exercise their constitutional rights, those rights will erode.

Nicole: There's a certain amount of inertia that if you don't have the momentum to act, why should you act? Even with us. We had initially considered, "Let's just pay the fine and be done with it. Let's move on with our lives." But we recognized that there was something greater at stake than just paying the hundred-dollar fine.

Jeff: In terms of the effect on our families, it took a little time to heal those wounds. I wouldn't call it a rift. There are bigger issues in our families than this, but it didn't contribute to family harmony. It caused a lot of sore feelings around Thanksgiving, especially right after the presidential election. That's for sure.

Nicole: Some family members took exception to the word "hate" on my T-shirt because they felt that's too strong a word. But "Love America, Don't Really Like Bush" doesn't really sound as strong. We also had family members comment, "Well, you should have expected that kind of treatment in West Virginia, and so we're not surprised." My attitude is that's all the more reason to stand up for what you believe in. I'm not sure what America they live in, but the America I live in, you're supposed to be able to do that.

Jeff: There has been a lot of good, too. Before the criminal trial, people would call the ACLU and offer their places for us to stay so we didn't have to pay for motels. They sent checks and supportive letters.

Nicole: While I was at the Charleston ACLU office, a woman came in one day and asked to see me. She was in her sixties. She was probably retired. She had tears in her eyes. She smiled at me and said, "Thank you so much for what you're doing. I want you to know there are people out there who appreciate you and are very proud of you." She hugged me and then handed me an envelope with some money. I asked what her name was, and she said, "No, my name's not important. Just know that people care about you." She then walked out of the office.

■   ■   ■

Political Protest Zones: Caged, Free, and Restricted Speech

The American Civil Liberties Union is representing Nicole and Jeff Rank in their suit against the government for violation of their First Amendment rights. The lead attorney is Senior Staff Counsel Chris Hansen who has been with the ACLU for thirty-two years after graduating with a law degree from the University of Chicago. "All I do for a living is sue the government," he says. And he is good at what he does. He was lead counsel in Reno v. ACLU, which successfully challenged two provisions of the federal Communications Decency Act of 1996 as violating the protection afforded freedom of speech by the First Amendment. For *Patriots Act,* Hansen discusses key legal issues involving freedom of speech and political protest.

I'm the lawyer for the plaintiff. The Ranks' suit is being heard in the United States District Court for the southern district of West Virginia. The government had moved to dismiss on the grounds that we haven't proven that the federal government was involved in the process. But first I need to explain that there are at least two or three phenomena that have taken place in the area of protest zones in the last few years.

The first thing that happens in these situations is that people who want to protest are put in a location that is so distant or so obstructed from their intended audience that their protest becomes meaningless. We saw this at the Republican National Convention in New York and at the Democratic National Convention in Boston—both of which were a serious problem. In Boston, protesters were placed very far away and under a highway overpass—literally invisible from the convention and invisible to all passersby, from every angle. In New York, there were lots of arrests, almost all of which have been dismissed. And there is litigation pending against the NYPD for the way in which they handled demonstrations during the convention. It's a mistake to say that this is all a Republican problem, or all a Bush problem. The ACLU sued over the almost identical problem in Boston, but there were fewer arrests in that city.

The second phenomenon is that people who are supportive of the event are given preferential treatment, as opposed to those people who want to express negative views. For example, anti-Bush people are put four blocks away; the pro-Bush people are put up close.

The third phenomenon that takes place is that both pro- and anti-Bush people are treated worse than pedestrians who aren't expressing a view at all. All of the protesters are pushed four blocks away but pedestrians are allowed to walk in front of the convention hall all they want. These are all examples of protest-zone problems.

Another big constellation of problems is ticketed events. Who gets in and who doesn't get in at a ticketed event. That is what the Rank case involves. The Ranks had tickets to get into what was an official presidential visit on the Fourth of July to the Capitol grounds in Charleston. And they were excluded from the event once it became known that they were wearing T-shirts mildly critical of the president.

There is no question that all the above are free speech cases. But the legal analysis is slightly different in each instance. I'm aware of at least five instances in which people were either forcibly removed, arrested, or both, from events in Denver, Cedar Rapids, North Carolina, and another one in Pittsburgh. I'm also aware of literally dozens and probably hundreds of instances in which people were excluded from events. The most famous one was during a campaign event when Vice President Cheney was speaking and people were not allowed in the hall unless they literally signed a loyalty oath before going in.

At some events where the president speaks, it is legitimate—in First Amendment terms—for him to exclude people. If the president is having a fund-raising dinner where it is a $10,000 a plate dinner, then you can't come in unless you spend the $10,000. He doesn't have to sell you a plate at the dinner, even if you've got the $10,000. He doesn't have to let you come in if he doesn't want to. And distinguishing between those events where he has a right to exclude people and those events where he does not have a right to exclude people is not always as simple as you might think. The thing about the Ranks case is that it was an official White House event where Bush was visiting as president and not as a candidate, not as a Republican leader, and not as a fund-raiser for the Republican Party. The event was open to the public. In our view, he can't exclude people who disagree with him. It's also my assumption that these ticketed events are designed to be televised ads anyway.

The Ranks were arrested by state and local cops, arguably at the direction of White House staff. What that means is not clear. The local cops and city officials dismissed the charges against the Ranks and apologized to them. So we decided we would not sue them. We are suing the state cops, the head of the Secret Service, and the head of the White House advance team—on the theory that it was one or all of them who were responsible for the orders that were issued—that nobody who was expressing criticism was to be allowed into the event.

The Secret Service's written formal policy is that it does not discriminate against people on the basis of their political viewpoint. Whether they follow this policy or not is an open question. What happens is that the decision to exclude people like the Ranks is made by White House advance people. But the White House advance people, like the Secret Service, are wearing suits and earpieces. And so, the local cops just assume they are Secret Service. The truth is that nobody knows. And the Secret Service has been astonishingly tight-lipped and the White House even tighter-lipped.

Every president has tried to restrict speech in some form or another. And every president has tried to restrict all kinds of speech. There was a famous ACLU case against President Clinton in which he tried to restrict the route of the inaugural parade down Pennsylvania Avenue to ensure that no one critical of him would be along the parade route. We sued. The court said you have to allow protesters along the parade route.

Every president has been resistant to hearing criticism at some point during his presidency. I think there is a more systematic effort in the Bush administration to limit the president's exposure to dissenting views and to make sure that he doesn't see people who disagree with him along his travel route or when he is going in or out of an event. And there is a much more consistent effort to make sure that no one attends any presidential event unless the person agrees with his policies. I think if it is a presidential visit open to the public, you have a right to attend. You should insist on your right to attend. And if they don't let you attend, you should call the ACLU.

All I do for a living is sue the government. About half of what I do is sue the government on speech cases. Even though the ACLU has a very good track record suing the government, you can't judge the likelihood of how a case is going to turn out by one's track record.

I work at the national headquarters office in New York City We also have a large lobbying office in Washington, most of whom are lawyers. We also have national offices in Atlanta, San Francisco/Oakland, and Connecticut. And then we have affiliated offices in every state. All told around the country, there's a couple of hundred full-time ACLU lawyers.

Bill O'Reilly has accused us of being an arm of terrorism. Bernard Goldberg published a book which named our executive director Anthony Romero as one of the top 100 people screwing up America. He was number five on his list. What more can I say?

Most of the people who work here at the ACLU are very proud of what they do. The truth is that we are not a liberal organization. We are a non-partisan organization. We represent conservatives all the time. We take positions that are more comfortable with conservatives in some instances. I can't tell you the number of times that police officers or FBI agents or evangelicals come to us to complain that their rights have been violated and ask us to help them out. And we do.

4

FIGHTING BIG OIL AND GAS

New Mexico cattle rancher Tweeti Blancett wants
the energy industry to clean up its act.

> "It's like living in the middle of an interchange
> on an interstate."

It's easy to imagine a television miniseries based on the life of New Mexico cattle rancher Tweeti Blancett. The modern-day saga spans several generations, and
would highlight many familiar themes of the American West found in dramas like
Lonesome Dove and *Into the West*. There's hard work, independence, courage,
love, tragedy, family betrayal, and greed.

Tweeti, sixty years old, has spent her entire adult life working the Blancett
spread with her husband, Linn, also sixty. Their 32,000-acre, leased ranch is located in the San Juan Basin in the northwest corner of New Mexico. This is high-
desert country. The 7,500-square-mile San Juan Basin also sits atop one of the
largest natural-gas reserves in the United States. Federal land that was once used
for grazing cattle is now an ugly maze of roads, methane gas wells, drilling pads,
and pipelines. While ranchers can lease surface-grazing rights from the government, underground mineral rights are sold off to third parties.

Widespread drilling arrived in the gas-rich basin in the early '90s. The energy
industry had perfected a new method to pump out methane gas buried deep beneath the earth. Nearly 20,000 wells have already been tapped. With rising energy prices, many more wells are on the way. In fact, the entire Rocky Mountain
region is awash with natural gas. Citing a government report, the *New York Times*
refers to this part of the West as "the Persian Gulf of gas, [which] has enough natural gas to heat 55 million homes for almost 30 years."

Unlike coal and heating oil, methane gas burns cleanly in our homes—something the gas industry loves promoting. But its extraction from the ground is a
messy, caustic, lethal affair. Drilled holes that can go as deep as 2,500 feet are
flushed with toxic liquids whose runoff causes irreparable environmental harm.

Livestock get sick after drinking the poisonous runoff that collects in pools around drilling sites. Vegetation is destroyed. Wildlife is endangered. Roads and truck traffic disrupt the natural habitats. "It's drill, drill, drill," says Tweeti. "It's unsustainable to raise cattle because the land is destroyed."

The energy industry has been indifferent to the environmental Armageddon it has created, while government agencies have failed to aggressively enforce regulations. Tweeti and Linn still have several hundred acres of private ranchland that have yet to be violated by big oil and gas. They might have had a lot more acreage, but a bitter fight with Linn's father ripped a hole in the ranch property—and a hole in both Blancetts' hearts.

Tweeti refuses to allow the gas industry to intimidate her. "They can be very nasty and very mean," she says. "They've threatened, 'We're coming to get you.'" She has stood at the locked gates of a private access road to her ranch when the big rigs show up with their drilling equipment. With Linn at her side, she has fought and defeated the gas companies and their well-paid legal teams in court. And now, with the support of organizations like the Sierra Club, which had once been implacable foes of ranchers, she has taken her legal fight right to the Bureau of Land Management for its lax attitude about protecting the environment.

She calls herself a steward of the land. *The Nation* and *Audubon* have written lengthy magazine profiles about her ongoing battle with the energy industry. She's petite, a grandmother, and also manages the Blancetts' thirty-nine-room hotel, the Step Back Inn, in Aztec, New Mexico. She's a Republican with strong party ties. So wouldn't this long-standing political affiliation endear her to the energy industry? Think again.

■　■　■

I was the Republican Party chairman for San Juan County in 2000 for George Herbert Walker Bush. But it doesn't make any difference. You go against oil and gas, you're *persona non grata*. The oil and gas boys tried to throw the unpatriotic route at me. I said, "Listen boys, if you just want to go that route, the reason the nation's Founding Fathers did what they were doing was to protect their land and the people on it. That is exactly what I'm doing, so don't throw that patriotic stuff at me. There's nothing more patriotic than a farmer and a rancher. I'm just somebody who's standing up for what I think is right."

We've been Americans for a long time. My ancestors came from Ireland, Scotland, Switzerland, and England—and that's kind of the mix. They settled in

the South. I don't have any Northern relatives. There were plantation owners on my dad's side. My mother's people were small farmers in the Carolinas. During the Civil War, they were very active on the Confederate side. Other people call it the Civil War. My family called it the War of Northern Aggression. I have one great-great-great grandfather who was captured at Vicksburg. The other one, whose name was George Washington Walser, died in the Confederate Old Folks Home in Austin, Texas. Both were sergeants. Just rank and file, good old, solid, hardworking farmers and ranchers. But they did own slaves, and they did have a belief in the Southern way of life. Both families lost everything in the Civil War, and so they moved into Texas, which had been a Confederate state.

My grandfather homesteaded and farmed in west Texas. He grew cotton and maize, and later when I was a young girl, he raised watermelons. West Texas is pretty windy and flat. I've always thought that there might be something just a little bit wrong with you if you like that part of Texas. My parents moved to New Mexico, where I was raised, so my roots are pretty deep here. On my mother's side of the family, I have thirty-two first cousins, and they all finished high school. That's a pretty good record, you know, for poor farming families. My mom's family was much poorer than my father's family, because there were so many of them and it was really hard during the Depression. But growing up she said that they never felt poor because my grandmother was just a very loving, caring, giving person.

All of my uncles, my mother's cousins, my dad, and my mom served in World War II. Dad got to Hawaii in January '42 after Pearl Harbor was bombed. He did instrument testing. He would go out with the pilots. My mom got there six months later. She was petite—we are about the same size—and she was trained to do aluminum welding of fuel lines that go in the wing of an airplane. She was like Rosie the Riveter. But if you knew my mother, you would have questioned that because she was definitely a Southern woman; she was definitely feminine. They spent four years in Hawaii and moved back to New Mexico after the war ended. They settled in a small community in southeastern New Mexico called Lovington. In fact, my two grandmothers lived a block from each other. We weren't a wealthy family, but we were rich in relations and we were rich in the fun things that big families do. Dad worked on airplanes at Holloman Air Force Base. Mom went back to being a mother and housewife.

All of our neighbors and friends worked out at Holloman. It was an enclave of German and American scientists. Many scientists from the Manhattan Project had moved from Los Alamos down to work at Holloman and White Sands

Missile Range. Later, there was pre-flight space testing with weather balloons and chimpanzees. The scientists' children went to school with us. We had an excellent education.

I went to college at Las Cruces. It's now called New Mexico State University. That's where I met Linn. He graduated with two degrees in animal science and range management, and I graduated with a degree in education. I also have a Masters from the University of New Mexico that I got after we married and had our children. After college, we came home to live and work at his family's farm and ranch in the San Juan Basin. It's a life that doesn't provide particularly good income, but it's a wonderful way to raise children because you generally all work together.

Linn's family came over from Colorado, where they had set up the first fur trading company—the American Fur Trading Outpost—west of the Mississippi. That was in the 1840s. They started migrating further west to more open country after it started settling up. When they finally made it to this valley in the San Juan Basin, a series of real strange events took place. All of the males in the line were pretty much killed off, and so the women with their small children just stayed on.

Here's what happened. The oldest of the males was Moses. He was appointed territorial marshal of this region. He had two brothers. One's name was John, and the other was Enos, who also had a son. They all served as deputies. They took care of the peace. One day, John was sent to serve papers on a man named Guadalupe Archuleta because he had supposedly stolen sheep or a wagon. When John showed up in this little Hispanic community south of Aztec, it was in the evening and they were having a big dance. But one must ask, "What was John doing serving papers in the middle of the night at a dance?" But to make a long story short, a gun battle ensued, and John was shot and killed. Well, some say he was shot in the back. The Archuletas' side of the story was that John had been messing around with one of the Archuleta women. After John died, they went and got Guadalupe Archuleta. They had a little trial underneath a big cottonwood tree, and they hung him.

Following that, the Archuletas placed a curse on the Blancett men. This sounds far-fetched, but there were a lot of *brujos* living in New Mexico. The curse said that the Blancett men would die off and every generation would be impacted. So, there's John, and he's already dead. Enos was later shot and killed in Utah. They never did find out who killed him. And then Moses, in 1891, while coming back to the homestead from Aztec, his wagon team runs away and he falls out of the wagon and he's killed.

Next to die was Moses' son, Marcellus. He was only thirty-three. He was bringing some cattle across a mesa just south of Aztec when he was struck and killed by lightning. Marcellus had three sons. His family had a drifter come through, and they let him stay in the barn — just like in the John Wayne movies. In his bed roll, he had a loaded pistol. One of Marcellus's little boys, who was eight years old, found it and pointed it at his little brother and said, "Bang!" He was shot and killed.

In the next generation, my husband's grandfather had three sons. The oldest son was going to school at Las Cruces. He had some heart problems growing up, though he had matured into a pretty healthy person. They were out at some place swimming, and somebody got in trouble and he dove in to rescue him. He saved the person, but it overtaxed his heart and he died. He was in his early twenties. My husband's father had three sons, and one of them died of whooping cough when he was three years old.

And then, my husband and I had three sons. We lost one son to crib death, which follows the Blancett curse. We then lost our second son when he was nine years old. It was a freak accident. He had hit his head and basically didn't have a mark on him, but it caused a brain aneurysm and he died. Our only living son is now thirty-seven, and he has two boys and a daughter.

The Blancetts don't have much of a family left anymore, but that's really a result of some real interesting changes we had over the last several years. There was this dissension in the family, which cast father against son and brother against brother. It's painful to think that my husband and I spent thirty-five years of our lives building toward something that has basically dissipated. In 1992, my father-in-law deeded to my husband the ranch that we've been building on since 1967 and working together on all my married life. We had bought our part of the ranch in '67. The entire Blancett private ranch was seven sections of 640 acres each and 200 acres of farm ground. My father-in-law also deeded land on the river where he lived. It was all tied together to this ranch that had been in the family since the 1800s. And then in '97, he met a woman the same age as me and Linn. Two years later, he married her. By the following year, everything was pretty much over as far as being able to work together as a family. He started making some estate planning, and said that the deeds he had given us were not valid even though they were notarized and signed deeds. At first, my husband tried to be congenial and put the family back together. It didn't work, and so the dispute over the deeds went to trial. My father-in-law said that it wasn't his intent in '92 to give the land to us. He said a lot of things in court that weren't true and just as hurtful, but when Linn had the opportunity to correct the facts, he didn't — because we didn't want to hurt the family any more than it already was. So we lost in court. We took it to the state's upper courts, but we lost there as well. And so, the land that we had fought for—the part that my father-in-law was going to give us—is no longer ours. It gutted the heart of the ranch.

My father-in-law doesn't talk to us now. This is a small community, so if we're at a funeral, it's like you're a tree stump. There's no communication whatsoever between this man and his son, my husband. They had worked together as close as any two people I've ever seen for over thirty years. Next to losing our two sons, it's the most devastating thing my husband has ever had to deal with in his life. He loved his dad. Linn's a very quiet, easy-going, loving person. Linn's brother didn't have any deeds, and so he went along with what his father said. He never stepped up and said, "Dad, now let's try to settle this."

What I really resent is all those years that I spent working with my father-in-law. I worked in the hay fields right alongside him and in the pens branding and doctoring cattle. We've always had at least one ranch hand, but most of the time, we did the work ourselves and as our boys got older, they helped out. We did the very best we could do, trying to defend the property and the legacy. The oil and gas industry was at the trial every day because they wanted us to lose! The new Mrs. Blancett, she's not very concerned about any of the land and the water resources.

Our farm's right on the Animas River. It comes right out of Durango, Colorado, and flows into the San Juan River. Our farm is about fifty miles from the original Blancett homestead. We had started protecting it immediately. We refused to have oil and gas come onto our property. We have fought them off for twenty-five years. Threats and intimidation are the nature of the oil and gas beast. There are a lot of verbal threats, trust me. I have letter after letter after letter documenting their threats. They'd say, "We don't have to do this. We can do whatever we want to. We're going to do this." And you know what I'd tell them? "Get it on, boys. Just come on! If you think you can do it, then get it on!" They do not want to be a good neighbor. They don't want to work with you. They want to go in and do what they want to do and abuse you in the process.

The government owns mineral and surface rights on federal land, but I have a grazing permit, which gives me a stake and has allowed me to fight them off. But it ain't pretty! They don't want me in court. Anytime they've been in court against us, they've lost. Once you get to court, their position is not what they tell you it is. I'll give you a little example. El Paso Natural Gas wanted to put on our ranch a piece of pipe that sticks out of the ground to allow liquids to escape. But I said, "No, you're not going to put any more structures there." And they said, "I guess we are. We're going to." They went and got a restraining order. So we went to court, and our lawyers stood up and said, "You know, Judge, these companies come onto the land, they don't take care of it, they don't compensate ranchers for it, and they treat it like they don't have to. Judge, we want you to look at all the damage that these companies have done on their ranches, not just on their private land, but on the federal lands, too. And we want you to uphold the Blancetts' right to lock the gates to their private road." We had seven different companies and probably nine different lawyers circling us during that trial.

Everything the oil and gas companies do destroys the environment. That's the problem. I was recently speaking with a reporter, Jim Carlton of the *Wall Street Journal*, and he said, "I can't understand. There's only 3,000 new wells that have been drilled in the last five years. There's a total of 19,000 . . ." I said, "Jim, stop, you're buying into the numbers. What difference does it make how many there are if they're not reclaimed and the land is not being taken care of. You're ignoring the cumulative impact to the surface."

The stuff they put in the drilling pits is caustic and deadly. There is no two ways about it. It's deadly to livestock. It's deadly to the wildlife. It is deadly to the environment and the soil. It is heavy in salt, heavy metals, and petroleum byproducts. When livestock or wildlife come into contact with it, they either die or they abort or they get real sick and lose weight. It's like poisoning. Sometimes they recover, but most of the time, they become sterile afterwards.

There are so many contaminants on the land that it's a killing field. The ranchland and pastures are so fragmented with trucks and rigs and fences down and gates open and cattle guards filled—you cannot manage a ranch enterprise. There's any conceivable environmental problem that you can have: air, water, soil, noxious weeds, erosion, watershed problems, contaminants. It's kind of like living in the middle of an interchange on an interstate. The air wouldn't be any good. The water wouldn't be any good. There's the loud noise from compressors. The lights are on twenty-four hours a day. You wouldn't see any wildlife. You wouldn't see any grass growing or any trees because the impact is so great that nothing has the time to recover.

I call our ranch "a sacrifice area." I even had a banner made with those words. The BLM wanted me to take it down. I said, "No!" We were sacrificed on the altar of corporate greed. It didn't really have to be that way—because they can do the drilling right. They just haven't. The ranch is completely gone. It's damaged. There is no way that you can restore it within our lifetime. And they are continuing the damage. They are going to double every well, every pipeline, every road on our leased ranch acreage. They are going after even more of it, because it is such a lucrative field. There's been an increase this year alone of fifty wells on our ranch, bringing the number to over five hundred. We have had 17,000 acres impacted, none of which has been restored, reclaimed, or reseeded. There isn't a single road in compliance. There are no paved roads. It's a complete mess. Last year during the rains, they had to shut the roads down because there was such a tremendous amount of damage to the surface. Nobody is enforcing the existing regulations.

The only place we've been able to keep them off of is the ranch headquarters. It's 200 acres. It's the only place that I know of in all of the San Juan Basin that has not been drilled. They would love to drill there, too. But we just fought 'em tooth and nail. If they decide that they're going to drill a well and they want to use my private road by the ranch, I won't let them. I tell them, "If you think you can come and destroy my farm, you're nuts; but try it if you think you're big enough." They haven't thus far. I'm waiting, though.

I am also trying to protect 400 acres on the high-mesa bench that is the only federal land that has not been impacted because they don't have any road access. It hasn't ever been breached. This is land above our ranch headquarters. There's juniper, pinyon, cedar. Lots of natural grasses. It's a sacred site for the Navajo. It is very pristine. There's elk, deer. It is also a wildlife corridor between Colorado and New Mexico because it is right on the state line.

Burlington Resources is the worst energy-industry actor in the entire San Juan Basin. They have a very public profile. They'll donate $75,000 to a local hospital for a heart machine or a lung machine. They are always giving away these little goodies. Of course, they are taking billions of dollars out of the county. Its main headquarters are in Houston, Texas. All the oilies are in bed with the Bush administration. But drilling actually started fifty years ago. They just hadn't gotten the technology down like they're doing today whereby they can really move with their drilling. With this type of methane gas drilling, the wells go down about 2,000 to 2,500 feet.

This type of coal-gas methane extraction started in the Clinton years. Both the Democrats and Republicans are bought and sold as far as I'm concerned. We have two senators in New Mexico, one a Democrat, one a Republican. Neither one of them has acted any differently. They both accept money from oil and gas in the same proportions. There isn't any care for the environment and for the ranching community when it conflicts with oil and gas. Consumers look at natural gas as a clean fuel. The environmental community was real helpful in that little theory because they were trying to get rid of coal-fired power plants, but they didn't realize what the methane extraction created on the surface and did to the water and to the air. We now have an administration that is certainly not going to back off. The Clinton administration didn't back off a whole lot, but they didn't roll back all the environmental regulations either.

The rest of the nation should know that when the gas bill plays out—it probably has another fifty years remaining—someone will have to restore the land. And it isn't going to be the oil and gas companies that are making all these obscene profits right now. It's going to be the American public and the state of New Mexico. Because the oil and gas companies are going to walk away, just like they have from every other place. This doesn't bode well for other areas in the West that haven't been drilled, especially with the current administration's lack of encouragement for its enforcement agencies. Agencies like the BLM aren't crossing the line. They aren't crossing the oil and gas industries which have already destroyed Louisiana and the Gulf Coast of Texas. So let's now move inward and spread the cancer to other places. They destroyed southeastern New Mexico and northwestern New Mexico. But they are moving to beautiful places in Colorado and Montana. They've even rattled their sabers in the Tetons area of Wyoming.

In the '70s and '80s, the environmental community showed a great deal of animosity toward the farm and ranch community. I'm not saying that the animosity is all gone. I mean, it's still alive and well in many parts, but I think that over the last ten years, we've come to the realization that we're both relatively small groups and in order to stand up and protect the environment, we'd better form alliances with people who are closer to our way of thinking than the oil and gas industry. But I have to be real clear that though we've joined hands with some of the environmentalists regarding oil and gas operations issues, there are other issues that we're not in agreement with.

The majority of federal-lands ranchers are the best stewards that you can have. The reason I say that is because it is in our vested interest to take care of the land. If we don't, then the land won't produce. We wouldn't have been on our own ranch for six generations if we had abused the land. We were here long before the BLM or big oil and gas. The American rancher—a good American rancher—is the best watchdog the public can have. Now I am not saying that there are not people who abuse the lands. A bad rancher needs to be moved off public lands or educated on how to do it right, because it's not right for public lands to suffer because somebody is not practicing the stewardship; but the majority of the federal-lands ranchers are very good because we're going to be here year after year after year.

I went to Washington, D.C., on a lobbyist mission to show photos of the damage to ranches in the area. The Bureau of Land Management officials were very polite. They would listen to me, and then when I walked out the door, I'm sure they probably said, "Well, I'm glad she's gone." The minute that I seriously started raising issues and went to the media and formed alliances with the environmental community, then I became very much ostracized.

My problem with the BLM is that there are regulations on the books to protect the land, and the BLM is not enforcing them as it relates to the oil and gas industry. If I did the same thing to the land with my grazing that the energy industry had done to the land with its oil and gas explorations, the BLM would have pulled my grazing permit a long time ago. The BLM allows oil and gas to continue damaging the land, but it doesn't pull their leases. It doesn't fine them with anything significant. The most it does is a slap on the hand. That's why I filed a private lawsuit in Washington, D.C., federal court against the Bureau of Land Management, which allowed oil and gas to destroy the rest of our ranch. Basically, the lawsuit says that the BLM did not carry out its responsibility to protect the land. There's a little-known regulation that says if one entity damages another entity, you can request that the lease be pulled. And so we're requesting that the drilling leases be pulled. What we are asking to be done has never been tried before. We're rattling our cages against the big boys. The New Mexico Oil & Gas Association hired the largest law firm in Colorado to intervene and try to keep this completely out of court, so we wouldn't even have a hearing. Our attorney is Karen Budd-Falen who is a top federal-lands litigator. She lives in Cheyenne, Wyoming. I'm paying for her. This is a personal lawsuit. Linn and I have nothing else to lose—except our money—and we're willing to fight for our land and our way of life and the legacy that was entrusted to us. Oil and gas made a real mistake in damaging everything we have. I'm not going to quit. They are not going to run me off my ranch.

I know that there are local people who disagree with me. They're thinking or saying behind my back, "Oh, Tweeti, she's just trying to wreck the oil and gas industry. She's trying to take all our jobs away." Which is ridiculous! You couldn't even beat them off with a stick! That's the craziest thing I ever heard. Then, many others believe that what I'm doing is very important, but they don't want to take the heat. They support me on the sidelines, but you have to understand that the gas industry is very punitive, very ugly. They get real nasty.

My favorite quote in the whole world is from Gandhi. This is what he says: "First they ignore you, then they laugh at you, then they fight you, and then you win." I'm at the fighting stage now with oil and gas. I haven't gotten to the winning stage, but I'm not quitting. I'm an American, and I have the right to my private property. I have the right to say what I want to say, and I have a right to stand up when our government isn't doing what's right. That is the cornerstone of my beliefs, and they're not going to take those rights away from me.

Our herd is down to twenty-five. That's all we have now because we won't turn anything out on the ranch that's contaminated and run the risk of losing them. These cattle are part of our herd that we spent our lifetime building. My husband Linn said to me the other day, "Maybe we should sell them." I told him, "If we didn't have the cattle, then what would we have for aggravation other than oil and gas?" Actually, we love our cattle. We wouldn't have it any other way. People who are ranchers and farmers, it's just a calling. It's our heritage.

5

FUNNY BUSINESS

Political satirist Mort Sahl has outlasted nine
U.S. presidents.

> "I had hoped to set an example. We were the
> guys who landed on Normandy. I put my body
> on the barbed wire. This new crowd, they are
> not about selling out. They are about selling in.
> Michael Moore is a long way from Che Guevara
> leading the resistance."

"I went to the kids when no one went." This boast by satirist Mort Sahl appears
in his memoir *Heartland*. He wrote the slim volume in the mid-'70s to settle past
scores and revive a stalled career in live comedy. "For a while, it was the only audience available to me, and I thought it was important to tell young people that
everyone twice their age is not corrupt. I did that. Alone. I accused the CIA of
murder. I write to you as a man whose conscience is totally out of control."

Sahl's stage personality was hardly out of control. For truly unhinged, there's
Lenny Bruce, Sam Kinison, or Andy Kaufman. Yet Sahl had popularized a new kind
of comic style, which he first unveiled at the hungry i in San Francisco's North
Beach in the early '50s. Wearing his trademark red V-neck cashmere sweater, he'd
walk out with a rolled-up newspaper and begin commenting on the day's head-
lines. With his staccato delivery, he riffed for the well-informed. He called it "postgraduate humor." He avoided vaudevillian shticks, gags, impressions, and wife
jokes. His comedic objective was to create "chaos out of the order" of the Eisenhower era. He channeled the repressed anxiety behind the conformity—and audiences loved him for his barbed apostasy. His patter had a digressive,
improvisational quality; it borrowed heavily from jazz. In fact, Sahl did the first college concert in the United States in 1953 with Dave Brubeck.

Many years later, at the age of seventy-seven, the remarkably energetic Sahl,
who lives in Bel Air, California, with his third wife, Kenslea, continues to perform

before live audiences. He has somehow managed to achieve iron man longevity in a young man's game that devours its young. After outlasting nine U.S. presidents, what's the point in quitting now? In 2005, he headlined at clubs, auditoriums, and theaters in Boston, south Florida, New York City, and San Francisco.

Political comedy is now a staple of our entertainment. Young people prefer getting their news from *The Daily Show*. Jay Leno, Rush Limbaugh, Bill Maher, Al Franken, and Jon Stewart have become household names. Yet the comic pioneer Sahl toils in the much quieter margins of the dimming limelight. Shouldn't there be a punch line here?

In his heyday, Sahl was the nation's chief jester. He was the go-to quipster at the 1956 Republican National Convention in San Francisco, with daily appearances on the *CBS Morning Show*. In Los Angeles, he hosted his own television show. He shared a *Time* cover in 1960 with Kennedy and Nixon. Sahl hobnobbed with Frank Sinatra, Hugh Hefner, Paul Newman, the Kennedy clan. When Joseph Kennedy wanted him to write "some things for Johnny," Sahl told the ambassador, "Well, I'll be happy to, but understand I don't endorse candidates."

Sinatra once remarked to Sahl, "You're a rebel. I'm a rebel. I'm really your brother. If you ever have a problem and don't come to me first, I'll break both your arms." Not surprisingly, Sinatra's recording label produced Sahl's first comedy album, *The New Frontier*, which skewered the Kennedy administration. Kennedy's associates referred to Sahl as a "bastard." The president agreed, but said, "He's a smart bastard." Sahl resisted being crammed inside predictable political categories of left, right, or moderate. He relished exposing hypocrisy in both Democratic and Republican camps: "If I serve any function, it is to raise questions—not answer them."

President Kennedy's assassination derailed Sahl's career. He had idolized JFK even as he attacked him. He believed that the Warren Commission was a massive cover-up. Justice had been denied to the American people. He became obsessed by the desire to find the real killers. He teamed up with New Orleans District Attorney Jim Garrison (resurrected from history in Oliver Stone's movie *JFK*), and for four years, they subpoenaed witnesses and investigated leads in an attempt to piece together the conspiratorial connections. "I don't know how anybody could have any theory about Kennedy's assassination, except one," says Sahl in *Heartland*, "and that's the CIA and the Pentagon murdered the president."

Sahl watched his annual income plummet from $1,000,000 to $13,000 during this gumshoe period. He had gone from emceeing the Academy Awards to scarfing down donuts and coffee with his comrade-in-arms Garrison. Upon his return to the stand-up circuit, he found that nightclubs where he once headlined now refused to book him. Audiences failed to share his enthusiasm for reading aloud passages from the *Warren Commission Report*. Late-night television shut him out because, as he explains, "all that time [I was being] suspected or accused of the most awesome crime of all in the eyes of show business—of not being funny and beloved any longer. My humor didn't stop. It changed. Politics isn't as innocent. What I had to say was no longer harmless when I discussed the news. Because the news had grown lethal."

Sahl would occasionally resurface on *The Dick Cavett Show* or *The Tonight Show*. Johnny Carson said one night, "Gee, we don't see you anymore." But Sahl never achieved his former notoriety. A younger, hipper generation of comics had emerged. Richard Pryor, the Smothers Brothers, and George Carlin were the new reigning rebels. Sahl seemed more like a moldy throwback from another era. Being slighted by Hollywood filled him with anger and resentment. Directly addressing agents and producers in *Heartland*, he wrote, "You can't bring me back. I never left. If you want to pronounce sentence, make it a death sentence." When Nixon moved into the White House, Sahl experienced only a minor career bounce. He blamed the Left for trying to silence him. "Even when the liberals found that Agnew and Nixon were repugnant," Sahl fumed, "no one called on me to satirize either of them. I was too dangerous to be on staff." He wanted to discuss on-air taboo subjects like Vietnam and the assassinations of Dr. Martin Luther King, Jr. and Robert Kennedy.

Sahl was forced to find work in Las Vegas, clubs, small theaters, and on college campuses. Sahl would often pair up with the late Senator Eugene McCarthy, whose strong showing as an anti-war candidate in the 1968 New Hampshire presidential primary led to LBJ's decision to drop out of the race. They jointly produced a live-audience recording called *America*. Sahl also worked as a screenwriter on studio lots. In the '80s, he began to write material for Reagan. He's also penned speeches for both Bush presidents and Senator Bill Bradley during his 2000 presidential bid. Sahl had one-man shows on Broadway and off-Broadway.

Uncompromising and fiercely independent throughout his career, Sahl believes that political humor keeps alive political opposition. That is why liberals enrage him. They cave into too easily. One of his long-standing complaints had been that "liberals were so busy proving they were not communists they became totally ineffective." Their second major offense was failing to rally to his side during his JFK murder investigation. The betrayal stings, and he still carries a grudge. Sahl plunged another shiv into his decades-old foe on NPR's *Fresh Air* in 2004. He told host Terry Gross: "A political satirist's job is to draw blood. I'm not a liberal. I'm a radical. The liberals, they made liberalism into a way station for people who want to cooperate with a right-wing administration and not lose their source of income and still be self-righteous. You know, have a dinner party at Barbra Streisand's but spend an equal amount of time with the guests and out in the kitchen talking to the Nicaraguans. That's really what's going on here."

Finally, what's the story behind the red V-neck cashmere sweater? Why did it become a permanent part of his act for over a half-century? "I buy them at Dick Carroll's in Beverly Hills," says Sahl. "I don't know why it became such an issue, but it became a fixture. I once wore a tuxedo to introduce Kennedy, and he said, 'When I got Mort Sahl, I wanted Mort Sahl—not the guy in the tuxedo.'"

■   ■   ■

I don't think there are any political comedians. Not to be facetious. But I can't believe what's going on out there. How these comedians represent themselves. They're puppets. Their topics aren't serious. And for them to discuss them is almost promiscuous. That's not politics there. Bill Maher has no politics. These people are animals with epithets. Dennis Miller became a born-again Republican. Al Franken is obscene because he's frightened. He should be frightened. His personality is frightening. But the audience won't laugh. So he is obscene. His stuff is extremely crude without being targeted: Republicans are bad; the subtext is Gentiles. And who the hell would that leave? Jon Stewart? Stewart is weak! You see, most good humor is a byproduct of a sense of irony on the part of a professional man. That's why Eugene McCarthy was great. And Adlai Stevenson. And John F. Kennedy. There is no sense of irony in any of these new guys. Why couldn't one of these comedians pick up on the Dick Cheney remark: "The Iranians don't understand they are not to interfere in the internal affairs of another government." Not a word! They're kinda star lovers. I don't like 'em.

Jon Stewart doesn't threaten the established order. He's a Judas, in effect. Just as *Saturday Night Live* is. And then we're told by the mass media that he is talking to the young people. I doubt it very much. I'd rather hear young people react to Seymour Hersh than Jon Stewart. He trivializes this fascism. Maybe he doesn't even perceive it. The problem is not the newscast of *The Daily Show*. It's whether or not satire really does an X-ray. And parody—which is what Stewart's doing—is a topical scratch. It's not satire. These guys reduce everything to entertainment! John McCain chastised Stewart for trivializing tragedy. I tell you something: a forty-six-year-old urban Jewish male should have more to say, not only politically, but about women. And about how we are being made into a Third World country. If it isn't already.

These young comics have no ambitions to radicalism. They just believe in economic success! So a shadow falls across whatever position they have. I mean, who asks the right questions? That's where the jokes come from. Well, if you're a real artist, you should be under the radar anyway. But they are not artists. They are there to distract the audience. If I were a Republican official, I would love *Saturday Night Live*, because instead of investigative reporting, you've got bitchiness. You've got envy instead of intellectual curiosity. You've got gossip, instead of news. Castro said recently that there will be a media struggle between the news that is put out by the governments of the superpowers and what young people hunger for and find on the Internet.

What do you see on television? It doesn't really offer anybody anything. Nader said the same thing. There's no labor channel. There's no left channel. There is not a real youth channel. It's only programs for made-in-the-lab young people. Television has depoliticized black people entirely. They put them on the shows that are like minstrel shows.

I had hoped to set an example. We're the guys who landed on Normandy. I put my body on the barbed wire. Growing up in a radical household. And not being afraid to come forward to the plate. I mean, where the hell are the jokes? This new crowd, they are not about selling out. They are about selling in. They are not threatening. They emasculated the Democratic Party. I tell you another thing about these new comedians: they're all too self-righteous. You have to come up with something satirical, not just walk around and yell at the next evangelical.

If you're aware of your country, I mean, you can make the jokes good and fast. When Larry Speakes was Reagan's press secretary and was standing up there and Bob Dole said, "They're falling on their swords for the president. They're good soldiers," I said, "Actually they're not falling on their swords. They're going to Merrill Lynch." Remember when everyone was talking about whether Bush was a hero, all I did was come out and say to the audience, "Bush's the Unknown Soldier. He was in the National Guard, but nobody could find him!"

Let's just say, Michael Moore is a long way from Che Guevara leading the resistance. But you know, the jokes all come as a byproduct of understanding issues and real politics. Not from righteousness. What emerged is that liberals have a chokehold on this country. What I call "social democrats." They pick their fights. They don't want to take on the fact that the CIA has embedded guys in the press and the guys in the press conferences. It's all righteous, and it's managed to alienate working people. Liberalism in the urban areas is a starvation diet. You can't count on it. They never elect anybody. Ah, the Democrats are the left wing of the Republican Party anyway.

Look at talk radio. You know, a country this diverse should certainly come up with someone besides Sean Hannity. He's like a robot. He's got a key in his back. Can't they find a real fascist for God's sake! Pat Buchanan can answer questions about NAFTA. And he can answer questions about immigration and he's got some passions of his own. Gordon Liddy has a good deal more vitality than the liberals. When I was there in the studio at Air America, Janeane Garofalo was waving her principles in people's faces: "she's liberal and she's good; the conservatives, they're bad." Like conservatives don't have children and they don't worry about them. It's all nonsense. It's like those rallies that they hold when the Hollywood gang gets Democrats together. It's safe. They are as good as the other side of bad. When you really get into an issue, they think they're dignified. A lot of them are guilty because they've had fortune and they've had minimal ability. They should feel guilty. Schoolteachers don't make as much money. But hell, it really comes down to trust. Can you throw a punch and can you take one?

I have written speeches for whoever comes along: Democrats, Republicans. It's not that hard to be independent these days. Humor is everywhere. When Pat Buchanan was at the Independent Party convention in Long Beach, he was asked, "So are you divorcing the Republican Party?" He said, "Yes. And they can have the kid." That is rich! He has a rich sense of humor.

I was at the Kennedy School of Government at Harvard. The director of the school asked me to recruit comedians to come to the school. I said, "What do you want them for?" She said, "Well, they're popular." I reminded her that a university's sacred duty is to resist what's popular. Change the taste of what's popular. I feel that way about television. The larger signs of success in this country such as *The Tonight Show* I don't jump at, because they are too formulaic. And they are run again by guys who are frightened. They're not free. They pretend to talk to youth, but they don't. You know what they're about? When it was Clinton, he was promiscuous and ate too many hamburgers. It's the same stuff that other comedians did in other eras. Dean Martin was drunk and Jack Benny was stingy. But it did not speak to the heart of America. If you keep it funny, you're there! I mean, it sets a very bad example. I work with Letterman, anyway. I'm on there two or three times a year.

We're in a political drought. It's not just a convenience. Look at the Democratic Party candidates. Gore certainly had more vitality than Kerry. He at least made an anti-war speech. Why doesn't somebody ask the liberals why they shot

Howard Dean and then said they were going to get somebody electable? So why wasn't he elected? It was bankruptcy. It wasn't logic. It was probably espionage. I don't believe in accidents. You know, if a bank gets robbed repeatedly, there must be an inside man at the bank. That's what a good cop would tell you.

I didn't think Dean was finished because of that speech in Iowa. But all the liberals were running around Los Angeles saying that he was bipolar. They've always got a reason to put the gun in their mouth and withdraw from combat. The reason is survival. Gene McCarthy said, "The first thing liberals do in a battle is shoot their wounded." The last liberal I knew was President Kennedy. I started the whole speechmaking racket with him. It wasn't my idea anyway. It was his father's. Well, the old man called me on his behalf. I knew the old man first. They write books about him being awful now, but they didn't then. There was a lot of sentimentality about Jack Kennedy.

Kerry is another guy who had bad luck. When his shadow was hovering over the presidential nomination, we found out he was a war criminal! All the good guys have bad luck. All the mediocre people have good luck. Barack Obama is like a roof-siding salesman. He makes Democrats feel good—the same way that they embrace Bill Cosby but not Dick Gregory. Because if it's somebody to move in next door, they'd rather have Cosby as their new neighbor.

You know what Joseph Lieberman reminds me of? That line from Clinton, who said, "If there is a Republican running and a Democrat who sounds like a Republican, the people will vote for the Republican every time." And that's it. That's really it. There is no difference between the parties. I can't think of any comedians saying that the Democrats favor abortion. The Republicans don't mind if you're born, that is, if you don't live long enough to collect Social Security. Before Bush was reelected, he said to me, "I don't want to fight terror either. I want to do other things. That's what you elected me to do." Then I said, "But we didn't elect you by that much!"

Well, the Democrats have been a fake since the Vietnam War. They ratified the lie. They went ahead with the war. What is it with our militaristic policy? Why did President Johnson quit? He quit because he couldn't overcome that military combine that said you had to stay there. If you don't want to stay there, get out. And he got out.

We've gone from Godless America to God Help America. That is the devolution. I think the country's knees are knocking now and it's breathing hard. The people feel futile here. Most of the people I talk to feel essentially powerless. The old thing you used to feel about making a difference is gone. You see, my own view is that President Kennedy was executed in public, because they wanted to fracture the spirit of his followers. The subliminal message was that if you do the right thing, you're on your way out. His murder cast a shadow again and again. Many good people have left our midst. And it's not a random phenomenon. Once they could do that, they could do anything. See, it's not the last bad thing that happened. They'll go as far as they have to. If they can stop you by character, they will. But they are gonna make sure there is nobody who believes what Jack Kennedy believed in the White House, and in any country that goes for social justice. I mean, what about Nicaragua? What about Cuba? What about Honduras? Who helped the death squads in El Salvador? What about Russia? After the destruction of the Soviet Union, Yeltsin comes in? With our approval. Then he quits—this man of boundless ambition—and names the other guy, who is not elected.

In the '50s, a lot of people were yelling about communists. But that was just a stopgap accusation. Nobody ever said to me, "How can you say that?" You have to be true to the audience and true to yourself. You've got to educate the kids. That's really what the job is about! I believe what I say, and I have an abiding belief in my heart that people will respond when you tell the truth. It is the only way to live. Because as Bertrand Russell said, "Conformity is death and protest is life."

6

THE DETAINEE

Syrian immigrant Nadin Hamoui was locked up for nine months by the Immigration and Naturalization Service.

> "Do we not belong anywhere? I am proud to be an American."

The roundups and detentions began shortly after 9/11. Through rigorous and selective enforcement of immigration law, the U.S. government targeted foreign nationals as the cornerstone of its anti-terrorism offensive. The majority of people caught in this dragnet were from Arabic-speaking countries. Many were deported or arrested. Detainees were kept isolated in twenty-three-hour lockdown with limited access to the outside world, making legal representation almost impossible. They were considered guilty of having ties to terrorism until they could prove their innocence. They were denied bail. They were known as "the disappeared."

Attorney General John Ashcroft championed this new draconian policy in an address before the U.S. Conference of Mayors on October 25, 2001: "Our anti-terrorism offensive has arrested or detained nearly 1,000 individuals as part of the September 11 terrorism investigation. Those who violated the law remain in custody. Taking suspected terrorists in violation off the streets and keeping them locked up is our clear strategy to prevent terrorism within our borders."

But what had Ashcroft actually set into motion? By manipulating immigration law to suit his public-relations agenda, he was seeking to reassure Americans that the government was making substantial progress in its fight against terrorism. Each week, the attorney general's office would proudly announce a running tally of arrests and detentions. But this practice stopped after critics started questioning why the Department of Justice refused to release detainee names or the crimes these foreign nationals had allegedly committed. In early 2002, Ashcroft signed into law the Absconder Apprehension Initiative, which concentrated on 2 percent of the 300,000 foreign nationals who were living in the U.S. despite outstanding deportation orders. This new crackdown specifically went after 6,000 people from Arab and Muslim countries.

"All the detainees were presumptively treated as terrorists," writes David Cole in *Enemy Aliens: Double Standards and Constitutional Freedoms in the War on Terrorism.* "They were denied bond even where the government had no evidence that they posed a danger or flight risk, and held for months while the FBI satisfied itself that they were in fact unconnected to terrorism. Many immigration detainees were initially arrested on no charges at all. The government's policy was to lock up first, ask questions later, and presume that a foreign national was dangerous even where there was no basis for that suspicion."

The Immigration and Naturalization Service managed to bypass public scrutiny because immigration law avoids constitutional safeguards guaranteed to defendants in criminal court. Cases could be heard in secret. Detainees were deprived of due process. The slightest infraction or technical violation, such as overstaying one's visa, could lead to immediate deportation or indefinite incarceration.

And just how successful were the attorney general's anti-terrorism policy measures? How many Al Qaeda sleeper cells were uncovered? Were Ashcroft's confident expectations met? The 9/11 Commission found that this immigrant detention policy had failed to nab a single terrorist. "Sadly, this program has been a colossal failure at finding terrorists," writes Cole. "Of the more than 5,000 persons subjected to preventative detention as of May 2003, not one had been charged with any involvement in the crimes of September 11."

It wasn't merely a question of what went wrong along the way that made a mockery of Ashcroft's boast to American mayors that he was "taking suspected terrorists off the streets." The entire program was excessively punitive. It was ethnically discriminatory. And its impact on detainees was severe. One celebrated case was the Hamoui family in Seattle. The father, Safouh, fifty-two, owned a popular Mediterranean grocery store in Seattle. He had been a pilot in the Syrian Air Force. He came to this country in 1992 seeking political asylum. The early-morning knock on Safouh's front door by INS and FBI agents came on February 22, 2002. With their guns drawn, a swarm of agents arrested Safouh, his wife Hanan, and daughter, Nadin, nineteen. The family was taken to an INS detention center in downtown Seattle. The two Hamoui women remained in lockdown custody for nine months before being released. Safouh was freed one month later. The Hamouis still live in Seattle, but Safouh was forced to close his grocery store due to the extended business interruption. He now manages a gas station. The family is seeking permanent resident status, which is a necessary step before full U.S. citizenship can be granted.

"A family cannot recover from the trauma of the government's unconstitutional civil jailing of the parents and the beloved second daughter," says Bernice Funk, who became the Hamouis' attorney after they were detained. "Fortunately, the Hamouis are a family of strong faith and keen intelligence, and a love of people—which is why the local community supported this family. If the family had had competent legal counsel, they would have been granted asylum in 1995 and been spared the pain, suffering, and trauma. When this information was brought to the government in early 2002, the reaction was unreasonable, and the anti-Arab, anti-Muslim prejudice was clear."

Here is Nadin's story in her own words. Her English is lively, spirited, and without any trace of a foreign accent. She sounds like any other twentysomething American with great dreams for the future. Energetic and ambitious, she currently works as a legal secretary at a large national law firm, but plans to enroll in a school for training in diagnostic ultrasound. "I always wanted to be famous," says Nadin. "But not because I was illegally imprisoned. Rather because I am a good dancer. You'll see me in Hollywood some day. That is my hope."

■　■　■

I was born in Damascus, Syria. I lived there until I was ten. Quite honestly, I don't recall my childhood there at all. I don't know why. I have no idea. There is no reason for this. My mother left Syria with me and my two sisters, who were five and twelve, and my two brothers, who were three and fourteen. We then lived in L.A. with my mom's brother for about six months. We then moved to Seattle to join my father who came to America later.

My mother had to leave Syria because my dad was a pilot and there was an incident. We didn't know of any of these problems while growing up. My dad wanted to keep us from knowing. We didn't hear about it until 2000. I knew he was a pilot. But I didn't know anything more. I just thought he had to stay behind because of his job. He wanted to shelter us from the fear. The Syrian government would torture your children and wife in front of you. It's been martial law there for over forty years. We were Sunnis and so was the government, but they worked very hard to clear everybody else out—the Christians, the different political parties.

My dad used to be a pilot in the Syrian Air Force. He held a position of high prominence. Lots of people worked underneath him. If you wanted to be a pilot, my dad was the only person who could let you go through. If my dad didn't approve you, then you couldn't be a pilot. He was very trusted and very respected, for twenty-two years. Then in 1991, he was flying the Syrian vice president to

Riyadh, Saudi Arabia, in a Russian airplane. There was bad weather. A lesser pilot could not have landed the plane at Riyadh. So the plane came down and lost its landing gear. Nobody was hurt. But my dad was falsely accused of trying to assassinate the vice president and people on board, even though he saved everybody.

The Syrian government locked him inside a prison cell for twenty-five days. The guards would bring him food. If they didn't, he would be without food for days. I know that they treated him very badly. He feared for us. I don't even know how he escaped. That is what I really don't care to know about either. He never went into any details with us. But he got out. And he came here to America. For our family, it was a life-or-death situation.

Once we were all in Seattle, we were never treated any differently. We never acted any differently. We were like all the other kids at school. We are Muslim. I didn't wear the head scarf to school. My mom hadn't worn it. She only started wearing it a few years ago.

My mom has Crohn's disease. It starts out with irritable bowel syndrome and can eventually turn into colon cancer. You have to have the affected part of your intestines cut out or you die because everything you eat ends up coming right out. She lost a lot of weight. It was hard on her. She once had a seizure. We took her to the hospital. She was there for about a month. She could have died. Afterward, she starting wearing the scarf.

She's a very strong woman. She is really tough, a courageous woman. I don't even know a lot about her life, but I do know how my mom and dad met. She was sixteen and a half. She was standing at the window; there were some bars on the window. My father was walking with his mom. They still believed in arranged marriages. They saw each other between the bars, and their families made marriage arrangements.

Here in America, my father couldn't get a job as a pilot. So he opened up a grocery store called Seattle Middle Eastern Market. It was the first Middle Eastern market in the greater Seattle area. He was well known. Everybody knew my dad. He was popular. We had a lot of friends. He was also an authorized dealer for the Dish Network, so he provided satellites for everybody.

Even though we lived at the same address for twelve or thirteen years, we were still here on a tourist visa. My dad had applied for asylum. We had some bad attorneys working on our immigration application papers. But I didn't know anything about this at the time because my dad still wanted to protect us. Right after September 11, 2001, my dad called one of the attorneys and wanted to know if we should be concerned. The attorney said, "Just keep living your life. Don't let it stop you." We had put all our faith and trust in the lawyers.

Then on January 26, 2002, Attorney General John Ashcroft signed an executive order. It was called the Absconder Apprehension Initiative. Why would you come up with such a long-ass name? Why couldn't you just make it a name that immigrants would understand?

February 22nd was the day when we were picked up. It was Friday, a religious day. That is when we do prayers. It was also the first day of Eid, which is our high holy day. You're supposed to fast during the day. My mom was up until four o'clock that morning, cooking and making special meals. At six o'clock in the morning, she heard a knock on the door. She woke my dad. They thought they were just friends of my brother or sister. So he went to the door and opened it, and these armed men just rushed him. There were about fifteen of them: three Immigration and Naturalization Service agents and the rest were FBI, police, and United States Marshals.

I was in my bedroom. I didn't know where the noise was coming from or who was in my house or what. I was half-asleep. It's like when you think you're dreaming but really the phone is ringing. So I got up. I was kinda sleepwalking. I was in the hallway, and I hadn't turned on the light. I then went around the corner, and this guy scared the crap outta me. All I see is this gun in my face. I am five foot and weigh ninety pounds. I put my hands up because that's all you know what to do. Not that I've been through the situation before. But you see it on TV. You throw your hands up. He asks, "Who is upstairs?"

My mother was in her bedroom. Not that she didn't want to come out. She just wanted to put on her scarf. And this guy is yelling at me, "What is she doing? Does she have a gun under her pillow?" He then went in there, and he walked her to the closet and watched her put the scarf on. She got really mad at that. He overstepped the boundaries.

My younger sister and brother were left at home with my uncle, while my mom and dad and myself were taken to the INS detention center in downtown Seattle. When we got to INS, they wanted my mom to take her scarf off again. They argued for a long time about the scarf, and she said, "Over my dead body. You will have to kill me first." They said, "I'd rather you cooperate." My dad replied, "Did you hear what she said?" They said, "Yeah, we heard what she said. And the scarf is coming off." I don't know what happened. My mother had a seizure after they stressed her. They finally said, "You can keep your scarf."

Then, because she had her passport in the bank, they took her back there and made her get the passport. We didn't know what we had done wrong. They wanted to put us on an airplane on Monday morning They didn't want to waste any time or money on us. They wanted us gone, back to Syria. They didn't interrogate us. Just my dad about September 11th. We weren't allowed to see him.

My brother Sam was finally able to make a quick phone call to Rita Za-waideh who is president and cofounder of the Arab-American Community Coalition. He briefly explained what was going on. She's very well known in Seattle. She owns a travel agency. She has great parties. Everybody goes to her house on July 4th. She was my dad's customer. My mom used to cater for her parties. Rita then got into contact with attorneys Julia Devin and Bernice Funk.

I was held in a cell with my mother. We were secluded. They didn't want people to know about us. Our front door had a tiny little peephole. I was able to be with her because they knew I'd be taking care of her. That if something were to happen to her, nobody knows her information better than her own daughter. If she were to have a seizure, I had her medical information. I knew all of it.

We didn't see our dad for several weeks. We were the only family in Seattle to be arrested. Everyone else in the INS detention center had already committed a crime. They had been in actual prisons. The INS looked at them and said, "Okay, you already committed a crime. We will kick you out of the country." And so, they were held at the detention center. But there was nobody else like us, who hadn't done anything. It was just so out of nowhere. I truly believe that after September 11th, what triggered it was the fact that my dad was a pilot.

We were kept in our cell for nine months. I cried a lot. My mom didn't stop crying. She prayed a lot. After a couple of months, I was staying up all night. The days were so much longer than the nights. There was nothing to do but stare at the walls. We had no books, no TV. I wanted paper so I could write. They wouldn't give us any. They wouldn't give us a pencil or pen because they thought I was going to stab somebody in the eye. I don't know *what* they thought. I have no idea what their reasoning was. I have no idea what any of it was about. The guards were trained not to have any kind of emotion. They can't get involved. They can't feel. They can't talk back to you. They'd get fired. They have to follow the rules.

There were Chinese girls locked up next to us. Some of them put paper through the cracks in the door, on the bottom. They showed us through the window how to do origami. The guards finally gave up and allowed us to have paper because they didn't want to fight with us anymore about it.

We had no idea when we were going to get out. We had already watched so many people come and go that it was starting to hurt. I also had kidney stones. It was very painful to pass them—the closest to giving birth in terms of pain. My mom was also sick a lot. An ambulance came out six times and took her to the hospital. They put her in handcuffs at first. She said, "I'm not going anywhere. I can't go anywhere. I'm not running. I'm not doing anything." They didn't get the concept of Crohn's disease and how bad it could be and that it's stress-related.

My mom had so many fevers. The last one was almost deadly. The officers were crying because my mom stopped breathing. There was nothing anybody could have done. I think they realized that she might never come out alive from jail. They were worried about all the local protests and that we now had great lawyers with Bernice and Julia.

On November 18th, 2002, some officers came in and told us to pack our bags. They were looking at my mom. I'm thinking that they were going to send her out by herself. They said, "You're going outside. You're being released." She asked, "What about Nadin?" They said, "We didn't hear anything about her. We only heard about you." So she started crying. "I'm not going without my daughter," she said. I'm also crying. I said, "Mom, please go. I don't want to watch you die in jail. Get out of here before they change their minds." It was all this huge chaos. About forty-five minutes later, they told me I was also to be released.

The INS people called the press and told them that the mother and her daughter were being released today—because, honestly, they wanted to look like the good guys. The press was waiting for us in the front of the building. But we were snuck out the back. My brother drove around to the back of the building and picked us up. As soon as we drove around the front, we started honking and the press saw us. We were later interviewed by reporters from NPR, AP, and the local media. My dad was released one month later. The delay was never explained to us.

I still consider America my home. I probably will always feel it. Especially if you are like me, and you can't remember your own country. What would you call home? Don't get me wrong. I still have pride of Syrian heritage and I always will. But I do not belong in Syria. I don't want to go over there. I don't like what they did to my dad. I don't like how they treated him. I don't like how they betrayed him. I don't like how they hurt him. People in Syria, they want to kill you. Are we not supposed to be in America? Do we not belong anywhere? I am proud to be an American. But they wouldn't let me be one.

I was invited to Washington, D.C., by a coalition of community groups including Council on American Islamic Relations, Hate Free Zone, and National Lawyers Guild National Immigration Project. I went with Julia. I spoke at a forum with congressional leaders on Capitol Hill. I got to meet Senator Ted Kennedy. I was in Washington for two days. I was seriously praying to God that I would run into some higher official from the INS or Justice Department and just have him look me in my eye and hear my story—not read about it or see it on TV or hear it from somebody else.

On my way to Washington, I wrote a poem called "February 22, 2002." Part of it goes:

> Is the day I will never forget
> Is the day, my family and I were degraded and discriminated against
> Is the day we were presented with cruelty, suffering, & heartache
> Because we happen to speak the same language as the terrorists
> Had we really been one of them?
> Or had Bush just been really mad at Bin Laden?
> I am an Arab and I am Muslim.
>
> Not only were we treated as criminals
> But also as people with no principles
> Six in the morning and people pounding on the door
> I swear my heart could have fallen to the floor
> I'd like for one night to sleep in peace and not fear
> That somebody's at the door, their guns cocking I hear
> I am an Arab and I am Muslim.

7

THE FIGHTING DEMOCRAT

Paul Hackett came back from Iraq and decided to run for Congress.

> "I called the president a sonofabitch, and the media just went nuts. But I was willing to put my life on the line for him. And that's as good as it gets."

In the final tally, just 1,751 votes stood between Paul Hackett and history as the first Iraq War veteran elected to Congress. The wealthy Cincinnati attorney and forty-two-year-old Marine reservist nearly pulled off an amazing political feat in the 2005 special election in Ohio's Second District when its representative, Rob Portman, quit to become a U.S. trade representative. After spending seven months in Iraq as an officer with the 4th Civil Affairs Group, 1st Marine Division, Hackett returned home to his family and law practice. His boots had barely touched ground at the Cincinnati airport when he decided to enter the race. Initially viewed as a long shot, the Democratic hopeful ran an insurgent's campaign, reaching out to voters in deep-red counties surrounding metropolitan Cincinnati. Hugging the Kentucky border near the Ohio River, this region is a Bible-loving stronghold where John Kerry pulled only 36 percent in the 2004 presidential race. Hackett's ultra-conservative GOP opponent was former state representative Jean Schmidt, the president of Southern Ohio Right to Life.

Early on, the bloggers took particular notice of Hackett's candidacy. His anti-Bush rhetoric appealed to progressive activists who rallied behind the political neophyte. Led by OH-02, Daily Kos, MyDD, Swing State Project, and Actblue.com, the netroots movement generated national interest, mobilized hundreds of campaign volunteers, and provided financial support. Around $600,000 was raised in online donations; individual contributions averaged around fifty dollars. The Democratic Congressional Campaign Committee spent another $200,000 after first refusing Hackett's request for monetary assistance. To meet this unexpected Web-based challenge, the GOP was forced to pump a million dollars into Schmidt's campaign coffers, dreading the prospect of losing a congressional seat that has been in Republican hands for over three decades. Hackett was the Republican Party's worst nightmare: an anti-war Marine vet.

Hackett prospected for votes at factory plants, county fairs, and neighborhood meet-and-greets. The tall, charismatic, and handsome Hackett was a natural crowd-pleaser as he spoke out against the president, Ohio's scandal-plagued GOP establishment, and job flight from the Buckeye State. His bluntness even resonated with independents and Republican voters who had grown dissatisfied with the White House's mishandling of the Iraq War. They liked his straight-talking ways, occasionally seasoned with profanity in that time-honored Marine style. In this sliver of heartland America, it certainly helped that Hackett opposed gun control and is an avid hunter. In stark contrast to what he calls "touchy-feely" Democrats, Hackett was pure lock-and-load.

His military credentials protected him from right-wing sniping. Nonetheless he attracted intense conservative fire after calling Bush a "sonofabitch." But Hackett refused to back down and apologize for this put-down. "What makes America great is we can have political dissent," he says. "That is what patriotism is all about." After Rush Limbaugh told listeners on election day that Hackett was a "staff puke who goes to Iraq to pad the resume," Hackett blasted away at this lie on Bill Maher's talk show on HBO, reminding viewers that Rush was a "draft dodger and drug addict." In one of several interviews for *Patriots Act*, Hackett adds, "Rush didn't know what the hell he was talking about. I never talked to the man. All I can tell you is that some of the Marines in my command—officers senior to me in my unit—heard him and called in to that show and I guess his phone screeners, when they heard the officers were calling to criticize Rush and defend me, the callers were just politely thanked and hung up on. The officers I served under and the Marines who served under me knew that the description of 'staff puke' was 180 degrees opposite of who I am and what I did in Iraq. I was not a desk jockey." In fact, Hackett survived shootings and roadside ambushes as a convoy commander in Iraq.

The special election in Ohio became the "summer's political sleeper hit," according to *Mother Jones*, which made Hackett its October 2005 cover story. In the end, however, he lost by four percentage points to Schmidt. Encouraged by his near win, Hackett subsequently decided to run for the Ohio Senate seat held by Republican Mike DeWine, whose $3 million campaign war chest has been fattened by Halliburton and the pharmaceutical industry. But Hackett must first defeat seven-term Congressman Sherrod Brown—whose district lies west of Cleveland in northern Ohio—in a bruising Democratic primary in early May 2006. (Before Hackett entered the Senate race, he met with Brown, who assured him that he was bowing out. Three days later, Brown changed his mind.)

Whatever the eventual outcome of the Senate race in this bellwether state, Hackett is part of a new trend within the Democratic Party: the re-emergence of the soldier-politician. Nine Iraq War veterans, who are Democrats, have entered 2006 congressional races, including those in districts in Pennsylvania, Illinois, and Texas. *Newsweek* has called this new partisan development "the Vet Strategy," which the Democratic leadership hopes will counter voter perception that Republicans own the high ground on issues of defense and national security. Electorally speaking, the war has come home.

■ ■ ■

I was born in Cleveland, Ohio, in 1962, but I grew up in Cincinnati. My family moved here when I was about four years old. My dad was an engineer who worked for General Electric at the Evandale Jet Engine plant. We always lived a good middle-class American life.

My mother started working at Cincinnati public schools when I was about six. When I was around ten, my dad went to work as a manufacturer's rep, also known as a traveling salesman, selling industrial equipment like pumps and valves. After about two years, he left the man he was working for and bought a small manufacturing rep business from a man who had a heart attack and had to retire. Like most Hacketts, my dad wanted to be self-employed. He really made a great little business out of it, and ran that business until about four years ago. It was just my dad, and he had a part-time secretary and a full-time salesman. My older brother Chris worked for him for a handful of years when he first got out of college. My brother now lives in Greenwich, Connecticut, where he is a private stock analyst.

First through eighth grade, I went to a private school in Cincinnati, Ohio. In ninth grade, I went to Indian Hill High School. I played baseball through eighth grade, then ran track and cross-country from ninth grade through senior year. I had nothing to do with student politics in high school. After I graduated from Indian Hill, I didn't think I was academically ready for college, so I went to Lawrenceville, a boarding school in New Jersey, for what's known as a PG year—a postgraduate year. It is one of the oldest boarding schools in the United States. When I went there, it was still an all-boys school—a good, old-fashioned, traditional boarding school. It was fantastic. It was everything I wanted it to be. Many, if not most, of the elite boarding schools in the East have PG years. They've got them for those who didn't get accepted by the Ivy League school they wanted to go to. They take a PG year to raise their standardized test scores and grades.

Back then, I was probably a younger version of what I am now. I wasn't looking to stick out, but I always did things my way. I had a handful of really close friends. I never felt peer pressure growing up. I wasn't opposed to getting into a fist fight if that is what was called for. I never walked away from a fight. I was pretty outspoken. I didn't have the tough-guy build. I've always been a tall, skinny kid. I stopped growing when I was fifteen and reached the height of six-foot-two. I weighed about 140 pounds probably until I was about twenty. But I had the tough-guy mouth. But these days it's a lot different. Kids who get into fights get tossed out of high schools. I dunno how many fights I got into in high school. Hell, even when I was in boarding school, I remember I got into a pretty good fist fight and bloodied the kid up pretty good. Back in the early '80s, it wasn't that big of a deal; it was just boys being boys. Yet in the spirit of full disclosure, I also got my butt kicked just as many times as I kicked somebody else's. It's not like I had a winning streak going there. It was probably break-even.

For college, I went to Case Western Reserve in Cleveland, Ohio. I thought Cleveland was a cool city when I visited the school. I found out later that was the only sunny day there in two months. My first year there, I was blown away by how much snow and rain there was. The weather is dramatically different in Cleveland than it is down in Cincinnati. I met my wife Suzi at Case Western. She grew up in Shaker Heights, Ohio.

While at Case, I signed the paperwork to join the Marine Corps in '82. My dad served in the Army during the Korean War and was stationed up in Newfoundland. I went through boot camp in the summer of '83 at Quantico, Virginia. The amazing thing about the Marine Corps is that you could pick up a book about going through Officer Candidates School in the '50s or '60s and then read a book like *Jarhead* set in the '90s, and it's the same deal with very slight variation. Our instructors in the early '80s were Vietnam vets.

My first week at boot camp was certainly very different than anything else I'd experienced in my life up to that point. I had worked some tough jobs and hung around some unusual people growing up. When I was in high school, I worked for a guy who made the mirror prizes you got when you threw the dart and hit the balloon at a carnival. I also ran a dart game for him a couple weeks each summer at the county fair. I also used to work changing tires at a large company here in Cincinnati called Tire Discounters. Before that, I used to string tennis rackets, and I carried golf clubs at one of the prestigious country clubs here in Cincinnati. When I was a kid, I had my own little jobs cutting grass, shoveling snow, and cleaning swimming pools. My dad emphasized the importance of work. And also for selfish reasons—I wanted to have some spending cash.

But back to boot camp. Remember the drill instructor played by R. Lee Ermy in *Full Metal Jacket*? Let me put it to you this way. That was routine. Ermy wasn't acting any more than any other drill instructor acts. He exemplified an old-school drill instructor, though at OCS we called them sergeant instructors and platoon sergeants. Boot camp lasted six weeks. You were there for screening and evaluation. Our dropout rate at boot camp was about 50 percent. You got trained if you survived. You then came back the following summer if you graduated from the junior program.

I graduated from Case in '85, then went to law school at Cleveland State. On my first day in law school, a guy named David Goshen was our first-year contracts teacher. He started off in a very traditional law-school way. There were about eighty of us in the class. Standing in front of us, he said, "Look to your left. Look to your right. Half of you will be gone before the end of this year, or won't graduate from law school." He was just going on with this rant. I raised my hand and asked, "When are you going to start teaching us?" Goshen told me to take a seat in the front row. I was within physical striking distance of him for the remainder of the year. Dave and I went on to be great friends. I had tremendous respect for him. I loved him as a professor, and I ended up taking his tax classes as electives.

After I graduated from law school and passed the bar exam, I did three years of active duty. I started at Quantico at the Basic School, which all Marine officers go to regardless of Military Occupational Specialty. It is a six month course. When you graduate, theoretically, you can go on to get further training to be an infantry or artillery officer. The concept in the Marine Corps is that all Marine officers are line officers. For example, if you're an attorney and you're in the Navy, you wear separate insignia on one side of your collar that has your rank, and on the other side it has some sort of symbol that looks like a grist mill and signifies that you are an attorney. That's all you can do. Well, in the Marine Corps, we wear rank on both collars. And you better damn well be able to go pick up another responsibility like a line officer. That was certainly a reality when I was on active duty between '89 and '92. I was an attorney for about two of those years and spent one of those years bouncing around doing deployments throughout Asia—Okinawa, the Philippines, Korea. I was training operations officers in the Philippines in the early '90s. When I was in Iraq in 2004, I sure as hell wasn't an attorney. I was a civil affairs officer.

As I was getting out of the Marine Corps in 1992, Suzi and I were trying to decide where to live. I wanted to move to Arizona, so we both applied for jobs at some of the Indian nations. We ended up getting job offers in Papago. We drove to Tucson, and I called up some former Marines who were practicing law as civilian attorneys. I was trying to get an idea of what it was that I wanted to do in the field of law. I realized that I didn't want to do hourly work, where I was tethered to a time clock, which is what defense attorneys do. Every defense attorney I spoke to told me it was a miserable existence. So after about ten of these informational interviews, I quickly concluded that plaintiffs' attorneys tend to be happier than the defense attorneys, so I decided that I wanted to be a plaintiffs' attorney. I did get the job offer at the Indian nation. I wanted to do it, but my wife had spent a year with me in Okinawa and she didn't want to be that far away from her family again. We had two options—Cleveland or Cincinnati. The deciding factor: Cincinnati had better weather.

I was wonderfully unemployed in Cincinnati. Of course, I am being facetious. I spent four months on the unemployment line. It sucks. Suzi and I were living in my old bedroom in my parents' house. She has a degree in school psychology and got a job pretty quickly, but I was unemployed. It definitely was not a positive thing. What it did for me was motivate me to never be financially hard-up again. Even when I branched off and started my own law practice, I became outrageously frugal for many years.

My first job was working for a guy by the name of Gene Rothschild, and he is still a good friend and supporter. I worked for him for about a year and a half. Then I said, "What the hell. I can do this on my own and make more money." So I opened up Hackett Law Offices in February or March of '94 , and I've been doing that ever since. Some of the clients I had when I was with Gene came over with me, which created some issues with Gene that we were able to work out over time. But it was one of the smartest business decisions I ever made in my life. You'll also notice a trend within my family. We tend to be all self-employed. My dad was self-employed. My brother is self-employed. I'm self-employed. My dad's sister is self-employed. Another sister is part-time self-employed. The Hacketts tend to be an independent breed.

I think of myself as a small businessman who has a law office. I do personal injury work. I represent the small guy against Goliath. I represent people who can't even afford to hire an attorney. The personal work I do is automobile-accident related. I have two attorneys who work for me. One of the attorneys does criminal defense work. When I was in Iraq, those guys were running the show.

I was in court the morning of September 11, 2001. The bailiff said something about the World Trade Center. I spent the rest of the day glued to the radio because we didn't have a TV in the law office. My wife's sister lived a couple blocks away from the Trade Center. I spent the next forty-eight hours doing nothing but watching TV since I brought a set into the office.

By then, I was completely out of the Marine Corps system. When I got off active duty in '92, I spent nearly three years serving in the Active Reserves as a communications officer. In 1999, I was honorably discharged from the Marine Corps. But after 9/11, as fate would have it, I started getting phone calls from former Marine buddies. By late 2002, it became very clear to all of us who had our heads screwed on tight that Bush was waltzing off to an invasion of Iraq. My position was that it was stupid to invade Iraq, because Iraq's got nothing to do with 9/11.

While the invasion of Iraq was going on, I was glued to CNN wondering how many of my friends were over there and what they were doing. Every now and then, I would read news articles about my friends. One of them from Okinawa, John Ewers, was profiled on the front page of the *Wall Street Journal*. He got shot up pretty bad in An Nasiriyah, one of the toughest cities, during the invasion. He was a JAG [*ed. Judge Advocate General*] and now he is a full-bird colonel. He was in An Nasiriyah to do some sort of follow-up investigation of something that happened the day before. He got ambushed and survived, but he got cut up bad.

So here I am, living this great life in Cincinnati, living in this big house. I got this law practice, and I am turning some really good coin while my Marine buddies were getting shot up in Iraq. Eighteen- and nineteen-year-old kids were going off to fight a war. And in the community of Indian Hill, where I live and which may have been the nation's highest per-capita donor to the Bush-Cheney 2004 campaign, many people thought invading Iraq was a good idea. But nobody was willing to go fight there. Yet they were the ones driving around with "Bush-Cheney" and "Proud to be an American" bumper stickers. Many had all these nationalistic attitudes, yet none of them were going to fight. And none of their kids were going to fight.

In February 2004, I decided to apply to get my commission back; I did the paperwork to get back into the Marine Corps. Both my wife and I were obviously aware of the tremendous risk and responsibility and hardship it would put on the family. We have three children, ages two, five, and eight. I was walking away from my law practice and turning it over to my support staff. I had run it completely myself. I had to teach my support staff to run the office, pay my bills, get into the checkbook. I didn't know if any of that would be there when I got back. I didn't know if I was gonna come back. I didn't know what I would be like when I came back. I didn't know if I was gonna have all my limbs, or any other problems. So I felt this huge responsibility to make sure that my family was taken care of. I also felt like I had this responsibility to set a good example for my kids, to give them a sense that when you have so much in life, that doesn't make you better, it just increases your responsibility.

I was at the top of the economic ladder. Certainly there are folks who are far wealthier than me, but I'm in about the ninety-ninth percentile. Guys like me have an obligation for service to one's country. When you look back at the greatest generation in World War II, what I did was common back then. People think it is such a big deal now. Yet looking at Bush's war cabinet, they were almost all draft dodgers. Sons-of-bitches, all of 'em. Not only does that piss me off, but it is in part why this administration has done such a poor job of managing the war in Iraq. Even making the decision to go to Iraq. They have an academic understanding of the military. But they have contempt for the military leadership—to the extent that they disregarded General Shinseki. And they disregarded General Tommy Franks who concurred with Shinseki until Franks decided he wanted to survive and then said, "Okay, we can do it with 150,000 troops." They disregarded Tony Zinni, the Marine four-star general who was the Mideast envoy for Bush. He cautioned Bush about going into Iraq. In fact, he had a quote something along the lines of, "If you take a look around, the only people excited about invading Iraq are people who have never worn the uniform."

In June of 2004, I got a call that I'd been accepted back into the Marine Corps at the rank of major, which I'd been in the reserves. I reported to active duty at the end of July. I did one week of training in Quantico, Virginia. Then I flew out to Camp Pendleton, California, where I did another week of training. I then took a flight to Kuwait. Spent a day in Kuwait, and then I climbed on a C-130 and on August 15, 2004, I landed in Taqquadam, Iraq. Everybody calls it TQ. It's a town between Fallujah and Ramadi.

My detachment was with the Governance Support Team, 4th Civil Affairs Group, also known as 4th CAG. I had two capacities. As part of the GST, I was the money guy who took charge in coordinating and getting the Iraqi provisional government payroll from Baghdad to Ramadi, which is the capital of the Al Anbar province. We did the payroll once a month. The government is the number-one employer in Al Anbar. And if the folks don't get paid, they aren't happy. If they aren't happy, they are rioting in the streets, and they are shooting at us. I would coordinate with Dick Arsenault from the State Department. He was a former 82nd Airborne guy. He was in Baghdad. Most of the time we would fly the money in the middle of the night in a couple of Black Hawk helicopters. I'd meet Dick with a bunch of Humvees, and we would start unloading the money and get the helicopters out of there as quickly as possible. We transported tens of millions in Iraqi dinars in boxes and sacks.

Two to three days a week, it was my responsibility as convoy commander to get our detachment from Camp Blue Diamond to the Ramadi government center in one piece and then back again. It was about six miles away. That wasn't a run you wanted to do unnecessarily. When I first got there, our Humvees were partly armored. They had hillbilly armor on them. They had open backs. Grenade tubs is what we called 'em. When I ended up in Fallujah, I was running around for three months in a canvas-top Humvee that had no armor.

Our Ramadi convoy survived two improvised explosive device ambushes. One IED detonated directly in front of my Humvee, just off to my right. And almost simultaneously, one IED detonated about three vehicles back in the convoy on the left. There was also small-arms fire. This happened on a run up from Baghdad to Ramadi in the middle of the night on October 21, 2004. There was a sandstorm that night. We were headed to Baghdad to pick up a truckload of shoes and give them away to the kids in Ramadi. Unbelievably, we blew through that ambush unscathed. The IED triggerman's timing must have been screwed up because of the sandstorm. If it had been a clear night, I wouldn't be talking right now. I had the closest miss on the IED. It exploded about twenty-five meters in front of my Humvee. The explosion would have killed me had we been going faster. It would have also killed my driver, my gunner, and my two backseat passengers. Either that or it would have fucked us up big time. We didn't stop. We drove through the debris field as it was still blowing in the air and falling on us. We later got on Route Irish, which is the road between the Green Zone and Baghdad International Airport, and is known as the most dangerous road in Iraq. We are doing this in the middle of the night. It is fucking black. We get up to the Green Zone around one o'clock. Let me tell you, we were happy. We all felt like Superman that night. Me and my buddy, Bill Reynolds, who is now Senator Arlen Specter's chief of staff, went over to the palace pool. There was a big party winding down. One of the World Series games was on the big-screen TV. We were covered from head to toe with dust and dirt. We still had our M-16s and assault packs. All our battle rattle. Grenades. The whole nine yards. We parked ourselves right on the deck of the pool. Some guy came up to us and said, "Hey, you guys aren't supposed to be out here. It's a private party. And there are supposed to be no rifles on the deck of the pool complex." Bill and I simultaneously looked at him and said, "Fuck you. Make us go away!" We later jumped in the pool in nothing but our skivvy shorts and basically cleaned up in the pool. We then whipped out sleeping bags from our assault packs and slept right there on the chaise lounges by the pool that night. I woke up to the sound of people swimming laps that morning. It was a beautiful thing.

I left Ramadi and took a night helicopter ride to Fallujah around October 25, 2004. I was in Fallujah before, during, and after the invasion. I was at a Forward Operating Base at the eastern entry point to the city. Right on Route Michigan which is the road to Baghdad. I was about eight miles down the road from Abu Ghraib. I ran a place called the Fallujah Liaison Team, which everybody referred to as the FLT. I was in charge of humanitarian assistance. I did all of the ID carding for citizens re-entering the city after the invasion. I also dealt with all kinds of issues. We spent one day picking up dead bodies. We came across a head and no body, and so drove around Fallujah with this head in a bag.

You saw bodies laying all over the place. Cats and dogs were running around with body parts in their mouths, sitting there eating insurgent bodies. Seeing all those dead bodies and body parts has yet to bother me. It's not that I'm inhuman. If it had been another day, maybe somebody would have been picking me up and shoving me in a body bag. I just tried to maintain a very professional view of it. It's not that I felt hatred towards these people. I'm a professional. They are trying to kill us. My fellow Marines are trying to kill them.

Combat was not my primary job. But I commanded those who did in a small way. My primary job was the hearts-and-minds aspect of the battle and to facilitate and coordinate reconstruction. Yet everybody was in peril over there. Everybody was at risk. One day in December, I was working on getting the Fallujah highway-patrol building back up and running, which involved multiple site surveys, getting water back in their water tank, and putting diesel back in their diesel tank for their diesel generator. This one particular day we went back to refill the water and diesel tanks. When you do that, you first gotta clear the building. I came back an hour later when we were filling the water tank because I wanted to make sure that all the spigots were turned off. The water tank was gravity-fed and if a spigot was open, we'd literally be pouring water down the drain. I was in the building by myself. As I was bending over to turn off the spigot on the last shower on the left down the hall of ten showers, I saw someone's shoes protruding from under the stall door. It was an insurgent we had not detected when we had cleared the building earlier. As I later found out, he was wiring the place to blow. All I had was my flak jacket, Kevlar helmet, and a 9mm on my hip. Seeing his shoes shocked me. I screamed. It scared the shit out of me. I shoved the door back on him, and he shoved it back on me. I wasn't even thinking except for survival. It wasn't as if I was going through this mental check-list: Is he armed or not? I was thinking, "I am gonna kill this guy." I shoved the door back. He shoved it back towards me. But I was bigger and stronger. I leaned into it and grabbed him with my left hand at his shirt collar. I started stepping backwards out of the shower stall while fumbling for my pistol. I kept dragging him towards me. He was pushing on me, so I just figured I'd use his power against him. I backpedaled. In the meantime, I drew my pistol and stuck it in his mouth. I have to be honest. There was a split second when I thought, "Do I pull the trigger? Or do I just keep my cool and see if I can't get this guy out alive so I don't have to visualize for the rest of my life his brains splattered on a shower floor?" I took him alive. I wrestled him to the ground outside, and once my Marines got there I holstered my weapon and they flex-cuffed him. I always travel with a digital camera, so I took a couple pictures of him sitting down. It was hard to tell his age. I tagged him as in his thirties. He was turned over to a unit for screening and questioning. They put him in the back of a Humvee, and he was shipped off to wherever was appropriate. Then I went off and had a cig-arette. I didn't smoke before I got to Iraq.

When Fallujah got opened up on December 26, 2004, I spent the day in a sea of Iraqi humanity checking IDs. We were concerned with what we called MAMs. Military age males. That is loosely defined as young teenagers to old men. We did our best to make sure none of them were armed or were wearing suicide vests. That went on for days. We did our best to do our job and screen these folks. We were professionals. I always felt I had a great working relation-ship with the Iraqis. I never felt animosity toward them. I would do my best with our interpreters to speak to them and explain to them what it was we were doing and why we had to do it, while extending my apologies for the inconvenience. But I hate to use that word apology, for fear it might be misconstrued. I was not apologizing beyond the inconvenience. I would try to explain to the people of Fallujah that it was in both our best interests to make Fallujah a safe place. Is-suing these ID cards would help not only the Americans but the Iraqi leaders in working together to rebuild Fallujah. They needed to get an ID card in order to re-enter their city to look at what was left of their houses or businesses. I wasn't apologizing for what we did to their city. Insurgents and religious fanatics had taken over their city, and it happened in part because the citizens of Fallujah were incapable or unwilling to oust those bad people.

At the end of my stay in Fallujah, I participated in Iraq's national election that was held on January 31, 2005. Because of my familiarity in working with Iraqis and my ability to hit the ground running, my team basically got put back together to track and receive Iraqi election poll workers who were coming in from Baghdad. They were put on Air Force transport planes and flown all over Iraq to work polls during the election. Many were Sunnis by virtue of the fact that they were coming from Baghdad. And probably many of them were Shias, too. Which is no big deal either way. They were very exuberant, very excited about participating. They were getting paid very well. But that doesn't necessarily mean that they were throwing caution to the wind and not taking into consideration the extreme risk to them and their families for participating in the elections. In my limited contact with them, I didn't notice this quiet fear. I mean, they were very social. I communicated with them through interpreters. It took a couple of days to count ballots and put them back in the boxes and ship them to Baghdad. We then made sure that the poll workers made it safely back to Baghdad.

I never walked around the city of Baghdad. Just in the Green Zone. It is a pretty large area, maybe ten square miles. People who live in the Green Zone talk about how dangerous it is. But when I was walking around inside the Green Zone, it felt like I was on vacation. There was some semblance of normalcy—unlike Fallujah or Ramadi. Yeah, they got some periodic mortar and rocket attacks. But, big deal. That happens all over Iraq.

While I was in Iraq, Ramadi was taken over by insurgents. It was a complete no-go zone. When you were on the roads in Ramadi, you had to be ready to fight. It was a complete fucking combat zone. RPGs would be shot at our convoys coming and going. You're going out there gunned up, ready to fight. Folks were looking for an opportunity to kill us. And that's every day. The only way you avoid that is by being supremely prepared, supremely briefed, and supremely trained to fight when necessary. And if you don't have to fight, you don't fight. If you gotta fight, you fight to kill. And just by having proper training and constantly working on it so that you have calm professional confidence, you diminish the risk of being engaged. You diminish the risk of failing to observe an IED that might kill or injure. It's like with hunting in that you develop a sixth sense that allows you to read indicators that you can't even articulate but you just know are there. I am righteously proud of the fact that none of my Marines were injured under my command or under my leadership as the convoy commander in Ramadi and Fallujah. I had probably gone outside the wire as commander a hundred times.

I left Iraq around March 16 and touched down in the United States two days later. I was met at the airport by my wife, our three kids, and about twenty other friends. One friend, Mike Brautigam, told me that our congressman, Rob Portman, had stepped down the day before. Before we left the airport, I said, "Yeah, I'll take a shot at running for Congress." I never sat around in my law office, saying one day, "I want to be a congressman." I hadn't even considered running for office while in Iraq. It's what makes America great. You don't have to have "experience" in politics. Look, I've got experience as an attorney and small businessman running a law office with five employees. I've got experience as a father and husband, and I've got experience leading Marines. I've got experience fighting for my country. In my life, where I don't act and when I don't make timely decisions, I either lose money or I lose lives. So I am intimately familiar with making decisions in pressure situations. Both in the courtroom on behalf of clients or on the battlefield with Marines. And what's the worst thing that's gonna happen to me if I lose the election? Big fucking deal. Again, if I lose in Iraq, I lose lives. That's a big deal.

It felt great to be back home. Every day is extra. I didn't even have jet lag when I got back. Went to bed at probably midnight. Slept like a baby. I got up around 6:30 in the morning. Put on my civilian clothes for the first time in eight months and hopped in my car and drove to Starbucks for a cup of coffee. It was a great ride. Couple miles away. It was just completely normal. I was so pleased. With that said, I was wondering about all that on my plane ride back from Iraq. What was it going to be like to drive down a road? Was I going to be paranoid or not? I think that we were all a little bit concerned when we were in Iraq. God, are we gonna get back? Is everything gonna be weird afterwards? I was concerned because we heard so much that there would be some readjustment. But there wasn't for me. To be honest, I was probably more calm and patient than before I left.

I was up early every day, working hard on the race. Traveling all over the district. Meeting as many people as I could. Answering all their questions. I tried to be honest and direct. I think people appreciated that I was comfortable saying what I believed in, though I met many people who disagreed with my positions.

I was not the guy running around saying, "Hey, I'm a Democrat!" But I can tell you this: I never voted for a Republican president in my life. I only began to identify myself as a Democrat, believe it to not, when Bill Clinton was impeached. I didn't vote for Clinton in '92. I voted for Ross Perot. I think Clinton displayed some outrageously poor judgment. Not only in his relationship with Monica Lewinsky, but how he handled it afterwards. If he had just said, "Hey, it's none of your goddamn business. Yeah, I had sex in the White House with a twenty-one-year-old. My mistake. Now get the hell out and let me deal with it with my wife," I think many Americans would have said, "Geesh. Not the greatest thing." But that would have been the end of it. He wouldn't have gotten impeached. But what happened afterwards was wrong. It confirmed my suspicions about how radical and misguided the Republican Party had become. If you had asked me before, I would have said I'm an independent, but I just felt at that point we gotta choose sides here.

I'll give you another example. During the run up to the elections in 2000, I was making deposits for my law office at my bank. I don't know how it came up. I was talking to this young teller about who she was gonna vote for, and I said, "Hell, I'm gonna vote for Al Gore. Who ya gonna vote for?" She said, "Oh gosh, I'm gonna vote for George Bush. I think he is great. He's gonna cut taxes." I replied, "Sweetheart, he's not gonna cut your taxes. He's gonna cut *my* taxes. He's not gonna do anything for you. Don't you understand? He's for guys like me, and guys like me shouldn't be asking for that kind of handout from the government."

During the campaign, my number-one issue was the economy, though it later morphed into the war in Iraq. I highlighted that Ohio has been misrepresented and underrepresented in Columbus and Washington, D.C. by our elected officials who were more interested in kowtowing to special interests who paid to have access. And those who weren't paying to have access were being disregarded. Ohioans are worse off today than they were five, ten, or even fifteen years ago, because our elected representatives were exporting good paying jobs out of state by subsidizing corporations who do not look first to how to contribute to local communities. And they should be. That's a basic American principle and value. Whether you are an individual or corporation, you serve your community. You serve your country. Part of that is giving back. It is not just paying your taxes. Paying taxes is simply a price of admission. There are times when taxes can be cut, and there are times when taxes need to be increased. That is an adult conversation. It's not, "I'm gonna cut your taxes." That's bullshit! It is! Do you ever believe a politician who says he's gonna lower your taxes? Look, if your taxes are lowered on the federal level, taxes are either gonna increase on the state and local level or you won't have the services that one expects from government. We don't have proper ambulance services. We don't have quality water. We don't have a quality electrical grid. And we start to look like a Third World nation. We are getting there.

My campaign message about the war became this: "Fight the war in Iraq to win or get the hell out." Bush's rationale that sacrificing more young Americans somehow validates the loss of other young Americans is bullshit! And when he talks about staying the course, I call on the president to tell us what the course is. What is the mission in Iraq? What is it? But because of poor Democratic leadership, they are not calling him on it. If you want to fight the war to win, then you've got to train the Iraqi security forces in order to take over. And they aren't doing it right. If you want to do it right, you gotta have a one-to-one match between Iraqi security forces and American military forces. Instead, a handful of American military advisers and interpreters would train three hundred or four hundred Iraqi troops. And the result was a complete failure. Just look at where we are today. On September 30, 2005, the Pentagon finally fessed up that after two and a half years there is only one Iraqi battalion capable of fighting on its own. A battalion has maybe three hundred to four hundred men. That is it. In the previous year, they were saying there were 180,000 Iraqi fighting men capable of fighting! And all of us on the ground in Iraq were saying, "Bullshit!" We would see these news reports talking about how well-trained the Iraqi security forces were. But we were working with them! These guys couldn't even handle their weapons safely, let alone fight safely! I mean it's just a complete disconnect with reality to say that there were 180,000 trained soldiers. Maybe there were 180,000 Iraqi men who went through some private or civilian contract. Or were hired on by Kellogg Brown and Root or some other war profiteer in Iraq to train "Iraqi fighting forces." And these men got a certificate. But they weren't qualified when they got spit out to fight. While in Fallujah, I had under my command eighteen to twenty-five Iraqi security forces, ranging from Iraqi National Guard soldiers to police commandos. At first, they really used to tick me off because of their complete lack of professional military bearing. But after a day or so of living with these guys 24/7, I got to like them. They were nice people, but they just were completely unskilled and untrained.

Given the cultural divide and civil war, the overall situation of training adequate Iraqi security forces to take over from us is not going to change significantly. I explained all this in my first political race after it became abundantly clear to me — as I think it has to most Americans — that the Bush administration has no desire to fight this war to win. Assuming it *can* be won. My bottom line is this: "The war is over. It is time to come home. Enough lives have already been lost." The Pentagon needs to develop a plan to get us home as expeditiously and safely as possible. And then let's carry out that plan. Please, White House, for once, rely upon the war-fighting professionals in the Pentagon to tell you what can and can't be done realistically with the military over there.

Iraq is now a terrorist haven. Whether we leave Iraq this year, next year, five years, or ten years, it's still going to spiral into further chaos. It's more chaotic and dangerous today than it was in 2003. The electric infrastructure is worse. The sewers, the water, the roadway—they're all worse. This notion that when we leave it's gonna get worse? Well, so what? No matter when we leave, it will then get sorted out among the Shia, the Sunnis, and the Kurds. I predict that eventually the Iraqi Shia and Sunnis will band together to oust the jihadist foreign fighters. But the Sunnis will again dominate the leadership of the country, because, in my perhaps politically incorrect take on it, they struck me as more culturally prepared to take over leadership. And the Kurds will revert to some sort of quasi-independent state that co-exists with the Sunnis and the Shias. Then the issue will become: Can Turkey tolerate this quasi-independent Kurdish state on its southern border?

I am, however, willing to go back to Iraq. It's what service is about. I am an American. As much as it saddens me to see my Marine Corps misused, they are my family. I fight first for them. I have a responsibility of contributing in whatever way I can to make sure that the young Marines who go to fight over there have quality leadership. I like to think I am a part of that quality leadership, to make sure that as many of these Marines return home safely.

Being the citizen-legislator political novice, I certainly never anticipated that people from all over the United States would get so focused on my congressional race. When I look back on it in retrospect, I understand how it happened. There was no other political race going on in summer. It was a special election. I'm a Marine who just got back from Iraq, which made me the first to take up a political race. People thought it was unusual that someone would sacrifice time with his beautiful wife and three beautiful children and beautiful house in Indian Hill and go serve in a war that he thought was a misuse of the military and then come back to run as a Democrat in the most-red district in America.

There was a five-way primary, and I won that on June 14, 2005. There were only 30,000 voters who turned out for the primary on both sides of the fence. I took 56 percent of the Democratic vote. I personally donated whatever my maximum federal allowance was, like 2,100 bucks. The rest of the money I raised online and with telephone calls. I did it the old-fashioned, political way.

The media interest picked up about three weeks before the general election—August 2, 2005—when CNN did a short piece on me. Then other news organizations started to take note. I called the president a sonofabitch, and the media just went nuts. The whole quote is not remembered. It's a quote I'm proud of. It was: "I don't like that sonofabitch. But I was willing to put my life on the line for him. And that's as good as it gets." USA Today ran a huge two-page color spread on me and that quote was in that article. The White House sent in the Republican National Committee the following day to back my opponent Jean Schmidt. The polling data suggested that we were in a deadlock. One of the RNC spokesmen said, "We are going to bury him," to which I responded, "Nice. My eight-year-old daughter read that in the paper and asked me what it meant because she didn't understand how the president could say that he was gonna send people to kill my daddy after I fought for him in Iraq."

The media's number-one question to me was: "Did you really call the president a sonofabitch?" I said, "Yeah, I said it. I meant it. I stand by it. I'd say it again." That's what makes America great: political dissent. I don't have to apologize, you know? That is what differentiates America from Iraq, Afghanistan, or Iran. We can verbally air our political difference any way we want to and go home at the end of the day. As opposed to resolving those political differences on the street at the end of an AK-47 or M-16.

When a guy like Rush Limbaugh takes on a guy like me, he probably loses a lot of people. I am not saying I'm pure as the driven snow. Christ. I'm a Marine. The Marine Corps is not exactly Aunt Fanny's Finishing School for Girls. But I am what you see. I am all about service. I am all about patriotism. I am all about serving my country. And when a guy like Limbaugh, who dodged the draft during his generation's war with some bullshit excuse that he had a sore ass, guys in the military think that's disgusting. When I was on the Bill Maher show on HBO, I said, "Look at Rush Limbaugh. What is he? He is a draft dodger, he's a drug user, he's a drug addict. He calls himself patriotic? What more can you say?" When we put on the uniform and fight when this country tells us to fight, we feel like we've earned the opportunity and the right to say whatever we want to say in criticism of whomever. Period. There is a caveat to that. And it goes like this: when we're in uniform, we smartly salute and proudly serve, but we don't criticize. I've always lived up to that.

Between TV, print, and radio I was probably doing over twenty interviews a day by the end of the congressional race. In the beginning, I had hired a manager, a fund-raiser, and a field coordinator—and that is all I ever hired. By the campaign's end, we must have had seven hundred volunteers around our little office. They came from all over the United States—Texas, California, Washington state. There was a Marine from Boston who quit his job and came out to work the last week. I had young Marines from my unit who were volunteering before they had to return to college. World War II vets were coming in to volunteer.

I think we just surprised the Republican Party in the congressional race. They were faced with this problem: "How do we categorize this guy?" When they tried to put me in a box, they realized that I was not your ordinary Democrat. I wasn't going to listen to their bullshit. They are used to taking a swing at Democrats who then become defensive. I'm a proud Democrat. And one of the things that irks me about the leadership in my party is that they are seemingly apologetic about what we stand for. That pisses me off. I think the Democratic Party represents what is best about this country. We are about fighting for the little guy and working Americans. We are about equality and fairness, and goddammit, I'm proud of that.

That's why I'm pissed off at the lack of leadership in the Democratic Party. They are afraid to stand up and call a spade a spade when attacked by Republicans. They didn't stand up and say, "You are unpatriotic if you say you cannot have political dissent." If political dissent is viewed as unpatriotic, that in itself is unpatriotic. There are parallels between this point in history and McCarthyism.

One of the reasons that independents and blue-collar workers have been voting Republican these days is that they are sick and tired of Democrats who are apologists. Who are touchy-feely. The Democrats as a national party are also wrong on the Second Amendment. People like me may not have a blue-collar job, but I have a blue-collar personality. I don't like Democrats who say they are gonna take our guns away. Maybe Democrats are not going to take away our guns. But they are certainly not proactive in making sure we have the right to enjoy our hunting and shooting sports. And as Democrats we lose a lot of votes because of that. I have an A-plus rating with the NRA. In southern Ohio if you want to be elected, you better have this position. I didn't arrive at that through calculation. It's just who I am. I am a responsible gun enthusiast. I own a wide array of guns. Handguns. Rifles. Semi-automatic "assault weapons." I've owned them for years, and I enjoy using them. I enjoy hunting, and I am not ashamed of that. Working Americans have historically enjoyed hunting sports and gun ownership. Democrats who whine and cry and continue to say, "Guns are bad, guns are bad," have probably never picked up a gun or shot one. They certainly have never gone hunting. And therefore, they do not realize how responsible we gun owners and hunters are. Gun control to me is when you hit your target. Hunters are environmentalists at heart.

In the end, Jean Schmidt, who is an absolute religious fanatic and is all about the government interceding into the private lives of regular Americans, beat me 52 to 48 percent, by 3,500 votes. Yet what was most troubling to Republicans and the religious fanatics and Karl Rove was not necessarily that I got 48 percent, but *where* I got that 48 percent. I won the four most rural counties in this district. I won Adams County, which is a county that was trying for years to erect tablets of the Ten Commandments and place them outside public schools until the Supreme Court shot it down. I won that county because I was honest about my religious views. I'm a Christian and make no bones about it. But that's a private matter, and we don't elect politicians to go to Washington to dictate how we live our private lives or how we worship our God. America was founded on freedom of religion. Why do I have to explain or wear on my sleeve my religious convictions? Our country was founded by people who came here evading religious persecution.

After the race, I was contacted by leading congressmen and senators in the Democratic Party and asked to run for the U.S. Senate. One of the incumbents is Mike DeWine, a Republican who is a career politician in the sense that he puts his career before his country. He's been an elected official since he was twenty-eight years old. I was originally under the impression that there were other elected officials from Ohio who were interested in his seat. One was Congressman Tim Ryan, from northeastern Ohio's 17th District. Big unions and steel belt counties are in his district. He had come down to help me in the final week of my congressional campaign, and we kind of hit it off. He's a bright guy. He's an attorney. He's another Irishman, and we shared a certain affinity. He told me, confidentially at that point, that he was thinking about that Senate race, but decided against it. He told me that Sherrod Brown, a congressman from an area west of Cleveland, was not gonna run. While I wanted to get back to my life, Tim encouraged me to run because "there is nobody to take up the mantle to fight DeWine."

But first, I took it upon myself to fly to Washington and meet Sherrod at his office and ask him if in fact he was out of this race. I told him, "Look, if you're in this race, I'm here to support you. I have no desire to run against you." He said, "I've just gotten remarried," and he assured me that he was not going to enter the race. He also assured me that if I decided to run, he would support my candidacy. I thanked him. We shook hands and parted ways politely. A couple weeks later, I heard he was telling people that he was getting back in the race.

Why did he change his mind? I suspect he saw the polling data of me versus DeWine and figured that he could have equally good polling data. Sherrod eventually called me, and I asked him, "Why were you dishonest with me?" He tried to tell me that he wasn't dishonest with me. I said, "Well, Sherrod, I hate to tell you, but down south here in Ohio, when you shake a man's hand, look him in the eye and tell him something, and then do the opposite, that's called a lie. We don't forget that down here. It doesn't go over well. I don't think it goes over well in northern Ohio either."

For the Senate race, I've got a campaign staff of about fifteen. I've got a national fund-raiser, a state fund-raiser, a finance director, a campaign manager, a scheduler, a personal secretary, a direct mail consultant, and a television media consultant. I probably left some out. I've got a driver who does all my driving. I personally purchased a large RV. Thirty-four feet. Brand new. We had it wrapped with a "Hackett for Senate" logo. We travel the state in the RV when we are on the road; it's a rolling billboard, an attention getter.

I plan to win this the old-fashioned way. My fight is for the citizens of Ohio. If Sherrod Brown gets between me and my desire to fight for Ohioans, then he is just roadkill. DeWine is the same in my book. I think that some of the leaders in the Democratic Party are scared shitless of me. I am not afraid to rail on the Democratic Party and my sense is that they don't like people who rock the boat. I have spoken to New York Senator Chuck Schumer a number of times. I will say this, if we grew up together, we probably wouldn't have socialized with one another. I doubt he'd want to go hunting with me. But the other night, Senator Henry Reid called me at home. He expressed his continued support for me. He asked me if there was anything that he could do. He has always been a stand-up guy. I don't know him that well. I think he shares my frustration with the fact that a state Democratic primary in Ohio has come about from all this. I won't get any fund-raising support from the Democratic Party until after the primary.

At the risk of starting to sound like George Bush, I happen to be who I am. And not in an arrogant way, but in a very regular way. I am not particularly special. I am the guy who graduated in the middle of my boarding school class, in the middle of my law school class. I am just a pretty regular American who's had above-average success. I have made some good decisions in my life, though the best decision I ever made was to ask my wife to marry me. I've got a debt coming to me somewhere that I gotta pay for getting her. I dunno what it's gonna cost.

Before I made the decision to get into the congressional race, I relished having an incredibly private life. Suzi and I went out about four times a year socially. Our social life was taking care of our kids and playing with them. And coaching soccer for me. We didn't want an active social life. I don't belong to a country club. I am not motivated by the notoriety of running for public office. I am motivated by the sincere desire to see positive change come to our state and our country. That is the correlation between Iraq and running for Senate. We have got to do better. We deserve better than this.

It all comes down to three words. Service. Commitment. Leadership. Which are not unusual in our Marine Corps. But they are a little bit unusual these days in politics. That is unfortunate. While there are professional politicians who put the country before their career, there are many, unfortunately, who are serving for less than the best reasons. That is not how this country got started. This country got started by citizen-legislators who were committed to serve and lead in the best interests of all Americans.

Moreover, those of us who served our country in combat believe that political dissent is at the heart of patriotism. On a day-to-day basis, those who served and fought were motivated by the fact that in some disconnected way, we are fighting for America's freedom. And that freedom is well-defined by political dissent. That is what differentiates us from rogue nations.

■   ■   ■

Postscript

Bowing to pressure from state and national Democratic Party leaders, Hackett announced on February 13, 2006, his withdrawal from Ohio's senate race and that he will leave politics altogether. He will return to his law practice. "This is an extremely disappointing decision that I feel has been forced on me," Hackett told the *New York Times*. "For me, this is a second betrayal. First, my government misused and mismanaged the military in Iraq, and now my own party is afraid to support candidates like me." Party leaders felt that Congressman Sherrod Brown, whose campaign war chest of $2.7 million was ten times that of Hackett's, had a better chance of defeating Republican incumbent Mike Dewine. Another factor was Hackett's outspokenness, which made high-ranking Democrats nervous. In January, Hackett had said that the Republican Party had been taken over by religious extremists who "aren't a whole lot different than Osama bin Laden." Even though Republicans demanded an apology, Hackett refused to back down.

8

TO THINK LIKE A TERRORIST

Red Team Leader Bogdan Dzakovic did his job too well working for the Federal Aviation Administration.

> "If there was a group of these air marshals on any of these planes on 9/11, the incident would have been over in one or two seconds; as soon as the terrorists initiated any action, they would have been dead."

It was his job to think and act like a terrorist. Bogdan Dzakovic was in charge of the Red Team, the Federal Aviation Administration's elite squad which investigated aviation security. His small, highly trained team conducted mock undercover raids as terrorists and hijackers. It probed airport security capabilities. With alarming ease and frequency, team members slipped bombs, guns, and knives onto aircraft during routine testing.

"We were extraordinarily successful in killing large numbers of innocent people in these simulated attacks," Dzakovic told the 9/11 Commission on May 22, 2003. "We breached security up to 90 percent of the time. The FAA suppressed these warnings. Instead, we were ordered not to write up our reports and not to retest airports where we found particularly egregious vulnerabilities, to see if the problems had been fixed. Finally, the agency started providing advance notification of when we would be conducting our 'undercover' tests and what we would be 'checking.'"

You won't find Dzakovic's critical testimony anywhere in *The 9/11 Commission Report: Final Report of the National Commission on Terrorist Attacks Upon the United States*. (Only a single footnote on page 441 lists his appearance before the Commission.) Yet no one better understood the threat of airborne terrorism than Dzakovic who was a fourteen-year veteran of the FAA's Security Division. And no one was more frustrated by the FAA's consistent effort to gloss over the airline industry's widespread problems related to thwarting terrorism.

Several days after 9/11, the FAA grounded the Red Team. "The FAA knew that the information we had within the Red Team was very damning to them," says Dzakovic. "The last thing they wanted to do was have us continue flying after 9/11, and continue doing work documenting that security is still as screwed up as it was before 9/11."

Deeply troubled by the FAA's questionable conduct, Dzakovic took the bold step of filing a whistle-blower disclosure in October of 2001 with the Office of Special Counsel. The filing—the first of its kind by an FAA Security Division employee—set into motion a lengthy and costly investigation by the Inspector General's office. But nothing really changed. As Dzakovic forcefully reminded the 9/11 Commission, no one at the FAA was fired or disciplined for mismanagement. In fact, many top officials were promoted within the newly formed Transportation Security Administration that had taken over many of the FAA's responsibilities in the Department of Homeland Security. And instead of rewarding Dzakovic for his whistle-blowing gallantry, the TSA punished him by reassigning him to a clerical position behind a desk. He spent months punching holes in paper and putting training binders together for new TSA employees. His expertise fighting bad guys was horribly wasted.

Single and living in a Virginia suburb just outside Washington, D.C., Dzakovic now hates flying. He also fears that another mega-terror attack in the sky is likely to occur. "Terrorists follow their own schedules, not ours," he says. He outlines a possible scenario: "If I were a terrorist mastermind plotting another big attack and I could muster up another twenty guys, I'd scatter them around to different airports around the country. I would give each one of them three bombs and three different sets of luggage. Some of those bombs will make it onto flights."

A chilling thought? Absolutely. His recommendation is that until the TSA combines human profiling with more sophisticated baggage-screening procedures, the country is still vulnerable. "What happened on 9/11 was not a failure in the system," he told the 9/11 Commission. "It was a system designed for failure. Our airports are not safer now than before 9/11. The main difference between then and now is that life is now more miserable for passengers."

■　■　■

My father came to the United States from Yugoslavia, and my mother came from Romania. My family was part of the working poor that immigrated from Europe after the second World War. They eventually moved to Cincinnati, where there was a Serbian community. Unlike nowadays, in which immigration is looser, back then you had to be sponsored by a family or a church. As I recall, my family was sponsored by a church in Middletown, Ohio, where I was born in 1954.

My father died when I was six and my mother died when I was eight, so I don't know a whole lot of my family history. I spent some time in several orphanages, and then in a foster home.

One of the orphanages, the Allen House, was pretty bad. It was a public institution for the homeless, neglected, and delinquent children, so you had a mix of behavior-problem kids and kids like myself who came from homes without parents. Some of the kids were already hard-core criminals. There were light beatings. One lady had cut off three feet of a hula hoop, and she used to go around whipping kids with that and leaving marks on them. I got hit a few times with that thing.

I wouldn't say I was terrified growing up, but it was not a pleasant childhood. Quite honestly, my experiences as a child had a direct bearing on my whistle-blowing. What little time I did spend with my parents, they did instill in me some concept of integrity and right and wrong; that was something that stuck with me my entire life. When I was confronted with the choice of becoming a whistle-blower, I had to weigh the odds and ask myself: How much is this going to hurt you personally? What are you going to accomplish? And I just started thinking back to when I was a kid. I had already been through the worst.

I next went to a Catholic orphanage, St. Aloysius Orphanage, and it was much better. In my age group, called the "Junior Boys," there were thirty kids. I got there when I was eight years old. Everybody slept in one great big room. And from that orphanage, I went to a foster home in Cincinnati, and I stayed with this one family for about eight years. They were a decent middle-class family, but I didn't belong there. I was a difficult kid, and there were already five children in the family, their biological children. I was not a behavior problem, but I did not do well in school. My teachers expected me to be a normal kid. The best analogy I can think of—as far as being an orphan, particularly at that age—is to imagine yourself breaking your leg on the school playground and not receiving any medical treatment. No matter how hard you try to run and play with the other kids, you just can't do it because your leg's broken; and no matter how hard you try, there's not only the pain, but the deformity. So it was always hard for me to study. The emotional pain was very lingering. It was a miracle that I actually survived grade school. I flunked the sixth grade and had to repeat it— and, obviously, I got through grade school and then high school. In my freshman year, I moved in with another family. They lived about eight miles away from the high school. I rode my bicycle to school every day for the final three years of high school.

When I started college at the University of Cincinnati, I lived on my own. I worked my way through college doing a lot of menial jobs: restaurants, working at a butcher's shop, cutting grass. For two years, I worked at a school for the blind where I was the night supervisor. I had no special training in dealing with blind people. I was there primarily at nighttime in case something happened, so there would at least be one sighted person.

I then went to Chase Law School, whose name was changed to Northern Kentucky University. I didn't last too long in law school. I had to drop out because I couldn't afford the tuition. I was working fifty-six hours a week at two different minimum wage jobs. I was stuffing boxes at a department store and worked as a bellboy. My grades suffered, so I ended up quitting and then joined the Coast Guard. I also found out from my birth certificate what my real first name was about this time. I grew up being called John.

I was on the Coast Guard cutter *Blackhaw*, whose homeport was San Francisco at that time. I was the operations officer. I was the third in command on the ship after the commanding officer and executive officer. There were fifty in the crew. Our main job was being a buoy tender, which means attending to aids to navigation. It may sound like a dorky job, but it was quite an art and science to maneuver this 180-foot and thousand-ton ship within a few feet of very hazardous conditions—rocks and shallow water—where you would put a buoy to warn other vessels.

We worked not only in the San Francisco Bay, but up and down the West Coast. We also went on search-and-rescue missions. I remember one time we had to go two hundred miles out to sea from San Francisco during a storm because a tugboat was having problems; they were taking on water and were in danger of sinking, so we just kind of milled around, but they ended up getting to port on their own while we escorted them. That storm lasted three days. We were a small ship compared to the Navy and the large freighters. Our ship was getting pounded really hard and roughly one-third of our crew was completely incapacitated from seasickness and exhaustion. The waves were thirty feet high. I got seasick after the second day. I was standing duty on the bridge. I was what they call the "officer of the deck," which is the officer in tactical command of the ship essentially. Seasickness is absolutely the worst feeling in the world. I was kneeling through the railing, throwing up every five or ten minutes for the entire four-hour shift. And after about three or four times doing this, there's nothing left in your stomach to throw up. When I got off my watch after four hours,

I went to bed. When I woke up, I had blood caked on my shirt because my stomach was just grinding so much that it actually tore the lining on the inside. I was spitting up blood just from the seasickness. It was a terrible feeling, absolutely terrible.

My second tour of duty with the Coast Guard was in El Paso, working with a joint federal task force: DEA, FBI, Customs, Immigration. We dealt primarily with marijuana smuggling. This was 1981 and 1982. There was a lot of corruption on the part of the Mexican police. There were two or three times when I actually saw Mexican police taking bribes from people. One time was in a restaurant, and another time was right on the border. There were drug gang problems back then, but nothing compared to what they have today.

Even though we were located in El Paso, we also had jurisdiction in the Caribbean for vessels that were smuggling marijuana. Our biggest catch was a hundred tons of marijuana. It was a large freighter. It had ten truck containers of marijuana. There was so much marijuana involved that we off-loaded the stuff in Guantanamo, Cuba—at the U.S. Marine base. When officials started burning this small mountain of marijuana, the flames and the fumes were so bad that they closed down the airport because they were concerned about pilots getting high.

After I got out of the Coast Guard, I moved to Boston and went to graduate school at Northeastern University where I got an MS degree in security administration in '84. I went back in the Coast Guard for another year's worth of service. I was then recruited into the Naval Investigative Service as a special agent. I joined the NIS because I wanted to be on the cutting edge of where the greatest threat was. In the mid-'80s, that was the Soviet Union, which was stealing military secrets from the Navy through espionage. They were primarily interested in the Navy because of its ballistic missiles and submarines. I wanted to engage in counter-espionage activities against the Soviet Union. And one of the reasons I later quit the NIS was because we did jack-shit in counter-espionage. I spent most of my time doing felony criminal investigations. I was based in Chicago at the Great Lakes Naval Training Center. It was a large base with around thirty thousand people. Basically, working for the NIS on a Navy base was like being with the detective department for a medium-size city. There were twelve of us on staff. We did surveillance and raids. For two years, I couldn't even begin to count how many muggings and knifings and rapes and child abuse cases I was required to investigate. I don't know if it's because sailors spend too much time at sea, but there was really a lot of sexual perversion that went on. There were rapes from males to females, males to males, even females to females. There was even bestiality. I remember asking myself, "What the hell did I get myself into?"

In 1987, a former NIS agent, who at that time worked for the FAA, recruited me. The one neat thing about the federal service is that you have a lot of good liaisons with other federal agencies. All this nonsense about agencies not talking to each other is not true; this was one of the criticisms by the 9/11 Commission. We talked to each other very openly. On the lower levels, with the street agents, all we were concerned about was getting the job done.

And so, the main reason I decided to join the FAA was to work as an air marshal and fight terrorism. The mid-'80s was the high point of aviation-related terrorism around the world. About every four to six months, I flew around the world for two to three weeks at a time. However, being an air marshal was only a collateral duty. The rest of the time I spent working as a special agent—which was basically doing security work at O'Hare International Airport as well as at airports in Ohio, Indiana, and Illinois.

As air marshals, we flew on United States major carriers: American, Delta, TWA, Pan Am. It was only international flights. No domestic stuff. Prior to 9/11, air marshals were not allowed to fly domestically. At all. Just another stupid decision that the FAA made. They supposedly didn't perceive the terrorism threat domestically. But that's pretty much bullshit. The main reason was that the airlines did not want to give up revenue seats for air marshals because they flew free.

We had to let flight crews know we were on board. We wore plain clothes. We were armed, but I never had to shoot anybody. There were a few situations when the pucker factor got up a little bit. I was going to Frankfurt, Germany, from Karachi, Pakistan. I was in the front part of coach with two other air marshals. One of them was pretty much next to useless. He was sleeping all the time. He was only there to travel. The other air marshal was a real gung-ho guy. In fact, we called him Terminator. He lived for guns. He was an outstanding shot. Anyway, there were three suspicious guys on board. One would go to the bathroom and then another one would meet him as soon as he came out and they would exchange a bag. Then the third one would get up and they would have a little consultation and go back to their seats. Then they'd be looking at each other. This went on for an hour. The lady sitting next to me was from Pakistan, and she was in tears. She thought something bad was going to happen.

I was sitting on the left side of the plane, on the aisle seat. One of the guys was actually sitting directly behind me. I kept eye contact with my partner, the Terminator. The third marshal was completely oblivious to all this. We both had the feeling this was going to be the big one. At one point, when the bathroom door opened and one of the guys got out, I immediately stood up and started walking toward the bathroom while he was walking down the aisle. I wedged myself between the seats so the two of us would have to touch each other in order to pass. I gave him a quick frisk. I ran my arms up the front and back of his torso just to feel if I felt anything hard. You know, a gun or a knife or anything. It was over in a second. Before he knew what was going on, I continued walking on. I didn't find anything on him. I then went to the bathroom. You could just tell by the looks on their faces that the shit was gonna hit the fan. At one point, when I was back in my seat, I kind of twisted myself around so I could keep the guy behind me in my peripheral vision, as well as the other two individuals. It's the only time I ever unholstered my gun on an airplane. It was a 9-millimeter Sig automatic.

I kept the Sig under my jacket but pointed it directly at the guy behind me. I was going to shoot right through the back of my seat if something happened. I knew the Terminator would take care of the other two guys, so I focused on the one behind me. I had my back to the lady sitting next to me. She was still crying. I don't know if these guys got wind of who we were because my partner and I were looking at each other with the same wide eyes that these guys were looking at each other. They may have picked up on us. But nothing happened. After a while I put my gun back in the holster. And everybody lived happily ever after. When we landed, nothing happened to those men from Pakistan. They weren't checked out. That is one of the problems we had. We had no system in effect to handle a situation like that.

Then there was one other time when some nutcase tried to get into the cockpit of a 747. I met him at the bottom of the stairs. I put my arm across the stairs so he couldn't get by me. It was me and another air marshal. We talked to the guy and he sat down for the rest of the flight. He wanted to complain to the pilot that he didn't like the seat. He wasn't drunk. Just agitated.

I was an air marshal until '92. And then I got out. The air marshal program was an accident waiting to happen. The training was not really good to begin with. The initial course was basic law enforcement. We went through drills on airplanes. The FAA had no concept of terrorism. It didn't even like the air marshal program. There was just too much deadweight in the air marshal program, which had numbered between three hundred to five hundred agents. While we had former Navy SEALs and Special Forces, roughly half the people in the air marshal program were FAA secretaries and overweight administration clerks and the like.

Take my very first week of training as an air marshal. This was early '88. The head of the air marshal program showed up at the training facility. As soon as I saw her being Ms. Pep Talk, I knew there was something wrong with the picture, at least with regard to physical qualifications for passing the ten-week course.

You had to bench-press your body weight. And here's this lady who is probably a hundred pounds overweight giving us this pep talk about shooting and physical fitness. That was my first negative inclination about the FAA. It went downhill from there.

There was another woman who could not pull the slide back on her Sig automatic while the barrel was pointed down range. This happened during practicing and qualifying on the shooting range. Somehow she'd twist her arms and point the barrel of her gun at the people to her left—of which I was one. Then she would flex her arms and pull back the slide of the gun. We flagged the range instructor and safety officer. We told them to watch her. And lo and behold, she continued doing it, but they weren't doing anything. Every time she reloaded, which requires dropping one magazine and putting another in, we would just stand back and let her go through this gyration and shoot. Yes, she passed. They didn't flunk anybody. Some of these people were too dangerous to be around a handgun. There was a joke among some of us who had some experience that if there was an incident on an airplane, we would just shoot one of these other air marshals and take their gun and the ammunition. We looked at them as gun-toters and ammunition-toters, in case we needed extra ammunition.

One other example of cluelessness involved an air marshal in my office in Chicago. He was playing with his gun in the office and fired it into the wall. The FAA didn't do anything to him. They didn't punish him. He should have been kicked out of the air marshal program. But the FAA made everyone else go through basic remedial firearms training again. The stuff you teach the Boy Scouts. This was how the FAA operated.

Things changed at the FAA following the bombing of Pan Am 103 over Lockerbie, Scotland, which killed 270 people. This was in 1988. Congress had compelled the FAA to hire a Marine Corps general named Orlo Steele to be in charge of security. He had once been in charge of the Marine's anti-terrorism program. This guy was really good. I have nothing but the utmost respect for Steele, nothing but glowing comments. He immediately got a grasp of how screwed up the whole program was. He started to transform the FAA's security division because it was a disaster waiting to happen. Pan Am 103 was indicative of how poorly security worked. One of the first things he did was transform the air marshal program into an elite organization. He got rid of all the deadweight—people who couldn't shoot and had no physical skills, who had no business being in the air marshal program, which meant that he got rid of all the fat slobs, secretaries, and the administrative people. We received a lot of training from the Marines. We had very high standards for physical fitness and shooting.

The shooting standards were so tight that we were tested with specially made timing devices that could measure from the point you're instructed to draw your gun and then shoot. It could measure your time up to a thousandth of a second. If you were off by one-hundredth of a second, you didn't qualify. The same went for the physical fitness standards. If you were one push-up short or one second short for the two-mile run, you didn't qualify. Because of these new standards, 90 percent of the people couldn't qualify; they just couldn't make it. By the time the new air marshals program got up and running, we had five teams of roughly ten to twelve people per team. I was in charge of one team.

For the duration under General Steele, who only had a three-year contract, we trained as small teams to take on the best that terrorists could throw at us. In training, as soon as a potential bad guy went beyond a certain threshold of either threatening somebody or displaying a weapon of some kind, we would respond appropriately at exactly the same time. If a bad guy stood up and suddenly grabbed a flight attendant and held a knife at her throat, he'd be dead shortly thereafter. If there was a group of us on any of these planes on 9/11, the incident would have been over in one or two seconds; as soon as they initiated any action, they would have been dead.

I traveled overseas about once every two to three months for about two or three weeks at a time. The rest of the time, I was either undergoing training myself or I was training other people. And when you're training with the same people, for the most part, you become a close-knit unit. We were fine-tuned as a fighting force, but unfortunately, when General Steele's tenure was over in '94, the FAA rescinded a lot of his policies. It was back to business as usual.

The FAA never liked Steele. The FAA was in the business of checking things like air traffic control, looking into flight standards, going to an airport and inspecting airplanes, monitoring the training of the pilots. But security was just anathema to them. Up and down the chain of command, the FAA's concept of security was: How many inspections did we do this year? How many tests did we do at a screening checkpoint?

Without General Steele, the air marshal program started to fall apart again. The managers and staff couldn't function without adult supervision. There was one time when I was asked to replace another team leader on a team known for being a party-animal team. They were competent when sober, but every single time we got on a plane to fly to our next destination—we were flying around the Mediterranean, from Athens to Rome to Turkey—these guys were either drunk or suffering from severe hangovers. I got so fed up with them. Lecturing and yelling at them had no impact. The mission lasted around three weeks. When the trip was over and I got back to the office, I wanted to start disciplinary action against most of the team, but my boss wouldn't allow it because these were his drinking buddies. He told me that I was out of line.

General Steele's replacement was a guy named Cathal Flynn, who was a retired Navy admiral. He was in charge of FAA security from '94 to 2000. He was just another political appointee. He was a former Navy SEAL. I guess his resumé looked good, but he had as much a concept of terrorism as the managers at the FAA did, if not less.

One of the training tools we had in the air marshal program was the "Shoot, Don't Shoot" video system used by law enforcement. For us, it consisted of actors on an airplane who would start some type of commotion. The video was shown on a wall in a darkened training room, so the figures would actually be life-size. Watching these videos trained you to do two things: one, it tested your judgment because you had to decide whether you should use lethal force against an individual or just let the situation ride out; and two, it measured your shooting accuracy, so you're actually shooting at life-size figures with a real gun. Each situation would play out in front of you on this big screen. Anyway, in some of these situations, you had bad guys stand up with a machine gun and threaten to kill people, and so you had to immediately take action and shoot them before they had the opportunity to shoot anybody else. If your judgment was off or if you didn't take action quickly enough, or if you missed the target, then you had to go back and do a lot of additional training to get back up to par. We had a lot of really gifted individuals in the program. It was the best job I ever had and some of the best people I've ever worked with.

Within a couple of months of becoming FAA Security Director, Admiral Flynn sent instructions that he did not want his air marshals taking any action on an airplane unless someone was already dead or in the process of suffering grievous bodily injury—and I mean this literally. We were prohibited under Flynn from taking any action. Judgment went out the window; we had no right to judge—like we had to just sit there and wait until someone got killed or was getting beaten to death. This was such an insane policy. Flynn's rationale was that the odds of air marshals actually being on an airplane with real hijackers was so remote that the FAA management would rather not have us do anything and instead just let us ride out a situation, unless someone got killed or was in danger of dying. We had been trained to kill a terrorist within a second or two; under Flynn, we now had to debate what to do when a person stands up with a gun. One day, my team and another team—there were about twenty, twenty-five people in the room—were watching one of the "Shoot, Don't Shoot" videos. We were trying to interpret this new policy. In one situation on the screen, a bad guy stands up with a great big butcher knife, and he starts yelling obscenities at passengers: "You people are going to die for Allah." He was flashing the knife around, and he's standing right next to passengers. Under the old system, as soon as he stood up with a knife and starting threatening people, he was dead. No ifs, ands, or buts about it. Under the new system, nobody in that room could figure out at what point can we shoot this guy or use lethal force. Anyway, Flynn walks in on us while we're debating this one scene with the guy with the butcher knife and one of my team members asks Flynn, "In your opinion, when can we shoot this guy?" And after a pregnant pause, Flynn said, "Well, the point at which you can shoot him is when he initiates his thrust with the knife." We're all looking at each other, thinking, "Who the hell is this moron?" Because we're not even allowed to confront the terrorist. We're not allowed to draw our gun and say, "Police, halt." What Flynn was saying was that from a seated position we were supposed to draw our guns out of our holsters, aim between the heads of the passengers that are between us and the bad guy, and then shoot him without killing anybody else in about the half second that it takes for him to stab somebody. Right after the video session was over, my assistant team leader quit.

I lasted a few more months in the air marshal program until I was recruited into the Red Team. This was in early summer of '95. Up until then, I was working as a good guy trying to kill the bad guys. Now the FAA was going to pay me to be one of the bad guys trying to kill the good people in simulated situations.

I really got into the work. I functioned as a terrorist would. I studied terrorism like it was a chess game. I had been doing this even when I was an air marshal team leader. I had my own terrorism database that I kept on my computer. I collected information entirely from open sources: no classified information. I had cross-indexed data by country, modus operandi, individuals, type of weapons used. I had over five hundred pages worth of data in my computer on terrorism by the time 9/11 happened. For example, one thing we did know, and which the FAA itself acknowledged, was that the favorite weapon of terrorists, when they weren't using a grenade or a bomb or a gun, was a knife of less than four inches in length. And these knives were specifically allowed to be carried on board by FAA regulations even though they knew it was their favorite weapon. Another thing I learned was that in every hijacking, passengers or flight crews recognized something "hinky" about the hijackers before the hijacking began, and this was either on the plane, on the ground before the plane took off, or when the passengers were still in the terminal building. Every single time the hijackers gave off warning signs.

The Red Team couldn't just go out and do whatever it wanted to do. We operated under very strict protocols. We were very careful about not disrupting the airline industry. We kept very close watch on the weapons and simulated explosives we used. We didn't just run amok. There was a lot of detailed paperwork involved in planning a trip.

We engaged in hijack exercises in which we flew on airplanes. However, everybody on the airplane was aware that it was an exercise: it wasn't a regular commercial flight. Our concern at the time, from a security point of view, was to prevent the hijacking from occurring, so once we got a weapon on the plane, that was the end of the scenario that we tested. It depended on the type of testing we were doing, but I would say roughly 90 percent of the time we would beat the system and get weapons on board.

I knew about the potential of using planes as bombs. The bad guys who hijacked that French airliner in '95 were going to crash the plane into the Eiffel Tower. That was a pretty good clue that the face of terrorism had changed. The plane was hijacked, I think, in Morocco. The pilot convinced the hijackers that they didn't have enough fuel to get to Paris, which is where the hijackers said they wanted to go to land. But French intelligence had indications that this was a suicide operation, and so the plane was diverted to Marseilles in the south of France where French commandos stormed the plane and killed most of the hijackers.

Pre-9/11, the FAA's attitude was that terrorists would hijack a plane and then land it and do a big dog and pony show in front of the press. There'd be negotiations and maybe one to two people would get killed. The FAA was simply and completely oblivious to the fact that something nastier could happen—which is inexcusable, because in 1994 we had the Bojinka operation, which was when terrorists were going to bomb a dozen U.S. civilian airplanes over the Pacific Ocean. What stopped those attacks—*bojinka* is a Serbo-Croatian term meaning loud bang—was a fire that broke out in the terrorists' apartment in Manila. They were building bombs and something went awry and the apartment caught on fire. The bad guys ran off, but the fire department showed up and found bomb-making equipment. They also found a laptop computer that had information about which planes they were going to bomb and when. So you combine just those two elements right there—the Bojinka operation and the hijacked French airliner—and that alone should have told the FAA that we've got to get our act together a little bit. But there's a political agenda at the FAA. It's like, "We don't want to ruffle any feathers and Congress is breathing down our necks and the airlines are complaining and so we'll just hope nothing happens and continue doing things the way they are." In either case, though, these people ought to be held accountable. The FAA used to say, leading up to 9/11—I don't know how many times I heard this when I would levy criticism about how they're doing things—that "we must be doing something right because there has not been a terrorist attack against the U.S. aviation industry since Pan Am 103." Well, the fact of the matter is the terrorists operate on their schedule, not on our concept of how they should operate.

The Red Team also did extensive work testing CTX bomb-detection machines. We went out of our way to try to get caught, but the system only detected one-third of our explosive devices. These results were so embarrassing to the FAA that my boss told me we needed to tell local FAA managers when we were going to test CTX machines at their airports. They, in turn, would tell the air carriers that we were going to be there; in some cases, they would give the air carriers our names so that when we checked in for our flight, they knew who we were and they would give our bags extra screening.

We did Red Team tests with checked luggage. Only 25 percent of the time did our checked-in luggage get returned to us when we intentionally didn't make our flights. It should be 100 percent if the airlines are doing their job properly. It's probably even worse now because they're screening every single bag. The one thing we determined on the Red Team was that in order for the CTX bomb-detection machines to be used effectively, you need to have the absolute minimum number of bags going through them because the machines aren't reliable for mass searching of bags. It has to be limited as much as possible to the most suspect people.

In August '98, I sent a letter through my chain of command to Jane Garvey, who was the administrator of the FAA and documented the general results we had in the Red Team. I tried to convince her that there was a dangerous culture of mismanagement within FAA security. I also put in the letter that the U.S. faces a potential tidal wave of terrorist attacks. I didn't go into a whole lot of detail. I was just trying to get her attention so that she would initiate an internal investigation. I also sent a copy to the Secretary of Transportation, who was Rodney Slater at the time. Garvey didn't even have the courtesy to acknowledge receipt of my letter; however, Slater did, and he sent me a letter acknowledging receipt. He also sent me a copy of the letter he sent to Garvey and said, "You might want to look into these issues." But there was no follow-up, and it was not an order. It was basically, "Here's something interesting you might want to look into"—and that was it.

For example, I had known that security at Logan International Airport in Boston was especially bad. Both planes that crashed into the Towers departed from Logan. They had a very poor manager at Logan who had no prior experience in aviation security. She was a former secretary who had been able to manipulate her way into a management position. The FAA agents in the office complained bitterly about her, not only through the chain of command of the FAA, but they sent letters to the Inspector General's office complaining that security is a joke—and primarily as a result of her. One agent said that security at Logan was a disaster waiting to happen. This was written in '99. She was later promoted under the TSA.

In May of 2001, Steve Elson, a former Red Team member and retired Navy SEAL, and a local Fox TV news reporter, Debra Sherman, did a story about the breakdown of security at Logan. They wanted to get Senator Kerry's attention so they asked me to hand-deliver a tape of the show to Senator Kerry's office, which I did. I never heard back from his office. Steve's the complete opposite of me. I tend to be kind of quiet, but he's very outgoing and aggressive. I've seen him yell at bureaucrats and politicians. Like me, Steve had gotten fed up with working within the FAA system because it was pointless. All you do is ruin your career by broaching negative information that management doesn't want to hear about. I had ruined my career early on. I knew I'd never get promoted. So anyway, Steve and I started working outside the chain of command, and we went to the Inspector General's office for the Department of Transportation and gave them several hundred pages of documentation about how screwed up the FAA was. I had several meetings with a senior manager in the Inspector General's office, and at one point, he got so exasperated that he threw his arms up in the air and said, "The FAA is so fucked up I don't know where to begin." Another time he said, "Unless you give me a dead body and a smoking gun, there's nothing we can do against the managers in the FAA because of the political situation between the Inspector General's office and the FAA." Now that they have three thousand dead bodies and a smoking gun—or cannon—they still haven't taken any action against these managers. Speaking of guns, there was a report that was filtered to the Operations Center of the FAA on 9/11 that there was a gun involved on one of the flights and that a passenger was shot. I have no idea where it came from, but this is what the 9/11 Commission should have really investigated. The way the Operations Center worked on 9/11 is that the only people who can call about information would be from another federal agency like the FBI or CIA. The 9/11 Commission said that there was no evidence that there was a gun involved. Of course, you could have had a Mack truck on one of these planes, and there wouldn't be any evidence because the planes were basically vaporized. I think it's a possibility there was a gun involved. What I would have done in the investigation is backtrack where this information came from. It is such a crucial piece of evidence that I would slam these people on a lie detector—the people who reported it—to find out if they did make it up or if they had changed their minds after the fact because somebody told them they could be fired if they talked about this gun anymore.

Steve and I, not being deterred, also went directly to six or eight members of the House and Senate, both Republicans and Democrats, who were on the various committees that oversaw FAA security and the aviation industry. This was from 1999 to 2001. Steve went to more meetings than I did. When you deal with Capitol Hill, you don't just show up on a congressman's doorstep and expect somebody to spend time with you. It took some cajoling with senior staff members, but we never actually talked to the elected officials themselves.

One thing that did happen on Capitol Hill before 9/11 was that the House's Committee on Appropriations—it oversaw the FAA—conducted a very high-level investigation into FAA security in 1999, partly as a result of what Steve and I did. We had provided them with documentation from the Red Team and other sources. The investigation lasted about nine or ten months. It then issued a scathing report reiterating our facts. I asked for a copy of this report from one of their investigators, but he said the reports are so highly classified that even committee staff are not allowed to read them; they are eyes-only for specific congressmen on the Appropriations Committee who requested the investigation in the first place. The committee didn't take any action either. All this information did not make it into *The 9/11 Commission Report.*

A day or so after 9/11, the FAA grounded the Red Team. I had proposed that we go back to the very same airports used by the hijackers and do the same type of testing, to see if security had improved. Obviously, they didn't want to do that. So they just grounded us. No explanation, nothing. On the other hand, putting National Guard units in airports across the country would have prevented nutcases from getting out of a car with an assault rifle and trying to shoot everybody—but as far as preventing another hijacking or a bombing, it was the wrong approach.

Two weeks after 9/11, some of the senior staff members on Capitol Hill whom I had been dealing with called me into their office—for two different meetings—to talk about where we go from there. At the end of both meetings, I asked staff members when the government was going to initiate an investigation into 9/11, and automatically—it's like they went to the same school—they both said almost the exact same thing, which were words to the effect of, "Our bosses," meaning the senators and representatives, "will do everything they can to make sure that there's *not* an investigation into 9/11 because it's going to open up a huge can of worms, which they don't want to deal with."

The fact that there was even a 9/11 Commission was due to the effort of some of the 9/11 victims' families. Still, the 9/11 Commission's investigation was a whitewash. It hid the enormous government problems that existed prior to 9/11. But anyway, after I had these meetings on Capitol Hill and was told that they were not going to do an investigation, I decided to do a formal whistle-blowing case against the FAA. I loaded up my documentation and submitted evidence in late October 2001 to the Office of Special Counsel, which is an independent government agency that reports directly to the president as well as to certain senators and representatives who are on the respective judiciary committees. The OSC accepted my case; they only accept about 15 percent of all cases. For the OSC to accept a case, it has to meet its criteria of gross mismanagement or a gross threat to public safety.

The OSC ordered Secretary of Transportation Norm Mineta to investigate my case. He, in turn, ordered his Inspector General's office to conduct an investigation. The investigation then went right back to the very same manager that Steve and I went to prior to 9/11! We had implicated him in our allegations and yet, he's the one investigating our case! The whole system is so corrupt. It took the Inspector General about a year to complete the investigation. It was the largest and most expensive investigation in the entire history of the Department of Transportation. When the case was done, it went back to the Office of Special Counsel; they then gave me a copy of the report and they allowed me to respond. This is just a procedural thing. I read the report. I then accused the Inspector General's office of falsifying this investigation. Several other people served as witnesses in my case. They provided documentation. I responded back to the OSC. The whole package was around five hundred pages long and my narrative portion of it was around thirty pages. The OSC, in February of 2003, sent a letter to President Bush about six or seven pages long. The key thing it said—it's on the first page—is that FAA security operated in a manner that was "a substantial and specific danger to public safety." That's fairly acrimonious information for a fellow government agency to say about another government agency. Anyway, I was in the press quite a bit. The 9/11 Commission obviously heard about me, and I was invited to testify at the second public hearing dealing with aviation security. They only had two sessions dealing with aviation security that I recall. Several other high-level bureaucrats and managers in the FAA also testified.

I was the last one scheduled to testify on my day, but I arrived early in the morning. I sat there for the whole day, listening to one politician after another, like Hillary Clinton who stood up and said how deeply she felt about the people who were killed. One congressman said, "This was a tragic event that has really affected the psyche of the American people." I became angry because this was not supposed to be a sentimental examination into how people felt; it was supposed to be a formal investigation into the aviation-security failures that contributed to 9/11 and how they were going to fix these problems.

When it became my turn to talk, I just threw away my written statement and began to ad lib, saying, "I will never cease to be held in shock and awe when I hear politicians and bureaucrats talk about how 9/11 could not have been prevented." I then outlined the entire history of aviation-related terrorism, beginning with the hijackings in the '70s. I then talked about the Red Team in which we proved that security was a joke and an accident waiting to happen. I explained that the Transportation Security Administration, which had taken over security from the FAA, had not improved matters. I said that the current TSA team that was supposedly engaged in what we did as the Red Team was not conducting tests based on the capabilities of the terrorists; it was testing based upon the capabilities and training levels of the screeners. It should be called the "Pink Team."

After I spoke for about twenty minutes, the Commission thanked me for my time, and I never had any other formal contact with them, except when one of the staff members called me. I offered him five hundred pages of documentation, but nothing ever materialized and none of my statement is included in *The 9/11 Commission Report*.

When the TSA took over operational control of aviation security in February of 2002, I was informed that very same week by my boss that I was no longer a member of the Red Team. He said, "When we want you to do something, we'll tell you." There was very little communication between me and management. From February of 2002 through the entire next year, I had nothing official to do. At first, I continued to input data about terrorism in my computer. I wanted to keep very close tabs on what was going on in the world of terrorism. So that's how I occupied myself intellectually, but at some point, my eyes were going bad staring at the computer all day. A colleague of mine was involved in training new federal security directors. He asked me if I'd be willing to help out with menial work like putting binders together and punching holes in papers. So I did that for several months.

I was eventually transferred to an aviation operations center near Dulles Airport where my main job was to answer the telephone on the graveyard shift. Because of the air-space restrictions around D.C. and other places, we received phone calls from pilots who were getting ready to take off. I would get half a dozen calls a night for an entire shift. I would document them and do some other administrative stuff, and that was it. That was my job for nine months. I was literally going crazy. If it wasn't for the fact that I read a lot, I would've gone totally berserk. I started slacking off on the terrorism stuff because I realized that it was pointless. I thought, "I'm never going to work in this field again and why waste time on it." I'm into martial arts, and I read a few books on that as well as on psychology. I got an undergraduate degree in psychology, and I'm actually giving half a thought to getting my Ph.D. in the field.

I still work in the general aviation area. I have an entry-level job that's little more than being a glorified clerk. I didn't lose any salary and I'm grateful to have a job, but you could get some high school kid on a work-release program doing what I'm doing and he'd be bored out of his mind. The TSA recently offered an early retirement, but the benefits are so minimal that I'd still have to find work. However, the problem is I'm blacklisted from getting a job in the area of my expertise. I'd rather be fighting the bad guys because I lived to do that. It was my passion. I regret that I'm not doing that, but my attitude is that I took an oath of office some time ago and my oath was to the people of the United States to fight, among other things, all enemies, both foreign and domestic. I emphasize domestic because I believe that the political system we have now is more of a threat to this country than anything that could be dreamed up from outside.

Looking back on it, I know if I did not take the steps I did as a whistle-blower, I would be more miserable now, wishing I had done it rather than doing it and suffering the consequences. I'm one of the lucky whistle-blowers. Most federal government whistle-blowers are fired—or else the situation gets so bad at work they're compelled to quit. I refuse to do it. I'm going to leave under my conditions, not theirs. People thought I was being disloyal for being a whistle-blower. I even had somebody coat pepper spray on my little desk fan at work. I received weird phone calls and about a dozen different packages and letters in the mail. These letters were not really a threat, but the words were cut out of a newspaper like a ransom note saying bad things about me.

Another time, one of the FAA managers was trying to give me fatherly advice. We were walking outside the FAA building. He said, "You know, you need to be careful and calm down your rhetoric because you just don't know what's going to happen to you." But when I became a whistle-blower, I decided that I was going full blast on this. I was not going to be intimidated by these people. So I stopped on the sidewalk, which is public property, and I pointed back to the FAA building. I said, "When you're in that building, I'm in your jungle; when you cross the line and get on the sidewalk and beyond here, you're in my jungle." I then just turned and walked away.

In 2003, both 60 *Minutes II* and *NBC Dateline* called me up in the same week and asked me to do interviews with them. I talked to producers from both shows and they each said the same thing: "We're not going to interview you if you interview with the other show, so you've got to pick one or the other." I interviewed with *Dateline* because I felt it was going to do the more aggressive show. I spent over two hours being interviewed by Stone Phillips. *Dateline* spent several other days over the course of the next month filming me. But they did not air it. I went through half a year talking to one of the producers and she just kept saying, "We're going to air it. It's real good. They love it." After five or six months, I could tell she was very uncomfortable every time I called her. For whatever reason, they got cold feet and didn't air my interview.

In August 2005, I appeared on a National Geographic cable special called "Inside 9/11." I make a five- or six-second appearance in a four-hour show, so if you sneeze while I'm on, you'll miss everything I said. One of the very last segments of the show featured 9/11 Commissioner Tom Kean who said that 9/11 was "a failure in imagination" on the part of the federal government. I went through the roof when I heard this because it didn't take any imagination whatsoever. All they had to do was look at the facts regarding aviation-related terrorism and the proof that aviation security was a joke. There were people at the FAA who actively thwarted improvements in security prior to 9/11 and who have since been promoted under the TSA.

The real problem, as I see it, is that the TSA is built on the same weak foundation as the FAA. It will always be at least one step behind the terrorists. Remember the shoe bomber? Right after that incident, the TSA made everyone take off their shoes at the screening checkpoints. Then we had the female Chechen terrorists who apparently hid explosives in their underwear. And so, TSA screeners started groping female passengers until a big public outcry brought that silliness to a stop. Next time the terrorists might put explosives in toothpaste tubes, and you can count on TSA screeners squishing out all the toothpaste from passengers' bags. If the terrorists had a sense of humor, they would put some kind of lethal chemical agent on toilet paper and make sure the government finds it. Then our government will outlaw toilet paper in all public restrooms.

Moreover, there are many objects you can bring on an airplane, or find on one, and use as a weapon. Things like a bottle of wine, a metal flashlight, non-metallic knives, a carabiner—a metal clip used by rock climbers that makes great brass knuckles—or a leather belt with a big metal buckle. The point of all this is that there is an infinite number of ways to smuggle weapons onto an airplane.

From my Red Team testing days, the only thing that ever really had me concerned about getting caught trying to sneak a weapon on board was a human being doing profiling. That means having highly trained individuals who are looking for the latest profile of what a terrorist or potential bad guy would be. Contrary to what the media says, profiling is not going after anybody who looks like an Arab; it's looking at very small anomalies and behavior like nervousness or other factors regarding ticketing and how someone answers questions. You don't simply ask a passenger yes-and-no questions. The journalist Paul Sperry, who has written several articles about aviation security's pitfalls, said that Islamic suicide terrorists will coat themselves with lilac as some kind of blessing it has for the next life when he's supposed to meet his seventy-two virgins. A real profiler should be looking for those subtle signs.

The bad guys are smart enough to test the system. In fact, U.S. troops found Arabic language translations of General Accounting Office documents describing how bad aviation security was in some of the Afghanistan caves used by the Taliban and Al Qaeda. The terrorists do a very thorough job before they undertake an operation. Because the 9/11 terrorists studied the system, they did not break any FAA regulation. They carried knives less than four inches in length.

The very nature of aviation security invites an attack. Aviation security must first and foremost "process" people and their luggage as rapidly as possible, while providing at least some illusion that effective screening is actually taking place. The FAA did a great job of maintaining this fiction, and the TSA is doing the same with billions of dollars of our tax money. There have been numerous reports in the press as well as official reports from the Department of Homeland Security's Inspector General and the General Accounting Office documenting how poor aviation security really is. All it takes to bypass these so-called layers of security is a little research from open sources. You can easily find the technical specs of bomb-detecting machines; many are published online by the manufacturers. With a rudimentary knowledge of chemistry and electronics, which the bad guys have proven they have, you can figure out how to beat every single one of these systems. The next step, as the 9/11 terrorists demonstrated, is to do some basic surveillance of the system just to see how things operate and get familiar with the airport environment. Then you do some dry runs. When Steve Elson and Fox News were doing their own undercover sting story at Logan Airport in the spring of 2001, the hijackers were doing their own dry runs at the same time and at the same airport.

In the mid- to late '90s, the FAA put into effect the Computer Assisted Passenger Pre-Screening System, or CAPPS. Initially it was called the Computer Assisted Passenger Profiling System, but political correctness forced a name change. The FAA proudly touted the fact that CAPPS made pre-screening selectees of nine of the 9/11 hijackers. The FAA felt that was proof that the system worked. Proof of what? The terrorists still got on the plane. What CAPPS actually does is make selectees out of thousands of people every day and they go through additional screening. Big deal. The terrorists had already tested the system and weren't concerned about this secondary screening.

The General Accounting Office later stated that CAPPS was deficient in some major areas, so the FAA (now TSA) came up with CAPPS II, which the GAO also stated failed to meet their performance standards. Now they've recently dreamed up Secure Flight, and I guarantee this isn't going to work either. If you are a terrorist and want to see if you are a "flight risk," or if you have been made a selectee by the pre-screening system, you just check in for a flight and see what happens. You're either made a selectee or you are not. If you are made a selectee, then you get to see up close what they do during the secondary screening. If you were already made a selectee or you find out that you're on the no-fly list, you just get a substitute bad guy with a clean record to do your dirty work. This has also been documented. Look at the London subway bombings: all the bad guys were clean.

That's why human profiling works—and why it must be used. Let me give you an illustration. In the late '90s, I was flying around Europe, testing human profilers at airports, among other things. I would go out of my way to give the appearance that something wasn't quite right with me as a passenger—things like my documents not being completely in order, not being dressed appropriately, and acting nervous and fidgety. Anyway, I was getting past profilers 100 percent of the time. They were terrible. I could have worn a T-shirt with lettering saying, "I'm a terrorist and I'm going to hijack the plane," and they probably would have still missed me.

But on my flight back to America as I was getting processed at the ticket counter in Paris, I happened to meet up with a good profiler. This was by sheer chance. Thirty seconds into the interview I knew I was in trouble. He made me a selectee, pulled me off to the side, and called the cops. He continued grilling me with a bunch of questions, while the cops were searching every square inch of my luggage. They also conducted a very good pat-down search of my body. I was tempted to just show them my Red Team credentials, which would have ended the whole process, but this was too good to be true. When the profiler finally found my credentials, which I had hidden in my luggage, he thought that he would be in hot water for bringing all this attention onto a U.S. government agent. But I congratulated him and asked to speak to his boss. I told him what a great job he did and that he should be used as a model for the other profilers. I then asked the profiler what it was about my behavior that had aroused his suspicion. He stated that he knew something was not right just based on the look on my face, but it was only when I hesitated for two seconds before responding to a simple question that convinced him that I was up to no good. But he didn't know what exactly, so he requested additional help.

This same profiling system can be modified to virtually every area of national security. On 9/11, the ticket agent who had checked in several of the hijackers later testified that he knew there was something wrong about them but there wasn't anything he could do about it. There wasn't a system in place to handle a situation like this. As it currently stands, if a person is subject to additional screening and he appears clean, he still can go on his merry way. So, nothing's really changed since 9/11.

Until they install some highly trained individuals doing profiling, aviation security is little more than window dressing. A little old lady with knitting needles isn't much of a threat; a person who looks like a member of an outlaw motorcycle gang carrying the same is altogether a different matter. But in the eyes of the TSA, who try to standardize everything, there is no difference between the two cases. Instead, the TSA should be focusing on who or what the real threat should be. Chances are that a hijacker is going to be male, within a specific age range, and in decent physical shape. And today, it is also very unlikely that a lone male is going to be able to hijack an airplane, because the other passengers would beat the snot out of him before anything could happen.

Within the first three years of the TSA's existence, we have already had three separate agency heads, and now we have a fourth. His name is Kip Hawley, and according to his official bio, he was a former executive with Union Pacific Railroad as well as a senior official in the Department of Transportation. Apparently, he was a key figure in the development of the TSA. I feel that he's bringing some pragmatism into the TSA, but he faces the challenge of a well-entrenched and broken bureaucracy. For example, I have occasionally perused the job announcements for TSA managers and federal security directors at airports. I couldn't find a single instance in which knowledge or experience of terrorism, security, or even aviation is a prerequisite for the job. Aviation security is not rocket science, but it is a science.

In early December 2005, Hawley publicly announced several changes in aviation security. He said that "the TSA will significantly increase the number of canine explosives detection teams." This is a great idea. A well-trained bomb dog with an aggressive handler is the major current deterrent to carrying a bomb into an airport environment. Provided, of course, that the dog isn't trained to do only random sniffing of people and their luggage.

Another change is adding more screeners and giving them better training to aid in their ability to find explosives. One can never get too much training. However, this is a major area of my concern. Prior to 9/11, our Red Team did extensive testing using a number of different types of explosive simulants and configurations. I am certain that the TSA trashed our team's conclusions and recommendations. We had observed that, while the overall detection rate of explosives was low, if one disguised or completely obscured a bomb, the detection rate was near zero. In the past, screeners were trained to find items that looked like a complete bomb; now screeners are being trained to recognize the individual components of a bomb—which is a major improvement.

Another TSA change is more intensive use of threat-imaging of bombs with x-ray machines. This procedure involves a computerized projection of an image of an explosive on the x-ray machine. During our own preliminary Red Team testing of the threat-image projection program, we determined that there was very little correlation between a screener's ability to notice a false threat image and the ability to find a "real" bomb. This was primarily due, I suspect, to the infinite number of ways to construct or hide a bomb. Training screeners to notice what appears as specific threat images is hardly a step above how Pavlov trained his dogs to salivate over a century ago. Obviously, using machines is a great asset, but not if they only work great in the laboratory yet have some serious operational problems. At some point, there has to be a real cost-benefit analysis. How many billions of dollars must be wasted on ineffective equipment? Tomorrow the threat may be chemical or biological weapons which could be much more destructive than any conventional bomb. Then we will have to spend additional billions on this technology, which will take years to develop. We will always be at least one step behind the bad guys with this mentality. The terrorists won't execute a mission until they are certain of success short of just having bad luck.

Hawley also announced that the TSA would conduct enhanced random passenger screening. He said that "predictability will be gone." But from the terrorists' perspective, this is a porous approach that's hit or miss. They can easily test airport environments to scope out the frequency and nature of these random searches. There's nothing unpredictable in this scenario.

The most widely publicized TSA change was altering the list of prohibited items that you can bring through a screening checkpoint. While the TSA is still banning items like box cutters, ice picks, knives, and lighters, you are now allowed to bring four-inch scissors, seven-inch screwdrivers, and other small tools through screening checkpoints. This, of course, opens up a lot more opportunities for bringing items of mayhem aboard an airplane. But the TSA's attitude is that a combination of more air marshals, hardened cockpit doors, and passengers themselves are a sufficient deterrent to nullify this threat. But the TSA hasn't listened to the complaints of pilots and flight attendants who want hardened cockpit doors that are double-doors. A single door doesn't offer enough security. When a pilot has to use the bathroom or a flight attendant brings food or drinks to the pilots, there are several seconds when a well-placed operative could force his way into the cockpit, particularly if he uses his seven-inch sharpened screwdriver. A double-door would require that the pilot or flight attendant first close one door before opening the next one. This would effectively prevent a forced entry. Of course, this added expense for airlines won't be accepted until the next disaster.

It was an unfortunate case of bad timing, but less than a week after Hawley's public statement announcing these major changes, the TSA was in the news again when two federal air marshals shot and killed a mentally disturbed passenger coming off an American Airlines plane at Miami International Airport because he had allegedly threatened to use a bomb. After the incident, nearly a dozen TV and radio talk shows called me for my reaction, but I turned down every request except for a background interview with a Miami newspaper. I don't really like trying to second-guess what happened without having all the available facts. But I do think the shooting was a very sad indication of how our government continues to regress. I believe that an innocent guy was killed for failing to follow orders.

After the Miami shooting, a federal air marshal spokesperson was quoted as saying that their mission is to stop the bad guys at all costs. This is a new concept, too. In my day, we had to use some judgment and common sense. That doesn't seem to apply now. When I was in the air marshal program, we had to follow three principles for rules of engagement regarding using lethal force. They were "means, opportunity, and intent." There either had to be a weapon or the person was so overpowering that lethal force was the only option. Also, potential victims had to be in imminent danger. I have a feeling that air marshals don't have any rules of engagement now. I remember a federal air marshals' video that came out right after 9/11 which said that their new motto was "control, dominate, intimidate," which means this is what air marshals can conceivably do to all the passengers on a plane, not just to the bad guys.

I have a suspicion that the guy in Miami was killed because he failed to be "controlled, dominated, and intimidated." Apparently, there had been a flurry of activity between the man and his wife that should have caught the attention of both marshals. It would have indicated that this was probably a domestic squabble. Furthermore, why did security officials wait an hour after the shooting before evacuating the passengers? If the marshals really thought that there had been a bomb, then they should have gotten people away from the plane as quickly as possible. If the situation becomes so serious that a person is killed, then you do an emergency evacuation of the plane including using the inflatable slides. News photos, though, showed people walking out of the planes with their hands on their heads. There's something wrong with that picture. It indicates how little faith the TSA has in its own screening process. Finally, I have never heard of a single would-be bomber shout that he has a bomb before he tries to detonate it. I understand that the guy was trying to leave the plane with the bag that allegedly contained the bomb. Even the passengers were saying that he did not mention the word "bomb." I found the Miami situation very disturbing. It represents a scary step by air marshals.

In an attempt to identify would-be terrorists, the TSA has also decided to implement a new strategy of training screeners who will engage travelers in casual conversations and see how they answer their questions. If the person appears nervous or evasive, extra scrutiny will be applied. While this system of behavior profiling sounds good in theory and is a baby step in the right direction, there are some serious problems with the TSA's approach.

For one thing, the TSA proposes using screeners to do the profiling. Big mistake. Screeners are already overworked. Giving screeners more time-consuming chit-chat and observation duties will only distract them from their primary job — which is basically just looking for stuff. TSA screeners weren't selected for their jobs because of their interpersonal and intellectual skills. I'd don't mean to demean them, but this just isn't going to work. It's kind of like asking truck drivers to do preliminary triage interviews in a hospital emergency room.

It's also imperative to keep airport and transit police out of the profiling business. Cops serve very crucial roles, but this task shouldn't be one of them. A police officer can notice any obvious criminal-type personality as well as the next person, but it's a big mistake to assume that he or she has some innate skill in detecting very subtle nuances that would betray a would-be terrorist. Airport and transit police are not trained to do this. Keeping them away from profiling will alleviate certain civil rights concerns. How many times has it been reported in the news since 9/11 when non-threatening and law-abiding people were arrested at airports merely for questioning inane procedures? This will only make things worse.

Instead, the TSA should select specially trained individuals to do the profiling. It should be their only job, not screening or checking luggage or whatever. I'd look for college graduates. Some foreign language skills would be a plus. These profilers need to have access to the latest intelligence briefings, say from the FBI or CIA, regarding what they should be looking for. Just sending these profilers to attend a two-hour course on how to notice signs of passenger nervousness is hardly worth the effort. A secret or even top-secret security clearance might even be necessary for these profilers.

To make profiling effective, there should be podiums before each screening checkpoint that every single passenger must pass through before proceeding to the next checkpoint. This is where the profilers would be stationed. There would be three levels of scrutiny for the profilers to use. Level A is for the vast majority of people. It would be the minimum level of security. Common sense alone could dictate this. A thirty-year-old mother traveling with two babies isn't much of a hijacking threat, no matter how nervous she or the kids are. An eighty-year-old man, same thing. Level B would be a step up in screening. People who just don't look right or who have an angry air about them. Their luggage would be sent through the latest bomb-detection equipment, and there would be a more careful screening of their body. This is basically doing what is currently referred to as selectee screening. Level C is the more serious type of screening. It is reserved exclusively for those persons who exhibit warning signs based on the latest intelligence data. There are pat-down searches of the body. Forget about using high-tech toys for screening their luggage. Every square inch of their luggage should be hand-searched. This is the only way to find potential chemical and biological agents as well as the dismantled components of a bomb or some other specially designed weapon. Only use these screening toys as a backup and not as a deciding factor in determining if something is a real threat or not. Do more extensive checks of the various law enforcement and intelligence databases that have been made available to the TSA. Call the cops only as a last resort or if a real threat is discovered. Get rid of the trusted traveler program or whatever its latest name is.

Let's look at 9/11 in the context of using the level C approach. Five terrorists arrive at a checkpoint at different times, but each one is getting on the same flight. Profilers may only select two or three of them for level C scrutiny. Hopefully, there would be some kind of database that would assist the profilers in ascertaining who else of interest might be getting on the same flight or is already on it from a previous location. It needs to be something more than a passenger manifest. If the level C terrorists are clean and not in any intelligence or law enforcement database, but they give off every signal that they are up to no good, what do you do? Let them go on their way? Throw them in jail? No, it may require that you split them up on different flights. Give them a coupon for a free meal to compensate them for the inconvenience. It would also be a good idea to have plainclothes profilers eyeing passengers in the boarding area, keeping special attention on high-interest individuals. All this will certainly cost some money to implement. But this would be a better use of resources than continuing to waste billions of dollars on high-tech toys that don't work very well. At the current pace, however, it will be twenty years before the TSA gets its act together.

So for the time being, I avoid flying if I can. I gave my career and my life to the aviation industry. I'm so sickened by it that I don't want to contribute money to the airlines. Barring a major change in their attitude, if they all go belly up, I could care less. I'm not so much concerned about a terrorist attack occurring when I'm on a plane because I know the odds are against it. I am not paranoid about a hijacking, but I'm prepared for it. I try to sit next to the emergency exit windows; in the event that something happens and the plane is still on the ground, I can get the hell out of there.

9

THE FLAMING LIBERAL

Randi Rhodes pumps up her listeners at Air
America Radio.

> "Republican callers hate me because I'm telling the
> truth. It goes against everything they've heard."

Randi Rhodes loves goading conservatives. From Air America Radio's studio in
New York City, the drive-time diva treats President Bush like a *piñata*. The popular
talk show host has compared the Bush family to the Corleones in *The Godfather
II*, with George W. perfectly cast as Fredo. She urged Poppy and Jeb to take
George W. out for a one-way fishing trip. Because Rhodes refuses to tread gen-
tly into the late afternoon and early evening hours, her right-wing critics have fired
back with equal verbal ferocity. They've called her "Osama bin Randi" and "Tokyo
Rhodes."

Rhodes is glib and liberal. She's opinionated, amusing, self-deprecating, and
has a pitch-perfect sense of how to frame political topics for her listeners. She's
on air to inform, entertain, and persuade. It's a fast-paced balancing act of reason and emotion. For show preparation, she downloads reams of articles from
the Internet, binges on C-SPAN, and studies committee reports from congressional hearings. Facts are a key ally for Rhodes, especially when she's scoring
points against Republican adversaries in talk radio land. In terms of ratings in
New York City, she runs practically mouth-and-mouth with conservative Sean
Hannity. Rhodes is heard in nearly seventy cities nationwide via the Air America
network.

Before she joined Air America, which launched in early 2004, Rhodes was a
popular talk-show fixture in southern Florida, first in Miami and then at a West
Palm Beach station. Unsyndicated, she was routinely beating Rush Limbaugh in
his own broadcasting backyard. The national press began to recognize her commercial potential. "Rhodes demonstrates every afternoon drive, a liberal talk radio
host can be just as bombastic, hyperbolic, and plain old nasty as a conservative

one," wrote the *New Republic*. With these credentials, she seemed like an ideal fit for the liberal talk-radio network.

In the beginning, it was far from smooth sailing for Air America, which ran out of cash within six weeks. Stations were silenced in Chicago and Los Angeles for unpaid bills. Matters looked dicey for the new Democrats on the dial. Fortunately, a new group of investors bailed out the fledgling network, brought in new management, and picked up syndication support from radio juggernaut Clear Channel Communications.

Rob Glaser, the chairman of Air America, is optimistic about his network's chances. "What happened on November 2 [2004] may have been bad for America," Glaser told the *Wall Street Journal*, "but it sure was good for Air America."

Conservatives used to take it as their FCC birthright that they had a near monopolistic lock on the talk-radio blabosphere. After all, a majority of all AM listeners are white male conservatives. Yet it can no longer be said that liberals lack the showbiz instincts to succeed in radio shout fests. Not only has Rhodes proven that she is one of the few golden-tongued exceptions, she earned her place behind the mike via a most improbable route.

■   ■   ■

I can't identify with one single Republican. I grew up in Brooklyn and eventually moved to Queens. It was one of those neighborhoods that happened because of the GI Bill. It created a whole new level of middle-class people. A lot of men were just getting out of college and starting families and Canarsie was just one of those new brick row-house type places. It attracted a lot of veterans from World War II. I remember hearing a lot of terrible things like, "Never sell to blacks." In my house you weren't allowed to say any of that stuff.

During junior high school we were being integrated with busing. Some of the parents were screaming about not letting these kids into the school and how stupid they were. Even their kids were starting to talk about how dumb the black kids were. I received this explanation from my parents: "They're not stupid, they're tired. If you hadda get up at 4:30 in the morning to get on a bus to go to school far away from your neighborhood and you didn't walk to school the way you do, you'd be tired too. That's why they're falling asleep in class."

In high school, I realized that if I was funny, people from both sides would let me live. The white kids and the black kids. I wanted to get along with everybody. I realized that no one would beat me up for being friends with the black kids and black kids wouldn't beat me up for being friends with the white kids if I was funny. There was a lot of ass-kicking going on by the girls. Everybody was calling everybody names. Everybody was like, "What are you looking at?" It became very elevated in gym class.

We were happy capitalists in my house. My dad worked for Polaroid and invented the flash cube. But he signed a thing when he went to Polaroid that said anything he invented, any ideas, belonged to Polaroid. So Mr. Land gave my father 1,000 shares of Polaroid stock as a bonus for his invention. It was twenty-five cents a share at the time, and my mom made him cash the shares out so she could buy new living room furniture. You know, I could have been as rich as a Dupont. But the living room furniture came first. Yeah, it was really ugly, too.

As a family, we never forgot that my father was a self-made man who had once put his life on the line. He was in Patton's Third Army. He was there at the end. He knew what liberation looked like in Europe. My father was badly wounded. After France, he went into Germany. One day he was hiding in an empty house, when somebody threw something in it and blew up the house. The blast threw him out of the house. He landed in the snow and got frostbite on both his feet. They were gonna amputate his feet, but he wouldn't let them do it. So his feet were always a mess. He was a Purple Heart winner.

I started tanking in high school when my parents got divorced—and life at home was a nightmare. After high school, I went to a community college, but I dropped out and joined the Air Force. When I told my mother I was joining, she said, "Are you a lesbian?" I was looking at my sister. Because she was the lesbian! I was overweight and didn't know what I was gonna do with myself. I just told her I had to get outta here. Nothing was ever gonna happen for me here. I wanted to see the world, and the recruiter told me I could go to Europe.

When I went into the Air Force, I tested high for mechanics. That is how I became a mechanic. You took an aptitude test. And they figure out what you're good at. I had dated a guy who used to soup up his car. We used to race cars at night in Brooklyn. We had this quarter-mile drag strip. It wasn't legal, but everybody used to meet there. And you'd work on the car all week, and you'd take it out on Saturday night and everybody'd do this quarter-mile race. It was kinda like *Grease*. Anyway, this guy taught me how to rebuild an engine. And so, I became a mechanic in the Air Force. I worked on C141s. Big cargo planes. Mine was a tedious job. Each panel on an airplane had a million little screws. So they give you this thing called a speed handle, and your job is to take off the panels. You are not touching anything that moves. You spend hours taking off every screw from the panel, and you do it with this handle.

I was there for seven or eight years. In my squadron, I was the only girl. There were 800 guys and me. When I got out, I was in Texas. I really had no clue how

I was going to get home. Or what I was gonna do. I thought, "Well, I know how to be an aircraft mechanic." But in the real world, you needed an air-frame and power-plant license. The Air Force qualified you for nothing in the civilian world. I mean *nothin'*.

So I became a waitress at a Mexican restaurant. Then I was a deejay at a country music bar called The Main Event in Odessa, Texas. I loved Odessa. It's a twin city with Midland. That is where Bush is from. Midland is upper crust, the people who own the oil rigs. In Odessa are the people who work the oil rigs. They are the ones who don't have fingernails. They are the ones who don't have hands. They are the ones who don't have arms. There are all these amputated guys in Odessa because of horrible oil-rig accidents.

I then became a full-time music deejay. I worked at KRKV in Seminole, Texas. I then worked at KOIO in Odessa and later at KUFO, which was a big rock station. Great call letters too. Great station. I had a lot of nice friends there. Then I moved to Mobile, Alabama, and from Mobile, I went to New York.

I'm always coming out of a small town and going to a big city. They always tell you that you can't do that. You can't go from a small market to a number-one market, which is New York. But that's a lie. You can. I worked at WAPP. The Apple. Rock 'n' roll. I loved Def Leppard, Elvis Costello, Frank Zappa. But you could never get them to play Frank Zappa. At WAPP, they wanted me to change my name. My then-married name was Randi Robertson. I had two choices: Randi Rhodes or Randi Rolex. I said, "I'm not a watch and I do admire Randy Rhodes—but he's Ozzy Osbourne's dead guitar player." I once was onstage with Ozzy. Because of my new radio name, I was scared to introduce myself to him. But he was great about it. His wife Sharon said, "Go out on stage with Ozzy." She pushed me out there. It was a long time ago, before anybody knew who Sharon was. She is a great girl. I sang *Wild Thing* with him. When we got to the part, "I wanna know for sure," everybody shut up. It was only me. I thought, "Oh my God." It was so much fun. The crowd got so rowdy that it turned our station van upside down in the parking lot. When the New York radio station was bought, the new people asked me to stay, but they wanted me to do Spanish pop stuff, like Latino urban. And they wanted me to change my name to Ramona. So I quit and moved to Dallas.

And from Dallas I went to Milwaukee to do a morning show with some guy. I was going to be the Giggle Girl. The one that laughs at really bad jokes. I started writing for him. I realized that I could do this on my own. I don't need this guy who tells Satan jokes and hates gay people. He was just really brutal. I lasted about six weeks and quit. I then got a job as a truck driver. I had a partner. Sometimes we'd haul beer, paper, bottles. We'd make trips from Milwaukee to St. Louis, from St. Louis to Houston, and back. I was terrified the whole time while I was out there on the road. But truck drivers are the nicest people. They are the salt of the earth. If they know that you are out there alone and you are a girl, they will protect you with their lives. It's that big-brother situation. They were great to me. I could never back a truck up to the loading dock. I still can't do it. It's hard to do. The cab is going to the left. Then the trailer is going to the right. I have no spatial reasoning, which is why I couldn't be a pilot. I would get where I was going, and I'd have to ask another driver to do it for me. And that is generally frowned upon. But they'd always help me. And they'd keep my secret.

After the truck driving, I came down to Florida. I was listening to the radio, and I wanted to see whose rock station sucked the most because I knew I was a great deejay. I picked this really bad one, and I went in there. I didn't have an interview or anything. I just walked past the receptionist. I know what radio stations look like anyway. I went into the sales area and asked a sales person where the boss's office was. So, I knocked on the door. I hear his voice. I open the door, and it's this jerk I worked for in New York who hated me. He's from Mississippi and I went, "Haw Slim!" And he goes, "Oh my God, what are you doing here?" I said, "What do you think I'm doing here? I need a job. I've done every format. You need help. I'm good at this. You know that. Hire me." He hired me for the Saturday overnight shift. I refused to play the playlist. I just got on the air and said, "It's the Randi Rhodes Rock 'n' Roll All by Request Party." And whatever someone wanted to hear I'd play it. I got in a lot of trouble. But this guy who hired me got fired about five weeks later. Then a new guy came in. He was from Connecticut. He phoned me, saying, "You can't call yourself Randi Rhodes." I said, "I know. He was Ozzy's guitar player." He said, "No. There is this great girl deejay in New York and she's unbelievable and you can't take her name." I said, "But that's me." He said, "It can't be you. Why are you working Saturday overnights?" I said, "That's my question for you." He said, "Well, prove that you are her." So I had to give him my WAPP tapes. When he heard them, he hired me.

Deejays don't make a lot of money. I was thirty. I thought I was old. I said, "I can't be thirty-five and playing rock 'n' roll records. This is ridiculous, you know?" I started going to a community college in Broward County in Florida. The very first class, my professor, Dr. Schindler, said, "You know why people become congressmen and senators?" Nobody knew, and he said, "So they can find out where the highway is being built so they can buy a Burger King at the exit ramp." I loved this guy. He gave me books to read, everything from Thomas Paine's *Common Sense* to Howard Zinn. It wasn't like an assignment. I just read everything he ever gave me. That is how I learned.

While I went to school, I took a new job working weekends with an FM station. It was easy-listening. It also had an AM station, which was talk. It was a really good talk station. I thought, "Gee, I want to work there." I started bugging the AM program director. It took about two years. I was also managing a band at the time. I got them a development deal, but they didn't get a record deal. Finally, one day at the station, the guy who worked eight to eleven at night went into the program director's office and told him to go screw himself. So the program director fired him. He called me up and said, "Come and audition." Now nobody auditioned in radio. That was ridiculous. But I did. He made me audition for the whole week. I was terrified. You don't have the confidence that it's your show, and you have to take abuse from listeners because you're new. Most people die under that pressure, and they go away. They don't make it. I lost ten pounds just sweating. On Friday, the program director called me in and said I had the job. And that was when I started doing talk radio.

The station manager Neal Rogers loved me. He hated everyone he worked with. He would take on our big company, Cox Enterprises, and just pillory them. He was funny, gay, and he was out. He was this big Jewish guy. He looked like the Michelin Man. He went to see his mother every Tuesday. He'd talk about it. He told the truth, and he stood up to the people in the workplace. He said the things you wish you could say to your ne'er-do-well boss. So I started doing the same thing with politicians. My thing was really talking to power. But political power.

When the Gulf War started, it was, "Oh my God!" We had been Saddam's ally for nine years when Iraq was fighting Iran. Throughout Iran-Contra, we were playing both sides of the fence. I knew we were selling TOW missiles to Iran. It wasn't just a happy coincidence that the day Reagan was being sworn in as president, the hostages were being released. I just thought, "Gee, this man is really powerful. He's not even president, and after 444 days they are releasing the American hostages. They must be scared of this actor." Yeah. None of it made sense. The Gulf War was really quick. It was, what, a hundred days? I just made fun of the video game that it was. The CNN videos. The green screen and everybody staring at it like they expected to see something besides a green screen and little flares. I made fun of everybody. The TV had already become flag-wavers, and Bush's approval rating was something like 91 percent. People were rallying around the flag and weren't asking questions. It was really upsetting. I was pissed. And then we told the Iraqis that if they rose up and overthrew Saddam we'd get their backs. It was disgusting. I was freaked out by the whole thing.

My time slot was eight to eleven at night. I had a big audience. I had an eight share in Miami. It was a big number. In New York, you get a two share, you get to work. Because a two share in New York is about 2 percent of eight million. An eight share in Miami is 8 percent of two million. My audience were twenty-five- to fifty-four-year-old men. They were valet parkers. They were people who drove delivery trucks. Since this was nighttime radio on AM, the signal powered down. If there was a thunderstorm, you could hear it in your headphones. I'd hear Cuban music playing. It was pretty wild.

After three years, I left Miami because they wouldn't pay me enough. It was killing me. I was making $42,000 a year; Neal Rogers was making a million a year. The lead guy on the afternoon show, which just sucked, was making $325,000. I couldn't get them to give me $100,000. That's what I wanted. I'm a middle-class gal. I drove a Toyota MR2 that wasn't new, and I was loving life. But they wouldn't pay me enough, so I had to go get another job—to use it as leverage. There was this station up the road in West Palm Beach which had a signal that got into Miami. I still would not lose my audience. Plus my sister had gotten sick, and I knew I was going to have to raise her daughter Jessica. I really had to make more money. The West Palm Beach station kept calling me. They must have called ten times. So I took a meeting with them. That was the first time I ever heard of Rush Limbaugh. They said, "We want you to come on noon to three. And we want you to beat Rush Limbaugh. Can you do that?" I said, "I can beat anybody! Nobody wins against me." They said, "Well, I'll tell you what. We'll give you a six-figure deal, and we'll give you big bonuses each time you beat Rush Limbaugh. But if you beat him by a tenth of a point, we'll pay you X amount of dollars." I didn't care. "Fine!" I said. "You fax me that. And if I get home and that is on my fax machine, I will quit my job tonight." It was Tuesday. I got home, and it was there. I got on the air. I didn't even offer the Miami station a chance to counter; I just quit. I said goodbye to my audience, which people never get to do. I told them where I was going, which you are not allowed to do. But I did have a non-compete. I had to sit out three months. But West Palm Beach paid me to sit out.

I went there, and I did my show. And then Clear Channel Communications came in and took over the station. It was changed over to Rush's station. I was put on after him, and I really got to hear him. You got to remember—I'd never listened to Rush before on the radio. I had no idea. Why listen to the competition? Everyone always says, "Know your competition." Bullshit. Be yourself!

Don't let anybody put you off your game for any reason. Then all of a sudden, I'm sitting in the studio doing show prep. And Rush is on the air because it's his station. I'm listening to this maniac. I'm listening to him call women Nazis. I'm listening to him talk about black people. I'm listening to the racism. I'm listening to the hatred. And he gets a TV show around this time. I watched the TV show the first few weeks it was on. I remember he had this show about welfare reform. He showed a big orangutan. All the baby apes were feeding off of the mother. And he said, "These are the welfare recipients." I just thought, "Oh dear God! I know this guy. I grew up with guys like that." I then found out that his father was some big lawyer in Missouri and his brother was a State Supreme Court Judge in Missouri. But, in some ways, he was just like me. He was a high school dropout. I thought, "Maybe he's just plain stupid. I dunno." But I couldn't stand the way he sounded. Even his voice irritated me. I always said, "I've made a living in spite of my voice." But this guy seemed to like his voice. You know, the golden microphone.

With Clear Channel, they told me they could never syndicate me because Rush would quit. What's really interesting is that the company behind him—Clear Channel Communications—believed what he believed. And they were willing to put him on every last station they could. Rush never came into our station. Not once. Not for the nine years I worked there. He did his show out of his house in Palm Beach. It's about a mile away. You know, the Denny's on Belvedere Road that he sent Norma Klein to go pick up his OxyContin at. That was also our Denny's—the radio station's Denny's. Rush is just a pompous, stuck-up pig. Why should he meet the local people when he was a national star?

In the early '90s when Clinton got into office, I'd talk about Gennifer Flowers. That Clinton was a saxophone player. That he was a womanizer. I rarely had guests. I did have Oliver North in the studio one day. When he walked in, he thought that I was gonna be a conservative, you know, one of them. He knew that 1290 AM was Rush's station. The very first thing he saw in front of me were Iran-Contra reports. I had Lawrence Walsh's book, *Firewall*. I had the executive summary of why North was convicted and why his conviction was overturned on a technicality because his immunized testimony broke an agreement. But he was guilty. Anyway, he wouldn't sit down. He stood there for the whole six, seven minutes he lasted with me. I asked him about lying to Congress, for crimes against our country. He said that I didn't understand the Constitution. We just got into it. His only defense was that he said he served his country and I hadn't. He then threw down his headphones and walked out.

Before I joined Air America, I was invited by Tom Athans, the husband of Senator Debbie Stabenow, from Michigan, to speak with other U.S. senators. Tom is involved in media issues. [ed. A founder of Democracy Radio, Athans is now Executive Vice President at Air America.] He contacted me and said, "They'd love to hear what you have to say about media and deregulation." It was 2002. Bush was in the White House. I understood that the Democrats would be a minority party for a very long time if they didn't do something about the media. I went to the Senate with thirty other broadcasters. They took us to all the committees. They brought us to Foreign Relations. They took us to Judiciary. I was excited to see Senator Patrick Leahy and meet Senator Tom Harkin. Because I watch C-SPAN, they are like rock stars to me. C-SPAN is my reality TV. Everybody got excited when Hillary Clinton walked in the room. I knew Senator Paul Sarbanes of Maryland. I knew how brilliant he was! I was at the Foreign Relations Committee, and Senator Carl Levin was there. I love Carl Levin. I think he is like a Founding Father. He even looks like a Founding Father. In my mind, when I see Levin, I think of Ben Franklin and John Adams. If you put those two together, that's what Levin looks like, you know, with the reading glasses and everything.

While we were sitting there at the Foreign Relations Committee, Levin gave an overview of the declassified intelligence that was going out on the airwaves about Saddam Hussein. He didn't believe half of this stuff was true, and yet we were going to invade Iraq. I was listening to him say this, and I knew what he was saying was true. I had been screaming on the air, "What does this have to do with Osama bin Laden?" Seventy-two percent of the American people believed that Osama was linked to Saddam Hussein. They couldn't tell the difference. And then Senator Biden got up, because it was his committee too. He said, "You guys in the media can say things we can't say. That's why we need you." I said to him, "Listen, we can say things that you can't say. Maybe. But why don't you just do what is needed here and call this president a liar?" Biden said to me that day in front of all these people, "Why do you have to pick the hardest thing to do?" I said to him, "The Republicans didn't have a hard time for eight years calling Bill Clinton a liar, a murderer, a dope dealer, the father of bastard children!" I could not understand it. And we got into it. I was furious.

Then, two years later, I was watching the Judiciary Committee confirmation hearings for Attorney General Alberto Gonzales on C-SPAN. I saw that Biden was not voting for Gonzales. In fact, the Judiciary Committee split along party lines. Eight Democrats, in unison together for the first time, voted "no" on Gonzales not to let it out of the Judiciary Committee and onto the Senate floor. This guy promoted torture. Next, I'm watching Biden get up on the Senate floor. This is what he says: "You know, I remember a couple years ago someone in the media said to me, 'Why don't you just do what you need to do and call this president a liar?'" I knew that Biden had been listening to me.

The Democrats have to start saying powerful things about dealing with truth and lies, because all these cable talk shows aren't journalism at all. They are nothing but hatchet jobs on the Democrats. So how should they counter? How should they defend themselves? There is not enough money in the world to buy enough time to counter 24/7 programming. You realize that when listening to Rush Limbaugh. He is nothing but hatred and meanness. "Hillary Clinton is a witch. Bill Clinton is a rapist!"

The first time I met Bill Clinton was in '96. Someone who used to listen to my show all the time took me to a very big fund-raiser that I couldn't afford to go to otherwise. She pushed me in front of Clinton and said, "Mr. President, I want you to meet Randi Rhodes. She's a liberal broadcaster." I didn't even know what I was going to say to him, and so I said, "Mr. President, it's an honor. But I really do have to ask you, sir. Why did you sign the telecommunications deregulation act? Look what it did to our ability to communicate with the American people?" He said to me, "Maybe I deregulated it too much." That said, he squeezed my hand really hard as if to say, "Shut up." Clinton was imposing. I felt intimidated. It took me an hour to tell the whole story on the air. About how long you have to wait to meet him. And what a rope line is. The whole bit. But that wasn't the only time I had a chance to talk to him. Since I've been on Air America I've had two conversations with him.

Before Air America, I was going to get involved with Democracy Radio. They called in their best fund-raisers. Then this lady from Palm Beach says, "You have no idea the power of this girl. She is unbelievable." I had started hearing people giving money, and it was like 250, 350. I thought it was dollars, but it was thousands of dollars. I felt like I was on the auction block, and it was very uncomfortable for me. I decided right then and there that I was not going to work for Democracy Radio because I did not want to be part of the Democratic Party. I didn't want to carry their water. I wanted to be free to criticize. I walked away from it. I gave all the money back to them.

I was then pitched by Air America's John Manzo, who was the program director. Now he's my executive senior producer. But Air America wasn't called that then. He told me that he wanted to have a whole network of people like me. Then he mentioned Al Franken and Janeane Garofalo. I was like, "Okay, show me a business plan. Show me what you are doing, and we will talk some more."

So, we talked for a year. I kept saying, "Make me an offer." Finally at the end of the year, they made me an offer. I said, "Okay, I'll move."

Janeane is just the nicest person. Al Franken gets all the great guests on Air America because he's Al. That's hard to deal with. Everybody will do Al's show. Everybody. But nobody will do mine. Al's a moderate. I'm a flaming liberal. That's why. I'm a half of a tenth of a point behind Sean Hannity. Hannity's got a television show to support his radio show. He has books he can sell because he's got a radio and a television show. I have none of that. I have one billboard in Times Square.

I don't have guests for the sake of having a guest on the show. I'm on for four hours. That is insane by the way. We ask callers, "What's your name? Where are you calling from? And generally what do you want to talk about?" But no one gets screened out. People who hate you listen better. Which is just a wonderful anomaly. Because you get to talk to people who would just scream at their radios. If you can make them have a thought that they've never had before, you're doing something.

We do get a lot of Republican haters calling. They hate me because I'm telling the truth. It goes against everything they've heard. At first, they are sure I'm making this stuff up. But I read the facts to them. I give them Websites to look up so that they can personally see that they've been lied to. A lot of callers will start out combative with me because it's nothing they've ever heard before. They've read all the lies for so long they think I'm lying. If they give me a chance and they look at something, they will call me back and go, "You know what? I changed my voter registration card. I'm voting Democrat." I get a lot of converts. A lot. I always tell them, "You're a real man." Or "You're a real woman." Because it takes a lot to admit you're wrong. And then to do it in public. So I'm really proud of those people.

The Republicans are good at telling everybody what they want to hear—not what they need to hear. Republicans will say things like, "You are just fine the way you are. There's nothing wrong with you. You're just overtaxed. I'll go to Washington and kick everybody's else's butt. I can get more money into your pocket. And you can continue to live the way you want to live." Republicans keep winning because they keep telling people that they don't have to do anything. And that's why people keep voting against their own best interests even though their best interest is to retrain for the new economy.

Democrats say, "You're not fine. You've got to retrain yourself. The Industrial Revolution is over. We're in the Information Age. You gotta go back to school. You've got to learn new skills. And if you'll do that, I'll pay for it. I'll get you money to go to college. I'll set up training programs for you in your own community. But you have to throw in with me." Well, Americans got so lazy, all they wanted to hear is how to continue to live the way they live. They didn't want to do anything. And it would all be all right. That was what the Republicans' message is. It's that, and pray for our country. The Democrats will say, "Pray for our country, but go to school."

Republicans feel that Bush is a tough, strong guy. They still feel that he is avenging 9/11. I don't think he inspires patriotism. You have to understand that this guy's crazy. He's terrible and he's nuts. I think that Bush is waiting for the end of the world. Those who believe in rapture think that Bush can actually make that happen. So they say, "I'm with him!" There are four million evangelicals out of 280 million of us. There are 100 million voters. In close races with a country so divided, four million is a ticket to the White House. In a close election, you need one ideological group that's going to stay together and vote for you because it can make a difference. We're choosing presidents by a margin of a few million votes or less.

Fox once did a whole week of shows about how I was inciting violence against the president. *The Today Show* called me. I said, "No, I don't want to go on your show." But they still did it without me. Joe Scarborough had a whole panel of people saying that I was dangerous and unpatriotic. They polled viewers with questions like, "Should we punish Rhodes some more?" and, "Has she had enough?" It went on for a whole week. Meanwhile Ann Coulter used to go on TV and say that she didn't know whether to impeach Clinton or assassinate him. Nobody said a thing then. The Republicans always point fingers. They like telling people who is to blame for their lot in life. They will also take someone and tear them to shreds. They will question their patriotism. They call me Osama bin Randi. Randi bin Laden. Randi Hussein. Tokyo Rhodes.

I haven't been threatened at Air America. But at Clear Channel, I used to get death threats. I contacted the FBI. They told me come in—bring the letter and put it in a plastic bag, and that's what I did. But when the threats come to your house, that is a little creepy. That's only happened a couple of times. One letter mentioned Jessica by name and told me to check on her and make sure she was in her bed sleeping. I found myself running upstairs, I was just so terrified.

If I had been a conservative, I would have been syndicated years ago. I would be hosting a show on Fox by now. I would have my own hour-long show on television. But I have self-respect. I have the courage of my convictions. I could never sell out. I just couldn't do it. Believe me, I was coached along the way that if I would just focus on the good stuff that the Republicans are doing, we can work with you. But by the way I dug my heels in, it was never gonna happen. And, on the show-business totem pole, radio is where the dog lifts its leg.

Now that Air America is being broadcast in Washington, D.C., I think politicians are listening to me. They need to listen—because there is a very rarefied atmosphere inside the Beltway. The Democrats invited me to the 2002 State of the Union speech when Bush gave his "Axis of Evil" speech. I walked out. I think I was the only one with balls enough to walk out. People wouldn't leave because of the majesty of it. They wouldn't leave the pomp and circumstance because it is all overwhelming.

Still, I'm very much a patriot. The flag means something to me. It's not something that just rises above the Constitution. It's a symbol of something really good. My father always had this special reverence for the flag. He trained me in flag etiquette. So I knew that an upside-down flag is not disrespectful. It means distress. You never let a flag touch the floor. I would tear up in the Air Force during reveille when we'd stand and they raised the flag every morning. You do cry. It's amazing, how emotional you get about this flag. But it's a wonderful thing.

I will also tell you this. The amount of parliamentary procedure and even the jargon and the lingo on the floor of Congress is almost military. The whole procedure brainwashes you into believing there is no world outside of this world. Because the American people don't usually get to visit their congressman's offices. The Senate is a very clubby place. The Senate would do well to listen to the national audience, which is begging for unity. They are begging for one voice from the Democratic Party that says, "We know the difference between right and wrong." Like in Iraq.

We need to get the hell outta Iraq. You can't train an Iraqi army in Iraq. That's just stupid. They're sitting ducks. The second they put on a uniform, even before they are finished with their training, they're dead! But U.S. troops can't leave until the Iraqi army has stood up. That's why the White House keeps lying about how many troops we've trained. Bush said 120,000 Iraqi troops during the presidential debates. It's a little more than 4,000. Of course, 4,000 in a county of 25 million, they are nothing more than targets.

So why are we doing this to our American troops? Why are we putting them at a disadvantage. The answer is because out of chaos comes the ability to steal: $8.8 billion dollars is missing from the days of Paul Bremer and the Coalition Provisional Authority. The money seemed to disappear the day that Bremer left. Look, you've got a country with no government in Iraq, and you're just pouring money in. Who's accountable? Who's watching the money? Who's distributing it? There's no government!

The people in the military who support the war in Iraq are doing it for one another. They're not doing it for any other reason. They are not doing it for the president. They are not doing it for their country. They are doing it for their buddies. See, when you are in the military, you learn liberalism, believe it or not. That's how they train you. What do I mean by this? They teach that you are only as good as the weakest person in your unit, because the weakest person in your unit can get you killed. So your job is to take the weakest person and make him as strong as he can be. And that's the essence of liberalism.

10

SUNDAY IN HELL

Max Mecklenburg was arrested during the Republican
National Convention.

> "The cop said, 'The Constitution gets abused and
> defended every day. What are you complaining
> about?'"

New York City braced itself for violence during the 2004 Republican National Convention. To meet this challenge, the city mobilized its entire law enforcement infrastructure. Ten thousand NYPD officers formed the backbone of this urban army, which was supplemented by personnel from federal agencies and a quick-response team of 1,500 undercover cops on motor scooters and bicycles.

"Manhattan turned into an armed camp," reported *San Francisco Chronicle* staff writer Anna Badkhen, "sealing off major streets with barricades of concrete and steel, and placing heavily armed police officers near major landmarks that could be potential terrorist targets. Bell police helicopters patrol the sky, and snipers watch the streets from the rooftops of skyscrapers. Heavily armed Coast Guard vessels look for suspicious watercraft in the East and Hudson rivers. Police officers in full riot gear cut through crowds of shoppers on Eighth Avenue, cradling M-16 machine guns in their arms, in a show of force some New Yorkers find disturbing."

For one week anyway, New York might well have been the safest major city in America—a distinction that offered little consolation to nearly 2,000 protesters, observers, journalists, or unlucky bystanders who were arrested by the NYPD during convention week.

Arrests started occurring four days before the convention got underway at Madison Square Garden. On Friday, August 27, the NYPD nabbed 260 cyclists during a Critical Mass bike rally which had shut down a number of city streets for several hours. Two days later, on Sunday, a mammoth gathering of more than 500,000 anti-Bush and anti-war protesters marched through Manhattan. While the police kept a watchful, respectful distance from the two-mile-long mobile demonstration, it exhibited zero tolerance for smaller protest tributaries branching off the flowing river of dissent.

Max Mecklenburg, who was bicycling with other riders alongside the marchers' route, experienced the sting of this zero-tolerance policy when he got arrested. The University of Chicago sophomore had participated in Friday's Critical Mass ride.

Mecklenburg, nineteen, grew up on New York's Upper West Side. In high school, he organized youth protest rallies and was a veteran of Critical Mass rides, which promote alternative transportation. "I generally go everywhere on my bike," he says.

■   ■   ■

There was a call for a Bike Bloc ride to accompany Sunday's main protest against the Republican National Convention. But because of the police violence that had occurred on Friday, people were scared. I witnessed police hitting people with batons. Cops were knocking people off their bikes and taking them and putting them into paddy wagons. People got "doored," that is, hit by doors of police cars. The idea was to divide and conquer.

Only about 150 riders showed up. We all agreed beforehand that we didn't want to get arrested; that we would prefer to ride around, support the demonstration. We were going to obey traffic laws and go by the book. Do it all legit.

About fifteen minutes into the ride, a bunch of meaty white guys on motorized Vespa scooters showed up. Some were dressed in blue jeans and Mets jackets and had short haircuts. They started buzzing through our group at full speed, knocking people over, deliberately running into riders and causing havoc. They didn't identify themselves as cops. There were also undercover cops on bicycles, and along with the cops on scooters, they formed a wall at one street which forced us to go onto a side street—which I guess was 36th. The moment the last person biked onto the side street, about a hundred riot cops converged from both sides of the street. Cop cars pulled in behind us, and then those guys got off their Vespas and started pulling people off their bikes, including me, and yelling, "Sit the fuck down!" "Shut the fuck up!"

I didn't say anything, although I tried to lock up my bicycle, which was apparently a big no-no. They wanted to confiscate it. I ride a Bianchi Pista. It's a track bike. It's a fixed gear, one speed. It's a steel frame. It weighs fifteen pounds, and it's really easy to maintain because there are very few parts and no wires. It retails for about $600 and is definitely the most valuable item I own.

They had us sit down on the ground behind these orange mesh nets, which they experimented with at the Republican National Convention. What we saw on Sunday were all these new crowd-control techniques. We sat there for about three or four hours, with plastic handcuffs on our wrists, our hands behind our backs. A big crowd had formed. People were yelling for legal aid. I was pretty furious. Then we got shoved onto a bus where we spent several hours. No bathroom, no food, no water, no air conditioning. We were brought to this old bus depot on 13th Street, our infamous little Guantanamo on the Hudson, which the Republican National Convention had rented out for the NYPD to hold demonstrators during the convention. It was a gross place where they set up these pens. There was diesel fuel on the ground.

I was standing in line with my cuffs still on, when some guy was wasting his time arguing with a cop, saying, "This is illegal, what you are doing. This is 1984! This is sick!" And the cop says to him, "The Constitution gets abused and defended every day. What are you complaining about?" I'm just eavesdropping, but I couldn't help but say, "You abuse and we defend?" The cop didn't say anything and walked away.

There are lawsuits going on about what happened. A lot of it apparently turned out to be illegal, but I think one of the crowd-control techniques that the NYPD learned is that the police can break the law as much as they want, and of course, there is no one to stop them at the time. And then what happens is a couple of months later, the courts say, "Oops, that was illegal," and the police say, "Oh, we're sorry. We won't do it again." And then, of course, it's all done again, and there are no sanctions.

We had our cuffs on for about seven or eight hours until we actually got into these pens. But I'm not sure about the time since they took away my watch. They like to keep you disoriented. It's the same reason that they moved us around. I would say that I was confined in about fifteen different places over the next thirty hours. They do it to keep you from sleeping, they do it to keep you from socializing with the people in your cell, and they do it to keep you feeling helpless.

There was a lot of solidarity going on in the pens. I'd say twenty-four was the average age. Everyone was pretty pissed off. There had also been a queer kiss-in at Times Square, and every single one of those protesters had been arrested. The joke going on in the pens was that we were the "queers and the gears." We started a Simon-says competition with the next pen over that was filled with mostly lesbians. They'd start, "Simon says, 'Say women are superior.'" Then the Simon-says game turned into a dance off. That's how we managed to amuse ourselves. We sang a few rounds of the Clash's "I fought the law and the law won."

We later received the only food you will see in New York City jails. Little cartons of milk and bologna sandwiches. The bologna was absolutely sickening, so I made a Go game out of the bologna and bread. I scratched the board in the dirt. Go is a very simple game. A minute to learn, a lifetime to master.

We were processed in the pens and then moved over to the Tombs, which is on Center Street. It's the Manhattan processing center. Depending on what you are arrested for and where in Manhattan, that is where you end up. The Tombs are multiple levels of cells. They would move us around periodically while doing all the fingerprinting and paperwork. We were probably treated better than your average criminal in the Tombs, so there was really nothing to complain about. One guy kept demanding, "Why don't we get blankets? We want blankets." So I told him, "They're not gonna give you a blanket." Then he actually managed to get a guard to come over. He asked, "Why can't we get blankets?" The guard said, "This isn't the Plaza Hotel." A typical cop answer.

We then found out that we could make collect calls. We called WBAI radio and did a jail cell interview. For some reason, I was one of the last people processed, and by the end, I was one of four people in the cell. At the beginning, there were probably twenty or thirty others with me.

The police really do try their best to humiliate and degrade you. The whole system is created to give one the impression that you're totally powerless and to make you feel like you can't depend on anyone and you're not going to get any help; they want to keep you scared and submissive. Your average detainee has a lot more trouble than someone who is arrested at a demonstration because he usually doesn't have the outside support network that we had. I remember going up the stairs where I walked past a barred window. Our cuffs were still on. About six or eight of us were chained together. All these people outside were cheering. The cop had specifically said, "Don't yell out the window." But because of the cheering I just sort of went "Yeeeaaaah" out the window. The cop said, "God-damn it! I just said it!" I said, "I'm sorry, I heard cheering and I can't help it."

We were then moved to another set of cells right next to the courtroom. There you actually mixed with the general population. It was always around twenty-five of us in the cell—about half Republican National Convention-related and the rest of the other prisoners were there on weapons charges and drug possession, the usual crap. These prisoners were alright, they really were. I met a very nice young murderer who had the same birthday as me. I didn't know he was a murderer until he got into the courtroom and they said that he had been found running from the scene of the crime with a knife that had the victim's guts on the blade. Hey, maybe he didn't do it.

We got lawyers to come in and talk to us and tell us about our rights. Again, the activists had a support network that the other prisoners didn't have. My lawyer was a guy named Bill Goodman from the National Lawyers Guild. He was great. I was fortunate because my mother was involved in all this activism back in the '60s and has all these friends. Once she heard I got arrested—when I was first getting cuffed, I yelled out to somebody, "Call my mother and tell her Max has been arrested!"—she made the trip downtown to the Tombs with my father. At some point, she must have run into Bill Goodman.

Bill had formerly been one of the heads of the National Lawyers Guild. He's part of a law firm that represented Fidel Castro and the Cuban government in America in the Elian Gonzales case. He is a very good lawyer, and it just so happens that he was one of these conscientious people who, upon hearing that all these people had gotten arrested, got off his butt and went downtown and offered his services. He laid out the possibilities for me. And the possibility that I chose, which I'm not particularly proud of, was that I should plead guilty.

Once I was in the courtroom before a female judge, it took twenty minutes. I was charged with five things: disorderly conduct, obstruction of pedestrian traffic, obstruction of governmental administration, parading without a permit, and reckless endangerment. They were going to let me plead to disorderly conduct, which was some sort of a misdemeanor; it was just a $95 fine. It meant that I didn't have to go to court, which was my main concern because I live in Chicago. So that's what I did, although if I had remained in New York, I would have sought to have all the charges dismissed, as many people later did.

After I got out of the Tombs, the first thing I did was get some Chinese food because it's right by Chinatown. I was absolutely filthy because I was covered in diesel fuel and I hadn't slept in thirty hours. I then went home and took a shower. The next day, I went to get my bicycle from a warehouse which was way out in Greenpoint, on the border between Brooklyn and Queens. When I arrived there, they told me that I didn't have the necessary forms. So I went back to Manhattan, trying to get the forms together. The next day I got my bike back.

I did not participate in Tuesday's big day of direct action where over a thousand people were arrested. A lot of people got close to the convention. People were doing sit-ins and civil disobedience and various other forms of direct action. The police deliberately slowed down the booking process in order to make sure that the last people were released from jail just as the convention ended. The whole thing was just preventative, to keep people off the streets and reduce the number of demonstrators.

I had been arrested once before. It was at an anti-globalization protest in Washington, D.C. It was in October of my senior year of high school. In a somewhat similar situation, I went to a demonstration early in the day when the police surrounded it and were going to arrest everyone. Then some windows got broken, and we rushed the cops. There were about sixty people who rushed the police line, and then we got away. We said, "Whoa, that was a close one. Let's go to this peace drum circle in Freedom Park. That sounds really calm and peaceful. We'll go there, just chill out, decompress a little bit, and not get arrested." Of course, no sooner had we gotten there than the whole park was surrounded by cops. Even the joggers who were in the park got arrested. And the arrest charge was even better: failure to obey. Because we were of a certain age, we were separated from the rest of the people who were arrested and released. They didn't want to deal with minors.

I thought the D.C. cops were cooler than the New York cops. The D.C. cops are seemingly more from D.C., whereas most New York City cops seem to be from Long Island. The D.C. cops were open about the fact that they sympathized with the protesters and that they were just trying to do their job. They didn't use as much unnecessary brutality. They were generally somewhat cooler. I don't want to overstate the case. They were still cops.

I went to Stuyvesant High School. It's on Chambers Street. The high school was in the news after September 11th because it was being used as a Red Cross center. In high school, I worked with a group called Youth Bloc, which was a coalition of New York City high schools and it formed around the Amadou Diallo shooting in which police fired forty-one shots and nineteen went into him. The cops had yelled at him, and he tried to pull out his wallet for identification. They thought it was a gun and unloaded almost every bullet they had into him. This happened in the Bronx. He was a West African immigrant. There was also this whole spate of attacks by the NYPD on the West African immigrants. There was the Patrick Dorismond incident, which was outrageous. He was an immigrant from a French-speaking country, and the undercover cop approached him and tried to sell him cocaine. Patrick told them he didn't want it and the cop kept pressuring him, and he sort of pushed him away and was shot to death. It was completely insane, but there were all these school walk-outs after the Diallo shooting. That was when the Youth Bloc was formed.

As organizers, we would stand outside high schools and hand out flyers saying, "There's a walk-out for this." Or we would try to find out if there was some sort of a social action organization and ask if they wanted to work with Youth Bloc. In many cases, we actually managed to get a lot of high schools involved.

Then we would organize demonstrations. We would set a time and date, and we would print up the flyers, do some press releases. We did a walk-out protesting school budget cuts. There was a lot of stuff against the Iraq War. There was a lot of anti-military activity where we had some groups setting up tables next to Army recruiting tables. We were concerned with issues that affected high school students.

It was punk rock that definitely got me into politics in a different way. A lot of local New York City bands provided me with contacts of people who later got involved in these causes. I was not a great student in high school. The thing about the University of Chicago is that my grades weren't so great, but they are very focused on essays and the interview. On my SATs, I got 1,470, which helped in the admission process.

My mother also attended the University of Chicago for three months before she was expelled for participating in a sit-in inside a campus building. This was January of '69, I believe. She was part of a protest against university expansion into the surrounding black neighborhoods. Then she briefly joined the Weathermen. She was involved in a women's action in Pittsburgh where she was arrested, but in the aftermath she was purged from the Weathermen for being overly bourgeois. She wasn't part of the Weather Underground; that's different. The Weathermen were formed in Chicago, actually. They wanted her to become a factory worker in Akron, Ohio, but she was resistant to this. I'm sure there are some great tire factories there; those are my mother's issues, not mine.

My mother is now a professor of history at Cooper Union University. My father is from Berlin, Germany, and traveled in the far left circles there. I know much less about his past. I don't think he was involved in any specific organizing activity. He's an archivist who works at a place called the Leo Baeck Institute, which is in New York. It's the study of German Jewry prior to 1933.

I have a younger sister. She goes to my former high school and is involved with the same student social action groups that I worked with. We definitely talked about politics in our house. I was not exactly rebelling very much by getting involved in social actions. My parents never wanted me getting arrested, but other than that, they were very supportive.

I've backed away from the activist scene, because the University of Chicago gives you a lot of work. I didn't really do much studying in high school, and instead the work that I actually did was organizing, taking notes, going to meetings and conferences. All of this was incredibly time consuming and, not to my mind, particularly pleasurable activity. I felt like I was doing some sort of good. Especially as a high school student. One thing that I have been sort of doing is vaguely making contact in Chicago with an anarchist group that I would like to work with regarding bus fare hikes. The budget for transportation has been cut, and of course, every single dollar of those cuts is going to the South Side and that means that we may lose these buses and we'll possibly get a fare hike. But right now, I'm giving my classes a chance. I have taken courses in legal reasoning, Islamic literature and image, German, and human physiology for everyday life. It is an odd mix; it's a mix of someone who doesn't quite know what he wants to do. I've never really thrown myself into schoolwork before, so I'm trying to see what happens if I do. As for my bicycle, it's downstairs right now. I ride in rain, ice, snow, whatever. I love my bicycle. I love my bicycle very deeply.

■   ■   ■

NYPD Crowd-Control Controversy

While the NYPD set a new record for arrests at a national convention, 90 percent of all cases resulted in acquittals or dismissal of charges. "In an effort to maintain tight control over protest activity, the NYPD too often lost sight of the distinction between lawful and unlawful conduct," said Christopher Dunn, associate legal director of the New York Civil Liberties Union (NYCLU). "Despite dire predictions that the convention would be the target of violence or even terrorism, the demonstrations were peaceful."

On the convention's year anniversary, the NYCLU published a detailed report, *Rights and Wrongs at the RNC: A Special Report about Police and Protest at the Republican National Convention*. The executive summary notes:

> Over the last ten years the NYPD has developed a comprehensive approach to the policing of demonstrations. This model of policing is based on the "broken windows" theory, which says that serious crime can be controlled by eliminating minor public disorders through a variety of zero-tolerance policing tactics. This "command control" model utilizes large numbers of officers, numerous barricades and protest pens, limited access to demonstration areas, and in extreme cases, the willingness to use force against non-violent demonstrators for minor violations of the law. In each instance of mass arrests, large numbers of people were peacefully assembled on public streets or sidewalks, and the police failed to provide any meaningful order or opportunity for people to disperse before arresting them. In each instance, as well as on many

other occasions during the week, the NYPD used orange mesh netting to surround groups and then arrest everyone inside.

Most arrests—totaling 1,200—occurred on Tuesday, August 31. That was the main direct-action day. In one demonstration, the War Resisters League planned to make a peaceful sidewalk march from Ground Zero to Madison Square Garden. According to NYCLU's report, "Demonstrators were informed that they would be allowed to march as long as they did not block pedestrian or vehicular traffic." Yet protesters had not even traveled a full block when the commanding officer on the scene ordered an immediate crowd dispersal. Within moments, cops surrounded everyone on the sidewalk with orange netting: all 227 individuals caught inside were arrested.

Again and again, these nets were used throughout the convention week, like fishermen hauling in a catch. "Not surprisingly, reliance on this tactic resulted in large numbers of wrongful arrests," says the NYCLU report. "While some individuals caught in the nets may have been engaging in unlawful activity, the nets snared hundreds of demonstrators who were acting entirely lawfully, people who were simply watching the demonstrators, and even passersby who had nothing to do with the protests but were simply in the wrong place at the wrong time. In each case, the police made no effort to distinguish between those allegedly engaged in unlawful activity and those simply caught up in the nets."

The NYCLU and National Lawyers Guild have filed federal and class-action lawsuits, respectively, against the NYPD on several counts: for its mass arrest tactics; the length and conditions of detention (some people were held up to three days before getting a court appearance); and the unlawful fingerprinting of those arrested for minor offenses such as parading without a permit or disorderly conduct.

Will other cities begin imitating New York City's zero-tolerance strategy? If they do, this bodes poorly for peaceful political demonstrations. As 5,000 Republican Party delegates trickled out of town, Police Commissioner Raymond W. Kelly told reporters how proud he was of the NYPD's performance: "I think the police officers were just absolutely amazing." Try saying that to someone who was trapped by one of those orange barricade nets before being carted off to the filthy detention-holding pens at Pier 57.

11

THE 9/11 BOMBSHELL MEMO

The FBI's Coleen Rowley addressed critical
shortcomings of a bureaucracy in denial.

> "You can't chalk this all up to 'failure to imagine,'
> when in mid-August an agent in my office was on
> the phone and saying to FBI headquarters, 'This is
> a guy who could fly into the World Trade Center!'"

Coleen Rowley was known as a serious and dedicated team player in the FBI's Minneapolis regional office where she was Chief Division Counsel. For Rowley, who was her family's breadwinner and mother of four, the FBI was like her second home. But in May 2002, Rowley did something seemingly out of character. She wrote a thirteen-page memo to FBI Director Robert Mueller that revealed how the 9/11 attacks might have been prevented if senior-ranking officials at FBI headquarters had been more alert and done their jobs properly. She hand-delivered the letter to Mueller's office in Washington. She subsequently gave copies to two senators on the Joint Intelligence Committee. Within days, someone on Capitol Hill leaked her memo to the press. One recipient was *Time*, whose June 2, 2002 cover story, "How the FBI Blew the Case," was based on what it called the "9/11 Bombshell Memo."

Rowley's memo provided a detailed timeline that exposed a maddening loop of administrative apathy and stonewalling that blocked key information from reaching the right channels. She described how agents in her Minneapolis office had been unable to obtain a criminal search warrant from FBI headquarters that would have lawfully given them permission to check the computer and belongings of a French-Moroccan named Zacarias Moussaoui. The foreign national had been detained by the Immigration and Naturalization Service on August 16, 2001 for overstaying his visa. "The Minneapolis agents," she wrote, "who responded to the call about Moussaoui's flight training, identified him as a terrorist threat from a very early point." Because Moussaoui spoke poor English and lacked flying experience, the agents obviously wanted to know why he was interested in learning how to pilot a jumbo jet. In *Time*'s summary of her memo, "Bureaucratic incompetence was, in part, to blame for 'stalling an investigation that may have led closer to the black heart of Osama bin Laden's plot.'" *[ed.On April 23, 2005, Moussaoui pleaded guilty in federal court on conspiracy charges relating to the attack.]*

Rowley ended her letter by addressing several personal concerns:

> *Although the last thing the FBI or the country needs now is a witch hunt, I do find it odd that (to my knowledge) no inquiry whatsoever was launched of the relevant FBIHQ personnel's actions a long time ago. I hope my continued employment with the FBI is not somehow placed in jeopardy. I have never written to an FBI director in my life before on any topic. Although I would hope it is not necessary, I would therefore wish to take advantage of the federal "whistle-blower protection" provisions by so characterizing my remarks.*

For bravely stepping forward and criticizing the FBI, which had elevated bureaucratic careerism over national security, Rowley shared *Time*'s Person of the Year award in 2002 with two other prominent whistle-blowers: former Enron Vice President Sherron Watkins and WorldCom auditor Cynthia Cooper. In December of 2004, Rowley retired from the FBI, and is now running for Congress in Minnesota's Second District, which stretches across the Twin Cities' western and southern suburbs. Her decision to campaign for public office was triggered by what she calls her "post-9/11 epiphany—the desire to bring change and new leadership to government as an independent-minded Democrat." Her opponent is second-term Republican Representative John Kline who is an ardent Bush supporter and former Marine colonel. "About the only thing I see eye-to-eye with Bush on," says Rowley, who is an accomplished runner and triathlete, "is that we have a mutual interest in keeping fit through exercise and sports."

■　■　■

I grew up in New Hampton, Iowa. It's in the northeast corner of the state. It's thirty-five miles south of the Minnesota border. I'm one of five children. My mother was a housewife. My father was a mailman. He walked a fourteen-mile route for thirty-one years. Our last name was Cheney. So am I related to the Cheney of the White House? Well, it's almost one of these things at this point in my life I would prefer not to know. My father's side determined that the Cheney family went back to William the Conqueror. One Cheney came over to the United States in the 1700s. So I am probably distantly related to Vice President Dick Cheney. The other reason for thinking that we are probably related is that we have a horrible history of heart disease in our family. My father had clogging of the arteries at age thirty-eight. And his uncles and grandfather all died young of heart disease. My father had triple-bypass surgery when he was forty-six, and he only lived another fifteen years after that.

Growing up, I always wanted to become an FBI agent. I was in the fifth grade when the television show *Man from U.N.C.L.E.* was such a big deal. I wrote to a question/answer columnist in my little hometown newspaper and asked, "When I grow up, I want to join U.N.C.L.E. Can you give me their address?" I thought it was something real. Someone at the newspaper wrote back, "U.N.C.L.E. is a fictional entity, but in the United States we have something similar called the FBI." And the columnist gave me the FBI's address. I then wrote to the FBI, and they sent me a pamphlet called "99 facts about the FBI." One of their "facts" dealt with this question: Why can't women become FBI agents? J. Edgar Hoover must have ordered some minion to write the lengthy convoluted explanation about why women could not handle the agent job. Hoover had very strong prejudices against women. After he died in '72, however, the FBI was not able to keep his wishes alive by keeping women out. Under threat of legal action, the FBI finally had to start hiring women agents. But between '72 and '78, only about six women were hired. At the time I applied, in 1979, there were probably fewer than a hundred. In both of my first two offices, in Omaha, Nebraska, and Jackson, Mississippi, for periods of six to seven months, I was the only female agent.

To get through the FBI's training at Quantico, Virginia, there were three components—academics, fitness, marksmanship—that had to be mastered. We had about eleven different types of academic tests, like constitutional law, search and seizure, and interrogation. I had just come out of law school—the University of Iowa—so the law tests were easy for me. As for the physical fitness tests, I had been running since high school, so I was in pretty good shape. I had been a high-school sophomore when Title IX came into play, and we got our first school track team for girls. In my senior year, in 1973, Iowa introduced the mile for girls. We had only trained a few weeks before running this event for the first time. When we were lining up to start the race, an official warned us, "Now girls, we don't know if you'll be able to make the whole mile. Pace yourselves and save yourselves for the end!" At Quantico, I held the women's two-mile running record for several years.

Then there was firearms training. We shot about 2,000 rounds, which makes a person become quite proficient. When I qualified, it was with an old

Smith & Wesson revolver, a .38 police special. That model had the shortest barrel, which makes it harder to aim and shoot. The FBI switched to automatics after two agents were killed in a shootout in Miami in 1989 with two bank robbers. The agents were horribly outgunned because the bad guys had automatic weapons and the FBI agents only had revolvers. And so, the FBI made the change. I got a Sig/Sauer 9-millimeter. I had the Sig until I retired in 2004, and then I handed it back because it was government property. In fact, I was happy to get rid of that gun. For one reason, I have four kids. For almost twenty-four years, I had to carry a loaded gun with me. My kids were never curious to try to find out about my gun, or to try to shoot it or anything like that. But it's always a worry when you're carrying a loaded gun. It is a tremendous responsibility. The FBI has rules about agents carrying a gun. It always has to be loaded. It can't be carried in a briefcase. It has to be right on you.

In Omaha we had about fifty male agents and in Jackson about forty. Some of the male agents were mad about having to work with female agents. They had a chip on their shoulders. Some wouldn't work with you. This isn't the case now, but back then, if you were trying to learn the ropes, you found the nice ones. In my first two offices, I was assigned to relatively easy jobs. In Omaha, I handled investigative leads. Then I went to Jackson, where I became the recruiter for the office. I went to colleges and gave speeches about joining the FBI.

When I was transferred to my third office in New York City, I was assigned primarily to Mafia and drug cases. I did a lot of transcribing of conversations from wiretaps and microphonic surveillance. These transcripts were used in court. One of the biggest investigations was called the Mafia Commission case. The bosses from four families had met to figure out their share of labor racketeering and any disputes regarding Mafia hits. Michael Chertoff, who is now Homeland Security Director, was the prosecutor. Louis Freeh, who later became FBI Director, was another prosecutor in this same organized-crime strike force. Other prosecutors, such as Barbara Jones, later become judges. That strike force broke the back of organized crime in the 1980s. There were about a hundred agents involved. Each squad had maybe fifteen to twenty agents and focused on one Mafia family. The squad that I worked on dealt with the Colombo family.

At the time, the Colombos in New York were controlling the high-rise construction industry. One of the *capos* in the Colombo family was the head of the concrete workers. We had maybe six or seven wiretaps at different times on this Colombo *capo*. He'd meet contractors in his car. We ended up having moving surveillance of certain cars. Then, after you listen to all the tapes—looking for clues and trying to figure out the conspiracies and connections, such as who is related to whom—you have to ensure the taped conversations are transcribed perfectly to play in court. Now this is the part that never makes it on the glamorized television shows or movies; there's a lot of work that goes into prosecuting.

Later on, the FBI sent me to the Defense Language Institute in Monterey, California, where I learned Italian and Sicilian for nine months. My Italian was pretty good back in the 1980s. Sicilian was harder to pick up. The dialects of Italian are almost as far off from one another as Italian is from French or Spanish.

There were two separate times when law enforcement officers on organized crime squads in New York City got shot and killed while I was there. One involved the Genovese crime family. This was in '87 or '88. There was a surveillance going on. Two New York City detectives, who were assigned to the FBI task force, were following three Genovese Mafia guys into a diner, but the Mafia guys unexpectedly came out and shot the two detectives. The male detective died. His female partner was shot three times but lived. Almost all of the agents working organized crime ended up getting involved on some aspect of this shooting investigation.

In 1989, because of my language skills, I worked on parts of what was known as the "Pizza Connection" cases. They were called that because pizza parlors were used for heroin and other drug trafficking. Most of the targets were first-generation Mafiosi from Italy. They spoke Sicilian or Neapolitan or Calabrese dialects of Italian. On my first day reporting to that squad, we had another shooting. The victim was not an FBI agent either. He was the only DEA agent assigned on an FBI drug squad. He was killed in an undercover drug deal by a guy with Bonnano family connections but who wasn't actually a "made" member. The killer, Gus Faraci, was also connected to a couple of other Mafia families. The shooting made national news. It appeared on *America's Most Wanted* several times. A lot of phone calls would come in. For a month or so, we then would have to go out, day and night, to try to resolve these leads. It sometimes meant we were checking out houses at 1 A.M. You'd have your gun out, ringing a doorbell, thinking that the shooter could be right behind the door. The DEA agent's killer was later rubbed out by his own Mafia associates, probably because of the law enforcement pressure we were putting on them. Eventually, they saw him as a liability. It happened about two years later. Faraci had dyed his hair and changed his looks so that it would have been impossible to recognize him.

In 1990, I was transferred to Minneapolis. The office was considered a medium-sized office, with somewhere between 110 and 120 FBI agents. I was the main legal adviser. I handled issues pertaining to freedom of information, the forfeiture program, and the victim witness program, which required law enforcement to provide information to victims to a much fuller extent than existed previously. Before 1982, it was common that law enforcement officials were often preoccupied in the prosecutorial efforts, but no one really seemed to care that much about the victims. And so, Congress mandated that certain efforts be made on behalf of victims and witnesses. At first, the FBI did not adhere to this law; it just kind of flouted it. In '88, another victim-witness protection law passed. Still, there was little adherence. But then in the early '90s, the Department of Justice started putting more pressure on the FBI to adhere to the Victim Witness Act. That is when we started a program to document every victim and witness, and if they were notified of their rights and if they were given their evidence back.

As legal counsel, I did not have direct command authority over agents. What I had was called an advising and teaching role. I would get calls all day long from agents in the field. They'd ask me questions such as: "What's the legal way of doing this?" Or, "I have this guy in custody, can I interview him after he said he wanted an attorney?" Those types of legal issues.

Many people think I was the investigator of the Moussaoui case because of the news coverage of me after the *Time* article. But I just had a peripheral role as the legal counsel. There were three agents involved in the case: an acting supervisor, lead FBI agent, and INS agent. They had written up a lengthy draft declaration seeking permission to go to the United States Attorney's office or to the secret court set up by the Foreign Intelligence Surveillance Act for a search warrant to probe the laptop computer they seized from Moussaoui and conduct a more thorough search of his personal effects. Because of the FISA wall you had to get permission first from the Department of Justice. You could not just contact your United States Attorney for a warrant. To understand why, you need to go back to the FISA wall's origins.

The FISA wall started to become a problem around 1995. The government was trying to create a separation between criminal matters and intelligence gathering. The FISA law and FISA court came into place in 1978 after the Church Committee's findings. Before then, it was thought that the executive branch had inherent authority to order secret surveillance in the name of national security. And this would have been fine if all secret surveillance had actually dealt with national security—like foreign spies conducting espionage. If the FBI had held to this narrow justification, probably there would have been no Church Committee and no FISA laws. But what happened in the '60s is that FBI Director Hoover abused the authority. He started the COINTELPRO, or Counter Intelligence Program, and agents began expanding on the definition of national security. There was surveillance of Martin Luther King, Jr. and the civil rights movement, anti-Vietnam War protesters, and even congresspersons. So these abuses were what the Church Committee addressed. Very few people knew about COINTELPRO until long after Hoover died in '72. And then in '76, information started leaking out; the Church Committee was convened to assess the problems. FBI supervisors started getting indicted because of these so-called "black bag jobs" done as part of COINTELPRO.

Consequently, the big quandary became how to conduct counter-intelligence. FISA was an attempt toward a compromise to give enough legal assurance to FBI agents that they wouldn't be prosecuted if their actions were authorized and they were just following the proper orders. Of course, these agents couldn't be ordered by the executive branch alone. There was a certain procedure that had to be followed before conducting national security surveillance: you needed to go to the Attorney General and the FBI director and submit your surveillance request to a secret court made up of seven judges. If one of these judges signed an order, then an FBI agent who then conducted the surveillance couldn't be liable in a court of law. So that was one of the reasons why the FISA passed in 1978.

You could go to the FISA court if you believed that someone was acting as either a spy or a terrorist on behalf of a foreign power. You didn't have to show a crime was committed. Now this worked pretty well, but here's the problem: in the mid-1990s, when international terrorist incidents grew in number, there were a couple of cases that gave the Department of Justice and judges on the FISA court a kind of an eye-opening revelation: what is to keep our secret court from being abused? And would the secret FISA court be used to bypass due process and therefore become an end-run around the regular criminal investigation process?

And so, the FISA wall started up, trying to separate intelligence gathering from law enforcement. It became more and more nonsensical as people began to pontificate about the FISA wall to the point where no one had a common understanding of what it actually required or entailed. The problem lay in the fact that the FISA Act was designed for stuff out of John le Carré novels. It was not designed for terrorists like Osama bin Laden.

Anyway, I knew that these three agents in our Minneapolis office were meeting this roadblock in their attempt to secure permission from FBI headquarters for their search warrant. I had talked to the agents from time to time in my office and in the hallways. And it's very fair to say that they were literally pulling their hair out. I think it was on August 22, 2001, that one of them was arguing very strongly with someone at FBI headquarters over the phone. The Minnesota agent said, "Don't you know? This is a guy who could fly into the World Trade Center!" And the guy at FBI headquarters said, "That ain't gonna happen." And this is the main point I later tried to explain in my memo to FBI Director Robert Mueller, that it wasn't really a failure that could be explained solely due to hindsight. Everything that had gone on pre-9/11 was all being glossed over because headquarters was saying that there was no probable cause to do anything. They were protecting literally everyone who had not done anything. The main gripe in my memo was that the FBI had not come clean and admitted to some of the problems and mistakes.

And while I was just the legal counsel and not a firsthand investigator in the Moussaoui case, I should have done something more when these agents met this roadblock. I should have picked up the phone and called the head of the FBI's National Security Law Unit, a chief named Spike Bowman. He was a couple of GS levels above me. He's a former Marine JAG. If I had done so, I would have probably learned something critical: Bowman had not read the draft declaration submitted by the Minnesota agents. He had relied upon a verbal briefing by a headquarters supervisor. No one knows what that verbal briefing consisted of, but it could have been all of a two-minute briefing. This supervisor might have said, "You know, Minnesota thinks they found something." So I personally should have called headquarters to find out what the logjam was pre-9/11.

At this time, the agents in our office knew nothing about the memo sent to FBI headquarters from a Phoenix agent also complaining of suspicious people taking flight training. And that Phoenix memo had gone to the very same people at headquarters. And now, they get a call from Minnesota with similar information? How much is it to put two and two together? Even if they were saying that they didn't have probable cause in our case alone, it should have been combined with the Phoenix memo. If you read *The 9/11 Commission Report*, the two supervisors at headquarters say that they never saw the Phoenix memo. I have no way of knowing whether that's true, but that was their excuse.

My immediate reaction when I saw the World Trade Center being struck on television was that I turned around and told someone in our office, "Oh my gosh, this must be tied in with our case here." And so, within just a few minutes, the case agent and I headed over to the United States Attorney's Office to try to obtain a criminal search warrant. It was finally signed late in the day on September 11.

About two days after 9/11, FBI Director Mueller made his first public statement that the FBI had no knowledge of any suspected terrorists in flight schools. Over the weekend, I heard him say it again on the news and quickly picked up my cell phone and spoke with different personnel I knew at FBI headquarters. I was trying to get a message to Mueller that this was not a smart thing for him to be saying—that the FBI knew of no one in flight schools—because this wrong information was going to be discovered and it would look like we were lying. There were other people in my office who also called their different contacts at FBI headquarters.

It was not even within the realm of plausibility for Director Mueller to have said that he didn't know about the case in Minnesota. Our office had already got a search warrant for Moussaoui's stuff. I am sure that someone in the Phoenix office, in the same way, was calling FBI headquarters. So all of this information was being funneled to headquarters. Still, Mueller went on saying for two and a half weeks, "We knew of no one training in flight school. Otherwise we might have been able to prevent 9/11."

Interestingly enough, one week before 9/11, our office had its special training day. This training day was mandated as a result of the Oklahoma bombing when all these additional documents turned up just two or three weeks before Timothy McVeigh's execution. It had caused a scandal that these documents had not been given to his defense attorney. FBI Director Louis Freeh had gone to Congress where he hung his head and said, "We will never do that again." But he never explained how or why the mistake had occurred. Every time a bureaucracy is caught in a mistake, what tends to happen is that it's glossed over. Officials think, "Well, if we tell the truth and explain it, no one will understand anyway—and so, isn't it just easier to move on?" With the Oklahoma bombing, the missing documents could have been explained quite easily. There were tons of documents that were provided to McVeigh's attorneys. These newly discovered "documents" were basically just irrelevant scraps of paper—mostly leads that had come in and were nothing important. The federal government does not operate with an open-file discovery the way some state courts do. In a normal FBI case, the scraps of papers with leads or calls that come in are usually never handed over to the defense. But instead of Freeh explaining all that, he told Congress, "Oh, the FBI is bad, and we will have a training day." Well, one week before 9/11, we had that training day. It was called Back to Basics Training. And one hour of that day was devoted to law enforcement ethics. One of the informational slides said: "Do not puff, shade, skew, massage, tailor, or otherwise firm up statements of fact." Of course, that's exactly what Mueller and others were doing after 9/11: puffing, shading, skewing, massaging, tailoring, and firming up.

Many other problems existed before 9/11. For starters, if you recall, Attorney General Ashcroft had ranked terrorism as his lowest priority in August 2001. After 9/11, he told the country that by seeking the death penalty of Moussaoui, real progress had been made in the war on terrorism. But what were we really doing?

We were forgoing possibly getting information from the only known source of information at the time. If you have an organized crime or a terrorist conspiracy, it doesn't help to request a draconian penalty such as the death penalty for the first person you catch. To make inroads against a conspiracy, you want to put pressure on somebody who seems to be at a lower level, and then get him to divulge what he knows about the criminal group. The Mafia had its own *omerta*, its own code of silence. And it's pretty strong. But it's not as strong as the terrorists' code because they have an ideological basis for keeping quiet. If you catch somebody and seek the death penalty right from the start, there is no motivation for him to cooperate. In fact, what you're doing is locking into the status quo.

And then, there was the problem of mass detentions and roundups of foreign nationals and immigrants with visa problems. I knew it was wrong. Our office in Minneapolis knew this policy was wrong. We resisted the temptation. We were under pressure every day to send in a report saying how many new people we had detained and how many searches we had done. And every day, in fact, if you didn't send in your report, they called you at home at midnight. And then, every day FBI headquarters compiled these reports. It was called the Daily Report. The FBI would put out a new press release under the guise of showing the American people that further progress was being made in the war on terrorism. In a way, this was its own cover-up. We wanted to look like we were on top of things. And when a mistake is made, you try to remedy it by overreacting. I have heard that none of those detained were charged with any connection to terrorism except for Moussaoui. All these other foreign nationals and immigrants were just at the wrong place at the wrong time. Some of them sat there in lockup in Immigration and Naturalization Service detention centers for six, seven, eight, even nine months.

During this time of roundups, Congress formed a Joint Intelligence Committee and hired Pentagon analyst Eleanor Hill and about twenty staffers to help her look into how the FBI, CIA, and National Security Agency had handled the 9/11 attacks. Her special staff included retired CIA, FBI, and Department of Justice people. These special staffers started to debrief current personnel who knew about pre-9/11 matters. In January 2002, the committee launched a formal inquiry. The FBI had started to prepare a timeline to show how all of these various events had taken place. Well, the agents in my office, and I, in a very peripheral way, were trying to assist headquarters in developing this timeline.

I was contacted by the staffers to come to Washington on May 21, 2002 to be debriefed. When I hung up the phone, I thought, "Oh wow. Now I get a chance to give my two cents on this whole thing." As the legal adviser in our office, I knew that our headquarters had been seeking to gloss over this whole FISA business. They were still trying to say there was no probable cause and that nothing could have been done—because if you go that route, then nobody made any mistakes. Everybody hides behind this big blanket defense.

Now I know that the hindsight defense does apply in a lot of cases. On the other hand, in this case, you can't chalk this all up to "failure to imagine," when in mid-August an agent in my office was on the phone and saying to FBI headquarters, "This is a guy who could fly into the World Trade Center!" And so, I was determined after I hung up the phone to tell the truth of what I knew from my peripheral role. I couldn't sleep that night, thinking of what I would say, especially about the problematic FISA wall. I took the next day off to help my daughter move back from college. I went to bed Thursday night, expecting that I'd sleep well because I hadn't slept the night before. But the same thing happened, and I was up again, thinking about what I should say and worrying that I'd leave something out. And so, at about 3:30 A.M., I thought, "This is ridiculous. I am just going to go into the office and start jotting down all the points I have to tell this special staff." I went into the office thirty minutes later and I started typing away. I got so far along that I thought, "You know what? This is a little more than just points I am going to tell the committee staff. I am going to make this into a letter to Mueller and ask for a further investigation by our own FBI internal affairs. I also copied the memo for delivery to two senators. Here's why. The special staffers on the Joint Intelligence Committee were split up between looking at the FBI, CIA, and NSA. The special staffer it had put in charge of the FBI portion and getting documents from the FBI was a retired FBI agent. Not only was he a retired FBI agent, but he was a thirty-one-year career guy. He had been an FBI deputy general counsel, and I knew that he was a loyal true-blue FBI agent. So I copied two of the committee's senators, Dianne Feinstein and Richard Shelby, directly on my letter to Mueller to eliminate there ever being a chance of the memo being toned down or altered. I didn't know who the heads of the two committees were, but I knew that both of these senators had previously asked good questions about national security.

I flew to Washington and met with two or three of the Joint Intelligence Committee's staff in a room next to the FBI press office. The entire time I had an FBI and DOJ minder with me. Both sat in on my interview. That is another thing people don't understand. When any government agency is under examination, even by Congress, there is huge mistrust and no government agency would ever let its lower-ranking personnel speak directly to a congressperson. The executive branch plays secret all the time. In fact, in many cases, executive branch officials think that when they sign a secrecy agreement, it actually does entitle them to lie if they are called on the carpet by Congress, like what happened with the Iran-Contra scandal. After I was done with my three-hour interview with the staff members, I was asked, "Do you have anything further to add?" I said, "Because I often leave things out, and I'm not that good verbally, I've written you a letter that kind of puts it all down." So I handed them my letter and then walked out of the room.

Then, I wandered around FBI headquarters trying to find the director's office. I dropped off a copy of the letter to Mueller at his office, and then I went to the OPR, or Office of Professional Responsibility, which is our internal affairs, and dropped a copy off there. I then went down to the street and caught a cab to the Hart Senate Building. There was still the post-anthrax mess going on. A long line of people was waiting to go through security. I had my gun, so I went over to the side and got a police officer. I showed him my badge, and I asked him, "You know, is there any way I can get in? I need to deliver these two sealed envelopes in a secure way directly to these two senators' offices." The security guard took me directly to Feinstein's office and then to Shelby's office. I just went into each office and said to whoever was sitting at the front desk, "Can you make sure that this goes right to the senator?" I certainly knew I would be getting myself into a lot of hot water by giving the letter to the senators. I figured people at FBI headquarters would be mad as heck for me bringing this up and trying to go against their desire to gloss over these issues. So probably what happened, and I am just guessing, is that either Shelby or Feinstein shared the letter with others in Congress and someone along the way decided to make it public. I don't know if they had altruism in their hearts or if they were thinking that it would save me.

The next day, I was back at work. Because our main media coordinator was out and I was the backup, I was taking calls from the press. Around six o'clock, somebody from CNN called and told me, "We are calling because we heard something about a letter written from somebody in Minneapolis." I said, "I have no idea what you are talking about." I hung up and thought, "Oh my gosh. This must be mine!" Until that point, I had no idea that the memo would be leaked to the press.

When I got home, my husband Ross was standing in the driveway. He had been watching C-SPAN, and he said, "Coleen, they must have read your letter because they were asking pointed questions along the lines of stuff in your letter." And in my heart, that was all I hoped for. To give Congress enough information so that they would be able to ask intelligent questions. Because up till then, they were all over the map. No one understood what this debate was about. They hadn't understood this FISA problem or anything, so I thought, "Well, at least I've achieved my goal."

Snippets from my memo started to leak out the next day in the press and on the air. So, someone from FBI headquarters in a position to know called me and said that he had overheard FBI officials talking about firing me. That took my breath away. I asked, "How could they fire me? What did I do?" He replied, "Because the letter was classified." I said, "Well, I didn't classify it myself, and it didn't have anything in it to make it classified." It turned out that FBI headquarters had classified it afterward in an effort to keep it from leaking. Based on two words in the whole letter! I had mentioned "a French intelligence agency." It's common knowledge that all countries have their own intelligence agencies, like our CIA. And I hadn't even named the specific agency, but headquarters had seized on that to make my entire memo classified.

They were basically grasping at straws. It didn't work though, because somebody in Congress gave the whole memo to *Time*. That weekend, both Mueller and Attorney General Ashcroft went on the Sunday talk shows. They were asked repeatedly, "Will Coleen Rowley be fired?" Under that media pressure, Mueller right away said that I wouldn't be fired because of my invoking whistle-blower protection. When I had thrown that in the letter at the last minute, I didn't know what federal whistle-blower protection even amounted to. As it turns out there is no real protection. The federal Whistleblower Protection Act of 1989 does not even apply as a statutory protection to anyone in the FBI or agencies in the intelligence community. By regulation, the FBI is supposed to give some kind of protection, but it depends upon the goodness of their hearts and lacks any enforcement mechanism. Mueller did write me a letter the next week saying that I was protected and wouldn't be fired and that he had forwarded my letter on to the Department of Justice's Inspector General for further evaluation. Ashcroft was tougher. He had to be asked two or three times on the news shows if I would be fired. Finally, by the third time, he kind of nodded in a way to suggest that I wouldn't be fired.

I was taken aback by all the publicity, but I was happy that the darn letter had been read by the right people and that they were on the right track asking questions. And I do think that my memo had a certain impact in leading to the 9/11 Commission inquiry. If we had not gotten past the blanket defense and the resistance to forming the 9/11 Commission, then what we would be seeing right now is continual surfacing of new dribs and drabs. History always comes out. It's just that it often takes a long time unless you have disclosures that speed up the process.

Judged by my memo about 9/11, I was actually viewed very favorably by the right wing. Because you know what? I was pointing out that we should be more aggressive investigating terrorists. *The O'Reilly Factor*, for instance, had its Top Ten Heroes and its Top Ten Villains for 2002. And I was third on its list of heroes. And FBI Director Mueller was first or second on its list of villains. Even I thought O'Reilly was unfair to FBI Director Mueller.

In my own field office, most of the people who knew specifics about the Moussaoui case were appreciative. I was basically telling their story. I didn't get any real criticism from the rank and file. The prosecutors on the case, however, weren't overjoyed—because in a prosecution, you want the least amount of information out about the case as possible. I got e-mails from other offices. People who had worked on espionage cases in prior years knew how the FISA wall had become a big problem. I compiled this feedback I got from other agents who worked in intelligence matters. And when the Senate Judiciary Committee invited me back to Washington to testify on June 6, 2002, I gave them a six-page statement with longer appendices. And in the appendices, I included some of the other comments by the agents. I removed their names of course.

The reason I was invited to speak before the Judiciary Committee was that Senator Charles Grassley, a Republican from Iowa, and Patrick Leahy, a Democrat from Vermont, were champions of whistle-blower issues. For years, both had listened to sad tales of executive branch employees who reported problems. For example, Frederick Whitehurst was an FBI supervisor who had worked as an FBI laboratory examiner. He saw all the different problems the lab had and tried to report them, but to no avail. FBI officials retaliated against him, and he ended up fired. I think he also suffered a mental breakdown. Eventually, Whitehurst was vindicated and improvements occurred in the FBI Lab, but it took years.

On the evening before I testified to the Judiciary Committee, I was at FBI headquarters and had a quick meeting with Director Mueller. It was about 7 P.M. He was still in his office. The head of the press office had asked me, "Would you like to meet the director?" Now I knew that when the agent from Phoenix— the one who had written the memo about suspicious men at the flight school— had testified a month or so before, Mueller had gone into the hearings with his arm around him. That agent told the committee, "I never expected my memo to be read. It meant nothing!" Hah! He was completely in bed by that time with the whole thing. Loyalty is a big factor at the FBI. In my chat with Mueller, he told me, "Oh, Coleen, I'm like you. I like mistakes to surface, and I'm critical-minded. Next time you see anything like this, please give me a call." I don't know if he said that he had an open-door policy, but he made me feel that I was free to bring any concern up to him.

When I testified before the Judiciary Committee the next day, I was in such a powerful driver's seat that no one in the FBI had even asked to proofread my statement. Nothing was censored. That is amazing. I had written this statement the weekend before while en route in the car to and from the Pigman Triathlon in Iowa. I even won my age division in the race.

I was there before the Judiciary Committee for about three hours. Mueller had testified earlier. He was grilled for about five hours. I didn't even get on until two o'clock in the afternoon. I got asked a lot of questions about some of the endemic problems facing the FBI in trying to combat terrorism. My responses were honest but not as articulate as I would have liked and were filled with "uhs" and "ahs."

Throughout all this, my husband was very supportive of me. I've been the only breadwinner since we've been married. I got pregnant the first month of FBI training and graduated three months pregnant. When we had our first baby, Tess, who's now twenty-four years old, we fell into these reversed roles: my husband Ross became responsible for bringing up the kids. He was "Mr. Mom."

It was my second letter to Director Mueller—writing about my objections to the looming war in Iraq—which Ross and I both knew could trigger far worse consequences, and it did. In February 2003, Mueller was standing idly by when Vice President Cheney lied his head off to the American people about the connection between Saddam Hussein and Al Qaeda. Cheney was often saying that the chief 9/11 terrorist, Mohammad Atta, had met an Iraqi intelligence agent in Prague, Czechoslovakia. Mueller knew that the FBI actually had a ticket stub that showed Atta was in the U.S. at the time. Atta did not meet the intelligence chief in Prague.

Then I brought up Waco in my letter. I basically said, "Mr. Mueller, shouldn't you bring up the fact that going to war is a lot like Waco? Where we had a rush to judgment because people couldn't wait any longer. And the children we were hoping to save at Waco all ended up dead?" The Waco analogy is really very apt with Iraq. There was no reason for rushing. Why couldn't the UN inspectors take their time? Even if these weapons did exist, why were the inspectors stopped and we had to invade just then? I also lumped in the fact that preemptive war is illegal under international law. Deadly force can only be used if there's an imminent threat. That's the correct legal term that's used in the FBI's own legal training about the permissible use of deadly force. You can't, for instance, go down the streets of New York and say, "There's John

Gotti. Our intelligence files show that he's a bad murderer. Let's just preemptively gun him down." You can't do that. It's the same with international law. If you know someone is going to attack you and you have no choice, no chance of avoiding it, then maybe you could make a case of "imminent threat," but otherwise no.

I e-mailed my letter to Director Mueller on February 26, 2003. I asked him to exercise caution against invading Iraq. I got no response from him. In early March, as U.S. troops were massing on the Iraqi border and it looked like the war was about to start, I more or less panicked. I gave copies of my letter to the *New York Times* and the *Minneapolis Star Tribune*. Both newspapers printed stories about my letter of warning on their front pages on March 7, 2003. I also did some follow-up interviews. But, of course, the war fever at that point was just incredibly strong, and my attempted warning fell on deaf ears and was completely unsuccessful.

I was vilified by pretty much everybody for my memo on the Iraq war. FBI employees are largely conservative. When the president said that there was a threat and we had to invade a country, everyone agreed. If somebody says this was a bad move, you're going to be shot as a bad messenger. One day after my Iraq letter was published, the FBI Agents Association called a special session and the officers unanimously voted to kick me out. I don't think that even happened with convicted FBI agent and Soviet spy Robert Hanssen. I was called a traitor—and for a little while became one of the most vilified FBI agents.

Our FBI office in Minneapolis is mainly Republican. I was shunned. I wasn't talked to. For a couple of weeks, I kept coming back to work and tried to do my legal job. But people were mad as heck. Not surprisingly, people in my office began marching to my boss and saying that they couldn't trust me as the legal adviser for the office. I had been a GS-14 Minneapolis Division Counsel for our office for thirteen years. And of course, I had the confidence of the whole office prior to the Iraq letter. Even the earlier 9/11 letter had not created any problems with me serving as the legal adviser in my own office. But agents kept pressuring my boss, and so at one point, she said, "Coleen, are you going to step down?" That idea had already occurred to me, as I thought the office needed someone that they could trust, even if trust was a subjective thing. So I stepped down from the GS-14 position in April 2003, back to a GS-13 agent. Once I stepped down, I think most of the people in the FBI got over it pretty quickly, and I actually ended up with a good job, albeit at GS-13 pay, handling human intelligence and confidential source compliance issues. In December 2004, I decided to retire from the FBI.

And now here I am, running for Congress! I've never run for an elected office. Even in high school. The closest I've ever come to anything political was in junior high when my best friend Jane ran for president of the student council. I wrote her speech and made her memorize it. She won.

I had voted for Bush and Cheney in 2000, not having any idea about the right-wing agenda that they apparently subscribed to, including their desire to "finish the job in Iraq" that was part of the Project for the New American Century. In the lead-up to the Iraq War that began in September 2002, it became clear that Bush and Cheney were about to dishonestly lead us into an unconscionable and counterproductive war. I predict that the Bush administration will go down as perhaps the worst in history. Their dishonest antics, once made public, are already making the Watergate scandal pale by comparison. Our children's future has been needlessly jeopardized.

The Republican incumbent that I am running against is a blind loyalist who has voted 99 percent in line with the Republican leadership. But I have a glimmer of hope. John Kline, my opponent, is a Karl Rove–schooled politician but not much of a people person. He chooses his audiences a lot like Bush. He will usually only speak to the Lions Club or the American Legion. He is so in lockstep with the Bush administration. He has fully echoed the misleading rationale for the Iraq War.

I'm basing my campaign on the need for ethical decision-making. We need to get rid of all this marketing stuff that is Orwellian about controlling the dialogue and public opinion. I have set down six or seven main initiatives that people have heard of, like "No Child Left Behind." Of course, we all agree that no child should be left behind. That's a wonderful, lofty goal that we should aspire to. But are the Republicans doing anything that effectively achieves this goal? Or take another example, the famous "Clear Skies Act." Who is against clear skies? Obviously, it's a great goal. We all want clear skies. Now, let's delve behind the rhetoric and see if the Bush administration is doing anything to achieve clear skies. No, in fact, they are just doing the opposite. They say that they are bringing democracy to Iraq. Who would be against democracy for Iraq? Okay, but actually they have brought huge chaos and horrible destruction to Iraq. "Defense of marriage" is another example. Who would not be for defending marriage? I'm for defending marriage. But examine the initiative and there is nothing in it that is related to defending marriage.

Our political system really needs fixing. If elected to Congress, I would like to be part of the process trying to pull this country out of the serious quagmires it now finds itself in. We will have to begin with the truth. It will be slow going and very, very difficult, but I don't think we really have any option. For example, every single person in the FBI and CIA who made mistakes pre-9/11 got promoted. Every single person who made mistakes about the weapons of mass destruction in Iraq got promoted or rewarded—even the highest level people. Former CIA Director George Tenet had said that WMDs in Iraq were a "slam dunk." He was later awarded the Presidential Medal of Freedom! I've had to argue with conspiracy theorists who say, "Oh, this guy was promoted in the FBI!" Well, that's nothing. They all were promoted. Every single person involved, usually in tacit exchange for keeping quiet.

George Tenet was also the most egregious example of someone making serious mistakes and then falling on the sword for the cause while engaging in complete denial. He only sheepishly admitted in the month before the 9/11 Commission disbanded that he had known about the case in Minnesota. He hadn't admitted that beforehand. He was having breakfast on the morning of 9/11, when somebody came running to him to report that a plane had hit the World Trade Center. The first thing out of Tenet's mouth was: "I wonder if it was that guy in Minnesota who was learning to fly?"

12

UNFRIENDLY FIRE

Speaking to the press was hazardous duty for Staff Sergeant Lorenzo Dominguez.

> "The base's upper command accused me of endangering the military and possibly aiding the enemy."

It is a well-known fact that the U.S. military is stretched dangerously thin in Iraq. The military must rely on a steady supply of National Guard and Army reservists to guard the checkpoints, patrol the roads, and assist in fighting insurgents. The tour of duty for these citizen-soldiers often comes at great risk, sacrifice, personal cost, and family and financial disruption. Moreover, they are plagued by poor battle and equipment readiness.

In late 2004, *Los Angeles Times* reporter Scott Gold wrote about the 1st Battalion of the California National Guard's 184th Infantry Regiment as it prepared for deployment to the Middle East. The unit was completing its training at a former World War II prisoner-of-war camp in Doña Ana, New Mexico. Gold described a battalion in disarray. It was hampered by low morale, poor equipment, and inadequate training. All but two soldiers quoted in the newspaper chose to remain anonymous. Little surprise here. The military's suffer-in-silence culture discourages airing its dirty laundry to outsiders. But Staff Sergeant Lorenzo Dominguez, forty-five, thought otherwise. As a squad leader with fifteen years of experience in the Guard and Marine Reserve, Dominguez believed that it was his sworn duty to protect the men under his command.

"Some of us are going to die [in Iraq]—and some of us are going to die unnecessarily because of the lack of training," Dominguez told the *Los Angeles Times*. "So I don't care. Let them court-martial me. I want the American public to know what is going on. My men are guilty of one thing: volunteering to serve their country." He also appeared on Deborah Norville's MSNBC show where he again voiced safety concerns. In civilian life, Dominguez is vice president at a mortgage bank in Alta Loma, California. He's a Republican, married, and has a daughter and young son, Reagan, who was named after the fortieth president.

Because of this unwanted publicity, the Guard command came down hard on Dominguez. It accused him of making the American military appear weak, especially in the eyes of the insurgents. As punishment, he was stripped of all his gear, weapon, and even his own squad. And yet, for all the grief and abuse he endured, Dominguez never made it to Iraq with his battalion. While in Kuwait, he developed a potentially fatal medical condition and was evacuated to Germany on a hospital plane. The army veteran is back home in Southern California with his family. These days, when speaking to Dominguez, you immediately detect a resigned weariness in his voice. This formerly gung-ho squad leader is sad, depressed, and can't sleep—an indirect consequence of trying to tell the truth publicly about the Guard because he wanted to save lives on the battlefield.

■　■　■

I decided to speak out because it's the difference between life or death. I'm very in touch with my mortality. It's the difference between being prepared and not being prepared. At forty-five, I don't feel like bullets can bounce off my chest anymore like I did when I was eighteen. That's why the military really loves teenagers who think that nothing bad can happen to them.

I don't know that by speaking out it was bravery. Maybe it was stupidity. It's just a matter of survival. I loved my men, and I didn't want anything to happen to them. I had to lead by example. How could I not put my name to my objections? I was responsible for nine men in my squad as their squad leader. I made commitments to them and to most of their mothers and fathers that I would bring them back home from Iraq in one piece.

The U.S. Army says that we train like we fight, but in reality, the National Guard does not get trained like we fight—because if we did, we'd have everything that you need up front. The quality of the training was so poor and pathetic in our dumb boot-camp environment. Our Humvees were breaking down all the time. Mexico has better equipment, and in certain instances, our Humvees were worse than the Mexican army's. I would have liked to take the battalion colonel, the command sergeant major, and Secretary of Defense Rumsfeld and put them in a light-skin Hummer and let them do the patrols in Iraq. See how quickly they'd get the proper equipment up front.

I've been a Republican since I was eighteen, and I have voted Republican since then. But I'm now very conflicted about what my political party stands for. My faith in the system has collapsed. I can no longer support my commander-in-chief. I don't believe that Bush was being truthful about Iraq, and I certainly do not support Rumsfeld because he has not been truthful with the people of the United States and he has certainly not cared for his soldiers.

I was willing to lay my life down for my country, and if anybody can question that, they're guilty of treason, not me. There's a price to pay, and I paid it. The only thing I wasn't willing to do was go to prison. I have a fourteen-month-old son, a daughter, and a wife. I cannot afford to go to jail.

I exercised my freedom of speech. Do you know that the majority of us on the base were not even allowed to vote in the recent presidential election? The system's so broken down. They passed around the roster for those who wanted to vote, and then they said they were going to obtain absentee ballots for us. Only a very few people wanted to vote. The majority of us did not receive these ballots. I personally went up my chain of command to notify them that I needed to get my absentee ballot, but they just kept passing the buck and the time came and went, and I did not get to vote.

I have never been this outspoken before. You might say it's out of character. I grew up in Southern California. I lived in Pomona and in Claremont and Alta Loma and Orange County. So I kind of moved a bit. I also lived in Mexico for about twelve years. I was five years old when I moved to Mexico. I lived there with my grandmother in Baja, in Ensenada, and when she passed away in 1973, I moved with my mother permanently back to the U.S. I had to learn to speak English.

When I moved in with my mom in junior high school, my first real job was delivering newspapers with a friend. I never went to college. I also worked at a convalescent home. I then saw an ad in the newspaper for a bank loan officer, and I went in and applied. I somehow managed to impress the executive of the company who interviewed me because he liked the fact that I was fluent in Spanish. He hired me as a loan-officer trainee, making $1,500 a month. That was a lot of money for someone with no experience. This was in 1987. That's when I got into the mortgage business. He then gave me a list of broker names and told me to call them and solicit them for business. Later on, I became an underwriter—that's the guy who approves the loans—and from there, I was made an underwriting department manager and sales manager, and before you know it, credit manager, and then vice president.

I've been in the military off and on since 1977. No one ever coerced me into signing my military contract. My first contract was signed at the age of seventeen; my mother had to co-sign. I started out in the Marine Corps Reserve. I was a load master on a C-130E; they are the big cargo planes. I've only been four years in this National Guard unit, which is based in Fullerton, California. Normally, you're scheduled to train one weekend out of the month and two weeks during the summer months.

The men in my squad varied in age. The youngest was nineteen and I was the oldest; in fact, I was the oldest in the platoon. I would say on average, they were in their mid-twenties. One of them was a Brink's armored vehicle security officer. There was a community college campus policeman. The rest were students. I loved them like they were my blood. I cared a lot for them.

We didn't need six months of training at Fort Bliss. Give us two months. Give us the right training and equipment and we will prevail. We went through a lot of really rudimentary basic training, such as going over the weapons. This is an M-4 rifle; this is what its maximum range is. Stuff that we already knew. It's okay to practice, because the basics are critical, but it's a little bit too late to be working on the basics when you're getting ready to go into combat.

My guys weren't even issued the proper weapons for training. We were using the M-4 carbine, and, of course, there's the M-16. The M-4 carbine is the most modern weapon that the Army has for an infantryman. But for the designated squad marksmen who can take down an enemy target at about 600 meters, the M-4 doesn't work that way. Neither does the M-16. An M-14 is what they need.

· The California National Guard is just broke. You're always short on training because there's no money for the state to support it. If you just look at your local National Guard armories in California, they're buildings from the 1950s and 1960s. They're dilapidated, falling apart. Unless you happen to go to a headquarters that's semi-new, everything else is garbage. Most other states support their National Guard. California is just absolutely horrific when it comes to that.

Another problem I found in the National Guard was incompetent leadership. The officers don't receive the same level of training in the National Guard as their active-duty counterparts do, and I'll tell you why. An officer right out of college joins the Guard, and he receives a commission and gets sent to officer candidates' school on a weekend basis. That is not intensive enough to ensure a high quality of leadership. The Guard is so short of men to fill its officer ranks that rather than demote or fire incompetent officers, it just transfers them to another position and then they get promoted. We have a lot of sergeant majors that way.

Everybody complains about the training and equipment in the Guard, but nothing really happens. I mean, you can complain to the chain of command, but the chain of command really doesn't care; they're here to make their rank or get the next star. I realized how cruel it really is when you just become another body to be thrown into the grinder. That's why I decided to speak to the *Los Angeles Times* reporter.

Once the article appeared, the base's upper command immediately accused me of endangering the military and possibly aiding the enemy. I was told by the public affairs officer that the *Times* article would probably be grabbed onto by Al Qaeda and Al Jazeera, and that we would be shown to be unmotivated and unwilling to fight. That's so untrue. You cannot be sending us to war if you're not going to give us the best of the best to fight it with.

A phone call was also made to my wife, Erlisa, that was threatening in nature. The person—it was a woman who was a family support coordinator for our company—had called on behalf of my first sergeant. She said there would be retaliation from "up."

The Guard command took away my gear and weapon. They were going to give me a conditional release, which would have released me from active duty and entirely from the Army, but to accept their conditions, it would have meant losing my pension. On December 6, 2004, the Guard sent me home on leave. I discussed their conditions with my wife Erlisa, and she felt that they were unacceptable. I then called the command sergeant major and told him that. Within three hours, I was notified that I was going to be retained in the same battalion, but transferred to a different company. That meant I would lose command of my squad and my men. However, I was told that I was going to be given another squad, but that never happened. So why did the Guard command back down and allow me to return? Basically, they were short a lot of bodies. I was able-bodied so rather than discard me, I was an asset. It's a numbers game.

When I returned to the base, the command sergeant major called me into his office, and the very first thing that came out of his mouth was "Redemption." And I asked, "'Redemption.' What do you mean by that, sergeant major?" Basically, he felt that I needed to redeem myself for speaking to the reporter.

The lieutenant colonel—our battalion commander—said to us at one of our formations that by speaking to the press, the only thing I achieved was that we would be labeled whiners and complainers. Instead of going out on patrols and doing infantry stuff, we would probably be relegated to doing security-guard-type duty in Iraq. He was blaming me. I was made the scapegoat for an entire company of over 600 men. Some of the men stopped talking to me. Several of them would give me the evil eye. Some of the men who understood the reasons behind what I had said felt intimidated because they saw what was happening to me publicly. So they immediately quieted down. These were kids.

On December 19, after we had a final formation before being released to come home for the holiday season, the lieutenant colonel ordered the entire battalion to fall out of formation and gather around him in a circle. He said to all of us, "You guys can go ahead, when you go home, and speak to the fucking media; it won't make any difference. You want to call the media? You want to give interviews? Go ahead! Has anything better happened? Has anything changed since you spoke to the media? Not a goddamn thing! Is anything going to change? You better fucking believe it's not! The only thing that we got out of this was silk panties." He was referring to our newly issued long johns made out of a synthetic material called Polartec, and so he attributed this additional gear as a result of my going to the media.

In early January 2005, before deploying to the Middle East, we spent two weeks at Fort Polk, Louisiana. They call it the JRTC, or the Joint Readiness Training Center. It was extremely cold in Louisiana, but I still didn't have any of my gear. It hadn't been returned to me. I was missing everything—my individual body armor, weapon, even all my sleeping gear. I only had my personal belongings and the uniform I was wearing. We slept in a tent, but it wasn't properly heated. The temperature was in the twenties, so I had to borrow poncho liners from some other soldiers to cover myself because I did not have a sleeping bag. I kept requesting a sleeping bag, but they told me that they didn't have any extra gear since it had all been shipped to Iraq. So everyone except me slept in their winter gear and winter sleeping bags. It was so cold that I could not sleep because my kidneys hurt so bad.

After arriving in Kuwait, we trained at Camp Buehring for another two weeks before going over the berm into Iraq. I still didn't have my gear, not even a weapon. I was given menial tasks to perform. I really didn't have a job. I was not given any particular duties which would be commensurate to my rank as a staff sergeant. And the entire time they had me sleeping in the same tent as the sergeant major and the colonel so I was within their control. I was soon transferred to brigade headquarters. I was finally issued a weapon. The entire time I was there, I fired six bullets from my M-4 carbine. That was the extent of my training in Kuwait. That's how many bullets it took for me to hit the target, also known as zeroing your weapon.

We never received the armored Humvees either. We were given what's known throughout the army as "Mad Max armor," and, basically, they are ill-fitting rusting steel plates that we were required to install on our vehicles. They afford you limited protection against small arms fire, but they will not protect you against IEDs, or improvised explosive devices. They will not protect you against any RPGs, or rocket-powered grenades. On the floorboards, we were given a directive to just put sandbags. Those things are just a stop-gap measure to deflect an explosion in the event that you run over a mine or some other form of explosive device.

I don't know if it was stress, but one day I was resting in my cot at Camp Buehring when I began to get chest pains. I went to the medic, and they found that I was having an irregular heartbeat, so they ended up evacuating me on a C-17 hospital plane to Ramstein Air Base in Germany.

In Germany they did a battery of tests and decided that I had an irregular heartbeat due to post-traumatic stress disorder, and so from there they evacuated me to Walter Reed Hospital in the United States, and then I was sent to Fort Bliss, Texas, where they told me that I was going to be stationed for the duration of my deployment on medical hold status, unless I refused medical treatment, in which case they would send me home.

I refused medical treatment by the Army. I was processed out and given a separation—not a discharge—from active duty. I came home April 30 and returned to my civilian work as vice president at the bank.

I still can't get these injured young men I saw on the hospital planes out of my mind. I saw horrible, devastating things on my flights back from Kuwait to Germany and then to the United States. I saw guys who were missing limbs. All the catastrophic injuries were due to IEDs. I saw a young man from my flight back to the United States with everything basically gone from his nose all the way down to his throat. All gone.

I still have an irregular heartbeat. It comes and goes. I could be sitting around or lying down; then all of a sudden, my heart begins to flutter. I'll start sweating profusely, and sometimes I get a feeling of claustrophobia. I never had any symptoms like this before in my life. I used to run a hundred miles a month. I have to take medication to put myself to sleep. Doctors gave me a drug called Ambien. I'm usually up until three or four o'clock in the morning.

I had a recent nightmare which involved me watching an insurgent take a chainsaw and neatly remove the top of a man's head. I stood there and heard the man's moans as his blood flowed freely and his life quickly ebbed away. The thick, iron-like smell of blood woke me up. I was drenched in sweat. I could not go back to sleep.

I'm in contact with one sergeant from my old unit. They're based south of Baghdad at Camp Falcon. Three days after they arrived in-country, a taxicab packed with explosives was parked on a road, and as my unit was driving by, the insurgents detonated it. A young man by the name of Corporal Watkins, who was part of Operation Iraqi Freedom back in March 2003, was killed. I knew him personally. He was in his late twenties. I felt anger, a sense of uselessness, powerlessness. I wanted to fly to Iraq to be with my men. But that's only a fantasy.

My wife is having a hard time. She's very supportive of what I did. She believes 100 percent in my having come forward and having stated the facts to the media. She was worried that someone would put a bullet in my back over in Iraq.

I'm not the same man that I used to be. I know I will struggle with this depression until my men come back from Iraq. I don't think that my mind will rest, and I don't even know if I will ever be able to rest. I don't have to duck bullets, but I'm ducking my own monsters. I'm a man of conviction. If I had to do it all over, given the same circumstances, and knowing ahead of time what I've been through, I would do it again.

The Army says that it encourages freedom of speech. I disagree. There is no freedom of speech in the military. I have paid the price for speaking out.

■   ■   ■

Postscript

Throughout the summer and fall of 2005, *Los Angeles Times* reporter Scott Gold continued writing about Dominguez's California National Guard battalion in a series of articles that exposed corruption and widespread misconduct by the unit's soldiers in Iraq. After allegations of prisoner abuse and extortion of local merchants surfaced, battalion commander Lt. Col. Patrick Frey was relieved from duty by military authorities. According to the *Los Angeles Times*, three sergeants were eventually sentenced to military prison and four other soldiers were forced to do hard labor for "their role in abusing Iraqi nationals who were taken into custody near Baghdad and apparently mistaken for insurgents. The abuse involved the use of a stun gun on men who were handcuffed." The beleaguered battalion also experienced one of the worst casualty rates of any Guard units in Iraq. By December 2005, there had been more than 100 wounded and 11 soldiers killed, including Colonel William Wood, a regular Army officer who replaced Frey as battalion commander. Wood died in a roadside bomb explosion after rushing to the aid of a mortally wounded Army captain by the name of Michael MacKinnon. The colonel was the highest-ranking American officer to die in the war.

13

DEMOCRATS READ HIM AND REPUBLICANS HATE HIM

Paul Krugman uses his *New York Times* column to lecture and reprimand the Bush White House.

> "I did have occasional contact with the Kerry presidential campaign, but the *Times* would've fired me in an instant if I were coordinating with them."

As an op-ed columnist for the *New York Times*, Paul Krugman is known as a harsh critic of the Bush presidency. The Princeton economics professor was described by former *Washington Monthly* editor Nicholas Confessore as "the columnist every Democrat in the country feels they need to read and every Bush Republican loves to hate." *Slate's* media critic Jack Shafer considers the topic more acidly: "Paul Krugman's wicked column proves that the paper doesn't mind employing human wrecking balls." Donald Luskin, who writes a finance column for conservative *National Review*, labeled him "America's most dangerous liberal pundit." Luskin even created an informal press club called the "Krugman Truth Squad" in an attempt to undermine his national credibility. (The squad relishes pointing out that Krugman once consulted for Enron and pocketed a hefty $50,000 fee for his efforts.)

Unlike the *Times's* razzle-dazzle wordsmith Maureen Dowd, Krugman's writing style lacks metaphorical flights of fancy. His prose is straightforward, precise, and can often tilt towards wonkish. To drive home a point, he will inject words like "lies" and "dishonest" into commentary about some White House misdeed or flawed policy. Longtime readers of Krugman's column recognize his familiar targets: tax cuts favoring the rich; health care crisis; privatizing Social Security; budget mismanagement; the mushrooming deficit; shameless gutting of environmental protection laws; special-interest cronyism; and, of course, the war in Iraq.

Before he became a well-known debunker of Bushonomics with its reliance on corporate giveaways and back room deal-making, Krugman flirted with the promise of Clintonomics and how to address the problem of income inequality. Rumors began to swirl around Washington in 1992 that Krugman was a leading candidate to head the President's Council of Economics Advisers. When he was passed over for this, or any other appointment in the new administration, insiders thought that the reason was due to his temperament. His outspokenness made him unsuited for Beltway politics; he also seemed unable to get along with Clinton economic transition team members Robert Reich and Ira Magaziner.

For a long time, Krugman exhibited little patience for economic policy entrepreneurs who contributed essays to popular magazines instead of engaging in serious academic work. But if he started out as an ivory-tower purist defending the esoteric world of economics and international finance, Krugman soon had a change of heart. Why sit on the sidelines and cede the public debate to unqualified individuals? And so, he began cranking out articles for *Fortune, Slate*, and *The New York Times Magazine*. In 1999, *Times* editorial page editor Howell Raines wanted to add a columnist who could explain finance and the new economy *zeitgeist* to a general audience. Krugman got the op-ed nod.

In the paperback edition of *The Great Unraveling*, which is a collection of his columns, Krugman writes that he "originally expected his *Times* column to be mainly focused on business and international economics, not domestic politics. But as the wreckage accumulated, I've found it necessary to try to explain why just our policies are so bad." He later discloses, "Few things I have written have generated as much hate mail as the columns in which I accused the administration of exploiting September 11 for political gain."

At the intellectual core of his political beliefs, Krugman is a big-picture optimist, a warm and fuzzy neo-New Deal softie. He grew up in Long Island, New York, then studied economics at Yale and M.I.T. (later joining each faculty). He is a devout believer in the self-correcting, healing properties of democracy. "I am convinced the American public will turn on the Bush people," he says, "because I believe that they are going to make such a complete mess of the country."

■   ■   ■

When I write a column that really bothers people, even something about Bush's personal character or, oddly, something that says that the economy isn't doing too great, I can get up to 1,500 hostile e-mails. I don't even know how many letters. There were a couple of times when I was giving a big speech to a couple of thousand people, and the organizers tried to make sure that they had someone there for security. But there has never been anything like a physical assault. There have been attempts to discredit me personally; trying to make a scandal out of nothing. Bush supporters are very hard, bold people. If I had anything in my personal life they could use, I'm sure they would.

I get very little feedback from colleagues in the industry. What makes me an iconoclast is that my life is that of a college professor. I live here in Princeton. I am rarely in New York or Washington. I'm simply not part of that set. I have an unfair advantage over journalists, which is that this is my second job. If I got fired, my income would probably go up. In some ways, I'm not subject to the career pressure, although I am frightened. If you're not a hard-line right-winger and you're not personally frightened by what America may be like and what the pressures on people who are critics might be, then you are just not paying attention.

I do feel like I've been out ahead on issues, but the funny thing is that what I've said on substance really shouldn't even be controversial. I often find that what I've said or written as crazy or radical becomes conventional wisdom six months or a year later.

The *Times* has maybe a couple of million people who read the paper, and not all of them carefully. I'd like to think that I actually shifted the 2004 election coverage a little bit. I feel best about what the column does when I see someone using one of my standard lines without attribution, and then I know that I've actually managed to shift the discourse a little bit. Surely this has been an object lesson in the limits of direct persuasion.

I did have occasional contact with the Kerry presidential campaign, but the *Times* would've fired me in an instant if I were coordinating with them. The *Times* still holds to that standard. We don't want to be like George Will, who coached Reagan before the debates and wrote after the debates about what a great job Reagan did.

I'm also on Air America Radio. I have fun for an hour with Al Franken, and I hope it does somebody some good. Franken is much more careful than your ordinary average news analyst. My problem is I don't know who listens to talk radio or how it works.

I'd say a good third of the American public really does more or less catch what is going on and is very revolted by what is happening; but it is not enough, obviously. It is a large electorate. If people really understood what was happening, we would have huge majorities of people saying, "Not in our name!" It is not occurring. The Republican Party is a very well-organized and very powerful coalition; there are schisms, but between the lure of power and the power of money, it holds together much more effectively than the other side.

I am extremely forgiving with the public and less so with the media. People have lives. They're busy. They have jobs and kids, and they pick up what's happening on the fly. If you ask the man in the street what was the surplus in 2000, or what's the deficit, it would appear that a very small fraction would give anywhere close to the actual numbers. They rely upon the media, particularly television, to give them a sense of what is going on. Watching the news on TV, what sense would you have of the severity of what's been happening?

If you are prepared to read the inside stories of the leading newspapers, you can naturally find out a lot about what's happening. But often not on Page 1. I have written at length about the propensity for the media to write even-handed stories, one side and the other side, even where there is no equivalence or there's a false equivalence. On one of those talk shows, someone used my line that, "If the Earth were flat, the headline would read: 'Shape of the Earth Viewed Different.'" That is a false equivalence. There are media organizations that are trying to have it both ways, and to be in the middle, but are in fact not just presenting a false equivalence, they are actually only presenting the right-wing point of view. Just after the 2004 election, CNN ran a piece about Social Security privatization, and they had two outside experts: one from the American Enterprise Institute and one from the Heritage Foundation. The notion now of fair coverage is to have one right-wing organization and one extremely right-wing organization comment on the issue. Fox News is probably beyond repair. Fox has been an enormous aid to the right-wing movement and its radical policies.

You don't want to lose sight of the fact that criticism of the right-wing will in time be vindicated by events. The majority of Bush supporters, according to some of the polls, still believe that the war in Iraq is going well, but that is not an illusion that is going to be sustainable over a period of years. Bush is still using the halo of defender of national security and obscuring the mess he has made of that. There will come a time when it is possible to capitalize on the truth, to say, "Hey look, these people have been leading us very much down the wrong track." The Bush people show an uncanny incompetence when it comes to actually dealing with real things as opposed to politics, and that will bring them down in the end. In the 2004 election, 51 percent of the public was blinded by the majesty of office, wartime rhetoric, and a heavy public-relations campaign. That doesn't last indefinitely. What does worry me is the abuse of the power of office and the basic machine of politics. Because of the combination of financial strangulation and intimidation of opposition, it may be very, very hard to change. Even though you have a very dissatisfied public, it may be difficult to challenge the Bush people. The whole point about the cult of personality around Bush is that to be patriotic means supporting and even adulating the guy in the Oval Office.

If I want to be downbeat, I'd look at my colleague, Larry Bartels, in the political science department at Princeton who has some statistical analyses which say that American voters really only pay attention to what has been happening in the last few months before the election, and even what you think of as the great realignments of history are only a luck of the draw. Even with Franklin Roosevelt. It wasn't that the people were demanding a New Deal; he just was lucky on the cycle. I'm not sure that view's right.

It is very hard to predict how long it will take, but somewhere along the line, there will be a growing backlash. There are many factors regarding how it will play out. There is Iraq, which is an obvious catastrophic sham. There is a dollar crisis. The U.S. is spending 5 percent more than it earns; that can't go on. The question is whether the process of the dollar's fall does a lot of damage to the economy. There is a lot of disagreement about that, but I've been swinging toward the catastrophic side the more I look at it. It's not going to be fun for anybody. It's going to mean probably lots of problems with people who have debts, especially adjustable rate mortgages. This is really uncharted territory.

We have never seen a First World country, let alone a country with the world's premier currency, be irresponsible on this scale. It is very hard to believe that the dollar crisis is going to hold off for four more years. I suspect the day of reckoning is coming during this presidential term, but who knows?

The right-wing's underlying ideology is starve the people. You undermine the revenue basis for the welfare state since Social Security and Medicare are extremely popular programs. You don't attack them directly; you cut taxes and say, "Oh, we don't have the revenue; we've got to have cuts." The theory is that when the dust settles, the right-wing gets what it wants. What I think will actually happen is that there will be a fiscal crisis and they end up being booted out.

We're being menaced by the right-wing coalition and partly by the religious right. It is really quite extreme on the religious side. They are scary people. There is nothing quite as bad as people who believe that their point of view is God's point of view and that any criticism is illegitimate. They have a deep level of intolerance. There were only a few times in American history when people were as intolerant as, say, Tom DeLay in that position of political power. We really have people who are deeply at war with modern America. Newt Gingrich was obviously somebody I didn't approve of, but he was not nearly as scary a person as DeLay.

The Democrats need some domestic issues if they are really going to stand for something. The truth is that health care is a very good one, partly because the system is cracking anyway. Kerry had a pretty good health care proposal in the

2004 campaign. I would like something even bolder. I wrote a column some-where back in the end of summer 2004 where I actually went through sixty days of network television newscast transcripts to see whether there had even been a single report that would have allowed you to get some sense about the differences in the candidates' health care platforms.

In terms of Social Security privatization, I am afraid that for the most part, I'll continue to be there to try to bully my colleagues in the media into report-ing that clearly, but it may not work. I suspect the press reporting will not be very good on that subject. The only thing you can say is that privatization might fool the voters, but it won't fool the financial markets. People think that they are going to have the freedom to invest the money as they like. As a practical mat-ter, it can't be done because the brokerage fees would be killing.

The individual accounts are too small, so it is going to be more like a giant mutual fund in which the manager of the funds decides how it goes. Money will be shifted to the stock market for sure. And then there will be all kinds of wor-ries: Will it be politicized? Whose stocks? A lot of questions haven't been an-swered. In fact, it was Social Security that radicalized me back in 2000 when I realized that Bush was lying about what the plan would entail—and nothing has changed. I was always a big fan of George Orwell. That was when I first began to use the word "Orwellian" to describe the Bush people.

In my other life, I spent a lot of time studying Third World countries, and there you often have really bad regimes that survive for quite a while by the combination of nationalism and intimidation and control of the press. But, on the average, the tendency has been that when the screw-ups got bad enough, there would be a public outpouring of anger and then the regimes are gone. In one of the columns I wrote before the 2004 election, I talked about Argentina, where you had a junta, which was brutal and incompetent, but nonetheless had a huge upwelling of public support because they managed to create a war psy-chology. Eventually it was thrown out. You do have a democratic government in Argentina. So stuff does happen. Even in the worst cases.

14

ARREST IN PEACE

Anti-war activist Kathy Kelly devotes her life to
civil disobedience.

> "If you want to understand poverty in our
> country, prisons are the place to go."

A wisp of a woman with an immense heart, Kathy Kelly has dedicated her life to
peace and social justice. The fifty-one-year-old Jesuit-trained humanitarian blends
compassion, pacifism, and social activism in both traditional and trailblazing ways.
She's taught school in Chicago's bleakest neighborhoods, ladled out food in soup
kitchens to homeless and drug addicts, protested outside the gates of the U.S.
Army's Fort Benning military base where Central American paramilitary units un-
dergo combat training at the School of Americas, traveled to Iraq as part of an international peace mission prior to the first Gulf War, and in 1996, co-founded
Voices of the Wilderness, which defied UN-imposed economic sanctions by directly flying in medical supplies to Iraqi citizens.

Her friend, legendary oral historian Studs Terkel, calls Kelly "The Pilgrim" because she "has visited more countries, cities and small towns than anyone I have
ever known. Her pilgrimages have one purpose: to reveal the lives of innocent
war victims." She's made more than twenty trips to Iraq.

Her civil-disobedience rap sheet is lengthy. She's been arrested over sixty
times. The first entry dates back to the Cold War era when she planted seeds of
corn at an ICBM missile silo site in Missouri. She spent six months in a federal
prison for that direct action. Her recidivism is inspired, in part, by the civil rights
movement. "What [civil rights] leaders would do," she once told a reporter, "is
communicate very clearly to the arresting officers that once they were freed, they
weren't going to go away. They'd come back again." By sticking only to peaceful
protests and demonstrations, she said that she "was appealing to a higher command, a love command. If you do it, do it lovingly."

Nominated twice for the Nobel Peace Prize, the once-married activist owns no car and is a war tax refuser. Despite her small size—she's five-foot-one and weighs around 100 pounds, except when fasting—she stands tall as a living legend in the peace community. In early 2003, following a month-long fasting-for-peace vigil outside the United Nations in New York City, she traveled to Iraq and was staying in Baghdad when the bombs began falling during the initial phase of the U.S. invasion. "I was sitting in a basement bomb shelter of the Al Fanar hotel shielding a little Iraqi girl in my arms," recalled Kelly in an interview with *Chicago* magazine, and "I whispered to her in Arabic the words to 'We Shall Overcome.'"

After leaving Iraq in May 2003, her next anti-war destination was the U.S. Navy's ELF/Trident transmitter site in the woods of northern Wisconsin, where she was arrested with eleven other demonstrators. ELF is an acronym for Extremely Low-Frequency waves, a system used to trigger cruise missiles, which were used during the shock and awe phase of the war in Iraq.

She spent the early part of 2005 serving a ninety-day federal prison stretch following a protest gathering outside Fort Benning. Within weeks of her release, Kelly was arrested yet again for participating in an anti-war sit-down inside Senator Richard Durbin's (D-Illinois) Chicago office.

Kelly is committed to using peaceful means to influence military policy. For someone who has witnessed so much grief and tragedy in war zones, she knows no other way to live. "The much more difficult thing to cope with is having been at the bedsides of Iraqi children who are not going to make it," she says. "The imploring eyes of mothers handing their baby to you. Not knowing what to say and then coming back to the United States and thinking, 'Well, if I don't say something, who will?' But somehow the voices of these children are, at some point, going to reach people's hearts. I still believe that."

■   ■   ■

I live in the uptown area on the north side of Chicago. I've lived in the same apartment since 1980. But when I moved here, it was literally one of the poorest neighborhoods in Chicago. It's now become quite transformed. I grew up on the southwest side of Chicago in an area that was fairly safe and secure. It was called Garfield Ridge. It was a working class neighborhood. Blue collar. It was Irish, German, Polish, Italian. I barely knew anybody who wasn't Catholic. It was a very homogenous sort of environment. People were concerned with raising kids. It also was a neighborhood where people did not want to lose their property value. They felt that if African-Americans moved in, that's what would happen. My family certainly did not have these attitudes. We would have been in a lotta trouble if we were to utter racist epithets at home.

We went half a day to a Catholic school and half a day to a public school. As it turned out in this little Catholic school, the teachers were quite young. Very energetic, very enthused by the Berrigan brothers and their actions in opposition to the Vietnam War. Very much taken with Martin Luther King's movement. We learned about all of that. It was interesting. It was exciting. It was at a time when it was unusual for people to impart those kinds of stories and ideas.

I can trace an emotional groove that was more or less instilled after watching the film *Night and Fog*. It was made by French artists and historians, who after World War II went to the death camps and filmed the remains. With narration and a very haunting mixture of classical music in the background, they simply showed mounds of blankets that were made from human hair and lamp shades made from human flesh. It seemed to me at the time that it would have made so much sense for people who lived nearby to do something to stop this. I remember hoping, wishing, yearning that I would never sit on my hands in the face of some unspeakable evil and do nothing.

I would have been a sophomore in high school, about fourteen or fifteen. I also remember reading Leonard Cohen's poems in *Spice Box of Earth* and just being utterly amazed at how important it was for people to speak up. But then, all I can tell you is, I went through the Vietnam War like *Brigadoon in the Mist*. I didn't get involved. I hung out with people who were conscientious objectors, but the idea of myself being active in something to try to stop the war was just beyond my horizon.

Even though I was a fairly late bloomer, I'm glad that there was time for a little bit of maturing on my part—because I could imagine I might have gotten somewhat in over my head. I'm glad that I had time to become very thoroughly grounded in nonviolence—as an ideal—before I started to become involved in activism. And I'm certainly glad that my activism intersected with meeting some of the finest people in the world.

Matters starting changing for me in graduate school at the Chicago Theological Seminary. I was studying for a theology degree. A lot of my course work was being done at the Jesuit School of Theology. At one point, what I really wanted to do was grab a truck driver or construction worker and say, "Can I take you out for a beer?" Just anything other than always exchanging ideas with other like-minded grad students in theology. It was a bit of an academic ghetto, though it was a privileged place to be in many ways. That would have been '77, '78. By then, I knew about the activities of some groups like the Catholic Worker. I had been reading William Stringfellow's *An Affect for Christian and Other Strangers in an Alien Land.* I knew about liberation theology going on in Central and South America, but didn't feel too compelled to move outside of a very comfortable zone. Finally two guys from the Catholic Worker on the North Side of Chicago came down to the South Side and left a note on my door saying, "Instead of sending checks, why don't you come up and visit us sometime?" I thought I better at least go up there and see what's happening.

They ran a House of Hospitality, a drop-in shelter for women in the daytime, and an alternative school. They made visits to shut-ins. Cooking in a soup kitchen, taking kids to summer camp, for me, it was kind of a relief to be able to help out and give some expression to this pent-up desire to try to make a difference. I was so impressed by what was happening that in two months I was living up there.

I met a man at the House of Hospitality. His name was Karl Meyer. He had run a House of Hospitality for thirteen years. He was a stalwart war tax refuser. His father had been in Congress. Karl had been in prison for two years during the Vietnam War, so he had that aura of the true radical. He was somebody whose articles I had faithfully Xeroxed and distributed to the kids in my class I was teaching at a Jesuit school. I had a huge crush on him. He came into the soup kitchen one night to help. I remember he was cleaning urinals or something and I very shyly let him know that I was using his materials in my class. He was pleased to know that. So I got to know him. Coming over to Karl's apartment, you'd get a chance to look at these old photos. He had this gravelly authoritarian voice, and so he really was wise. He was in his forties.

And then at one point, another activist named Roy Bourgeois had moved to the neighborhood, and we all loved him. Roy was very important to many of us. He was sent to prison for six months for having thrown blood on a pillar of the Pentagon after affixing a poster protesting the murder of Bishop Oscar Romeo in El Salvador. So we held vigils praying for people in El Salvador and praying for Roy. We were very pious. I remember Karl coming in one day on his roller skates and he said, "Wow, you can all pray, but I'm going to do something that Roy would do if he were at liberty." That was at the time of the draft registration, so we went with Karl and sang songs inside the post office. Our singing echoed throughout the post office, and we were arrested for disturbing the peace. It was my first time ever being arrested so Karl nursed me through arrest, trial, court — and they were really of no consequence. A slap on the wrist was all that one got. But it meant a lot in the Jesuit school where I was teaching. It branded me. As soon as we were let go, we'd go back and do it again. I'd been arrested five times with Karl. By then, we had gotten to know one another much better, and we married in 1979.

I didn't care about income very much. I didn't know anybody at the time who owned a car or who would darken the door of a firsthand store or think about having job security. All of us were much more concerned with how we could effectively become tax refusers and organize our time so that we'd be able to take our shifts at the shelter and cook for the soup kitchen. I really couldn't imagine having been together with a more dynamic or interesting group of people. And then there were the people who were on the streets. They also became friends and dropped by. You see, the wonderful thing about the Catholic Worker is what we learned from Karl, and that is not wanting to fix people. Just admire and enjoy people where they're at. If you don't have to try to fix people, it's a big relief really. If a person knows you are approaching him or her with respect, curiosity, and ready affection, I think that makes a big difference and allows for much more crossing the divide that separates you.

By then, I was no longer teaching at St. Ignatius College Prep School in Chicago, which I had done for six years through 1986. I was now teaching in a high school that had been started by this do-gooder's ghetto group. It was a very small school. We had about fifty kids. They were Hispanic and black primarily, some Appalachian whites. Each year, there would be at least three kids killed. Drive-by shootings. Standing on the wrong corner peddling drugs. There would literally be more funerals than graduations. And then one day when I came into school, I could tell that everybody was bracing to tell me more bad news. It involved a young boy by the name of Shaun Powell. I think he was selling drugs and got a bit greedy and thought that if he stood on another corner he would be able to make more money; someone from an opposing drug-selling group must have killed him. When I heard about Shaun's death, I just remember sitting down and realizing, "I can't pretend that this is normal. I can't go on like this." Shaun was tall. You looked at this kid and thought, "God, he must be an incredible basketball player." Very handsome face. His eyes were always kind of blazing. His mom was a prostitute. He'd sit out on the front porch and wait until it was okay to go inside. He really could write. He also had a horrible temper. He would go into sulking fits. But he could be cajoled. He knew that I admired his writing quite honestly, and he liked reading. He wasn't an easy kid to work with. I had all the kids keep a three-ring binder of their writing. Shaun would make me hang on to his, because I think he knew that if he died, he wanted to make sure I'd have it to give to his mom. So his death was the real turning point for me. It was the recognition that there was never enough that we could do to try to create a better world for Shaun or any of the kids. They'd committed no crime except being born into situations of real affliction.

I knew some very fine people, some of them from the suburbs of Chicago who had been going out to Missouri and to the missile silos that surround Kansas City. There were 150 ICBMs. Those missiles were aimed at women and children in the Soviet Union, and their missiles were aimed back at us. The Cold War was a reality. Two local heroes of the civil rights movement, Jean and Joe Gump, had gone to the missile silos. They had done an action. She got an eight-year prison sentence and her husband, Joe, in the next year got a four-year sentence. I'd been a support person for Joe when he did his action. It just seemed to me that it was my turn.

I was accompanied by about twenty-five people from the Milwaukee-Chicago-Madison group. We had met consistently throughout the year. Our action was to go to nuclear missile silos and plant corn on top of the sites. We had mapped out all the missile silos throughout the Midwest in North Dakota, Missouri, and Kansas. There are 1,000 buried in the Midwest. But we knew the Kansas City area quite well. I went by myself to this site the first day. There were four soldiers who came and surrounded the site. They had their guns out and ordered all personnel to clear the site. They opened the gate. I was kneeling on the ground. The soldier behind me had a gun aimed at me. I asked him, "Do you think the corn will grow?" He said, "I don't know, ma'am. But I sure hope so." It was a nice moment. I remember that very, very much. That young guy was exceptional in his desire to be kind. As soon as we were taken to jail and let out, we went right back and did it again and again and again. So I was looking at a potential thirty months. I was pretty relieved when I was sentenced to only a year in prison.

I served that year in a maximum security prison in Lexington, Kentucky, at the Lexington Federal Correction Institute. While we were all in prison, we compiled essays that later went into a book called *Prisoners on Purpose: A Prisoner's Guide to Prisons and Jails of the United States*. We all had an easy consensus. County jails were, by far, the worst. If you could manage your way through two months in a county jail, federal prison would be quite a bit easier in terms of conditions.

There is no oversight in the county jails. The people who run them get a contract from the federal government to house prisoners. The conditions inside the jails are Dickensian. They are really bad. In that Kansas county jail, the bullpen—which had once been the holding pen for male prisoners—was converted into the living quarters for women prisoners. It was a very small place with just enough room for six bunk beds and an occasional extra mat on the ground. It had a chow hatch, table, and a TV that never stopped. Fluorescent light that never went out. One toilet, exposed to anybody who walked by. Three sides of the bullpen were open to the guards; no solid walls. A miasma cloud of smoke because everyone was smoking. We never went outside for two months.

When I walked into that cell, I often joked that I looked like a poster girl for what the Soviet Union did to their prisoners. I was ninety-five pounds. My hair was standing on end. I had pink eye. I had a respiratory infection. I'd just come out from major surgery. I had diseased tissue on my lungs from a congenital problem, and I had a collapsed lung. I had a broken rib from surgery. I could barely stick my mattress inside the pillow-case type of slip. I was sneezing and obviously not well. One of the women prisoners rolled her eyes and asked what she ever did so wrong to be "locked up with this white motherfucker." I would say that I was quite nervous. I thought, "Oh no! These women are not going to be too charmed to have this crowded cell filled with my germ warfare here." I remember calling Karl and saying, "I'm not sure I can do this." And he said, "Well, you've done things you didn't want to do before when you did have a choice. I don't know why you wouldn't do this now when you don't have a choice." That was just what I needed to hear. It kind of got me. The rudder was okay. Within three days, I was their mascot. The women were extraordinarily kind, interested, conversant. I got to know them. We came from different backgrounds certainly. They were curious why I could have made bail, but chose not to do it. That was hard for them to understand. They couldn't afford bail or weren't allowed bail. They would have liked to be with their children and sorting their lives out and not be held in a county jail. I told them that it was up to the government to hold me. I didn't think I had committed a crime. The missile silos were the crime. The jail system was a crime.

If you're white and educated, you'll be insulated to some extent from the punishment and misfortune that befalls people like these women. They never got an economic stake in the community by any stretch of the imagination. And so, they got involved in the drug trade. Some became addicts. Their lives went out of control. Violence was a part of their lives. But if I were to ask, "Who poses a threat to you, to me, to anyone in this country now?" it would not be the women I've met in prison. It would be the people who are manufacturing acid rain, the people who are manufacturing nuclear weapons, the people who are ravaging the topsoils. There are many ways in which environmental degradation and corporate stupidity jeopardize people's lives in very real ways. Oh, I'll admit that I am by no means virtuous when it comes to consumption. To bring it closer to home, we are all consumers of stuff that is bad for us much of the time. But it's not the person who is doing a back-alley drug transaction that is threatening your average person in the United States.

I would wake up as early as I could in the county jail, four in the morning if I could possibly get myself out of bed, because then it would be completely quiet for a while and I could read Howard Zinn's *The People's History of the United States*. Then I followed that up with *Bury My Heart at Wounded Knee*. I was reading Scriptures pretty often too, and exchanging letters with other friends who were in other prisons. I remember feeling connected with them because I'd taken my own activism about as far as I could.

If you're in a county jail, there almost reliably will come a minister rapping on the bars asking if you want him or her to pray with you. Most of the time it will be a right-wing evangelical offering a fundamentalist interpretation of Scriptures. I would see people almost beating their heads with their Bibles. It was a view that disturbed me. They felt they were wrongful people and deserved to be punished. If God didn't want them inside this prison, they wouldn't have been here. It was this sort of fatalism that I was happy to have moved away from.

At one point, a woman had come into the cell who had been given a driving-under-the-influence citation. For some reason, she had to spend the night in our bullpen. As she was leaving, I asked "Could we have your newspaper?" And she said, "Oh no, honey. This is yesterday's. I'll get you today's newspaper." I said, "No, we'd like that newspaper. Because when we don't have toilet paper, we use newspaper." She was so offended by prisoners not getting toilet paper that she slapped a lawsuit against the jail. The guy who ran the jail was furious. He came bursting in, yelling, "Which one of you bitches had the nerve to say we don't give you toilet paper?" And all the other women in the cell said, "It must have been Missiles." They called me Missiles for short. They said, "She thinks she's living in a hotel." I was amazed. By then, I thought we had a camaraderie. Then I saw everybody point the finger at me. The guard then polled every person and asked them, "Did you ever have any experience where your every need was not met in this here bullpen?" And each of the women said, "Yeah, you take good care of us." I was dumbfounded. When it came to me, I said, "You don't give us toilet paper. We don't get sanitary napkins. We scream and holler all day to get paper towels. There are no cleaning supplies. The shower curtain is ripped. The lights are on all night. We haven't been outside for two months. You shouldn't be running a kennel for dogs much less a place where humans live." So he got pretty angry. When he left, I couldn't understand why nobody agreed with me. Then a cup of Kool-Aid spilled on the floor and it was sticky and everybody was screaming for paper towels that never came. Finally when I was in federal prison, I asked one of the women, "What was going on that day?" She told me, "Don't you get it? The guard could have taken away your good time, or made it impossible to see a lawyer." I couldn't believe that I was so dense not to have figured that out. But I learned so much from those women. It taught me that if you want to understand poverty in our country, prisons are the place to go.

When I entered the federal prison, there were fifty-eight of us and we were given a sixth-grade literacy test, and twelve of the fifty-eight passed the test. So to whom much is given, much is required. I spent a lot of time in the library typing letters for people. Actually, sometimes reading letters for people. I did a fair amount of reading. I had a boatload of correspondence to catch up with. I was assigned to work in the courtyard picking up cigarette butts. I tended the flowers a little bit. I was very extroverted. I got to know a lot of the women quite well. I wrote profiles of five of the women I got to know best. Those profiles are finally seeing the light of day in a book I just got published called *Other Lands Have Dreams*.

After I left the federal prison in 1990, I became a part-time volunteer teaching sixth graders. Oh boy! Very, very difficult. It was in a neighborhood in Chicago that was close to Cabrini-Green. A very bereft area called Horner Homes near Madison and Ashland. It wasn't my class of sixth graders. I was helping someone out who had just about thrown in the towel.

There were quite a number of Central American refugees who had moved into our neighborhood. Karl and I always kept what others called a crash room. There was always someone living with us. Those who were in the process of seeking asylum, often having been arrested and tortured in the past. We had also housed a young Nicaraguan boy who wanted to avoid the draft into the Sandinista army. His family was more sympathetic to the Contras. But we said that we would support anybody, whenever we could, who wanted to avoid picking up arms and killing other people. I used my war tax refuser money to pay for his tuition at a Catholic high school. I felt there was some balance there.

The Jesuits had been highly regarded in El Salvador. They helped to educate the young. But then Archbishop Romero had been slain and four nuns had been raped and killed. This sent shock waves here. There were also massive killings of union leaders in Honduras and Guatemala; you couldn't just look away. The U.S. government was worried that the Sandinistas were going to come over the Texas border and harm us. Meanwhile, we were massively destroying cultures. The Christmas season became unbearable. Congressional legislators wanted to go home for Christmas; they went ahead and rammed through one more law: supporting the mercenaries, supporting the Contras, supporting the death squads in El Salvador. And meanwhile, everybody would go to church and say, "Wasn't King Herod bad?"

The situation seemed to beg for further action. So, for twenty-eight days, I became involved in a water-only fast in front of Fort Benning, Georgia, where the School of Americas—a military combat training school—is located. Graduates of this school were also on the list of people who had been convicted of crimes ranging from massacres and disappearances to torture. The military would like to say that there were a few bad apples. But it's really not the case. There were many people. All you had to do was to compare those graduation lists from the school with some of the people who'd already been convicted or identified as perpetrators of these crimes. So it was the logical spot to go protest.

It was also a great retreat for me. There was a sense of relief in being able to fold into the community of people who were fasting in front of the base. Twenty-eight days spent with lots of time to read and reflect. Because we were just fasting, there really wasn't anything else to do—except read and learn from the others who were there. There were about a dozen of us. They had experiences as missionaries. They were well-versed in history. For me, it was also a time of readiness for I didn't know what.

At the time, Iraq had already invaded Kuwait. Economic sanctions had been imposed. It really seemed likely that the United States was going to be at war. I was waiting to get word that I could join the Gulf peace team. They were a group of people living in London who had the idea to bring a large group of people from different parts all over the world right to the borders between Kuwait and Iraq, and Saudi Arabia and Iraq, and put camps on each side of the border, and have unarmed people say, "We don't want this war!" It was a dramatic kind of risk-taking. We were a peace movement going forth to the region unarmed and calling for negotiation and dialogue rather than war. And if there was about to be war, we'd be on the border to have one more chance to say, "Please don't come any further!"

I am no fan of Saddam Hussein. He made a huge blunder in the Iran-Iraq war. In Oriana Fallaci's interview with Kissinger, he said, "Things couldn't be better. Both sides are killing each other and they are using our weapons to do it." And Rumsfeld had gone and shaken hands with Saddam. I think also there is a possibility that, to a certain extent, Iraq had been suckered into entering Kuwait. Iraq had amassed a huge debt from its war with Iran, and in his egotistical misreading of the world situation, Saddam had thought that the other Arab countries were going to rush to him with their thanks and help relieve him of that debt. And Kuwait, instead of being thankful, said Iraq had to repay every dinar. Kuwait lowered their own price for oil against OPEC agreements. That meant Iraq was going to make less money with their oil. Iraq also believed that the Kuwaitis were siphoning off their oil by slant drilling. At any rate, Iraq still thought of Kuwait as the thirteenth province of Iraq. Saddam Hussein had said to April Glaspie, the U.S. ambassador to Iraq, that he was thinking of retaliating against Kuwait because he believed Kuwait was waging a war of economic aggression. And Glaspie cabled back to the United States this, and she was told to say to Saddam that the United States would not meddle in the affairs of the region. Saddam took that as a green light. So that's why we wonder: was he suckered into invading Kuwait? Anyway, he did. Nobody thought he was going to go clear through to the middle of Kuwait. The Kuwaitis certainly had grievances. The United Nations and the Arab League might have been able to arrive at some kind of a negotiated settlement.

In March of 1991, our peace group spent the first two weeks out in a desert camp. We were on the Iraqi side of the Iraqi-Saudi border. It was called Usadat Arat, an absolutely desolate spot. But then we were taken to Baghdad by Iraqi officials. We didn't see ourselves as hostages. In fact, there were thirty of us. We said, "Please, may we move in with families. Don't keep us in a hotel." We were only in Baghdad for four days. Then a big bomb hit really close. So, we were on a bus the next morning and driven to Jordan, but those of us who had asked to move in with families were told we could come back in. We put the word out in Jordan that if we could be equipped with small trucks and pharmaceuticals, enough to make some sort of medical relief convoy, we would try to keep the road safe by traveling between Amman and Baghdad, and hopefully the United States would not bomb that road because U.S. and U.K. citizens were riding along it. So we assembled these motley humanitarian relief convoys. We were later credited with helping to safeguard that road, but I don't know if that was true or not.

After the cease-fire, I was absolutely dizzied with confusion. We headed to Karbala. I have no idea why we were allowed to go to Karbala by Iraqi officials. It's about an hour and a half drive south of Baghdad. We were taken by van, and as I calculate it now, it was probably one to two days after the Shiite uprising had begun. They were encouraged by President George Bush to overthrow Saddam Hussein. They expected that they might get some air cover from the United States. But the United States had also told the Iraqi government, "Yes, you can keep your attack helicopters." And so, Iraq's air power was able to brutally mow down the people who had begun the uprising. Then the people were rounded up and put into prisons and tortured.

We visited a hospital in Karbala. Literally, our feet stuck to the floor of this hospital because the blood was so thick. Honestly, we didn't know who did this. Why did this happen? And then we saw bullet holes on the top of the building; we couldn't figure out who had been firing. It was just atrocious. Atrocious. And Karbala had been such a beautiful city. It was wrecked. The palm trees were cut down, and there was smoke rising from the rubble. A woman pulled us aside and said there was a mass grave. It was clear that doctors were petrified to be asked questions by us. We honestly did not know what was going on.

And then from there, we went back to Baghdad and we were told there was a bomb shelter in Amiriya that we should see. While in Jordan, we had seen the news about a bombing—a direct hit by the U.S. on this shelter. Anyway, I remember stepping out of a van and seeing the Amiriya shelter. I had a big lump in my throat. A little girl came up to me and she put her arm around me and I looked down at her. This beautiful gleaming face, bright eyes. She wore a little white headdress. She said, "Welcome." Then her brother came out, and somebody must have had tea brewed or something. Next thing we knew, this little child was bringing us little cups of tea. Then a woman came toward us with two other women. She made eye contact with me and I said what little Arabic I knew: "Ana afifa." Which is trying to say, "I'm sorry." And she said, "La la la la," which means "No no no no." She then said through an interpreter what we heard many times: "We know that you are not your government. Your people would never do this to us." We learned that she had lost all of her children. Except one. I met that woman again and again. Every time from 1996 on. I've always felt very close to her. A hard-bitten journalist will say, "Well, you people were taken to the shelter because Saddam wanted to make a show." But an Iraqi woman facing you a month after what happened and extending warmth and friendship is remarkable.

From 1996 onward, I have gone twenty-one times back and forth to Iraq. And each time I went with a delegation to break the UN sanctions. Every person traveled with duffel bags filled with over-the-counter medicines or antibiotics or medical textbooks. We wanted to deliberately challenge laws that were directly punishing the most vulnerable people in Iraq. Particularly children who were sick. Elderly people. Poor people. We wanted to say, "Look, you can't hold these people responsible for the actions of their government. And in fact, they are going to suffer much more than the high-level government people." The country's infrastructure was already so badly deteriorated from the 1991 Gulf

War. Some UN coordinators rebelled against the sanctions, calling them a geno-cidal program.

An August 1999 United Nations report claimed 50,000 excess deaths of children under the age of five because of economic sanctions. And this report, when it was released with a full press conference, occasioned one-half of one sentence in the *Wall Street Journal*. Those deaths were generally attributed to malnutrition, water-borne diseases, or a combination. Or respiratory diseases and then cancers and chronic diseases, because they couldn't get medicine. And so, we organized a nonviolent campaign. We just hoped it would spread as far as possible through the United States and eventually the United Kingdom. It did spread. Seventy delegations went to Iraq, and every group that came back to the United States hit the ground running, telling people what they knew was happening to ordinary Iraqis. It was our responsibility then to make sure people knew. The sanctions needed to be abolished. We tried very, very hard. We tried every trick in the book. We sat out by Congress's doorsteps in D.C. in the middle of a blizzard. We had gone on a 230-day partial fast. We walked from the Pentagon to the United Nations carrying banners saying, "Our grief is not a cry for war," and "Walk away from Saddam." We fasted in front of the U.S. mission to the United Nations; we would carry lentils and ice and untreated water to its steps every Friday after the fast. We said that we would break the fast if they would only come down and talk to us about what we had seen and heard in Iraq. Then we would be arrested and thrown in jail. We constantly begged legislators to travel with us. We finally took legislative aides over to Iraq in August of 1999. We wrote their reports for them. We put out newsletters. We did cross-country bus tours. We constantly asked people to contact their legislators because the sanctions against Iraq were brutally and lethally punishing their people. I honestly don't know what more we could have done.

In the months leading up to the Iraq War, we did our best to go to all the different civilian places in Iraq that we believed could potentially be bombing targets. We clarified that it would be a war crime to bomb this electrical facility or bomb this hospital or bomb this school or bomb a particular sanitation facility. In early 2003, I was in Baghdad that entire time—except for a couple trips to Basra, and to a place south of Basra called Abu Falooz. I was trying to help bring a young girl to the United States so that she could get a prosthesis. Her arm had been chopped off by a missile blast. She was fourteen years old. She lives in Los Angeles now with her father.

During the initial bombing campaign in March, we remained in Baghdad. It was an ethical decision. It would have been very difficult to walk away from people who befriended us and often welcomed us into their homes and who believed that we cared about them. And for us to say, "Well, yeah, we've got to get out of town, since this looks pretty dangerous," that's disingenuous. We had all along said that we didn't want war to sever bonds between us and ordinary Iraqis.

We were in a small hotel called the Al Fanar Hotel when U.S. tanks rolled into Baghdad. In fact, the tanks parked immediately outside of our hotel along with their Jeeps and Humvees. It turned out that this was where the U.S. military decided to set up their headquarters for the initial days of the invasion. When we saw them arriving, we were standing on the second floor balcony. We had strung a big peace banner. And we hung old pictures of Iraqi children and families from every floor of our hotel. The newly arrived Marines called out some questions and we answered them. I remember turning to one of my friends who was holding a banner with me and saying, "These guys look pretty thirsty." She said, "Of course." She dropped her end of the banner and went and got two big six packs of bottled water and brought them to the Marines. I probably thought about it for a minute or two and then thought, "Yeah, she's right." For me, it was the beginning of ten days of steady conversation with many different Marines. I don't know if I had changed anyone's minds over there. But if they had a presupposition that they would dislike the peace activists, then they probably dropped that idea pretty quickly. They liked us fairly well. They were interested in what we had to say. We were interested in what they had to say. They were very congenial conversationalists. Quite a few actually said they wished they could be part of rebuilding Iraq. Or that they were sorry to see that the Iraqi people had suffered so much.

The Iraqis had been so beaten down economically before the war. If the United States had tried to lift economic sanctions and encouraged other countries to think of ways to build up Iraqi society, I think it would have been very possible that the Iraqis, who were weary of Saddam Hussein, would have found ways to oust his regime. Who in the United States would have lost if there was no war? Halliburton. Bechtel. Boeing. Raytheon. Alliant Tech. The makers of the bombs. The makers of the jet fighters. The makers of the materials to reconstruct the country. The owners of the groups that were providing security. There are many people who profited a great deal. Big corporations were encouraging the United States that the only way to go forward was to declare war. They wanted that war so badly they fixed the facts to suit the war movement.

Americans are only 6 percent of the world's population. Among that other 94 percent, people are wondering, "How do you stop the Americans? They are too incurious to figure out the world around them." But that's not the approach to take if I'm trying to understand a right-wing Christian fundamentalist. Or to change things. Instead, we have to figure out how to communicate to people who for one reason or another are quite frightened or quite willing to accept this enormous expenditure on the military. So it's person by person. Bit by bit. We've grown accustomed to a pretty cushy way of life. It becomes almost unimaginable to live with less. The TV is constantly telling people, "Buy this!" "Have that!" The first President Bush put it really well. At an energy conference in Rio where he rejected any conservation protocols that would change the American way of life, he said, "The American way of life is non-negotiable. We won't give this up. We won't even think about it." It's as though the national religion is shopping and it gives people a sense of meaning and a sense of choice.

Currently, to earn money, I rely on going out and giving talks. I work out of my home, in my apartment here in Chicago. So, any income I generate I turn over to Voices of the Wilderness. We always manage to make ends meet. I haven't filed taxes since 1980. I recommend people go to the National War Tax Resistance Coordinated Committee Website. It's a long process of discovery and decision to become a war tax refuser. It will take research. There's a manual that talks about ways of doing it. One should connect with somebody in their area who is a war tax refuser. For me, initially, I just lowered my salary beneath the taxable income level when I taught at a college prep school. That was about $2,500, or somewhere in that vicinity. The school was willing to accept money I didn't take and send it out to charitable organizations that I wanted it to go to.

The IRS contacted me many years later. Because their computers weren't up to speed, they contacted me in 1995 or 1996. An IRS agent came to where I lived. At the time, I was a full-time caregiver for my dad. He is dead now. The agent asked some questions. I said, "Obviously, I can't go out and start earning an income. I live with my dad. I can't leave him alone. I don't own a car. I don't know how to drive one. I don't have a bank account. I don't want one. I rent this apartment. I don't have any income other than my dad's. And if I did, I wouldn't pay the taxes." The agent wrote me off as uncollectible. I think I still have that status with the IRS. There was a spike in war tax refusal during the Vietnam War. But it went down. Then it spiked up again when Ronald Reagan began to talk about nuking Russia. Then it really hasn't spiked up again despite constant war.

In late 2003, it made sense to me to nonviolently challenge the U.S. Army's School of Americas at Fort Benning, Georgia. The United States had trespassed into a sovereign country on the theory and argument that Iraq had weapons of mass destruction. And here in this country, graduates of the School of Americas had been indicted for terrible war crimes. There were about thirty-four of us.

After we were arrested, I was anything but afraid. I felt like I was at an airport terminal going through security. In a previous year, it was almost as if the military at the base had staged a picnic for our processing. This time, we were taken into this big warehouse for processing. I was told to go to Station J. I walked over there. I got to Station J, and there were five soldiers and a woman officer giving orders. She was screaming. I suppose I went into high-school study mode. I turned to her and looked her in the eye and said, "Could you help me understand why you are screaming at me?" She screamed back at me, "Keep your eyes straight ahead! Don't say anything! Keep your eyes glued on the person in front of you. Raise your arms higher! Spread your legs farther!" That was followed by a very aggressive search. Jabbing. Poking. Squeezing. Hands inside of clothing. And it didn't take very long for me to think, "I am not going to go along with this." So I very quietly lowered my arms and said, "I'm sorry. I can't cooperate with this any longer." Whooh! I was thrown down to the floor. I got a black eye from the impact. My wrists were bound. My ankles were bound. My wrists and ankles were bound together. I was hogtied. Then someone was kneeling on me. Referring to me as "this fucker." Even as I was moaning "I can't breathe," the person kneeling on me wasn't getting up. I started to wonder. I am not getting a full breath. I've had a collapsed lung. I can't breathe. These folks don't seem to get it. I was thinking, "What country am I in?" I was waiting for the dogs on leashes and the flashlights. I was kinda wondering: Where are the others? Unfortunately, my friend, Joe Mulligan, a Jesuit priest, thought that I'd had a heart attack and they were giving me resuscitation. He only heard this muffled groan coming from underneath five big soldiers. A thought flashed in my head: "I might die." I've been in Sarajevo and Nicaragua and Haiti and Iraq and Israel and Palestine. I've been in war situations when bombs are falling. I've had my share of tough moments. But I wouldn't call my reaction at Fort Benning fear. It's something else. More like curious. I thought, "Oh my. This is pretty bad." I think several minutes went by as I was still moaning "I can't breathe, I can't breathe." Finally, the person kneeling on me got up, and then I was okay. Just five minutes later, another soldier who was taking me to the place where they photographed us said, "To take your picture, I have to remove the hair from in front of your eyes. Is that okay?" I said, "Yeah, that would be fine." And then he very gently squeezed my shoulder. I just need to make sure I remember that squeeze on the shoulder every bit as clear as I remember the other soldier kneeling on me.

You know, it's been my constant experience, even while dealing with the Marines who arrived in Baghdad, and God knows what they'd experienced on the way there, that they were quite ready to turn to us and be like the boys next door. I think people are vulnerable to being persuaded to be their best selves and to be kind. In my everyday ordinary experience, I don't meet people who are predisposed to be cruel and vicious. We just need to treat other people fairly.

I'm kind of astonished in the short history of this country by the succession of extremely valuable and hardy and brave movements. To go back to the efforts of the abolitionist and women's suffragist movements and union movement efforts and the effort to end the Vietnam War and the civil rights movement. There is a real resiliency and creativity and problem-solving and desire to make a difference that's residual in American culture. I'm deeply happy to be part of it. I feel a responsibility to identify with the best of what has been developed in this culture, and which has been represented by the Reverend Dr. Martin Luther King, Jr. and Cesar Chavez and Dorothy Day. People who didn't try to accumulate personal wealth. They tried to share what they had with others and to be of service and experiment with nonviolence. That should be the first thing you think about when you get out of bed every day: How can I better identify with what they represent because it's so needed right now.

15

POLITICAL FREEDOM AND NATIONAL SECURITY

Civil liberties advocate John Dempsey takes the
country's temperature.

> "Intelligence investigations generally do not result
> in criminal prosecution. They are conducted in
> absolute and perpetual secrecy."

In the Age of Terror, the nation finds itself confronted with an eternal nightmare—endless war. Our global jihadist enemy won't spare our children's children's children. Future horrors await in ambush—both at home and abroad. As dread and denial vie for emotional primacy, Americans place their faith in the government to protect them from potential harm (while often criticizing its incompetence).

Right after September 11, 2001, congressional lawmakers felt compelled to move decisively before the next attack on native soil. The Capitol Hill anthrax scare added to this national security urgency. Legislation was hastily passed. The USA PATRIOT Act of 2001 greatly expanded government surveillance and law enforcement powers. Many in Congress admitted that they were simply unable to read the 300-page proposal submitted by the White House at the eleventh hour. Casting the lone dissenting vote in the Senate was Russell Feingold (D-Wisconsin) who objected to its absence of adequate safeguards protecting privacy and civil liberties.

The act's name—USA PATRIOT—was a bold stroke of marketing and political genius. PATRIOT was, in fact, an acronym for Providing Appropriate Tools Required to Intercept and Obstruct Terrorism. Critics of the proposed bill were denounced as unpatriotic. Opposition was easily thwarted. As former U.S. Attorney General John Ashcroft testified before the Senate's Judiciary Committee: "To those who scare peace-loving people with phantoms of lost liberty, my message is this: Your tactics only aid terrorists, for they erode our national unity and diminish our resolve, giving ammunition to America's enemies."

Pending its reauthorization, the PATRIOT Act was scheduled to expire at the end of 2005. This time, deliberation by lawmakers proceeded at a much slower, thoughtful, and uncertain pace. Discussions regarding the breadth and scope of granting increased surveillance powers to the government were deeply partisan, and involved dozens of hearings and non-binding resolutions by over 400 communities which opposed anti-privacy measures such as checking public library records. Only after being unable to muster enough votes to make the law permanent (which the White House pressed for), Congress passed a one-month extension right before it went into holiday recess in December.

"The PATRIOT Act is a lightning rod," observed *New York Times* reporter Eric Lichtblau, co-author of the long-delayed *Times* scoop that exposed Bush's granting approval to the National Security Agency to conduct warrantless domestic spying. "The debate over [the Act's] future amounted to a national referendum between fighting terrorism and protecting civil liberties."

As executive director of Center for Democracy and Technology, John Dempsey often found himself on the front lines of this political debate. "Dempsey has been one of the leading watchdogs of FBI surveillance initiatives," writes investigative journalist Robert O'Harrow in his book, *No Place to Hide*, which is a fascinating look inside the nation's security industrial complex. "Dempsey is a reasoned and respected civil liberties advocate routinely summoned to the Hill by both political parties to advise lawmakers about technology and privacy issues. [After 9/11], he was swamped. Reporters, other activists, Congressional staffers—everyone wanted his take on how far the Justice Department and Congress would go in reaction to the attacks." Dempsey was getting up to fifty calls a day.

Dempsey grew up in Waterbury, Connecticut. "It was a dying mill town," he says. "All the factories closed, all the jobs went away; they turned all the factories into shopping centers. My father worked in a factory. My mom worked in a bank. I went to Yale undergrad and Harvard for law school. I wanted to work in New York, my wife wanted to work in Boston. So we compromised on Washington."

For the next ten years, starting in 1985, Dempsey was assistant counsel to the House Judiciary Subcommittee on Civil and Constitutional Rights. He then joined the non-profit Center, whose mission is to "promote democratic values of freedom of expression, access to information, and citizen participation in government decision." In late 2005, he relocated to San Francisco with his wife, who planned to teach at Hastings College of Law. As of January 1, 2006, his new title at the Center is policy director.

Dempsey's modest background in Waterbury has made him, as he puts it, "very sensitive to power and powerlessness. People should be empowered and have control over their lives. They should have avenues of redress." He believes that citizens need to stay alert to even the slightest erosion of their civil liberties. "It's a little bit like the frog in the pot of hot water," he says.

■   ■   ■

After the first plane hit, I was just hoping that it had been an accident. In our office on the television, we saw the second plane hit in real time. As soon as the second plane came onto the screen, I just knew it was Al Qaeda or some other Al Qaeda-related terrorist group. My reaction was, "Fuckin' FBI. I can't believe they missed this." Obviously, it involved a lot of perpetrators, which meant that they had to have communications. They had logistics. They got here. They moved around. They coordinated. They used cars. They rented things. They lived places. They had telephones. They had airplane tickets. They came into contact with other people. It turned out that some of them lived with an FBI informant. They could have then been on a watch list. Given the resources at the FBI's disposal and given the kinds of cases they have pursued after the Oklahoma City bombing and after the 1996 Counter-Terrorism Act, the FBI had this awesome set of powers at their disposal. It was shocking and disturbing and outrageous that they missed it.

The FBI had too much of the wrong kind of information. They clearly were drowning in information. I don't want to come across as an FBI basher. A lot of them were themselves devastated and upset to learn that they had missed it. It was very traumatic for people who had been very close to those investigations. Obviously, they were people of good faith working very hard defending their country. They still missed it. I am afraid to say they probably still have an inability to prioritize, to separate the wheat from the chaff.

Soon after 9/11, in an almost knee-jerk way, some members of Congress began to say the government needs more power to prevent these attacks. That raises the whole question of what power they already do have. What power were they lacking that could have helped prevent the 9/11 attacks? What would be the significance of the powers that were being proposed? In my view, the government before 9/11 had substantial power—and to this day, I see no evidence that there were any additional powers that the government needed that would have prevented the attacks. And so, reporters were calling me, asking me, "What does that mean? What is the wiretapping law? What is this Foreign Intelligence Surveillance Act, or FISA, we are hearing about? What are the guidelines currently in place on terrorism investigation?" I was serving both as an advocate and as a source of objective analysis. One of the frustrations of the governing issues pre-9/11, but even more so post-9/11, has been the black and white nature in which the debate was presented. For those of us who are more deeply engaged in it, it is not black and white at all.

The first civil rights abuses in the United States government's response to 9/11 have occurred outside of the PATRIOT Act. The PATRIOT Act pales in comparison to the detentions in Guantanamo and the abuse at Abu Ghraib; the president's claim that he can hold United States citizens in military prison indefinitely without criminal charges; the use of the material witness statute to hold people the government really has no intention of actually questioning; the roundups after 9/11 and documented abuses that occurred; the use of rendition to transfer people to countries known to engage in torture: all of these things occurred purely on the basis of a presidential claim of power outside of the PATRIOT Act—with no Congressional approval.

Congress has not responded to any of this. It has done essentially nothing to bring Guantanamo under the rule of law. It has done nothing about the president's claims of extraordinary powers. The Supreme Court did reject, during the summer of '04, the more extreme claims—including White House claims both regarding Guantanamo and regarding U.S. citizens it had declared to be enemy combatants. But even since then, the administration has resisted the implications of those Supreme Court decisions, and the lower courts have sided with the administration in giving it more discretion than it seemed the Supreme Court believed was appropriate. So, in comparison to those things, the PATRIOT Act really represents relatively minor changes in the law. Significant, but comparatively minor.

Attorney General Alberto Gonzales is one of the authors of the administration's policy on terrorism. He is a staunch believer, it seems, that the president can do no wrong—and that in the name of national security, the president's powers are at their zenith and largely not reviewable and uncontrollable either by Congress or the Judiciary. By the same token, Gonzales is more likeable than Ashcroft—and in Washington, that actually makes a difference.

A number of the provisions of the PATRIOT Act had actually been proposed by Clinton and rejected by Congress, such as sneak-and-peek searches. Some of the Internet proposals began percolating during the Clinton administration. So there is a certain permanent government. Clinton was fairly conservative, or at least moderate, on law enforcement issues. Congress was more liberal than Clinton was. There is a very left-right coalition on civil liberties issues. There are libertarian conservatives and libertarian liberals. There are also big-government liberals and big-government conservatives. Pre-9/11, the mainstream liberals and libertarian liberals and libertarian conservatives worked particularly against surveillance issues. In '96, when Clinton was president, he got the Terrorism Act of 1996 passed, which severely curtailed the right of *habeas corpus*. But by and large, as a result of the sort of left-right libertarian coalition, that '96 law does not include a lot of provisions on surveillance.

Leaving aside any action by the government, and without any changes in the law, the trends in digital technology—largely driven by consumer interest and market forces—have meant that more and more information about our daily lives is generated in digital form and is easily accessible both to commercial users and to the government. Most people now carry with them their own location tracking device. Some people have two or more location tracking devices, which the government can use to track their whereabouts. Combine your cell phone with your building entry card, easy passes, and your credit card and, hey, it will give a very full picture of where you are day by day, hour by hour, sometimes minute by minute. This comes out in individual court cases. The government is able to prove that somebody is identified as having been at that toll booth at such-and-such a time, which is inconsistent with what he claims. Or this person is tracked using his cell phone. We saw that the London subway bomber was tracked to Italy using his cell phone. Nobody has ever shown the scope of this. It is not theoretical.

I am not sure that we will be having as many surveillance cameras as England. They went particularly camera happy. As we know, they are not that good for preventing crimes. And in the case of suicide bombers, they are worthless. But I can't predict how many cameras there'll end up being in the United States.

We now have a de facto national ID card in the form of the state driver's license. There's a greater standardization of the state driver's license. In essence, we are using a decentralized approach to the national ID card in the form of the driver's license. There are two different issues involved. One is the process of issuing the driver's license, which is a true point of vulnerability. If you can bribe a clerk to issue you a driver's license, then that's the real point of vulnerability. The Center for Democracy and Technology issued a report two years ago on problems at DMVs nationwide. There's been insider fraud. There have been break-ins at DMVs, where the objects of the thieves were machines and blank cards. Then there's the card itself: how much and what kind of information the card carries in addition to the text and what kind of biometrics the card carries. A photograph is a form of biometrics.

I don't think that one should demonize all information services companies. The byproducts of the information security industry are very convenient and beneficial. Like any other sales force, people at those companies hype what they have to offer. They oversell the government. Matrix, for example, has had a checkered history. Matrix is really a system for law enforcement—and not primarily useful in counter-terrorism. And yet, partly in order to sell it, the initial creators of Matrix called it an anti-terrorism system and emphasized its anti-terror value. That was just a case of overselling and overpromising. Hank Asher, the founder of the company, tended to talk about the Matrix system as a profiling tool. Law enforcement officers tended to look upon it as an information-sharing and retrieval tool.

Former Admiral John Poindexter's Total Information Awareness program failed because he oversold it. It should have been correctly described as a set of research projects centered around challenges of analyzing and extracting meaning from large quantities of data. Poindexter claimed that he could find unknowns based upon the analysis of transactional data generated in the course of everyday life by everybody. The whole concept of Defense Advanced Research Projects is experimental. It's research. And yet Poindexter was claiming that he already knew the answers. His main theory was that if you sucked in enough information about travel and ordinary daily activities, you could spot the signatures of terrorists. Terrorists, in order to operate, need to do certain things. They need to engage in certain kinds of legitimate conduct. But that leaves behind a signature. Poindexter claimed that with enough data and enough computers he could find that signature. Now, that is a proposition worth testing. I'm skeptical. I don't think it's possible. But I'm willing to support testing of it. But Poindexter claimed that he was running a research project and already knew the outcome—and that's not research.

There has also been a serious misinterpretation of the Foreign Intelligence Surveillance Act that had grown up in secret, between the secret FISA court and the office of the Department of Justice to process FISA surveillance requests. And the FISA wall that had grown up was quite a misconstruction of the statute. It came to be over-bureaucratized and overinterpreted. By the time of 9/11, it clearly offered very little protection of civil liberties—because the government, if it wanted to prosecute somebody, would go ahead and do it.

We have always had domestic spying. There is nothing wrong with domestic spying per se. But the government has always claimed and Congress has always recognized that there are two sets of investigative powers and authorities available to the government. One is the criminal investigative power, and the other is the foreign intelligence and counter-intelligence power. Terrorism is a crime. Supporting terrorism is a crime. Planning attacks is a crime. Conspiring with others to carry out attacks is a crime. Raising money for other people to carry out attacks is a crime. Sheltering terrorists who are planning attacks is a crime. And they are subject to investigation as a crime. But when those activities are inspired or controlled from abroad, those are also matters of a national security concern and also fall under the FBI counter-intelligence and foreign intelligence responsibilities.

Counter-intelligence, in some ways, is very different from law enforcement. Law enforcement investigations focus on crimes—which are defined by Congress and result in a trial. The government can only take action against a person by arresting them and charging them with a crime. And at that point there, the government's actions are subject to the intense scrutiny of the adversarial process. And the defendant is entitled to the full protection of the Bill of Rights: the right to a jury trial; the right to confront his accusers, cross-examine them, challenge the evidence. The burden of proof is upon the government. The individual is entitled to a lawyer. The trials are open. All of those mechanisms protect against the state's overreaching abuse.

Intelligence investigations generally do not result in criminal prosecution. They are conducted in absolute and perpetual secrecy. They are not limited to the investigation of crimes. Intelligence investigation can investigate lawful activities. It can even investigate First Amendment–protected activity. You cannot be arrested on the basis of your First Amendment statements; but you can be investigated on the basis of them if you are acting on behalf of a foreign power, or under the direction and control of a foreign power—which includes a foreign terrorist group. And the information collected in the course of an intelligence investigation is primarily not against individuals, but against foreign powers. They inform the president's development of foreign policy, his negotiating posture, relationships with foreign governments, the whole structure of the Defense Department, the procurement of major weapons systems, and the negotiation of treaties. All of these things are where foreign intelligence is used.

And in the sort of spy vs. spy context, often the targets of intelligence investigations have immunity from prosecution. The most the government can do is expel them—in which case they simply go on to continue to work for their governments in some other post. We spy on them. They spy on us. And it's all in the shadows, because the intelligence investigations are secretive. Absolutely secret. Because they are wide-ranging, they are not limited to the investigation of criminal conduct and can include the investigation of legal conduct. The feeling has been that the information collected there should not be used against an individual—and that is the concept of the FISA wall. When the government is invoking the broader, less-strictly-controlled secretive investigative powers that it has available to it under its counter-intelligence and foreign intelligence authorities, it should be doing so for the purpose of intelligence, foreign policy, national security, or diplomacy—and not for the purpose of arresting individuals and putting them in jail. That was the concept of the FISA wall. The wall was never intended to be as rigid as it came to be viewed. Espionage is a crime. You investigate the spy. You may collect evidence of a crime. You may expel the foreign diplomat. But you may prosecute the American citizen who was passing classified information. The FISA wall always allowed for the passing of information between intelligence authorities and law enforcement authorities. There was never any legal prohibition on intelligence agencies sharing information with law enforcement agencies. But the concern over the protection of sources and methods became an overly rigid concept. The CIA, for example, did not pass information to the FBI, fearing that it would end up in court and their source would be compromised.

I don't believe in open borders. This country has the right to patrol who comes into the country, but it should be on a non-discriminatory basis. We have probably eight million illegal aliens in the country. The government post-9/11 chose to focus its resources disproportionately on illegal aliens of Arab and Muslim heritage. That was wrong. It ruined their lives. It was unfair. The government was haphazard in the roundups. It thought they might be terrorists. It couldn't prove it. But it found they were still here illegally, and therefore subject to deportation. So, just to be safe, it was "get them out of the country." Many were deported on immigration charges even after it was determined they had no links to terrorism. Government effectiveness in national security and human dignity demands better, more accurate decision-making when disrupting people's lives. Unlike what happened in World War II with Japanese-American internments, there was a very different public reaction. The numbers were much smaller, but the public outcry was quicker.

In the history of our country, the overall trend has been an expansion of our freedoms and civil liberties. I'd rather live today than in, say, 1810 or 1890. Certainly if I'm black, any kind of immigrant, or a woman, I'd far rather live today than any other time in history. Overall, when looking at the population as a whole, the opportunities of freedom and liberties today are greater than they were before—although I can't predict the future because technology augments the power of the government in a way that was never possible before.

16

THE HONEST CHIEF

U.S. Park Police Chief Teresa Chambers was fired for defending our national monuments and parks.

> "Because I wouldn't agree to waive my rights, I was now being terminated for the same things that I wasn't going to be charged with a week before."

On March 17, 2003, tobacco farmer Dwight Watson drove his John Deere tractor towing a small trailer into a pond on the Washington Mall. Mounted on the trailer was a metal box containing what he claimed were "organophosphate bombs." He wanted to call attention to U.S. tobacco farmers whose livelihoods had been threatened by the $200 billion anti-tobacco settlement. Foreclosure procedures had already commenced against Watson's North Carolina farm, which had been in his family for more than a century.

Watson's protest took place during an especially tense time in the nation's capital. With U.S. military forces about to invade Iraq any day, a heightened terrorist alert was in effect. The FBI, U.S. Park Police, SWAT teams, and local cops rushed to the scene, but Watson threatened to detonate the explosives if they came too close. Police evacuated nearby buildings and barricaded streets in a ten-block radius. The siege caused a massive downtown traffic tie-up for two consecutive days and inconvenienced members of Congress. One lawmaker suggested that a police sharpshooter take out Watson, whom the press nicknamed "Tractor Man." When the standoff finally ended after forty-seven hours, no one had been injured, and Watson was led away in handcuffs. He was later tried in a U.S. district court where the jury found him guilty. While handing Watson a six-year prison sentence, the judge said, "Whatever your intentions, this city regarded you as a one-man weapon of mass destruction." The bombs, as it turned out, were just two cans of bug spray.

For her key role in ensuring a nonviolent resolution of the Tractor Man incident, U.S. Park Police Chief Teresa Chambers received generous praise from D.C.

officials and her colleagues in the Interior Department. She told reporters, "Mr. Watson was a troubled man who was seeking a way to air grievances. While the Park Police regrets that motorists were inconvenienced, no traffic tie-up can justify the taking of a human life."

Chambers, forty-six, was the first female chief in the Park Police's 212-year history. Hired several months after 9/11, she recognized the importance of using the press to reassure jittery Americans that it was safe to visit our national monuments. The U.S. Park Police provides security and protection for the Statue of Liberty, the White House, the Washington Monument, the Lincoln Memorial, the Jefferson Memorial, as well as federal parkland in the D.C. region and areas near the Golden Gate Bridge. But a new Homeland Security directive mandating beefed up protection of the nation's most-treasured icons severely strained the resources of Chambers's overworked 621-member department. She addressed her safety, budget, and staffing concerns in an interview with *Washington Post* reporter David A. Fahrenthold. In the December 2, 2003 article, she was quoted as saying: "It's fair to say where it's green, it belongs to us in Washington, D.C. Well, there's not enough of us to go around to protect those green spaces anymore. My greatest fear is that harm or death will come to a visitor or employee at one of our parks, or that we're going to miss a key thing at one of our icons." She recommended doubling the size of her staff and increasing the department's budget by $12 million.

Chambers's candor with the *Post* reporter apparently embarrassed her bosses because within several days they retaliated. Her gun and badge were taken away, and she was placed on paid administrative leave. On December 17, 2003, she received a formal written notice of her proposed dismissal, which listed six violations including "failure to carry out a superior's instructions," "making improper remarks regarding security on the Federal Mall," "improper lobbying," and "improper budget communications."

Chambers was floored by their reaction. She insisted that the charges were absurd. Speaking to a reporter from a southern Maryland news weekly, Chambers said, "[The *Post* interview] was not really different from any other interviews that I had held in the past. In fact, my press officer and I were almost giddy with how we had crafted our message."

Crying foul, the media rallied to her side. *Slate*'s Timothy Noah championed Chambers and her plight in an eight-part series called "Gagging the Fuzz." She appeared on CNN, Fox News, and dozens of radio talk shows all across the country. The *Washington Post* wrote two pro-Chambers editorials. An excerpt from the first, titled "Punished for the Truth," read:

What was the chief's transgression? She said her understaffed department had to curtail critical patrols in Park Service jurisdictions beyond the Mall, such as major parkways and crime-ridden U.S. parkland in neighborhoods, because of Interior Department orders requiring more officers to guard downtown national shrines. Ms. Chambers should be commended for speaking up for public safety. The Interior Department underlings trying to muzzle her are the ones who should be on their way out the door.

Once the initial shock of her suspension dissipated, she fought back to reclaim her $135,000-a-year job. She applied for federal whistle-blower protection through the Office of Special Counsel. She also sought redress from the Federal Merit Protection Board; within several hours of that filing, the Interior Department officially terminated her.

Taking on her former employers became a full-time mission for Chambers and her husband Jeff. They've appealed the Merit Board's decision. "There is no time frame within which they are required to respond," says Chambers. She filed a lawsuit against the National Park Service, citing attempts by the department to destroy positive job review documents that she believes will exculpate her; she is seeking $2.2 million in monetary damages for wrongful acts by its top officials.

The Chambers use their Website, www.honestchief.com, to keep the public informed of their tireless battle against a powerful bureaucratic foe. The site has received close to 50,000 e-mails from supporters around the world. A non-profit alliance of law enforcement and environmental professionals, Public Employees for Environmental Responsibility, created The Honest Chief Fund to help pay her mounting legal bills.

Chambers's story reads like a Kafka parable. Whenever she had previously attempted to bring up budget, staffing, and safety issues with her Interior Department bosses they would either ignore or downplay her valid concerns. But as she explains in *Patriots Act*: "Never once in those briefings did somebody say, 'Hey, I appreciate the information, but please don't ever speak about that outside of this room.'" That is why her termination leaves her baffled. And it helps explain why she and her husband are determined to keep fighting. "We will prevail," she says. "I mean, we're just not budging. We're not going away."

■　■　■

My family moved to the Washington, D.C. area when I was ten years old. We were from the mountains in Western Maryland. My dad was a mechanical engineer. He worked for Allegheny Ballistics Laboratories, which made parts for the space program. Times were tough up there. It was a coal-mining community. The economy was not great. It was very rural. We lived near the town of Frostburg, which has a couple thousand residents, except for when the college is in session. The Cumberland Gap is ten miles away.

I'm the youngest of four children. I have two brothers and a sister. I was a tomboy from the start. I knew how to watch my mom bake bread. My interest in policing came from working as a legal secretary while I was still in high school. I did that through my senior year and then for about a year after I graduated until I began actual police work. I didn't go to college until I was working full-time. I got my Bachelor's Degree at the University of Maryland's University College, which has adult nighttime courses, and then I got my Master's Degree from Johns Hopkins University.

I was a cadet for two years in Prince George's County Police Department. When I first started in 1976, there were over nine hundred officers, eleven of whom were women. The county sits right on the southeast side of Washington, D.C. It's rural and urban. It has five hundred square miles, with nearly a million residents at that time. It's a tough area to police, too. During my twenty-one years there, we buried thirteen officers. The deaths came sometimes from auto accidents, but very often by gunfire. It was a community where, yes, you faced potential violence every day. When I first started, we carried Smith & Wesson revolvers. First a six-inch, then a four-inch, and then finally a two-inch.

You got street smart very quickly. To survive, you learned how to use your brain more than your brawn, especially as a woman who is small-statured like myself. In fact, I should mention that there was a height requirement to join the police force. I had to do stretching exercises to gain another eighth of an inch because the height minimum was five feet, four inches.

Criminals would initially respond to me with some confusion. Seeing a woman in uniform helped us make an arrest rather quickly. For example, while growing up, there were rules for my brothers in our family—you couldn't hit your sister, and you couldn't pick on people smaller than you. Well, there's no guarantee that the criminals are going to follow those same sets of principles, but gender does play a role here. There were several times where male suspects would fight male police officers and yet very willingly comply with my command. I'd get handcuffs on them before they could think about what was going on.

When I later taught at the police academy about gender roles in policing, we used to discuss the television show, *Police Woman*, with Angie Dickinson. *Police Woman* influenced my era. Before that show, there was *Adam-12* and

Dragnet. If you saw a woman in uniform, she was getting coffee and answering the phone and taking notes for a meeting. *Police Woman* was one of the first television shows where it at least took the role of women in policing to a different level. Still, she wasn't quite allowed to do what her male counterparts would do. When they chased somebody down the sidewalk, she couldn't quite keep up with them because she was in her high heels, and when she got to the chain-link fence, her male partner, of course, had to bound over the fence because she would have ripped her pantyhose.

When I got promoted to lieutenant, I had eighty officers under my command. I was responsible for a large geographic area around the University of Maryland and the surrounding communities. I retired after twenty-one years because I could also get a chief's job elsewhere and still draw a monthly retirement check from the self-funded retirement system. I started checking the professional ads to see what was out there.

In January of 1998, I got hired as police chief in Durham, North Carolina. I had about six hundred officers and civilians under my command. It was a very violent community, but also a very welcoming community. It was close to the universities and used to diversity. The police department was anxious to try new things. After my four years in Durham, there was a 26 percent drop in violent crime.

I decided to leave Durham because a police chief's job in this country generally lasts three to five years. If a person is smart, he or she will go in, make their mark, and move on. We generally answer to political appointees or elected officials. So when the opportunity came up to compete for the position of chief of the United States Park Police, which is highly sought after in the law enforcement profession, I applied. If I got the job, it would also allow me and my husband to move back to the area where my parents and my husband's parents live. My husband is also a retired law enforcement officer. He was a sergeant in one of the local police departments. He used to tell people, "Hey, I'm just two steps away from the Chief." What has continued to make the marriage so strong is we have a love of the profession.

I was interviewed for the position by the National Park Service two months after 9/11. They were intrigued with having a current chief of police who could hit the ground running and who didn't need to be trained. I already had twenty-six years of municipal policing. During the interview, there were six people sitting around the conference table. I was asked what seemed to be programmed questions. I later learned that there were about eighty candidates; I don't know how many they actually interviewed.

The United States Park Police is more than two hundred years old. George Washington himself set up the Park Police as park watchmen in Washington, D.C. They were actually called park watchmen. The Park Police grew from there. It is more of an urban arm of law enforcement than the National Park Service. Our jurisdiction includes the Washington Mall, Ellis Island, federal parkland in and around Washington, D.C., and area near the Golden Gate Bridge. We're set up almost exactly like a municipal police department.

My starting date was February 10, 2002. There was a big gala for my swearing in on Valentine's Day. It was held in one of the auditoriums at the Smithsonian's Natural History Museum. Secretary of the Interior Gail Norton was there. She is the first female Secretary in the Department's history. Fran Minella, who is the first female Park Service Director in the history of the National Park Service, was also there.

My first year as chief was both awesome and challenging. The Interior Secretary had made it known that she didn't want any monuments to fall on her watch. I also had to deal with old guard issues. Some people were just not willing to accept change. Part of that was due to gender; it was also related to my work ethic. I demanded work from my employees.

Our first big test was the first post-9/11 Fourth of July celebration on the Washington Mall. Over a million people showed up on the Mall. There were only 621 police officers nationwide in the Park Police. So we had to rely on other agencies. We brought in their people and had them sworn in as federal marshals for the day and then gave them police powers.

I found myself as a spokesman for patriotism on that Fourth of July. With the White House and the Washington Monument in the background, I told the national media personal stories about my dad taking me down to the Mall when I was a little girl and listening to the marching band. And now here I was many years later, telling people to stand up in the face of terrorism and to safely celebrate America's Independence Day. I had live interviews, sometimes on the set of CNN. I was walking around and pinching myself, thinking, "I cannot believe I'm being paid to do this job. I'm still serving law enforcement, which I love dearly, but for the first time in my life I'm serving my country in a very real way."

I met President Bush a total of three times. The first time was at the White House. The Secret Service agent in charge of his security detail thought it would be important for me to have an opportunity to meet him face-to-face, because the Park Police has an important role with regard to dignitary protection.

I was with him on September 11, 2002, when he spoke to the nation from Ellis Island. He saw me and some of my staff on the island that night. He's drawn to uniforms, and so he came over to us. I got a hug from him.

I saw President Bush one final time. It was the night before I was sent home by the Park Service. It was at an annual event in December on the White House south lawn where the national Christmas tree is lighted and there's a festive program to start the holiday season. President and Mrs. Bush were going back up the White House steps, and as he looks over, he sees me and then comes over and shakes my hand. He said, "Gee, how are you doing? Great job. Continue the good work." We wished each other a Merry Christmas and up the steps he went.

I never had contact with President Bush again. When I was finally terminated in July of '04, I did a telephone interview with CNN, and I remember being asked, "Do you think that the White House was involved in this?" I don't know. What I do know is that thousands of supporters had written to the White House. Where those e-mails and letters go is anybody's guess. My case had a lot of local visibility, and the fact that the Interior Department took on the *Washington Post* was one of the dumbest things it could have done. I am sure that the White House gave its blessings to my suspension at some point.

But I am jumping ahead here. Starting in midsummer of 2003, I was involved in a series of meetings and briefings at the Department of Interior to alert folks to the fact that our current funding was insufficient to protect our primary icons and memorials and do necessary law enforcement in the parks. I had data, pictures and charts, but I was pretty much ignored. Never once in those briefings did somebody say, "Hey, I appreciate the information, but please don't ever speak about that outside of this room," or "If you're ever asked publicly . . . ," or "If you're ever asked by Congress . . ." If they had said any of those things, that would have given me reason for concern, but I could have at least made a decision about my future with an agency that didn't value honesty and openness.

On November 20, 2003, a reporter from the *Washington Post* approached me for my response to information about staffing issues that he had received from police union representatives—the Fraternal Order of Police. In fact, the Fraternal Order of Police Chairman for the Park Police had written earlier to Interior Secretary Gail Norton: "We're concerned over the long hours, the no days off, not even so much as a bathroom or a food break on some of these assignments for twelve-hour shifts." And so I confirmed this information to the *Post* reporter; it was information that he already had. My point was not to be the complaining employee, but to offer a more balanced perspective and yet still be very candid.

I had spoken on record to the *Post* dozens of times before. I mean, that was part of my job. But after talking to this reporter, I realized that he was looking into some issues that were larger than just the Park Police. For example, the budget as a whole in the Department of Interior and who got what slice of the pie. And so, as a courtesy when I finished my interview that night, I contacted my immediate supervisor, Donald Murphy, who is the Deputy Director of the National Park Service, and told him about the interview. I asked him if he wanted me to notify his boss, Director Fran Minella. He said no, he would do that. Between the time that he and I spoke and the time that the article actually came out two weeks later, I received a phone call from Secretary Norton's press officer. He asked me a little bit about the interview. He said Don Murphy had told him that the interview had taken place. He asked me what types of things the *Post* was interested in, how much information did they have—and so we talked for five or ten minutes, and he says, "You know, I really don't like having more than one spokesperson on a topic like this. If there are any follow-up questions from the *Post* or if there are subsequent media interviews from other print media or television or radio, we want you to remain the sole spokesperson for the Department of Interior on this matter." So not only did they know I had done the interview, they had no criticism based on what I told them.

When the story appeared, I thought that the police union was probably going to be glad that its issues were highlighted. As I was driving into work, a local talk radio show, WTOP, wanted a live interview—which I did from my car. When I got to our headquarters, I was surprised to see that there was a bank of cameras from all the local television affiliates.

My press officer stood there with me as I answered questions from reporters. We were hoping that the Secretary of the Interior and the Director of the Park Service themselves had seen or heard some of my interviews, because we thought that they would be pleased with my overall message. I mean, there was no indication that they wouldn't be. I wasn't saying anything that would be embarrassing to them or to the Bush administration. I had supported my officers by talking about the good work that they do every day, but I also acknowledged that there's not enough money to go around for everything that needs to happen in our government. After 9/11, whether it's the federal or local government, everyone's short on resources. And so, our job in law enforcement and protection was to prioritize and to look at those things that needed our primary attention, which were those very visible monuments and memorials. And that meant sometimes the Park Police had to pull officers out of the neighborhood parks—it didn't mean that they went without police protection—but they may not have had as many police officers as they did before. I felt that it was important for the public to know that. In the world that I came from, that is to say, community policing, you've got to empower the neighborhoods; you've got to tell people what's going on. So, my press officer and I were thrilled with how that came across in my interviews. My bosses apparently weren't.

The first ax fell about twelve hours later, around six o'clock that evening. I had done no fewer than a dozen interviews so far. But there was no feedback from my bosses all day long. That evening, I found two voice-mail messages from my boss Don Murphy, who said, "Trying to get hold of you. Director Minella and I have spoken, and we don't want you to do any more interviews until we have a chance to talk with you. The message that you're putting out about the budget is not consistent with the message the Department wants. Please get back to me." I called him back immediately and told him I was a little shocked and not sure what went wrong, but I was anxious to have an opportunity to get together and get matters straightened out. He asked me if I would be at work the next day. I said, "Sure." He said, "Good, I don't know what the calendar looks like. I know that the director is in town and she'll want to be a part of this meeting, so just stay available and I'll give you a call the following morning." I said, "Can you give me some hint? What is it that has gotten folks' attention so late in the day?" And he used for the first time a phrase that I had never heard before. He said, "You just can't talk about the president's budget." I said, "Well, I'm sorry. Where did I talk about the president's budget?" And so he read a sentence from the *Post* article, and I could tell this was not the time to argue. Well, I then called my press officer, told him what I had just learned. I said, "I have no idea what he's talking about. What does he mean, 'president's budget'? And why would I worry about the president's budget? I have my own budget to worry about." Much later in this process, I learned that there is a term called the president's budget, which is the entire federal budget. Even so, there's nothing in the *Post* article that talks about the president's budget. The reporter had asked my opinion as to whether we were underfunded, and I answered, "Yes, we are." My calculation of twelve million dollars in overtime was only my opinion versus a budget fact.

The meeting that Murphy promised the next day never took place; it didn't take place on the third day; it didn't take place on the fourth day. On the afternoon of the fifth day, I was called to a mandatory meeting that was supposed to be with him and Minella. I was to bring my second in command. Well, I've been a cop for twenty-six years. I knew something was up. I thought to myself, "They're going to take my command from me."

I went to the meeting. Murphy was there. Minella was not there. I was told that I couldn't see her. There were also three armed special agents from the National Park Service and one of the head attorneys for the Department of Interior. I was handed a piece of paper and told that I was being put on administrative leave. I asked, "When is somebody going to tell me what's going on? What have I done wrong?" So finally, Murphy said, "Well, there's violations of federal regulations and insubordination." I had to bite my lip not to say anything. I then said, "Well, can you tell me when I fell on my head or did something and failed to do what you told me?" And he says, "Well, we're researching that." I said, "Let me get this right. You're going to now go back through two years of my work performance and hope to find something that I've failed to do to now substantiate what you're doing tonight?" He said, "Well, we're not going to tell you any more." I responded, "What regulations have I violated?" He replied. "Well, we're still researching that." I said, "You're hoping to find something after the fact?" He replied, "We're not saying anything else." The last thing I said to them was, "Does the term 'whistleblower' mean anything to the two of you?" And I got no answer. I was then forced to surrender my badge and my gun. I was still in my uniform.

There is no more demeaning action in law enforcement against a uniformed police officer than taking his badge and gun. You can strip him of his clothes and walk him naked down the hall, but that still is not as demeaning. Because they also took away my vehicle—an unmarked Impala—one of my employees took me home in her car.

So this was a power play. Murphy was a political appointee. He's a Republican. But so am I. He worked as the Director of the State Parks in California. He started out as a park ranger and came up in that system. Minella was also a presidential appointee. It was the second time in Park Service history that a Park Service Director was actually picked by the president. She was Director of Parks in Florida under Governor Jeb Bush.

After being sent home, I spent the next week wondering what I had done to deserve this treatment. I was driving my attorneys nuts about why couldn't I get an answer from the Interior Department. I wanted to know: Why won't they tell me what's going on? And is there a criminal investigation? I mean, can you imagine the paranoia I was experiencing? I'm thinking, "Oh, my God! Somebody has told them I robbed a bank! That must be what it is!" Because you never take a policeman's gun and badge unless he's accused of being involved in criminal wrongdoing. I'm thinking, "Somebody must have planted evidence in my office!"

Seven days went by before the Department of Interior contacted me and my attorneys. They informed us that they wanted to meet us at a secret off-site location to talk about what it would take to bring me back to work. We agreed, and so I went with my attorneys and drove to the site. All of us met there, though Don Murphy was segregated in another room with his attorney. I was presented with a draft proposal of their charging document. I'm reading the draft, thinking, "If it weren't happening to me, this would be a sitcom because it is so unbelievable." For example, it said, "You're charged with telling the *Post* 'where it's green, it's ours . . .'" I'm thinking, "What law or whatever did I violate?" Once I finished reading the document, my attorney says, "Okay, well, here's the deal. They're willing to shelve the charging document and not put it into formal action if you agree to certain stipulations." I asked, "What stipulations could there possibly be?" He said, "Don Murphy has some things he wants to say to you, but only in front of his attorney and your attorneys. There's some things he wants you to agree to, but we're working on that now." For example, there was going to be a joint press release that said "we're all living happily ever after." I replied, "Let's see what all the stipulations say before we agree to anything." So this took several hours of back and forth. The attorneys kept coming in with handwritten lists from Murphy. The first few things got my goat, and I didn't say anything. It was just very much a power issue. One of the things that he and I had disagreed about was his transferring one of my top executives out of the Park Police. I'm like, "Okay. He can do it anyway. He's the boss." But as I got down to numbers four and five, I pushed the paper back to my attorneys and said, "Impossible. This doesn't work for me or for anybody else." One point concerned contact with Congress. Any conversation or meeting that I had with a staffer or member of Congress would have to be approved in advance both as to contact and the content of what I would discuss. The same with the media. I rolled my eyes and said, "You know, first of all, this is insane that anyone would believe that a police operation could operate this way. Secondly, Congress should be incensed to find out that before I can answer 'yes' or 'no' to them or one of their staffers, I have to ask permission to tell the truth, and that's just from an operational standpoint." I gave them the example of Chandra Levy, the intern whose remains were found in Rock Creek Park in Washington, D. C. When her body was found, I was called to the scene with the Chief of Police of Washington. When I got there, it was the largest bank of cameras I had ever seen, everything from international and national outlets to the local news. And so can you imagine, just for a moment, that I now would have to say, "I'm sorry, you want to know where the bones were found? Hang on a second. I have to pick up my cell phone and call my boss and say, 'Excuse me, they want to know where the bones were found.' Of course not. You can't do it. It wouldn't work. Not for me.

Not for any other chief of police. This can't happen. I'll find a job working for somebody else without these stipulations." I decided to let them chew on that for awhile. The meeting was over.

Seven days later, I was served with my proposed termination papers. Which meant I was being put on paid administrative leave. But the really interesting twist to my case is that it implied that because I was such a valuable employee I wouldn't be charged with anything as long as I was willing to waive a few constitutional rights. And then I could come back to work. That's how insignificant whatever it was I was alleged to have done wrong in the first place. There wasn't even going to be a letter of reprimand! There wouldn't be any charges against me! There wouldn't even be a paper trail! But because I wouldn't agree to waive my rights, I was now being terminated for the same things that I wasn't going to be charged with a week before. So at least I now knew that I was only being charged with administrative stuff.

Originally, there were six charges. The charge of "inappropriate budget communications" was based on my answering a question from a congressional staffer. She had asked me something about a consultant study. As it turns out, my answer was very different from what she was getting from Minella and Murphy, so they didn't like that. Another one was "lobbying." I had told the *Post* reporter that, why yes, we could use more funding and more personnel—and my remarks were printed in the newspaper, which then a congressman might read.

There was also insubordination and violating a chain of command. Another had to do with releasing information that they believed was law-enforcement sensitive, such as giving out the number of officers guarding a monument at one time. My point is that anyone can see officers standing there; the public is not seeing what we don't want them to see; they're not seeing different levels of surveillance or undercover officers or regular patrols. I used to give quarterly briefings to the city council in Durham where I had to tell them how many officers I had and where they were stationed. It's a rather typical thing and is public information in every law enforcement setting that I'm familiar with.

One of my two original attorneys is a retired career federal employee who held undersecretary positions in the Department of Defense. He's old school and would try to help me understand the mind-set of the federal government. He said that "the charges were baseless and silly." He told me that it is typical in whistle-blower cases for the government to add trumped-up insubordination charges against the whistle-blower.

My husband and I spent most of those first two months crying around the clock. We had no tree on Christmas day. We had no presents. We only put up a tree on December 26 for general principles. But we decided to fight back no matter how long it takes. I said to the media at one time, "If it takes eight years or eight days, I'm going to fight it." Well, now those eight years or however long it might take seems like a reality because the process moves so slowly.

On January 9, 2004, we submitted our first appeal—a fifty-six page appeal—to the deputy assistant secretary in the Department of Interior. Why Fran Minella wasn't the appeal person, we don't know to this day, but they kept her out of it perhaps because she was a presidential appointee. They have done their best to keep her away from my case.

The Interior Department waited until July 9, 2004 before officially terminating me. Here's what happened. The Office of Special Counsel, which handles whistle-blower cases, didn't act for whatever reason on my case. Maybe the OSC had asked the Department of Interior to not move forward while it was investigating my case, but it seemed clear to us that the OSC was dragging its heels and that it was not going to give us an answer any time soon. Well, after a certain period of time, the employee has a right to go directly to the Federal Merit Systems Protection Board, and so on June 28, we decided to file with the Board. On July 9, we presented a very comprehensive Motion for Stay to enable my immediate return to work. We laid out all their dirty laundry, pretty much saying that I was suspended for doing what I'm pretty much told to do. Within four hours of our filing, the Interior Department—after holding off on my termination for seven months—decided to make it final. I learned about it from WTOP on my car radio just as I was pulling into my attorney's offices. I heard that my termination was effective at midnight! So yeah, it was, "Let's retaliate against the whistle-blower one more time!"

The Federal Merit Systems Protection Board did dismiss two of the administrative charges—"inappropriate budget communications" and "lobbying," which the judge saw right through. The other charges weren't dismissed.

In our appeal to the Board, our petition runs 250 pages. It states over forty errors that we believe the first judge made. So this isn't just a five-page brief that they have to look over. If they're serious about doing a proper review, they've got a lot of paperwork to go through, and who knows when they can get to it. They have no time frame whatsoever. It could take forever. It looks as if it takes about a year for their average case. My case isn't average. Maybe they've been pressured not to get to it during this presidential administration. We have no way of knowing.

Our attorneys' fees have been very, very costly. We are about a hundred thousand dollars in debt so far. I have applied for other jobs. One was actually for my old job—the Interior Department opened up the position of chief of the United States Park Police. I applied. I didn't get the courtesy of a response, which they pride themselves in saying they will do. And I applied to be editor of an on-line newspaper that's law enforcement related. But I questioned how I'd also be able to manage my case, which is a full-time job. This is why the federal government has such a high success rate in delaying, and defending against, cases like mine. They have all the resources. They've got as many salaried attorneys as they need to work on a case.

I stay out of Washington, D.C. to the extent that I can—for a lot of reasons. One is, you know, I can't protect myself as a police officer. Here I am, one of the more recognizable law enforcement faces in the nation, and I don't have a way to protect myself. So no, going downtown is not one of the things that I do. I used to go bike riding on the Washington Mall after work. Of course, I had my gun if I needed it. I wouldn't go bike riding without it.

I don't believe there was anything I said to the *Post* that was inappropriate. Just the opposite. I took my role as a manager really seriously in supporting my bosses and my troops. In fact, there are fewer police officers in the U.S. Park Police today than when I first raised the alarm.

17

THE SHOT SEEN AROUND THE WORLD

War correspondent Kevin Sites captured explosive
footage of the Fallujah mosque shooting incident.

"If we bury the truth, then all the things you
are fighting for don't mean anything."

Over 50,000 results will show up by Googling "Kevin Sites" and "Fallujah." The
listings span the globe and ideology. They range from military and peace blogs to
op-ed commentary. They refer to an incident Sites witnessed as a freelance NBC
correspondent embedded with the U.S. Marines seeking to regain control of Fallujah in late 2004. Thirty-five miles west of Baghdad, Fallujah was a flashpoint of
resentment against the U.S. occupation. Its population is primarily Sunni, and the
city is remembered as the place where, on March 31, 2004, four American defense contractors were ambushed in their SUV, and their incinerated bodies were
left hanging from a bridge.

On November 14, 2004, Sites followed a squad of battle-weary Marines into
a mosque that the insurgents had used as a firing position and a place to store
weapons. The men found several dead and badly wounded insurgents. A young
Marine walked up to one of the wounded and pumped an M-16 round into his
head. Sites captured the scene with his camera. Forty-eight hours later, the killing
was broadcast worldwide.

As expected, the reactions varied. Anti-war groups were incensed. To viewers in the Arab world—Al Jazeera and Al-Arabiya ran uncensored footage, unlike
NBC—the incident was further evidence of American disrespect for Muslims. The
shooting raised suspicions within the U.S. military that the press could no longer
be trusted. Right-wing talk shows and bloggers questioned Sites's patriotism,
maintaining that he had handed the enemy an unwarranted propaganda coup. But
within the journalism community, Sites was lauded as a hero for refusing to shirk
from the ugly realities of war. Despite knowing that there would be repercussions
from its airing, he responsibly stood his ground by not destroying the tape. It was

a brave, gutsy move that also served to highlight a moral dilemma often experienced by war reporters when they are caught between conflicting loyalties: fealty to truth, or to one's military.

Sites is no stranger to danger or controversy. Working in the field as a producer and correspondent, he spent five years covering conflicts in Afghanistan, Colombia, and Kosovo. His Balkans war reporting netted him an Emmy and an Edward R. Murrow Award. During the early days of the war in Iraq, *fedayeen* briefly held him and his crew hostage; the abduction became its own minor news story. But Fallujah raised Sites's profile to an entirely new level of visibility. It also isolated him in a reporter's no-man's-land. Though he posted an open letter to the Third Battalion, First Marines, also known as the "3.1 Devil Dogs," on his blog, in which he laid out all the facts about the shooting, he chose to duck all press inquiries and interviews. And for the next seven months, while the military conducted a formal investigation into the shooting, Sites maintained a public silence.

On May 5, 2005, in a statement to the press, Maj. Gen. Richard F. Natonski, commanding general of the 1st Marine Expeditionary Force, claimed that a review of the evidence on the shooting showed the Marine's actions in the shooting were "consistent with the established rules of engagement and the law of armed conflict." The corporal was not going to be charged with murder. In short order, Sites appeared on NPR and *The O'Reilly Factor*, eager to tell the nation his version of the incident.

"It had been a tough year," said Sites during the first of four interviews for *Patriots Act*. "It's my job to see and report the truth, what happens in front of my camera—and that is what I did. My job is to bring the realities of war to the public." That goal is now being further expanded with the Yahoo-supported Website called "Kevin Sites in the Hot Zone" (http://hotzone.yahoo.com). The Hot Zone is a pioneering effort to bring a new kind of solo war reporting into the digital age. It was launched in late September 2005, with Sites reporting from Somalia, the Congo, and Uganda in quick succession. In the span of one year, Sites—who is equipped with a PowerBook, satellite phone, Canon digital still camera, and three small video recorders—plans to travel to thirty-six war-ravaged countries and file personal reports via video footage, blogging, audio and written dispatches.

■   ■   ■

I always wanted to be a journalist. My very first job was as a still photographer for my hometown rag, the *Geneva Free-Press*, in Geneva, Ohio, which is ten miles east of Cleveland. At fifteen, I got a camera. I just started snapping pictures. I went into the paper and said, "I'm a photographer." They said, "Okay, great. Show us your book." So I had to put some prints together. I came back. They said, "Okay, come back in the fall and we'll talk to you about it." I thought they were just bullshitting me. But sure enough, I went back and then they hired me. I lied about my age. I was only fifteen at the time; I didn't even have a driver's license. So I had to ride my bike to take the pictures. For the next two years, from my sophomore year to my senior year, that was my job. I worked probably fifteen to twenty hours a week. I started writing for them too, doing newspaper stories. I went off to college, Ohio Northern, for two years. It's near Toledo. Then I transferred to American University in Washington, D.C. I finished my bachelor's degree there. Then I worked for five years.

I was fairly politically active at the time. I worked in some Democratic politics. I worked on the political campaigns of Gary Hart when he was running for president. I really thought he was going to be in the White House. He was the right kind of progressive Democrat. He actually thought out his position on issues. He was the New Democrat; progressivism with muscle. He wasn't some namby-pamby guy; he was forceful. But maybe his temperament wasn't right. He could have done all the things that Clinton would have done, and with the same kind of mandate. Hart was much more serious in a lot of ways. But he was not a genial man. He had a kind of dual perspective about life. He wanted to be president—the most popular man in the world—but he also wanted to be the pure Irish author and go off somewhere in Dublin. There were conflicting aspects to his personality. I guess we all have that. But his were very apparent. I mean, he's a smart man, and like all smart, powerful men, there was a certain tad of arrogance. It was heartbreaking when the Donna Rice thing happened. I had been dating one of his schedulers, and there were rumors about his infidelities. But I had no personal knowledge of it. I liked him. It was very difficult for so many of us who thought we were going to change the world.

I also worked as press advance on a lot of large international aid campaigns, including Hands Across America and Farm Aid. But I ultimately realized my true passion was reporting. I wanted to get back into journalism and start reporting again. And so, I went to Medill journalism school at Northwestern.

My first job after Medill was being an on-air reporter in Gainesville, Florida. I did TV-20 News there. It was a local network, an ABC affiliate. I was a general assignment reporter covering everything that happened. There were property and farming issues. It was really tame stuff. Eventually they had a series of grisly murders—people were getting beheaded—but that was after I left.

I wasn't certain I was going to be able to make the long climb as an on-air reporter. People on air were certainly more polished than I was. I grew up in a small town. I didn't want to be in a small town forever. So I took a job as a writer and producer for FNN—Financial News Network—in Los Angeles. It was right at the time of the first Gulf War and so we covered defense contractors and oil issues, and it gave me a real economics education. Then KTLA Morning News hired me as a producer. It gave me my entrée to the network. I had a contact at ABC and sent tapes of stories that I had written and produced. They hired me as a producer. I moved with my wife to Washington, D.C. I worked for ABC for three years on *This Week with David Brinkley* and *World News Weekend* with Carol Simpson. And then NBC hired me to produce for its well-known correspondent, Fred Francis.

Fred Francis spent thirty-five years at NBC. He began as a bar bouncer and then worked his way up to cameraman in Miami, and then ended up a network correspondent. It was a meteoric rise. He was very much the maverick correspondent, not your typical blow-dried, Ken doll–looking dude. He was a bulldog. I think a lot of who I am as a correspondent certainly came from working with him. I learned a lot from him. We were a good team. We did a lot of law and order stories initially. We were based out of Washington, D.C., but we traveled all over the country. We covered the TWA 800 crash and the Centennial Park bombing in the Atlanta Olympics.

The last story I covered for NBC was Kosovo. We won a national Emmy for our war coverage there. I came back from Kosovo, packed up my house in Washington, and my wife and I drove across the country. I took this job teaching in the fall as the broadcast lecturer at California Poly in San Luis Obispo. Its journalism department was a mess. When I first got there, I almost felt like these kids should get their money back. I was shocked to see what I had to work with. I had a couple of broken-down VHF editing machines and non-working cameras. I went to the dean, and I said, "This is horrendous. We've got to do something. Give me ten grand. Let me buy ten consumer level cameras at a thousand dollars each." I then went to Apple Computer, and I asked them to give me computers that my kids could edit on. At the time, I really didn't know how to do too much shooting and editing, because I was a producer. I was directing people to do that. I had to teach myself very quickly how to do all these things because I had to teach my students. Within that two-year period, I honed my shooting and editing skills. I was also well on my way to getting a divorce. So right after 9/11, and with my teaching contract over, I ended up going over to Afghanistan as an

NBC producer, but I was also equipped to actually report. I had a camera, videophone, and laptop. And I knew how to edit and shoot.

I was in Afghanistan prior to the fall of the Taliban. I was with Northern Alliance soldiers for more than three months in that little sliver of territory in the north that they held. The Northern Alliance operated as if they were a government in exile—which in some ways they were. They had been beaten by the Taliban and they took what political structure there was with them. Their land was only a thumb of territory. I don't even know how many square miles, but tiny. We had to get a passport stamp and everything from the consulate that the Northern Alliance government was running in Uzbekistan. And then we went to Tajikistan.

As an NBC producer, I had a crew and a correspondent. I was in charge of my whole team, about six people. That was a fascinating period, I have to say. Today, there is only one Western newspaper that has a full-time correspondent in Afghanistan. Back then, there was a huge desire to get into Afghanistan because everyone knew that there was going to be a war. Some reporters were actually with the Taliban. But a lot of the press was coming across the northern border from Dushanbe, Tajikistan. You'd cross the Amu Darya river at night. The Russian army was still doing security for Tajikistan. To get across the river, there were these rafts and a cable going from one side of the river to the other. We poled and pulled ourselves along this cable to the other side. When we got to the other side, there were the Northern Alliance soldiers. They took us to our encampment.

Our drive to the encampment was a surreal experience. The roads are not really roads at all. They are pockmarked, carved paths through packed-dry desert soil. It felt almost like we were on a lunar landing surface. We are driving in and out of ruts and swerving back and forth across the road to avoid these huge potholes. They were sometimes the size of the vehicles themselves. It was completely dark. None of us had slept for days. We were tired, we were hungry, we were grouchy. We got to the location, and some of the other NBC team was already there. There had been a sandstorm. They were wearing gas masks. These guys were so dirty, tired, and hard-bitten by this point, they just said, "Come and try to find a place to sleep."

It was the most primitive place I had ever been in my life. This was camping out to the extreme: cooking on open fires, eating MREs [ed. U.S. military term for meals ready to eat]. The only thing modern in Afghanistan at the time were the weapons. We were bringing in cases of water. You did what you could do. You drank a lot of tea. I never got sick in Afghanistan until the day I left. It was probably due to sheer exhaustion and my body had shut down. You couldn't afford to be sick there. People obviously got parasites, things like that.

We were with the Northern Alliance for four to six weeks in Khodja Bohaudin. It's a refugee area. Their commander and leader, General Massoud, was killed just prior to my being there. I stayed in Massoud's house and headquarters in the very place that he was killed. One portion of the house had been sealed off. The Northern Alliance soldiers had put up plywood around the windows, but you could still see black outlines from the flames of the explosion that had fanned out. Massoud was a hero to them. These Northern Alliance guys would plaster so many photos of him on the windshields of their vehicles that they could barely see around them to drive. It was crazy.

We would go to the front lines every day, usually in old Russian jeeps. The U.S. hadn't launched its invasion yet. There wasn't even U.S. bombing. It was simply fighting between the Taliban and the Northern Alliance forces. Then the bombing started, and it all picked up. There were U.S. Special Forces. We didn't see many of them, because they were very good at hiding out with the Northern Alliance forces. They avoided the press like the plague. The only time we actually saw them was when we actually got to Tora Bora much later in the conflict. And then, they really didn't want to be anywhere near us.

Being on the Northern Alliance front lines was very strange. It was what I might imagine trench warfare to be like in World War I. There were these dug-in positions. The campaigns were slow-motion volleys of mortar fire and small arms fire, until the massive United States air campaign began. That was the only time you saw movement. Then the Northern Alliance pushed across the former Taliban front lines and started heading south. That is when four journalists were killed. There was a French journalist and a German journalist from *Der Spiegel* and two others. It was the same day that we got mortared. The mortar wounded a *National Geographic* producer. He was standing right next to me. I was unscathed. The shrapnel cut through his lower thigh and his butt, close to the femoral artery. He could have bled to death very quickly. It was a real wake-up call. So I had to make a decision at that point. What do I do? Do I bandage this guy or do I shoot it? I've got my video camera in my hand. I'm still rolling. I've got the whole explosion. This was the first ground contact that anybody has really seen where someone got wounded. Especially an American. So I do both. I shoot it for a second. And I put the camera down and I pulled off his scarf and tied off his leg. We then got him out of there. NBC aired this, but the only thing we see is the impact of the mortar round coming in. We don't see the guy getting wounded or any of the aftermath. But because we put the entire footage on our affiliate network, which has cross affiliations with CNN, everybody got to have it. And that's what happened. NBC lost the initiative on it. Then *National Geographic* did a whole special on it, using my footage.

We then got into Kabul after it fell. It was a five-day drive to Kabul. A horrendous drive. We were going around land mines and sleeping in houses along the way. It was very slow progress. It seemed to take forever. The Kush is this huge and terrifying but beautiful valley and mountainous route you had to drive through. We flipped a Jeep. The brakes went out on one of our vehicles. Just lots of little trauma everywhere we went. When we finally got to Kabul, we rented this house, and we were all excited because there was water and we'd be able to take showers and wash up a little bit. It seemed to be a pretty good house in a nice Kabul neighborhood. Most of my team moved in there. I went to the Intercontinental Hotel. It was untouched. I took a room there, but there was no water. It was like living in a kind of terrarium. You had a room, but it was cold and you couldn't really get clean. You bathed with Baby Wipes.

The home we had rented in Kabul seemed okay for the first couple days. We wanted access to the whole house, but the owner wouldn't open up the pantry door for us. So one of our fixers/translators, who was up on the roof of the house, saw a hole through the roof. "What is that?" he asked. The hole seemed to be right over where the pantry door was. So he finally forced the owner to unlock the pantry and open it up and show us what was inside. Right there, embedded in the concrete at a jaunty angle, was this unexploded 500-pound American bomb. It had dropped through the roof. It had been part of the bombing campaign. The UN came in later, removed it, and detonated the bomb.

From Kabul, we went to Tora Bora as the campaign kicked off to try to find Osama bin Laden. We weren't getting a lot of information because the U.S. military wasn't telling us what was going on. They weren't there in the way they were conventionally in Iraq. They were depending on the Northern Alliance and what they called the "Eastern Alliance fighters"—people who were more in cahoots with the Pakistanis. There were reports that the British had Osama and his men cornered, but the Americans told the Brits to back off because they didn't want them to touch him. They wanted victory for the Americans.

Being in Afghanistan was almost like a field commission for me. I became a regular correspondent for NBC. I was also doing producing duties. They hired me to go back to Afghanistan about a month after I had come home. I was still pretty burned out. But they made me an offer I couldn't refuse: to be a correspondent for them. This was during Operation Anaconda against the big counterattack by the Taliban. They had regrouped. The Americans went in hard. This was around March of 2002. That was a pretty tough campaign because it was still cold and we were sleeping in houses without windows. Plus it was a very unfriendly area. It was Pashtun. Our fixers were scared to be down there, because they were mostly Uzbeks and Tajiks—people from the north. The Pashtun are tribal warriors. All these guys have been fighting for so long; it is second nature to them. Everybody has a weapon slung over their shoulder. You walk around in that environment long enough it seems like human life is really cheap. People die constantly. You are living in a constant state of war. Their environs are destroyed from twenty-five years of civil conflict and hundreds of years of wars. The warrior ethos is revered there. At the same time, it doesn't have any glamor. It is such a dirty, long-term war of attrition. It is painted on their faces—and you wish to God that somehow they could get some relief from this life they are living. But for so many of them there is no hope. This is what they know. It is ultimately all they know. They will live and die in war. They must support themselves by becoming part of a warlord's militia. Subsistence farming is another aspect. Poppy farming is the third. There really is very little else for them to do. They can become merchants if they have enough capital to set something up.

My second tour in Afghanistan lasted about six weeks. I stayed there until Anaconda was over. I then came back to the U.S., and CNN hired me. They liked what they saw. They were preparing for Iraq. They knew they wanted me for that.

During the early days of the Iraq War, I almost became a victim. It's something I will never forget. It's shaped and defined me in a lot of ways. I had a photographer, a security guy, and a translator working with me. I was covering northern Iraq, and I got dropped into northern Iraq with three other very senior CNN correspondents: Brett Sadler, Jane Arraf, and Ben Wiedemann. All three of them were bureau chiefs in the Middle East. Sadler was a bureau chief in Lebanon, Jane Arraf was the Baghdad bureau chief, and Ben Wiedemann was the Cairo bureau chief. I literally had to compete with them for stories. I was a solo journalist for the most part. Covering things on my own. I was also very junior in the CNN structure. I was just hired. So, it was a strange situation. I covered this smuggler's town called Chamchamal. It was on the Iraqi front lines until the U.S. bombings. The Iraqi troops fell back to Kirkuk and then withdrew from Kirkuk as well. CNN's regular correspondents had Kirkuk covered. CNN talked to me about going to Mosul. I said I hadn't been covering Mosul. I didn't know what was going on there. At this point, Tikrit was the big story: Tikrit hadn't fallen yet. So I told them I wanted to go to Tikrit. They told me no. But we told them that my team was only going to check the perimeter. So we headed south toward Tikrit.

We ran into an Iraqi army patrol about twenty kilometers outside of Kirkuk. This wasn't the *fedayeen* yet. This was a regular Iraqi army patrol. They were packing up their trucks and trying to get out of there as fast as they could. They saw we were journalists. They could have captured us and taken us right there. But I think they realized we didn't pose a military threat to them, so they just said, "Get out of here." They were in the process of rapid withdrawal. So we set up about 10,000 yards away and began transmitting: "Kirkuk has fallen, but there are Iraqi soldiers right behind us." So we got a story out of it. We decided the next day that we were going to Tikrit no matter what. It hadn't fallen, and we were going to get there first. Brett Sadler, the other CNN correspondent, wanted to get to Tikrit as well. He had a larger entourage. He had about six vehicles, and he had a satellite dish. His security man and my security man—he had been in the SAS in Britain—were in contact with each other. We knew each other's locations by the GPS readings which they were sending back to each other. Whether each of us was acknowledging it or not, we were racing each other to be the first to get to Tikrit to report on it, even though we were from the same network. We also had another vehicle that was following both our vehicles. It was our supply truck. They were both Kurds in that vehicle.

We were moving down the road and making great progress. But about three hours later, we hit a *fedayeen* checkpoint. We basically thought we could talk our way out of it. We had just talked our way out of the regular Iraqi army patrol. But these guys were more like thugs and thieves. I was videotaping this guy who comes up to our vehicle and begins yelling at us. My translator, Tafiq, says, "Kevin, turn around. We need to get out of here." One of the *fedayeen* guys says, "We are the soldiers of Saddam." That is the term they use for one another as *fedayeen*. He points his AK-47 at my head and says, "Get out of the car!" And so Tafiq says, "This is not good. This is not good." My security man and photographer are in a vehicle behind us. They are forced out of their vehicle as well.

That was not the first time I've had a gun pointed at my head. I still thought we could talk our way out of it. But when I got out of the vehicle, I didn't know what this *fedayeen* guy had said. Tafiq, my translator, told me afterward. He said he looked at me with contempt and said, "This one is surely a spy." Meaning me. Then he fired an AK-47 round right between my legs. And it's funny because I didn't flinch—and it's not because I wasn't afraid. Again, I was kind of shocked. I didn't realize that this was going to be as serious as it really was. Then we were forced down on the ground. I honestly thought, based on my hostile environment training, that once that happens—once you're on your knees or you're down on your face—you will be executed. There will be a muzzle against the base of your skull, and you're gonna be shot.

Now, I'm very scared. I'm lying next to my security guy. I'm gonna make up a name for him. He doesn't want to be identified. I say to him, "What do we do now, Mac?" He just looks at me. I realize that my mouth is as dry as it's ever been in my life. It feels like the desert itself, like sand.

When you truly face death, your body just compensates for everything that is going through it. You don't have any fight or flight anymore, because at this point your fate is in their hands. So I just stayed calm and submissive. Tafiq, who is older, begins to negotiate with them aggressively. They pull him up and start to take him out into the desert. And we all think, "Oh, this is fucked up. They're gonna kill us." Whenever they separate people, that is also a sign that you're gonna get killed. So we swarmed around him; we grabbed onto Tafiq. We held his arms and legs and said, "He's our father. He's our father!" Even in English, we wanted them to know that this man was important to us. He is not just an employee. He's our family. We were trying to make that connection. At that point they punched and kicked my cameraman. Mac grabbed the foot of the guy who's kicking the cameraman. It was really a brave move. They started hitting and punching Mac instead. They didn't hit me but they tied my hands behind my back. I was the only one they tied up.

Then they threw us in this truck. They kept on saying that they were going to take us to Tikrit to the intelligence headquarters of the Iraqi army. Tikrit hadn't fallen yet. But something happened. When the Kurds in the supply truck had seen us captured, they turned around and drove away. We thought they might have gone to get help. Tafiq told the *fedayeen*: "You're gonna be sorry now if you don't let us go. Those guys with us just went back to get the Coalition Forces. The *peshmerga [ed. The Kurdish fighters and militia]* are gonna come here, and they're gonna bomb you back to the Stone Age."

The *fedayeen* really didn't care about that, for the most part, because they're thugs. They're like any other gang. They may or may not have lived in that village near where they stopped us. They might just have been manning the checkpoint there. But one of the *fedayeen* was from that village. He became concerned. So he started having a discussion with their leader. He said, "Listen, before we take these guys to Tikrit, we need to check with the tribal chieftain, with the elders." And that decision probably saved our lives. Because at that point, instead of taking us directly to Tikrit, where they probably would have killed us and thrown our bodies outside the city, they took us to the tribal chieftain. He became very concerned that if he let the *fedayeen* take us away, then the Coalition Forces would come back and turn his village into rubble and kill them all. That is what my translator Tafiq told me. He capitalized on that fear and used it against them. And so the chieftain negotiated with the *fedayeen*, who released us to him instead.

We were then put in a gas station and held there until the *fedayeen* took off. The *fedayeen* took everything: both vehicles, all our equipment, probably about $15,000 in cash that I had, and $10,000 another guy had. They had taken our watches earlier. I had a Citizen watch my brother had given me for my birthday. I had worn it through a couple of conflicts. One of our guys had a watch that his young daughter had given him. These were important things. They were also our last vestiges of our humanity, what connected us to the world. When they were taken from us, I had thought that they were just going to strip us and kill us. But when we were turned over to the tribal chieftain, he made them give us our watches back. Tafiq is the bravest man I know. He was totally unafraid. He is a Kurd. He lives in the north. I love him like an uncle. He has five children. He was a widower. His wife had a heart attack. Though he appeared almost a little frail, and overweight, he began negotiating. "Not only do I want our freedom, I want our gear back." We didn't get our gear, but we did get one vehicle back. And that is the vehicle we used to drive back into Coalition-held territory. With our lives. We didn't really celebrate. We were so exhausted by the process, and so overwhelmed. We were humiliated to such a degree, that it just almost makes you silent. Truly it shocks you into this place of silence.

CNN told me that they were happy we were back. At the same time, there was a certain amount of consternation because we had disobeyed them. If we had gotten into Tikrit and reported from there first, they would have loved us. But for us, the war was over at that point. We were sent out of the country fairly quickly because we had no gear left—even though we all asked to stay. Baghdad had already fallen. We sat on our hands for about three days in Kuwait. On the leg of the flight home we went into Dubai. I didn't want to go to my home in central California. I was still kind of reeling from the whole thing. I had an overwhelming sense of failure. We didn't complete the job. We were there to get a story, but we became the story. It was the last thing I wanted. I was here to report on this war.

I got plenty drunk in Dubai. People were telling me, "You need to come home." I didn't want to. I wanted to go back to Iraq. But at the same time, I was in this limbo. Dubai is kind of a limbo anyway, the crossroads of the Middle East. It's very Westernized in the sense that there is a lot of shopping, lots of concrete. It's like a mall in so many ways. I just wanted to get lost in limbo for a while. I just wanted to hang out. My girlfriend at the time was begging me to come home. In fact, I just kind of pulled away from contact. I didn't email or phone anyone.

Well, I had to come home eventually to Pismo Beach, California. Still feeling like a failure. I started doing domestic stories for CNN. I covered immigration. There was a group of vigilantes on the border with Mexico. I was doing solo reporting. But CNN wasn't really sure what they wanted to do with me. They weren't very happy with me—partly because of the capture, but also partly because I had started a blog that was independent of them. CNN felt that if their correspondents all started their own blogs, independently of them, how would they maintain a certain coherence in the objectivity of their reporting? I certainly wasn't being political in the blog. But I was being much more casual, and I was using the techniques of narrative nonfiction to tell stories that were much richer in character detail and content than my television reporting. They felt that my blogging was going outside my purview as their employee. So I shut it down and ended my relationship with them. I talked to NBC again.

I headed back to Iraq for NBC. It was late October 2004. I embedded with the Marines for about three weeks prior to their invasion of Fallujah, which led to one of the bloodiest chapters of the Iraqi conflict. I was with the Three One, Third Battalion, First Regiment. They are based in Camp Pendleton, California. We developed this relationship that was really strong and trusting. When I was with them, they began to trust me in the same way they would with somebody in their unit. I was living the same way that they were living. Living in the dirt.

You experience the same things they do. You can wear the same sort of protective gear, and so on. For me, specifically, I got a little superstitious after I started covering war conflicts, like in Afghanistan, Kosovo, and Nicaragua during the civil war. Every time I got into a situation where I came close to being killed, I never had a helmet on, I never had a flak jacket on. I got to the point that I just didn't want to wear them. Again, it was more superstition than anything else. I'd wear a flak jacket, but I'd take the plates out. The Marines didn't want to be responsible if you did get hurt. But at the same time, I think they respected the fact that I had experienced probably more combat than a lot of them had. I'd been covering wars the good part of five years. I am forty-two. I was twenty years older than most of them.

I'd go on combat patrols with them. They were called "feints." They would probe the outside of Fallujah. They would go in with their weaponry and try to draw the insurgents out. Once they knew the location of the insurgents, they would fire on their positions. They would go in Humvees; they would sometimes go with tanks. Then they would go in and make a full-scale attack.

On the same day as the mosque shooting on November 14th, we had been walking back down a road. It was a road we had cleared the day before, meaning we had cleared out all the insurgents. But we started taking fire from some of the houses. So we had to go back up that road. The Marines threw a couple of grenades into one of these houses. It was almost like a police raid. They'd bust in the door and then run up on each side. I would follow them with my camera. At this one particular house, they threw a couple of grenades. The Marines went to the right, and I went to the left. And when I went to the left side of the house, I saw that the grenade had ignited boxes of ammunition. It caught fire, and I had to warn them they needed to get out of there. We all cleared the building. Then the ammo started doing what is called a burn off—burning off and firing.

You're part of a unit. You don't want to see anybody get killed. It's your responsibility. If you see danger coming, you can't stand there and do nothing about it. I think that is part of the process. You can be neutral but can you live with the fact that someone may die if you don't do something? And I can't necessarily live with that as a journalist. I was operating, to some extent, as part of that unit—not doing their job, but working with them, experiencing what they experienced.

I kept following the unit into the same area that was cleared the day before. I ended up going with one squad while another squad was moving around the back and going into the mosque. I heard gunshots—M-16 shots—while we were waiting outside. I followed the second squad into the mosque. We had gone in the mosque the day before; there had been a firefight where the insurgents had used the mosque as fighting positions. The Marines killed ten of them in a firefight—legitimate, justified. They wounded five. They treated them. Their wounds didn't seem to be life-threatening, and so they left the insurgents behind in there. They told the insurgents that they were going to get picked up later since the Marines were going to move forward to places where they thought there was other insurgent activity.

When I went back into the mosque on Saturday, I was surprised to see not only those dead bodies, but also the five guys who were wounded the day before. Four of them had been shot again. They were very much alive when I left that mosque on Friday. They had gunshot wounds, usually to their extremities. I remember specifically this guy in a red *kaffiyeh*. He and another man were against the corner wall and they were bleeding to death. It was dramatic because his wound was fresh, blood was coming out of his nose and his mouth. He was maybe in his late fifties; the other man was probably in his late thirties or forties. His head was lying on the older man's lap. They were both bleeding to death. So I began videotaping them—and then this Marine walked over to two other insurgents against the wall who were also bleeding to death. And he said, "This guy's faking. He's fucking faking he's dead." And then as I heard that, I raised my camera. I wasn't sure what he was going to do. I thought he might be covering them to check for weapons, if that was the fear he had. He was three, four feet away from the guy. His gun's at waist level. He raised it to his shoulder, took aim, and then he pulled the trigger. The shot blasted through the guy's head.

I'm about twenty feet away. There are dust particles in the air, some light streaming through the windows. It was very powerful at the moment. I had seen guys killed in combat, but not this way. I felt shock. I was very surprised that it happened. I didn't expect it. But I didn't know what I expected. I dunno. In some ways, maybe, it stunned me to an extent. But I didn't run up and confront him or anything like that. I continued to shoot from my position. And strangely, like I was completing the sequence for some strange reason, I panned the camera back to the guy with the *kaffiyeh* I had been videotaping initially. He didn't have any reaction. He was bleeding to death.

I went up to the Marine afterward and said, "Why did you do that? What's going on? They were the same guys who were here yesterday. They were wounded." "I didn't know, sir," he said. "I didn't know." And then he walked out of the mosque.

That is when I started talking to this insurgent who popped up in a blanket. He was the only one who had not been shot again. He tried to talk to me. I couldn't understand what he was saying. But I could assume that it was something about the day before. "You saw us," he said. I had it translated later.

I was not happy that I had shot the video. I knew it really was going to be volatile. I left the mosque right away. There was a vehicle going back to the battalion rear, which is where the lieutenant colonel was. I needed to talk to him. I needed to make a decision. I knew the story I had was explosive, and that it was going to have far-reaching repercussions. It needed to be reported responsibly. Part of the responsibility was having a discussion with the chain of command. What are the rules of engagement? Is this shooting allowed? Is this something that would be accepted? I needed to show them the videotape. I wanted to get his response. I showed it to him.

The lieutenant colonel's comments were mostly like, "Ah, this is so bad." But this was still a very hot shooting war going on. We were not that far behind the lines: two miles. It was a crazy period. It couldn't happen at a worse time for them, because they were really in the middle of a huge fight. The colonel of the brigade looked at it. Then it went up to a one-star general. Then the two-star general who was the commander of the Marine Division. It went all the way up the chain of command. But they fully cooperated every step of the way.

They asked me, "How long can you give us? We want to do a full investigation." I had no problem with them. I called NBC right way. I got the three top foreign news officials. The guys who are in charge of its foreign coverage. I needed to safeguard myself. I had very conflicting feelings. I thought, "If no one knows about this, I might be tempted to destroy the videotape or just forget it exists." I wasn't thinking very clearly as a journalist. I was thinking about the possible repercussions from that videotape airing—such as Al Jazeera getting ahold of it and using it out of context as a propaganda piece. Or the Marines could become the victims of the same type of fate if they were captured. The insurgents would say, "Okay, here is retribution for what you did in the mosque."

The tape was released after forty-eight hours. My desire was to hold it for seventy-two hours. I wanted a full investigation. But since I was a pool reporter, I had a responsibility to the pool. When the actual battle for Fallujah began, we were required to send all of our video to a clearing house—and by clearing house, I just mean a satellite dish—where everybody could use it. I sent a full version where you actually saw the shooting. And I sent a blacked-out version. I argued for blocking out the actual shooting part. I even argued initially that the tape shouldn't be shown at all, that we could just tell the story. I really feared the damage it could create. One of my core principles is to minimize the harm.

As a member of the pool, I had to release the video to really everybody in the world. But I had a lot of misgivings about having to do that. The American networks managed to show the blacked-out version of the actual shooting itself. But many of the Middle Eastern stations, Al Jazeera included, showed the un-blacked-out shooting over and over again. There wasn't a proper context. It was just the video over and over again. And in some ways, I thought it was very hypocritical. Because they weren't reporting on the beheadings and the executions that the insurgents were doing. It did seem like it was a double standard by members of the Middle Eastern press. My Arabic translators in Baghdad told me that they felt relief that an American journalist would actually shoot and release this videotape. There was some sense that perhaps the United States does have freedom of the press.

In the U.S., the right wing got behind the Marines fairly quickly. Whether they had seen the video or not, their initial reaction was to always support the troops, regardless of circumstances. Yet there wasn't an understanding of the full context of what happened—or even the potential consequences of enlightenment through this video that served the U.S. in informing its allies that it is a country that walks its talk.

By and large, a lot of conservatives are suspicious of what they call the mainstream media. And they believe that most journalists are indeed liberal. To some extent, they thought I epitomized the liberal media, and that the liberal media was once again trying to undercut the military and the administration in the middle of a very sensitive and difficult fight offensive in Fallujah. So that enraged many people.

The Marines I was embedded with felt like they were tainted with the same brush by the actions of that one individual. Many of them didn't know the specifics of the shooting anyway. They weren't all in that mosque. They may have felt that this Marine was being unfairly charged, that it was a justified act. Remember, their friends and comrades had died on a regular basis. There was no outright animosity against me, though some of the prior good will I had built up began to evaporate. I think it was more like they wanted to know, "Wait, you were with us. How could you report this?" I had to explain to them, "It's not just my job; it's our responsibility to the truth. If we bury the truth, then all the things you are fighting for don't mean anything."

I stayed in Iraq probably for another two weeks. I finally left for a break. I went to Thailand. I was there prior to the tsunami, then I ended up in Cambodia. When the tsunami hit, I went back to Thailand to cover it. The strange thing about it, I had been so shell-shocked by the whole last half of my experience in Iraq that I had sent my camera home. I had to cover Thailand using some of the wire-service footage, until I eventually got a camera.

When I covered the tsunami, there was death everywhere. Everywhere I pointed my camera. And it was a horrific thing. But in some ways, it was easier for me than the killing that I'd seen in war. Because it was nature. There is no recourse with nature. Nature will do what it does. And it wasn't man-made. People were coming together to help each other. In war it's about violence, animosity, and killing. There are aspects of war that can be very attractive and seductive. Once you start covering war, there's the danger of addiction. You become overstimulated. Chris Hedges mentions this in his book, *War is a Force That Gives Us Meaning*. There is a mythology that goes with it. You are exposed to things that are so powerfully dramatic that in some ways everything else pales in comparison. You are exposed to the most heightened moral and ethical dilemmas imaginable. That makes it difficult to transition to normal society. That is why you see such a heightened level of alcohol and drug use among long-term war corre-spondents. You see a high attrition in their personal relationships.

Looking back, that incident in the mosque, surprisingly, has never given me nightmares. While that is one of the worst things I have ever seen, I have seen things that were more bloody. But this time, there was the moral dilemma. When that incident happened, I was surrounded by a lot of self-doubt and con-cern. There wasn't a good ethical answer. If I had destroyed the tape, then I would be trying to destroy the truth—and there's never any good that comes out of that because you can't destroy the truth. If I released it, the tape could be-come a propaganda victory for insurgents as well as a potential increase in dan-ger to the Marines that I was with. Both looked like just bad endings for me all the way around.

It had been a long year dealing with a lot of people who were being very hateful about this whole thing. A lot of them had justifiable anger because they don't know the full story. It was particularly difficult for me in the months right afterward. I got death threats. I got hundreds of hate e-mails. I would get e-mails that said, "We know where you live"—and they would give my address, and it would be the address of an ex-girlfriend. I knew that I was somehow putting other people in danger as well.

I was taking the hits, but I wasn't really defending myself. The Marine hadn't been cleared. It was an ongoing investigation. I didn't want necessarily to influ-ence the outcome. In the end, they decided not to prosecute the Marine. In lay-man's terms, they felt they didn't have enough evidence to prosecute—despite the video. It's not my role to decide whether justice was served in that particular case. It's my job to see and report the truth, what happens in front of my cam-era—and that is what I did. My job is to bring the realities of war to the public.

In spring of 2005, I got to speak at West Point during a panel discussion with CNN's Christiane Amanpour, John Kifner of the New York Times, and Paul Holmes of Reuters. It was the first time that I showed the full video to any audi-ence since I had returned from Iraq. There were 900 people in the audience. These men and women are going to be guiding the American military forces in the future. I knew that if I did speak to these young military leaders, I would be able to make my case in a very clear and succinct way without a filter of other media. There was silence when it was shown. It stopped everything on the panel pretty much cold. The fact that this shooting was reported and an investigation began immediately and that this particular Marine was pulled off the front line certainly showed to a lot of people that America believes in its democratic prin-ciples—and most importantly, in my particular situation, the free press. Someone didn't put a bullet in my head and take that tape away, or simply not allow me to air that tape, or slap me in irons and throw me in prison—as is done in some nations that don't have a free press.

But as war correspondents, we've done a very poor job of educating the public about our role in society as journalists. We need to be independent of the government and the military. Our role should be that of a watchdog. Although it's not always a pleasant one, it's indeed a role that is necessary for democracy to function effectively. You cannot rely on the government and military to tell you the truth about what's happening in instances where they have an ingrained interest to promote something, or spin it in its most positive way.

Journalists are there to sometimes do the dirty work of revealing the unglamorous truth. And so, fulfilling that role is not always the easiest thing to do. In some ways, we are the ones with the shovel cleaning up behind the elephant in the circus. I think that the mainstream media has failed viewers in a tremendous way. They haven't been able to provide real context for the war in Iraq. The public is not getting the full truth. Stories both good and bad are going unrecorded.

The reporter must be transparent, vulnerable, and empathetic. That's what I am hoping to achieve with Yahoo and "Kevin Sites in the Hot Zone." I'm doing solo reporting, but I've got a team of two: producer Robert Padavick, who worked at NBC and CNN, and researcher Lisa Liu, who came over from Panasonic. They are my mission control in Santa Monica and help me nail down stories with interviews—and also do some post-production on the materials that I send back. The idea is to cover every armed conflict in the world within one year. Just myself.

When you go to Yahoo's news site and punch up my page—"Kevin Sites in the Hot Zone"—you'll see on every single day the following: a six-hundred- to eight-hundred-word dispatch; a five- to ten-photo slide show; a piece of video that day; and toward the end of the week, a video package. And there's also audio blogging.

I brought this concept to Yahoo. This is an incredible opportunity to do the kind of reporting that no one else is doing—and do it in a way that maximizes the new digital technology on the news gathering side and reach an audience that transcends national borders. This is Yahoo's first attempt at actual content producing: news gathering rather than aggregating news. It's the compilation of every type of media that you could see out there—television, radio, press, and even interactive—maximized in one delivery system. It's the nexus of technology and independent reporting that can happen outside the mainstream media. But it's not just the technology that makes this different; it's concentrating on the human narrative, which makes stories fascinating. It's the story in front of the conflict and behind the conflict; for example, the story about the child soldier who is being reintegrated back into society after having to rape and kill before he turned twelve years old.

Without a doubt, everything that I've ever done in my career has led up to the "Hot Zone." I certainly didn't feel like I wanted to jump back into a war zone, but this opportunity has given me more focus than I've ever had before. And if I can help other reporters embrace these techniques and use them to become better journalists—then people will understand and appreciate our profession that much more.

18

THE WHITE HOUSE DEFECTOR

Rand Beers, special assistant to the president for combating terrorism, quit five days before the war in Iraq began.

> "If I was protesting anything, it was the ineffectiveness of our terrorism policy. It just turns the pit of my stomach. That's why I left."

Rand Beers was a government lifer. He specialized in foreign military affairs, terrorism, intelligence policy and operations, counter-narcotics, and law enforcement. His globe-trotting career dated back to the Nixon presidency. With each new administration, he continued climbing the rungs of success until he reached the northernmost latitudes of the State Department and National Security Council. His responsibilities took him all over the world, from Africa and Asia to Central and South America.

In late 2002, he became senior director and special assistant to the president for combating terrorism. Privy to the nation's highly classified secrets, Beers analyzed threat-matrix reports funneled to his staff by the CIA. He kept a black secure phone by his bed in his Washington, D.C., home. Yet he began to privately chafe at Bush's military obsession with Iraq, believing that it would dilute the government's counter-terrorism resources and priorities. As war fever intensified, he addressed these concerns with his longtime friend, Richard Clarke, who once held the same White House counter-terrorism post. Their conversation, held in late March 2003, is summarized in Clarke's best-selling memoir, *Against All Enemies: Inside America's War on Terror.*

> *Beers called from the White House and asked if he could stop by my house for a drink and some advice. "Randy, since when have you started calling before you dropped by? See you in a few minutes." We had been*

giving each other advice and counsel for years, but I sensed there was
something wrong, maybe there was new information about another
planned Al Qaeda attack. I sat on the stoop of my old Sears catalogue
house and opened a bottle of Pinot Noir. When Beers sat down next to
me his first words were, "I think I have to quit."

I thought I knew why, but I asked. His answer flowed like a river
at flood: "They still don't get it. Insteada' goin' all out against Al Qaeda
and eliminating our vulnerabilities at home, they wanna fuckin' invade
Iraq again. We have a token U.S. military force in Afghanistan, the Tal-
iban are regrouping, we haven't caught bin Laden, or his deputy, or the
head of the Taliban. And they aren't going to send more troops to
Afghanistan to catch them or to help the government in Kabul secure
the country. No, they're holding back, waiting to invade Iraq. Do you
know how much it will strengthen Al Qaeda and groups like that if we
occupy Iraq? There's no threat to us now from Iraq, but 70 percent of
the American people think Iraq attacked the Pentagon and the World
Trade Center. You wanna know why? Because that's what the Admin-
istration wants them to think! I can't work for these people, I'm sorry
I just can't."

Beers resigned two days after his talk with Clarke. That was also just five days before the start of the war in Iraq.

Two months later, Beers made another bold protest statement. He joined
John Kerry's presidential campaign as a national security adviser. "I can't think of
a single example in the last thirty years of a person who has done something so
extreme," Brookings Institution scholar Paul Light told the *Washington Post.*
"He's not just declaring that he's a Democrat. He's declaring that he's a Kerry
Democrat, and the way he wants to make a difference in the world is to get his
former boss out of office." Syndicated columnist Robert Novak snarled that Beers
had turned into a "turncoat."

Shortly after Kerry's loss in the 2004 election, Beers moved from the campaign trail to the classroom. He co-taught a seminar on terrorism with Clarke at
Harvard's John F. Kennedy School of Government. Their class had ninety-five students—including Army majors and lieutenant colonels—who had come there for
a year or two of graduate work. "We had healthy and lively discussions about Al
Qaeda, Iraq, Iran, terrorist acquisitions of weapons of mass destruction, the
spread of terrorism to other countries with affiliated organizations, and homeland

security," says Beers. For course reading material, they used *Against All Enemies*, *The 9/11 Commission Report*, and *Defeating the Jihad* by the Century Foundation.

These days, Beers, sixty-two, is busy launching two non-profit organizations: the non-partisan Coalition for American Leadership and Security and the Valley Forge Initiative. "Their goal is to support specific candidates and promote strong, smart national security policy," says Beers. On the family front, his wife Bonnie is a school administrator at a special education school in Rockville, Maryland. His oldest son, Nathaniel, works as a pediatrician at D.C. Children's Hospital, and his younger son, Benjamin, was an AmeriCorps and Peace Corps volunteer in Honduras, but is now a medical student at the University of Virginia.

Does Beers have regrets about leaving the Bush White House? "Not at all," he says without hesitation. "But I sometimes miss having some of the intelligence information as a counterweight to what I read in the press."

■   ■   ■

I was born in 1942 in Washington, D.C. My father came from the Midwest, although he was born in Boston. He was the son of a preacher—a Methodist preacher—and moved all over the Midwest. Being a preacher's child was something of a challenge, and somewhat inhibiting. I have the same lineage on the other side of my family. My mother's grandfather was a Congregational preacher. My parents divorced when I was four. My mother remarried a naval officer, and we began moving around the United States. By the time I was thirty-four and came back from Belgium after my first and only Foreign Service overseas assignment, I had moved between cities seventeen times.

I wanted to go to West Point, but ended up at Dartmouth with a Navy ROTC scholarship. After two years and a summer cruise in the ROTC, I switched to the Marine Corps because I thought naval life was somewhere between challenging and boring: you're on four hours and you're off eight hours, around the clock, and then you go to port and you sort of let loose. My stepfather, of course, wanted me to go to the Naval Academy; he was a career military person. He retired as a commander. He was a supply officer who worked at a number of logistic facilities around the country during his career. I never felt any criticism from him for joining the Marine Corps.

By the fall of 1965, I knew I was going to Vietnam. I had a naïve vision of the warrior. I was anti-communist, but I wasn't a McCarthy anti-communist or anything close to that. My mother and stepfather were Republicans; my father and stepmother were Democrats; and I was a Democrat by 1960. I was a

Kennedy supporter. So sometime in that period, I became more clearly a Democrat than a Republican, and things really haven't changed after that.

Once in the Marine Corps, I did a tour in the Mediterranean aboard an amphibious vessel doing landings in Spain, Italy, Malta, Greece, and Sardinia, so I ended up at sea anyway. I came back to the U.S. I was then ordered to go to a unit that was mounting out to Vietnam—it was a military police battalion. We were supposed to help relieve the pressure on the line infantry units in Vietnam. We ended up guarding the Da Nang airfield, plus running the brig and a few other ancillary tasks. I did that for about six months. Then I became a regimental operations officer.

When I was in Da Nang, there may have been a few stray shots, but nothing serious. That was the first six months. The second six months, I was at a place called Camp Carroll, just south of the demilitarized zone, with the Third Marine Regiment. During that time, I was a battalion operations officer for about four or five days when the command group was wiped out. What happened was that this battalion—the Second Battalion, Third Marines—got ambushed north of Camp Carroll, but south of the DMZ. The battalion commander was killed, and the battalion operations officer was wounded and evacuated. And so, our regimental executive officer was sent in to command the battalion. I was sent in to be the battalion operations officer in order to get them out of the field. In a normal battalion, you've got four rifle companies of about 150 and a headquarters company of as many as 200, so it can be 800 people. In Vietnam, they weren't always at full strength. The first thing we did was walk the whole battalion out of the field. Literally. We'd made sure that there were no other engagements that we weren't ready for. We primarily relied upon ourselves. As it turned out, the ambush was the extent of the North Vietnamese effort. They had intercepted information on the location of the command group and had laid down this ambush very artfully.

I don't know how many died. But it was significant because normally a command group surrounds itself with support. So this was a very rare occurrence. There were probably twenty casualties, with between five and ten killed in action. I knew both of the top two people in the battalion—one was dead and the other wounded—so that had an effect on me.

At the end of my Vietnam tour, I extended for an additional six months in return for a promise to command a rifle company, because I really hadn't had any command experience and hadn't really served in the field, except for that very brief experience. I went home for thirty days and came back and started off commanding the headquarters company; but after a firefight in which the commander of India Company, Third Battalion, Third Marines, did not perform to the satisfaction of the battalion commander, the two of us traded places and I became its commanding officer. This was in August of '67. When I took over the company, our troop strength was depleted. We were probably down to 120 because of the constant rotation, as well as casualties. We later got several drafts of recruits, straight from basic training.

I was twenty-five years old. It was an awesome responsibility, and shit happens. While I was the company commander, I lost as many people—Marines killed—to friendly fire as to combat. We were in two firefights. We were shelled by enemy mortars and rockets maybe another six times, and had four or five killed from combat. That was the episodic nature of combat in Vietnam. But two of our people were killed when the battalion operations officer mistakenly plotted the position of our perimeter and called in registration fire from an 81-mm mortar, and it landed inside the perimeter. We also lost somebody to a short artillery round; that's when the powder is faulty and doesn't send the shell as far as it should. And we lost two Marines when a nighttime bombing mission dropped two 500-pound bombs on our battalion perimeter. We had three people killed in one firefight after we ran into a North Vietnamese platoon that was dug in near our battalion position to observe what we were doing, probably in anticipation of an attack by a larger force. We had several nighttime probes of our position before that run-in.

Another time, I was walking along the trail on a battalion sweep operation and someone ahead of me in our formation set off a booby-trapped land mine. This one was set up so the lead person hits the tripwire, but the explosion kills somebody farther back in the column. The unit commander or the radio operator is the preferred target. I was not the closest person to that mine, but the shock wave staggered me and it killed a guy two people behind me with a piece of shrapnel right through his helmet. We evacuated him. I don't know whether he was already dead when they took him away.

I came home in January of '68. Tet occurred a week later. I felt enormously guilty because I was safe and my men were in danger, and they had some rough times. War is a significant bonding experience. The war literature suggests that, for a large proportion of a unit's members in combat, it is the most significant experience of their lives. You don't find a lot of people who talk about their combat experience. It's very personal.

I was then stationed in Norfolk, Virginia. I was the guard officer at the Norfolk Naval Base. I was the third-ranking officer in the unit. There were maybe a hundred people who had 24/7 shift duty. By then I was married. My wife

Bonnie and I met in 1964, when I was a senior at Dartmouth and she was a senior in high school. We met in Macon, Georgia. She was a naval officer's daughter and was born in Bremerton, Washington. She moved all over the world like I did. Her family is from Fairfield, Connecticut. It was a pretty typical marriage by sociological terms: officer meets his future wife on a military base.

While I was in Vietnam, I believed we were doing the right thing. When you're in combat, you're just looking at your job and the people whom you're trying to protect. I changed my mind about Vietnam during the tumultuous spring and summer of '68—assassinations, withdrawal of Johnson's candidacy, Democratic National Convention, the time of deep soul-searching in the country. After Tet, it seemed unlikely that we could ever apply enough military force to win.

After I got out of the Marine Corps in August of 1968, I arrived at the University of Michigan in Ann Arbor to study military history. I wanted to do a dissertation on career patterns in the United States Army and Air Force between 1900 and 1950. So there I am, still in my short Marine Corps haircut, on one of the prime anti-war campuses, with organizations like Students for a Democratic Society. I went to some anti-war rallies with my wife and wrote letters against the war to the White House. But I was not a big anti-war activist.

I wanted to go into the Foreign Service. And so, in '71, I left Michigan and came to Washington and began my government career in the Foreign Service through '83, and then became a civil servant. While I was in the Foreign Service, I did go to anti-war demonstrations. Secretary of State William Rogers would not divulge the names of known protesters to the Nixon White House. I presume they didn't know about my going to anti-war protests. No one ever told me that they knew about it. I once ran into a Foreign Service officer who was not participating in the march, but he saw me. I waved to him. I certainly wasn't hiding anything. The ability of the government security apparatus to monitor the momentary activities of members of the government, even those in highly classified positions, is an impossible task. There has to be some probable cause to draw their attention, and the people who do counter-intelligence have enough things to look at.

As the deputy political adviser to the Foreign Service, I had one overseas tour in Belgium. It was at the Supreme Headquarters of Allied Powers Europe in Casteau, Belgium, working as deputy political adviser for General Andrew Goodpaster at the end of his tenure and for Al Haig, at the beginning of his tenure. Alexander Haig was prone to pontificate. He had already developed his political ambitions and sought to embellish his record. He was somebody who wanted clearly to be seen as in charge, and proved it by talking as opposed to leading by example. Remember after Reagan got shot, he said, "I'm in charge here." He was secretary of state. The vice president was in charge. The speaker of the House of Representatives is higher than the secretary of state. We weren't at war. If it were a crisis that required an immediate meeting of the National Security Council, and if the vice president was not present, Haig would have been the ranking officer of the executive branch, but that's an academic issue. Anyway, I didn't have that much contact with Haig in Brussels. I helped the international staff on the political side. We wrote a NATO exercise program. This is late Nixon, early Ford. We were doing the SALT talks during that time. You can call it the Kissingerian period in American foreign policy.

After I came back from Belgium, I took an economics course at the Foreign Service school in Arlington, Virginia. It was the equivalent of a master's degree in economics. I then worked in the State Department's Office of Population Affairs before going to the Bureau of Political/Military Affairs. I took eighteen months off to finish my dissertation, but I ran out of money. It was time to decide whether I wanted to stay in the Foreign Service—and so I got a really good job doing arms control in August 1979.

The Bureau of Political/Military Affairs is like the Pentagon inside the State Department. I was working on Star Wars—anti-satellite arms control. SALT II had been signed but not ratified by the Senate. SALT III was believed to have a life. We were looking for a way to protect our satellites from being attacked by the Russians so that we wouldn't be blind, and at the same time, we wanted to preserve a yet-to-be-developed capability to take out opposing satellites in time of war. And then with the Soviet invasion of Afghanistan, coupled with the Senate hearings, SALT II and SALT III collapsed. I suddenly became a regional specialist working on Afghanistan and Pakistan and then the Persian Gulf and the Middle East. I had one long trip there in 1983–84 and then some later trips there in '86, '87, and '88. In 1988, I got my first supervisory assignment as a deputy officer and then as office director. Much of my time spent working on this region involved terrorism and crisis management.

The counter-terrorism office in the State Department wasn't big during the '80s. So whenever there was a crisis, we got involved. Normally, you have a regular watch in the operations center, and it is manned twenty-four hours a day. For crises, you bring in additional people. You want people who actually know something in detail about the region where the crisis is occurring. The Bureau of Political/Military Affairs was always drawn upon to help man the crisis watch because we knew how to find the right people in the Pentagon to get things done. In addition to the regular twenty-four-hour watch, the State Department sets up a task force. It meets in a separate room and it has four to ten people and they read all the cable traffic and intel and answer the phones and keep people informed. These crises all tend to have a military content to them. We dealt with the *Achille Lauro*, TWA 847, Pan Am 93, and the Tripoli bombing in response to the bombing of the German disco. I also worked on the Iran-Iraq war. We supported Iraq at the time.

In 1988, based on my experience in terrorism, I got a new job with the National Security Council as director for counter-terrorism and counter-narcotics. I'd never worked on the drug issue before. The National Security Council staff's offices are in the old Executive Office Building. There's about a hundred on the NSC staff. There was no one under me, but it's a near flat organization. The lowest rank is director; the next rank is senior director and special assistant to the president. When I first went to the White House, part of my briefing was, "Are you registered with a political party?" I said, "Yes, I'm a registered Democrat." It wasn't a secret. They could have gone and found it out in public information. I have no idea what the political leanings of the career people were on the NSC staff. We just didn't talk about it.

I sat in the office that Oliver North had used. I did not know North, who was several years behind me in the Marine Corps, until he got to the NSC. He was a very disruptive influence in the government. He was a rogue of the first order who found it very difficult not to embellish his stories and renditions. He inflated what actually happened, whether he was directly involved or not. I never felt I got a straight story from him in conversations. I never had long or frequent contacts with him, but I once flew to Honduras and back with him for a set of talks with the Honduran government about our access to their military facilities. It was clear that he had come along in order to tell the Honduran military that this was not a discussion about the Contras. We had a straight-up base agreement with them, which said that we could have a permanent presence at an airfield and have U.S. aircraft come and go. This would allow the U.S. to have a location in the region as a stopping-off place in order to move military forces around. The Hondurans thought they could get extra leverage with this agreement, such as more financial support, because they were allowing the U.S to run the Contra program in Honduras. North's purpose on the trip was that if they tried to bring up this matter, he'd explain that we'd handle that aspect separately. That's really all he came along for. Even though he was a lieutenant colonel and they were Honduran generals, they all knew him.

By engaging in Iran-Contra covert activity, North caused our government to rewrite the procedures for doing covert actions. What's now required is an interagency review of the process, including at senior levels, to make sure that all the issues are on the table and that there's buy-in and that it isn't done secretly by the White House. North had also basically undermined the notion that the NSC doesn't participate directly in operations; on behalf of the president, the NSC directs other agencies to do operations. The NSC does not order embassies around directly—the State Department does that, even if the order comes from the president. And subsequent NSCs have sought to avoid being perceived acting in such a hands-on role.

The NSC staff members who generally meet with the president do country or regional jobs. They are often the note-takers in meetings that presidents have with foreign leaders. I never met with Reagan. I did meet the senior Bush, both when he was vice president and when he was president. He was a very nice gentleman who knew a great deal about the issues. He also welcomed information and asked questions. He cared a lot about international affairs.

In the spring of 1988 at the end of the Reagan administration, Congress passed a bill establishing a drug czar. Reagan had delayed the initial appointment because Vice President Bush was the lead person on the drug issue and the presidential campaign was in full swing. That's why, when he became president, Bush appointed Bill Bennett as the first drug czar.

There are a series of different ways of fighting drugs: You try to reduce demand; you go after the leadership; you go after the drugs in the field; or you try to disrupt the transportation system. But as these efforts progress, the drug traffickers become more sophisticated and so the traffickers begin to use larger aircraft. We attempted to counter them in the air, either by tracking them until they landed, or eventually trying to shoot down the aircraft. On the ground, there was an increasingly larger effort to cut down or spray the coca while providing some form of alternative livelihood to the *campesinos*. It's a highly profitable cash crop, and that's part of the reason the *campesinos* grow it.

For four years, I spent a fair amount of time in Bogotá in southern Colombia, and then I spent somewhat less time in Peru and Bolivia. To get these governments committed to going after the traffickers, you had to counter the corruption. The drug traffickers were able to push a great deal of money at underpaid government people.

In 1992, I went back to the State Department briefly as deputy assistant secretary. I worked on Middle East arms sales. My office was responsible for licensing the sale of arms by U.S. firms to foreign countries. There is a lengthy list of things that are required before licenses to sell are issued. The government keeps track of who the arms are going to, and in fact, it can veto them going from the original recipient to another country. I didn't spend a long time in that job.

I left and went back to the White House in February of '93 with the Clinton administration. For the first two years, I worked primarily on peacekeeping in Somalia and Haiti. I also helped out those who were working on terrorism and narcotics, and I began working for Richard Clarke.

I flew to Somalia with former U.S. ambassador to Somalia Robert Oakley to obtain the release of the downed Black Hawk pilot, Warrant Officer Michael Durant. He had been held hostage for ten or twelve days. We asked to see warlord Mohammed Aidid. Those we talked to were instructed to tell Aidid that it would be of no value to him to hold this guy hostage. Aidid was not a stupid person, so he agreed to see us, knowing that we had come to deliver a message from Clinton to get Durant out. I was also with Anthony Zinni who was chief of staff of our military forces when they initially entered Somalia at the end of 1992. We drove to a place where we were met by some other people who then led us to Aidid's compound. We didn't have a lot of security with us. The whole point was to show our gesture of goodwill. If Aidid wanted to get out of the situation that he found himself in, here was an opportunity. We simply told him that it was in his best interests to give up Durant and that if he took any further action, the United States was going to come after him in a very determined fashion. Over the course of six trips to Somalia to try to craft some kind of reconciliation and government of national unity, we met with Aidid probably three or four times. Somewhere in my pile of stuff, I have an autographed copy of his biography. It's in English. Durant was not handed over to us at that time; he was turned over later. When Aidid later died, his son took over his clan. That's an interesting story in and of itself. The son had actually become a U.S. citizen; he was in the Marine Corps and went to Somalia as part of the humanitarian relief operation because he spoke the local language. Anyway, after he got out of the Marine Corps, he returned to Somalia.

When we traveled to Somalia, we flew on small jets. From Andrews Air Force Base, we would take a small executive jet to the Ramstein base in Germany, where we would be met by another jet, and from there, we would fly to Cairo for refueling, and then, generally speaking, we'd stop in Ethiopia and meet with Ethiopian President Meles Zenawi to talk strategy, and then we'd fly into Mogadishu. The plane would always have enough fuel so that it could take off immediately and go someplace else like Nairobi, until we needed it again. We didn't want to leave the jet on the runway in Mogadishu. The runway was subject to being shelled or attacked. The planes that came in didn't stay.

I never heard a hostile round fired at me in Somalia. I knew enough about taking care of myself—I wore my flak jacket when it was appropriate. We traveled a lot in different helicopters, including at one point a Ukrainian helicopter that the UN had rented.

During the Clinton administration, I was in ten or twelve meetings with the president. Again, I was working in an office that tended not to meet with the president. I found him to be very smart, very informed, very engaging, and very much a political person in the sense that he just loved wading into crowd. He loved telling stories. It was easy to see why he was effective as a vote-getter.

In early 1998, I was now the assistant secretary for international narcotic and law enforcement affairs, which is the State Department bureau that's responsible for reducing the international supply of heroin and cocaine. It's also responsible for law enforcement training, both for peacekeeping operations like Bosnia, Kosovo, or Afghanistan or trying to improve the quality of law enforcement in countries like Nigeria or Russia. We started with a $200 million budget. I understand it's more than $2 billion today. I traveled to Colombia, Peru, Bolivia, occasionally Ecuador, Venezuela. I went to Nigeria, Thailand, Indonesia. In Nigeria, they have a police problem. They also have a lot of organized crime. We were told not to take our credit cards with us and to pay for everything in cash, including at their best hotels, because credit card fraud is so big there.

I held the assistant secretary position from January of '98 until September of 2002—almost five years. As an assistant secretary, I served at the pleasure of the president. It was a confirmation position. In the second Bush administration, staying on was a pretty straightforward process since I had served in the first Bush administration. They walked me right through the process. Colin Powell had hired me in '88 to be on the NSC staff. When Powell became secretary of state, he wanted clearly to demonstrate that he valued career professionals. Almost all of the career assistant secretaries were asked to stay. I think there was only one instance when a career professional was replaced by a political appointee. What he was trying to do was win the loyalty of the Foreign Service and career professionals.

Powell was very effective as a leader. In terms of the positions that he argued in favor of, they were generally issues I agreed with. He was thoughtful and cautious. He sought advice from his friends, but he obviously didn't fit in with the major players in the Bush administration. He was sort of the odd man out. But he was a team player. He was very loyal. When it was known that he had lost a particular fight, he would tell the staff not to worry because there were good days and bad days.

On September 11, 2001, I was in Peru with Powell. We were having breakfast with President Toledo of Peru. When Powell found out about the first plane hitting the tower, it sounded like it was pilot error and that it was a small plane. When the second plane hit, it was clear that it was an attack, and Powell ordered his plane refueled. That was going to take some time because we weren't supposed to leave for several hours—you don't leave a plane totally fueled on the runway when you're not about to take off. So as they refueled, I had a meeting with the justice minister; Powell gave an address to the Organization of American States assembly. We then all went back to the plane, got on, and went back to Washington. It was somber on the way back. Powell was on the phone most of the time involved in NSC meetings. We literally had no information about the attacks because we had no media contact.

The magnitude of the attacks caught me unaware as opposed to the fact that there was an attack within the United States. I mean, terrorists had tried to blow up the World Trade Center before, and they failed. At the Murrah Federal Building in Oklahoma City, a domestic terrorist attack had happened. We had the millennium plot that was thwarted. We knew that Al Qaeda was coming after us. We had bombings in Tanzania and Kenya, and there was the attack on the USS Cole. There was all that information during the summer about how heated the situation was and how bin Laden was coming after us, so the attack itself wasn't a surprise—just the inventiveness of it.

We landed at Andrews Air Force Base and drove back into the city. Very eerie; no cars on the road. We were in a convoy of cars because Powell had a police escort. He was going to the White House for meetings. I went around and talked to people at the State Department about their personal reactions. People were suffering from post-traumatic stress. Some had seen the Pentagon burning, or they heard the impact of the plane when it hit the building.

In this period after 9/11, everybody was just attending to their own jobs and trying to be supportive of the larger effort as it unfolded. At the most senior level we made decisions about going after Al Qaeda in Afghanistan. One of my early tasks was how to shore up Pakistan's border with Afghanistan. There was an initial reluctance to engage the Pakistani military because of its association with the Pakistani nuclear program and the Musharraf coup. I ended up working with Ambassador Wendy Chamberlain—she used to be my deputy—to beef up a border security program. That included buying aircraft and economic development programs for sparsely populated areas along the border. I proposed a figure of around $75 million, and that was something we did fairly quickly in order to fortify our relationship with the Musharraf government. Border security was necessary to prevent Al Qaeda and the Taliban from withdrawing into Pakistan, or returning. But these programs take time. They don't get made overnight. The

Pakistanis would administer these programs because they didn't want U.S. forces in Pakistan in any visible fashion. That's what it comes down to. Obviously there were U.S. forces in Pakistan prior to the invasion of Afghanistan, and some are undoubtedly there now. But they were not the main operating forces; they were intel types and Special Forces. Let's also remember that Pakistan's northwest frontier is governed differently from the rest of the country. The tribes have never fully recognized Pakistani sovereignty and don't regard the border as a border; it's just land that they live in, though occasionally the military has to go there and remind people that Pakistan is actually in charge. You can say the same thing about our Saudi ally. While they're prepared to receive assistance from us, they have political problems about having that embrace be too obvious, in the sense of an actual large-scale military presence. They could take our help and intel, but they want to do it themselves. That's not necessarily a bad thing. We shouldn't have to do all the work. The question is: can the Saudis, in fact, actually do the work and do it well?

Post 9/11, we were also looking to raise money from international donors for Afghanistan. Because I was in charge of the law enforcement programs—which involved trying to create a police force, legal system, and narcotics enforcement in Afghanistan—I worked with the UN, the British, and the Germans. The Germans were in charge of the police program among the Allies, and the British were in charge of the narcotics program. The Italians were in charge of the justice program; the Japanese were in charge of demobilization, disarmament, and re-integration of the militias. We had a number of meetings in Tokyo, Washington, and Paris to try to move the programs—but they were slow in starting. The urgency of restoring order was not evident to many of the international players.

Shortly after I arrived at the NSC for my final tour in September 2002, national security adviser Condi Rice asked me to suggest courses of action to deal with Afghanistan's opium problem, which was already beginning to show up. The farmers had planted opium in the winter of 2001 and harvested it in the spring, after having essentially stopped growing it for a whole year under the Taliban. The British sent a delegation over to Washington to talk about this issue. They sent their Afghan coordinator and narcotics coordinator from the foreign office, along with an interagency team of intel and defense types, and they said, "We will organize a counter-narcotics strike force to eradicate parts of the crop in order that people understand that there's not a free ride and that they will actually consider alternative development." The British called this strategy Alternative Livelihood. Rather than growing opium, the farmers would be encouraged to switch to something else. Because the U.S. had the largest military presence there, they requested us to be backup in terms of rescue forces if significant violence occurred, helicopter mobility for the eradication forces, and provide storage areas on our bases for their equipment. The British would still run the program. And so I coordinated an agreement at senior levels in Washington, and a cable went to London informing the Brits about what we agreed to. The Pentagon was also supposed to send out the cable through military channels to Afghanistan. The British narcotics coordinator then went to Kabul, but the cable had never gotten there. It had either been quashed in the Pentagon—even though they had agreed to it—or it had been quashed at U.S. Central Command, because they regarded any kind of activity of this nature as not central to their mission. I know for a fact that Rumsfeld did not think that the Pentagon should be involved in counter-narcotics activity, because at the beginning of the Bush administration I had a conversation with him on that subject. It was very clear that he did not think of counter-narcotics as a military mission.

Recently, however, the Pentagon has reversed its position. It finally came to the same conclusion that a number of us were saying all along—which was that the opium activity is a multi-billion-dollar slush fund for corruption and instability in Afghanistan. We never had any clear evidence that Al Qaeda skimmed money from the drug trade when they were in Afghanistan as the guests of the Taliban, but the Taliban did. The Taliban took Kabul in '96. They taxed the drug trade and did not institute their opium eradication program until the 2000–2001 crop. The Taliban probably were using their eradication effort to win international recognition for their government, but they were also hedging on the opium crop because the drug market had become glutted.

In 2005, the opium situation is completely out of control in Afghanistan. The country has had a long drought which has hurt other agriculture, while poppy is less stressed by drought conditions. As a crop, it dominates the water market because it is the most profitable. Poppy grows on little water, so whatever water is left is then diverted to it. The last time I saw a map, the crop had spread like measles all over the country. We always thought that the Northern Alliance got some of their money from the drug trade, but it was never a significant element of poppy production in Afghanistan until a couple of years ago.

I don't know what the Bush administration is actually doing about this problem; there was a big debate on whether the U.S. ought to engage in aerial eradication. My understanding is that the folks who wanted aerial eradication lost that debate. Afghanistan is a much more difficult environment for aerial eradication than Colombia. The terrain is more hostile in the topographical sense, but it is also more hostile in the sense of an armed peasantry. The poppy culture is going to require a serious and sustained program to deal with it. The alternative is prolonged instability and a potential for the return of the Taliban.

I didn't spend a lot of time working with Condoleezza Rice. She came to the job as national security adviser with limited experience in a lot of things that the U.S. did on a global basis. She was a Russian expert. She spent two years working for the government during the first half of the first Bush administration—and the rest of her time was in academia where she took on administrative as well as academic positions. Now, she read a lot, she knew issues, but she didn't know them in the kind of fine-grain fashion that Dick Clarke certainly had. Had she heard of Al Qaeda? I would think she had. But I would probably bet that Al Qaeda wasn't all that familiar to her. Remember, the Republicans came in worrying about China and a phoenix-arising Russia. They didn't think as much about non-state actors like Al Qaeda. That was not their world view.

I was in a couple of meetings with George W. Bush. The first meeting was in the State Department, and he was on his way to Mexico for his first foreign trip. He came over to be briefed. He knew things about Mexico. Powell wanted him to be briefed by junior officers, so they did most of the briefing and he engaged in a very interesting set of discussions with them. The second meeting was a cabinet-level meeting to look at our counter-terrorism effort. When Rice and Tenet and Wolfowitz talked about the need to reduce Al Qaeda's recruitment of terrorists, the president sort of dismissed them by saying that victory in Iraq would take care of that problem. He thought that our victory in Iraq would undermine Al Qaeda's ability to recruit. Bush said in this conversation: "Victory will take care of that problem." I'm giving you my interpretation of what he meant by that very short phrase. He believed that victory would be so overwhelming and with Saddam removed from the scene, it would make clear to other states that they had better cooperate with us. He equated military victory with political victory because it gives you power to move people in your own direction.

I stayed on as special assistant to the president for combating terrorism for seven months. In January 2003, I told people that I was leaving. Rice knew that I wanted to leave. I was asked to stay until after the military campaign aspect of the Iraq War. In March, I realized I could no longer stay and do the job that the president deserved from a member of his staff. Rice asked me if I was leaving in protest of the war. I said, "No, I just want to leave." If I was protesting anything, it was the ineffectiveness of our terrorism policy. It just turns the pit of my stomach. That's why I left. I felt that the Bush administration wasn't as serious about the job as the threat warranted. They were focused on Iraq. They had a decision-making process involving the senior-most people. It was not clear what kind of input they wanted from their staff. On top of that, they were beginning to execute our policy toward Iraq without building the kind of a coalition that George Bush, Sr. had built for the first Gulf War. It seemed to me that we were getting more and more into a situation that was going to take our eye off of the terrorism effort and maybe end up creating a lightning rod that would make it easier for terrorists to recruit. They also weren't spending much time or effort on homeland security. The organizational effort to create that department was really not moving forward in a way that would make the department able to function properly.

I got complete support from my family for my decision to leave. My son Benjamin said, "You've taken spears for the team long enough," meaning I'd been a loyal government servant long enough. So after I left the Bush White House, I signed up with the Kerry presidential campaign. I'd never met him before. I wanted to work on a political campaign. I wanted to participate in an effort to change the leadership in Washington. I had looked around the field, and he was the person who I thought was best qualified and most likely to be able to defeat George Bush. I thought Kerry would make a better commander in chief. He had a broader experience and perspective on the domestic side as well.

The Bush campaign undermined Kerry's national security credentials very effectively. As a result, national security issues like fighting terrorism never got the traction needed. It was one of the enduring struggles that the national security team faced in the campaign. Some of this was our inability to communicate as clear a vision as we should have, and I bear some of that responsibility. Some of it was due to a reluctance on the part of Kerry's political consultants to focus on national security in a presidential campaign when domestic issues—the normal winning issues for Democrats—needed to be addressed. Some of it was due to the difficulty Kerry sometimes had in communicating why he voted to authorize the war in 2002, but was against the supplemental funding for it in 2003—a position that the Republicans exploited. Another problem was that the press always wanted Kerry to say something new; there was a constant struggle to find new things to say as opposed to simply saying the same thing over and over again.

Kerry spent most of the time talking about domestic issues. Although Kerry did talk about national security issues, the war on terrorism and Iraq became more prominent in the last forty-five days of the campaign. But the final push wasn't sufficient to counter all the negative remarks put out by the Bush administration. I suspect that the video by bin Laden had some effect in the campaign. And even though Kerry clearly won the presidential debates, the Republican

Party and the president were successful during the length of the election campaign in branding John Kerry as weak on terrorism, Iraq, and national security. I know it's uncommon to change leadership in a time of war, but the president's stewardship on the range of national security issues was horrible. And the president's economic policies certainly did not find favor with the majority of the American people. In the end, however, enough people felt Bush was just somebody who they were more comfortable with than Kerry. Kerry's not as much of a down-home sort of person as George Bush—and that's an important characteristic for many voters. The devil you know is better than the devil you don't know.

Looking back, I really did what I wanted to do, which was to leave the Bush administration and try to do something political, something which I had never done before—to change leadership in the country. Running for president is a huge undertaking and being involved in a political campaign is also a huge undertaking, which I hadn't truly appreciated before. I felt very blessed to have been able to participate in that kind of an effort. It was a good campaign; we just didn't run hard enough to win against some of the things that they did to us— and I sure wish we had.

Taking on headfirst the Islamic extremism should be the defining issue for the Democratic Party. I think that Al Qaeda will continue to try to carry off a terrorist attack on the United States, given bin Laden's predilection toward big events. It takes a long time for them to organize such actions. They have to get the people here, they have to have a plan, they have to get their weapon for the destruction, they have to do all that without being detected, and they have to make sure that there are no glitches in their plan. So they tend to be very deliberate. To some degree, we're doing some things right. It was easier for them to attack before 9/11. We're a lot more watchful now, but we are not perfect.

As for Iraq, the basic ingredients of a successful exit strategy are becoming more and more questionable. The basis of that strategy is that there will be enough force and commitment for stability to overcome the forces of chaos. You don't have to have an overwhelming force to produce chaos—but you do to produce stability. I don't like to use Vietnam analogies because they tend to be a little simplistic, but with the Vietnamization Program, the idea was to train the Vietnamese well enough to take over for themselves. South Vietnam didn't collapse until 1975—about two years after we departed. However, the South Vietnamese never had sufficient will to fight for themselves to be victorious. This is a different situation. There's an overwhelming number of people in Iraq, demographically, who are in favor of stability. But will the Shiites and Kurds actually come out and fight for a unified or even a federated Iraq? Or will they just sit on the sidelines? A civil war may be the ultimate result. A fragmentation into quasi- or wholly independent states in constant friction with one another is a possibility. It's hard to feel optimistic. What effect will Iraq have on the Republican Party? It depends upon the nature of the end. Nixon was brought down by Watergate, not by Vietnam.

I fear for the Republic now. When I see Bush, Rice, or Rumsfeld on television, I find myself thinking that if these are the people who represent the United States, we as a nation are so much more than they are. Politically and philosophically, America is a much richer country and has so much more to bring to the world than this administration.

19

REAL BAGGAGE

Federal aviation security expert Jay Stroup was buffaloed.

> "Most of the screeners were hired right off the street. They had no experience with passenger baggage screening operations."

The Buffalo Niagara International Airport has been a case study of airport security in disarray. Baggage screening violations were frequent. Supervision was lax. Its slipshod operations even caught the muckraking attention of *Mother Jones* magazine. But, as federal employees at the airport soon realized, if you wanted to hold onto your job, it was unwise to complain about security problems or personnel issues to higher-ups in the Transportation Security Administration. The airport's federal security director, Jay Stroup, learned this lesson the hard way. Not only were his warnings and complaints ignored by his supervisors, they forced him to resign.

Stroup is now trying to fight back through legal channels. With the assistance of his attorney, Stroup filed for whistle-blower status with the federal government, but it could be years before a verdict is reached. Nor will it be an easy road for the aviation security expert. He's been blacklisted in the industry, his family savings are depleted, and to make ends meet, he's pushing a broom and cleaning toilets in a plastics factory.

■   ■   ■

I brought the Transportation Security Administration to Buffalo as its first federal security director. My date of hire was October 6, 2002. Prior to that, I worked for Raytheon for a little over a year where I did testing of Federal Aviation Administration air traffic control systems. And before that, I was in the U.S. Navy for twenty years. I was a chief petty officer. My last assignment was down on the Patuxent River in Maryland where I was the liaison for the chief of naval operations.

My primary responsibility in Buffalo was to administer security policy. I wrote out baggage and passenger screening operations as well as conducted regulatory oversight responsibilities. There were approximately 320 screeners when I got here. Buffalo is a very big Category 2 airport, though it has been re-designated a Category 1 airport.

Buffalo was one of the regional training centers. We trained Buffalo screeners as well as screeners from airports in Ohio, Pennsylvania, and Syracuse and other parts of western New York. Most of the screeners were hired right off the street. They had no experience with passenger or baggage screening operations. TSA had contracted out the hiring process for screeners to a private company who was responsible for doing the background checks. I didn't have any say about who got hired.

A lot of the screeners had problems with their screening managers. And the screening managers had problems with the director of screeners, who was my subordinate. In July of 2003, some screeners came to me with complaints. They put these into writing and signed their names to them. The complaints dealt with deviation from security directives. A lot of it was just plain irresponsibility. For instance, one of the complaints was that the assistant director of screening would take the day off and go golfing. He would take a screening manager and a couple of screeners with him and force other employees to work overtime.

Harassment was another issue. The screeners didn't like being harassed by the local police departments at the airport. The Buffalo airport has its own transit authority police department. A few of their officers harassed and harangued the screeners on a routine basis. It wasn't based on gender or race. It was mostly based on a power-play thing. But that is one of the issues I wanted to get Internal Affairs to investigate. An officer tried to go off an exit lane at the airport without showing his airport ID pass. Officers in uniform are allowed to go in the opposite direction in an exit lane in response to an emergency, but they still have to show ID badges. That is required by federal law. One of the screeners asked if he could see his ID badge. The officer got pretty irate with him.

Another time, we had three screeners who fell asleep in the bag room. This happened during baggage screening operations. As far as I know, the bags went on the airplane unscreened. The three employees were probationary employees. I recommended to headquarters and to the employee relations director that they should be terminated. Well, when I was forced to resign in October 2003, it wasn't a month later that those three sleeping screeners were brought back to work.

So why did they force me to quit? Well, I had asked Internal Affairs for a formal investigation of our assistant director of screeners, as required by TSA policy, because there was a violation or suspected violation of federal regulations and security directives. But my request was blocked by my superior in the northeast director's office, who told me on the phone that he didn't want lawyers involved. He said that he was going to have his own management inquiry. It was going to be in-house. These were operational issues, not legal issues, he told me.

Well, it turns out that the investigator, who was sent by management from Syracuse, didn't do anything about the assistant director of screening. You know what his prior job was before he became a career federal employee? He sold men's clothing. I don't even know how he got hired. Aviation management is a big old boys' club. People get hired because of who they know—not what their experience is.

Anyway, the investigator didn't look at any of the charges. He didn't even read the screeners' statement. Instead, he just conducted an inquiry on me, based on an anonymous letter dated July 28, 2003, which happens to be the same day that I put the assistant director of screening on administrative leave. Obviously, they didn't want me around. I was a probationary employee; we all had to serve a one-year probationary period. I believe that they wanted me out of Buffalo so they could give my job to someone else. There was a lot of cronyism, people hooking up buddies.

I was handed my letter of termination on October 1, 2003. They gave me this option. They said, "We will accept your resignation." I said, "Why should I resign? I shouldn't be terminated." Their response was, "Well, you're a probationary employee. You have no grievance or any kind of rights to complain about this." They told me that if I ever wanted to get a job in Homeland Security or anywhere else in the federal government, a termination would prevent that from happening. They gave me twenty-four hours to resign. They called it an involuntary resignation. I chose to resign rather than be fired because I thought that was the best thing for my family. I wanted to get another job in security. I turned in my badge, along with other equipment like phones.

Since then, I've sent out resume after resume, application after application, to other federal agencies and non-federal organizations. But nothing. People in the TSA are so vindictive toward me, they've been willing to tell prospective employers something that would keep them from hiring me. They took away more than my job in Buffalo. They took away my whole livelihood. It was my family's future.

I am forty-three. I have three children, two daughters and a son. We had college savings for them, but that is gone. Our retirement savings are gone; it's all gone to attorneys. I had a decent job with Raytheon, which I didn't have to leave. My job in Buffalo was at the GS-15 level. The base pay was $75,000. Out of thirteen people they had interviewed for security director, they said that I was the best candidate. I'm a guy who spent his life in aviation in the security arena. I went through Navy SEAL training in 1990. After that, I moved into aviation tactical operations and aviation assets for amphibious assaults, and then from there I moved into naval base and aviation security issues. But now I can't find work in my field. I'm making less than ten dollars an hour working for a temp agency as a janitor in a plastics factory. Every time I pick up that broom and that mop I get angry.

Looking back, I'd still do it all over again. Just like many others in the post-9/11 era, all I wanted to do was make sure that the Transportation Security Administration worked properly. That's all I wanted to do as a whistle-blower. I wanted to make sure that airport security went to the next level of efficiency. I could have just looked the other way and allowed the screeners to sleep on duty. I could have just looked the other way and allowed security directives to be totally ignored. I could have looked the other way and allowed the screeners to be harassed by the police. But I didn't do that. It would have been a violation of my duties.

Back in 1776, people said, "Enough's enough." They went against the establishment, the British. Now I'm not anti-government. I am pro-government. But the TSA has wronged people. I don't see anyone in government—a congressman or senator—standing up and saying, "This is wrong. You did this to my constituent. Why did you do this to him?"

My family extends all the way back to before the Revolution. I was born and raised outside of Pittsburgh, Pennsylvania. Most of my family lives in Pennsylvania. On my dad's side of the family, we have relatives buried at Gettysburg. I wanted to serve this country with honor and dignity.

I am cynical toward the TSA, because I question its motives. The TSA has become nothing more than a bureaucratic screening agency. The TSA has been watered down to focus on passenger screening. The airport management staff is now responsible for airport security—just like it was back before 9/11. For instance, an airline agent will ask security supervisors to speed up the baggage-screening line or will try to bring a group of passengers through quickly. I don't think the airports have done much of anything to make themselves safer. We were on the right track, but then bureaucracies and the old paradigms took over. Screening operations and airport security have regressed back to pre-9/11 levels.

20

TRUTH, LIES, AND WAR

Daniel Ellsberg straddles history, theorizes about
human aggression, and contemplates nuclear war.

> "Within a couple of months into the Iraq war,
> I could see that this was going to develop
> like Vietnam."

It's difficult to neatly summarize Daniel Ellsberg's life. "To anyone over a certain age (forty-five?), Daniel Ellsberg needs no introduction," wrote Nicholas Lemann four years ago in the *New Yorker*, "but it would be quite a challenge to explain Ellsberg to someone who had never heard of him." Lemann proceeded to list career milestones. Following his example, here's another compressed biographical overview. Ellsberg was born in Detroit. Third in his class at Harvard. Marine infantry lieutenant. Joined Rand Corporation and specialized in nuclear war-gaming. Left to go work at the Pentagon on Vietnam policy, serving directly under Assistant Secretary of Defense John McNaughton. Went as a State Department official to Vietnam for two years where he evaluated "village pacification." Leaked Pentagon's top-secret historical study of U.S. policymaking in Vietnam to the *New York Times* in 1971. Enemy of Nixon, who demanded that Attorney General John Mitchell "haul in that son-of-a-bitch Ellsberg right away." Subject of the most intensive FBI manhunt since the Lindbergh kidnapping after briefly going underground with second wife Patricia. Criminal defendant in federal court on multiple felony charges. All charges dismissed after government misdeeds surfaced during trial. Author of national bestseller, *Secrets: A Memoir of Vietnam and the Pentagon Papers*, which won the 2003 American Book Award for nonfiction. Focus of FX cable movie, *Pentagon Papers*; James Spader of *Sex, Lies & Videotape* and *Boston Legal* played Ellsberg. Civil disobedience activist. Arrested seventy times. Opposed nuclear weapon proliferation, U.S. military involvement in Central America, and war in Iraq. Holy man of the left.

Ellsberg, seventy-four, continues to display the stamina of a man half his age. His calendar is booked giving anti-war lectures, attending peace rallies, and mentoring government whistle-blowers like former FBI translator Sibel Edmonds, who is president of the National Security Whistleblowers Coalition. He's working on a book about nuclear disarmament. His intellect remains intimidating, probing, and challenging, though he admits with a self-deprecating chuckle, "my short-term memory is not as good as it used to be." He lives in Kensington, California—a quiet enclave of expensive hillside homes next door to Berkeley. He's been married to Patricia for thirty-five years. They had met in Washington, D.C. She interviewed newsmakers for her syndicated public radio show. Their first date was April 17, 1965, which was also the same day as the first big Students for Democratic Society anti-war march. Even though he still worked at the Pentagon, Ellsberg went with her to the rally. He has five grandchildren.

Ellsberg's evolution from academic to analyst to activist can be traced by a visit to www.ellsberg.net. This is a fifty-year trove of interviews, lecture transcripts, published articles, and scholarly papers. One recent addition to the site is an op-ed piece he wrote for the *Los Angeles Times* (July 3, 2005), whose title is "I Wrote Bush's War Words—in 1965." It begins:

> *President Bush's explanation Tuesday night for staying the course in Iraq evoked in me a sense of familiarity, but not nostalgia. I had heard virtually all of his themes before, almost word for word, in speeches delivered by three presidents I worked for: John F. Kennedy, Lyndon B. Johnson and Richard M. Nixon. Not with pride, I recognized that I had proposed some of those very words myself.*
>
> *Drafting a speech on the Vietnam War for Defense Secretary Robert S. McNamara in July 1965, I had the same task as Bush's speechwriters in June 2005: how to rationalize and motivate continued public support for a hopelessly stalemated, unnecessary war our president had lied us into.*

Ellsberg had an intimate view of how the American government prepared the nation for war. That education in deception began on his first full day—August 4, 1964—at his new job in the Pentagon. He found himself monitoring urgent traffic reports from a U.S. Navy commander in the Gulf of Tonkin off the coast of North Vietnam. The cables reported North Vietnamese patrol boats firing torpedos at two American warships. (These alarms later proved inaccurate; choppy seas had affected interpretations of sonar readings.) President Johnson nonetheless had his smoking gun; he announced to America that this was "unprovoked" evidence of

North Vietnam's "naked aggression." Johnson said that the incident demanded immediate retaliation. His Tonkin Gulf war resolution easily passed Congress; only two Senators opposed it.

Why did LBJ risk military escalation with North Vietnam? And why did he mislead the public by saying he sought "no wider war"? The answers rest with domestic politics. He couldn't afford South Vietnam being overrun by communists on his watch, but calling for the wider war that Republican presidential candidate Barry Goldwater championed would have imperiled chances for a landslide victory, which he saw as critical in generating sufficient political capital for his Great Society proposals. But, like his predecessors—Truman, Eisenhower, and Kennedy—LBJ privately knew that the war in Southeast Asia was unwinnable. Each one recognized what happened to the French in 1954. If LBJ wanted to avoid the humiliation of losing, he still wasn't prepared to try to win at all costs. The political price was too high.

In 1965, Ellsberg vacated his E-Ring office at the Pentagon and spent seventeen months in South Vietnam on a State Department fact-finding mission. He toured the countryside. He went along on combat and recon patrols. He made careful notes about "village pacification." But his observations contradicted what passed for highly classified intelligence back in Washington. Pacification seemed like a complete failure. Hearts and minds weren't being won over. Field reports were being doctored, enemy casualties inflated. Furthermore, the South Vietnamese government was riddled with corruption, and its army suffered low morale.

When he returned to the U.S., two years went by before he began living a double life as a Pentagon insider briefing top officials, including National Security Adviser Henry Kissinger, and participant in anti-war gatherings. He was a man whose loyalties were split right down the middle, that is, until he made that irrevocable decision to copy the 7,000-page top-secret Pentagon study locked in his office safe. "I saw [Vietnam] first as a problem, next as a stalemate, then as a moral and political disaster, a crime," he writes in *Secrets*. At first, he tried to get anti-war senators like William Fulbright interested in the Pentagon Papers, which documented a consistent pattern of exaggeration and deliberate falsehoods about Vietnam policy dating back to the Truman administration. After being rebuffed on Capitol Hill, Ellsberg went to the press.

Did the papers' publication actually shorten the Vietnam War? At the outset, they became the center of an intense freedom of the press struggle. The Justice Department sought an unprecedented injunction to prevent the *New York Times* from printing them. When the Supreme Court voted 6–3 in favor of the *Times*, it was a victory for the First Amendment, though their continued publication in the

Times and eighteen other newspapers failed to generate the impact Ellsberg hoped they would have. He explains why in *Secrets*:

> *Starting the day after Christmas 1971, [Nixon] launched a thousand U.S. bombers during five days of bombing against North Vietnam, in the heaviest raids since 1968. Thus, six months later after the publication of the Pentagon Papers, when people asked me at the end of the year what I thought I had accomplished, I said, 'Nothing.' Nothing in regard to the war, my overriding concern. It wasn't public opinion I had been ultimately seeking to change. It was the bombing, the war, Nixon's policy. None of those had been influenced by American public opinion since the start of his term in office, as far as I could see, or by the release of the papers.*
>
> *Most Americans in truth had wanted out of the war long before the papers were published; a majority had come to regard it as immoral. In the face of that majority sentiment, the president had kept the war going by reducing ground troops, while he increased the bombing, and by recurrently convincing the public that he was on the verge of a settlement.*

While the papers stopped short of covering the years of his own presidency, Nixon feared that Ellsberg or others might come out of the woodwork with potentially damaging evidence. Nixon wanted to plug these leaks. This led to the creation of a new cloak-and-dagger unit called the Plumbers. Its first covert mission was breaking into Ellsberg's psychiatrist's office to find dirt to use against Ellsberg. It was this same group—Cuban exiles working for E. Howard Hunt—who later bungled the break-in of the Democratic National headquarters at Watergate.

Ellsberg's trial for leaking the papers lasted five months. He faced 115 years in prison if convicted on all the charges. But on May 11, 1973, the judge dismissed Ellsberg's case outright. He cited "improper government conduct" (illegal wiretapping and evidence tampering came to light). On that very same day, Nixon sat down with his chief of staff, H.R. Haldeman, in the Oval Office and vented his fury. An excerpt from that secretly taped conversation appears on the last page of Ellsberg's memoir:

> *For example, on this national security thing, we have the rocky situation where the sonofabitching thief is made a national hero and is going to get off on a mistrial. And the* New York Times *gets a Pulitzer Prize for stealing documents. They're trying to get at us with thieves. What in the name of God have we come to?*

The Senate Watergate hearings commenced the following week. It was the subsequent cover-up, not the crime itself, which set into motion Nixon's resignation. (The articles of impeachment that were then being drafted included the Ellsberg break-in.) The war ended on May 1, 1975, under President Gerald Ford. Would the Plumbers have even existed if Ellsberg hadn't pulled off one of the most important whistle-blowing acts in American history? Would there have been a Watergate? How much longer would the war have lasted? How many lives were ultimately saved?

In Iraq today, the echoes of that past war keep resurfacing. Our nation is once again experiencing the painful, slow drip of tragedy and mounting casualties. "Sometimes I feel I'm waking up to the world I left 40 years ago," Ellsberg told the *San Francisco Chronicle* in 2004.

In a *New York Times* op-ed piece (September 28, 2004) called "Truths Worth Telling," Ellsberg encouraged other officials in the Bush administration to step forward with documented claims detailing how the White House misled the American public into supporting the war. Citing himself as an example who had failed to act until it was too late, he described a conversation he had in 1978 with Senator Wayne Morse of Oregon, one of the two senators who had voted against the Tonkin Gulf resolution:

> *Seven years and almost 50,000 American deaths later, after I had leaked the Pentagon Papers, [Morse told me that] if I had leaked the documents then, the resolution never would have passed. That was hard to hear. But in 1964 it hadn't occurred to me to break my vow of secrecy. Though I knew that the war was a mistake, my loyalties then were to the secretary of defense and the president. It took five years of war before I recognized the higher loyalty all officials owe to the Constitution, the rule of law, the soldiers in harm's way or their fellow citizens.*

■   ■   ■

James Spader doesn't look like me in the movie, but he caught my intensity. Patricia and I watched it hand-in-hand. We loved its love parts. I asked her, "Did I really look that good?" And she said, "Better."

I have one child with Patricia. Michael is now twenty-eight. He's a writer actually. He is up most nights writing. He is writing a memoir, of all things. His growing up. Various intellectual and emotional concerns. He is a very good writer. And a savage editor. Michael slashed *Secrets* almost in half. He calls himself Jack the Ripper. My older son, Robert, is editor-in-chief of Orbis Books. He did a lot of editing on my book. In the movie, Robert is running the Xerox machine, and my daughter, Mary, who was ten, is cutting the "Top Secret" off the documents. That really happened.

FX never approached me when they made the film. I am sure one reason was not to pay me any money. The other was probably to not get any interference from me—which I would have almost had to do because every scene was wrong essentially. My former wife did not come to the place where we were copying documents and confront me.

At the beginning of *Pentagon Papers*, Spader is speaking to the camera and more or less quoting a description in an essay that I wrote in which I quoted from *Toilers of the Sea*, by Victor Hugo, about people walking into quicksand. As usual in that movie, he gets it almost exactly backwards. My essay is called "The Quagmire Myth and the Stalemate Machine." It got a prize for the best paper presented at the American Political Science Association in 1970. Its thesis was that the notion we got into Vietnam as into a quagmire—without noticing that we were getting deeper in and it was harder to get out of—was a myth. Whereas the movie says that is how we got into Vietnam. What I said in my paper, which has been reprinted a lot, is that it's a very arresting image and very plausible, but is wrong in every respect. It is *not* how we got into Vietnam. It may have been how the public thought we were getting into Vietnam. It was told that we were about to win any day. But inside the White House, the president was never told that. Never. Never told it was gonna be quick or easy or cheap. Nor that the next step would be sufficient to win.

I was also rather furious at the movie's end. It ends by my character saying, "If my greatest act of patriotism was an act of treason, so be it." Two or three times in the movie, I'm heard using the word "treason." "Gee, this is treason." And "I'll be tried for treason." I was, of course, not indicted for treason. I did not expect to be indicted for treason. I really don't appreciate people legitimizing the idea that what I did was treason. When people do say it, I correct them. So for my character in the movie to say it was an act of treason again reverses my actual attitude.

As we approached going to war in Iraq, I realized that whistle-blowing by officials was really very urgent, as it had been in Vietnam. My message was: "Don't delay telling the truth to Congress and the press. Not just Congress, because without pressure from the press, Congress doesn't move on these truths. They just hold them to themselves and keep silent about them. Don't wait years into a war. Don't wait until the bombs have been falling. Don't wait until thousands more have died, if you know that the administration is lying to the public, is deceiving the public, is leading them into a wrongful, unnecessary war."

When I released the Pentagon Papers, I was trying to avert a disaster. It has nothing to do with wanting to be a martyr. And in my case, of course, Nixon failed in his efforts to martyr me. You might say, I didn't suffer any major loss. There was the loss of friendships; my friends having had security clearances. That was a loss. But it wasn't what Nixon had in mind for me. What he had in mind was 115 years in prison, or even before that, beating me up. Slandering me. But he didn't succeed in any of that.

I am not claiming to be totally prescient about the Iraq War. But within a couple of months, I could see that this was going to develop like Vietnam. Which is a thoroughly stalemated war. It is a quagmire. It's not a question of our being driven out, but of it being impossible for us to eliminate the insurgents. As was true in Vietnam. We got into Vietnam with our eyes open internally as to how bad it would be. In this case, the military could see that there would be a terrible occupation problem. General Shinseki, of course, was strongly rebuked as chief of staff of the Army for saying that it would take several hundred thousand troops to occupy instead of the 130,000 that they were sending over. Wolfowitz said that's wildly off the mark. And Shinseki's replacement was announced. He didn't retire immediately, but was made into a lame-duck general. Now, looking back, I'm sure that Shinseki had a six-foot-high stack of studies telling him why you needed several hundred thousand troops. I wished he would have released those at the time. They are documents that need to be leaked.

The *blitzkrieg* part was done very competently. Very effectively. And it was a Nazi-like *blitzkrieg*. Very well-executed war of aggression. To look back at what my judgments were in May 2003, I wouldn't know one way or another how Iraq was going to develop. By the fall, I could see that the insurgents had an effective tactic here—the suicide bombing. Effective in a military sense. That's not to excuse terrorism when it's targeted on civilians, which is murder. Suicide bombing is like precision-guided munitions. Where you want it. And it is very hard to stop. It was also very clear to me right away that we were not getting intelligence from the people who knew about those ambushes. In other words, we were facing the same ambush problem that the French faced and we faced in Vietnam. The Iraqis weren't prepared to give information to a foreign occupier in order to save any of the lives of the foreign occupiers. My Vietnam experience prepared me to think, "Okay, this is a war that can go on forever." People say, "Oh, you're prejudiced. You're just looking through the lenses of the past." Well, I was using my own experience, but I wasn't confined by it. I was just ready to perceive similarities. People ask me, "But aren't there differences?" I say, "Sure. It's a dry heat. The language we don't speak is Arabic rather than Vietnamese. And the ambushes are in the city rather than the countryside." But the similarities are more important than the differences.

It was obvious to me that we were being lied to about the reasons for going to war. Even though I did think they had WMDs. Trying to say that Saddam Hussein, after ten years of sanctions, is the number-one threat to the U.S. and world security was an absurd statement. It was just ridiculous. In a world where Russians have loose nuclear weapons, and with India and Pakistan facing each other with nuclear weapons, to say that Saddam was the number-one threat, I could not believe Powell believed that. I felt he had to be consciously lying.

The press had been compliant right along. They are getting a little critical now. There is a synergy between public dismay and disillusion and the press. When there is more unrest in the public, the press gets a little nerve to criticize the president. But they have been very dismayingly compliant—and essentially passing on government handouts and cheering things on.

It was the same thing with the Democrats in Congress. They were afraid of being called names. The fear is a well-justified expectation that they would be called unpatriotic by the White House. Dick Armey was calling Tom Daschle unpatriotic and giving aid and comfort to the enemy by criticizing the president or questioning strategy.

People like Bill O'Reilly and Ann Coulter and others are great name callers. Coulter writes a book with the title *Treason*. And I am in that book not only as a traitor like everybody else, but she also describes me as a felon. That is interesting. Isn't Ann Coulter supposed to be a lawyer? You don't have to be a lawyer in America to be aware that you are *not* a felon if you haven't been convicted of anything.

I can't sue anybody for libel as a public figure. That is an aspect of our First Amendment here—which the British don't have—and for our not having an official Secrets Act. I am a little envious of their libel laws, to tell the truth. My First Amendment friends are very down on libel. Because I am a public figure, the tests for proving libel, I believe, are insurmountable.

I don't want to label Republicans in general, but these people are extreme slanderers. They are very vicious. These people are unusual. In many respects we have a White House now that is extremely dangerous. And among other things, I would say very anti-democratic. They don't believe in democracy, in my opinion. And that's why I am very, very concerned that they will exploit the next 9/11. I expect there to be another 9/11. They will use that as a Reichstag fire to close down democracy very seriously in this country. I don't use that analogy lightly either. We really are in a pre-authoritarian situation here.

This is the time for people to show courage. People have more courage than they realize. It is the situation that challenges them. I think a lot about what happened in Germany in 1933 and I also wonder what people could have done in '32 to try to avert that in Germany. With each year it got much harder, and after that it was very hard to do anything about it. It took increasing courage. Now is the time for people to show that courage, and one thing specifically that I would like to see is a lot more whistle-blowing.

For the past three years, I have been calling for whistle-blowing and truth-telling within the government. One obvious example was the Downing Street memo, which was leaked to the British press. It revealed that Prime Minister Blair had been briefed in July 2002 that President Bush had decided on a war against Iraq and that intelligence was being fixed around the policy. It got almost no attention over here. Nearly a month went by before anybody even mentioned it. The *New York Times* eventually gave it a certain amount of discussion. But very little from the media. It almost blanked out. Second, the Downing Street memo was written in July of 2002. If it had been leaked then, instead of several years later, that probably could have prevented the British participation. Although Bush was so determined to go in, he would probably have gone in alone even without the British. The same is true of a lot of the stuff that came out from Richard Clarke in his book, *Against All Enemies*. Or Mike Scheuer of the CIA who wrote a book under the name "Anonymous." Both are good books and definitely worth having even at this late date. But there is nothing in them that they could not have told back in 2001! Let alone in 2002. If they had put out documents that backed up what they later said in those books, I believe either one of them would have prevented this war. They probably would have gone to prison if they had put out those documents. But you can't tell somebody, "You should give your life. You should go to prison. You should do this." But I do tell people you should consider doing that when there are so many lives at stake. And I wish they had.

When Clarke was speaking before a congressional committee, someone asked him, "You told us a year ago that the president was doing a great job against terrorism. Now your book is saying he wasn't doing anything that needed to be done, that he was tremendously incompetent and wrongly directed. Which should we believe? How can we believe you now?" And so Clarke said, "Well, I'm not an official now. I'm not being told what to say. If I had told you then what I am saying in my book, I would have been fired before I got back to the office." That's probably true. But given the stakes, should that have been an absolute bar to telling the truth?

I don't begrudge him the money he got from the book. But I do wish that it occurred to him to put the book out before the war, rather than wait all that time. I'm not being invidious when I say that, because I behaved the same way in '64, '65. I had information in my safe in the Pentagon from the weeks I started in August of 1964. I had information that we were being lied into a war. Although I was not against the war at that point, I was very much against the way I saw it was going to be prosecuted by heavy bombing. From the very beginning, I was against the bombing of the north. Again, I didn't object as I might have, because the president was facing a candidate, Goldwater, who in all sincerity was calling on us to enlarge the war. So I thought it was important that Johnson beat him, and it wouldn't have occurred to me to undercut the president at that time by exposing him as a liar. That's the way I felt.

But I don't admire my actions in retrospect. My conscience and prudence about my career told me to keep my mouth shut. But I was wrong. What I am saying is that conscience is so much socially constructed that even your own conscience should be looked at skeptically in situations of life and death. If you find you've been wrong, change the decision you made there. Change direction.

As I get older, I realize that people act according to their conscience most of the time. And it isn't always the right way to act. One's conscience is very much shaped by society. Very often people put obedience at the height of their conscience and values. Obeying the president as a matter of conscience. Keeping a promise, even when that promise turns out to involve you in participating in great social evils and war. Promises to keep secrets—which of course are made many times in the government, and which I ultimately broke.

I have done a lot of lecturing—for thirty years—but for a long time, I didn't speak about whistle-blowing specifically because it seemed as though I was blowing my own horn. I was being defensive about what I did, or in effect, saying, "Do what I did." Most people in my audience were not in a position to be a whistle-blower ready to go to jail. But then I realized it is one of the most important actions a person can be called on to make. I now like to complicate the lives of people who hear me speak by encouraging them that they should not regard promises or expectations of obedience or silence as absolutely obligatory. The meaning of whistle-blowing is to warn people. Policemen were equipped with whistles. If there was a wrongdoer in the neighborhood, the policeman would shout, "Help me get him! Stop this man! Don't let him get away! Watch out! You're in danger!"

The thing that keeps people in line is very much like what they used to say to us in the Marine Corps: "You volunteered. You stepped over the line. Now you have to stay. That is the price of signing up in the Marines." I did observe combat enough. I was with the State Department in Vietnam using my Marine training. I walked with troops under fire in combat. And you see great courage all around you. Routinely. And that's taken for granted. A very small percentage of people get medals for it. Civilians somehow seem to think it is almost not right for them to risk their careers. Or to risk their family's livelihood and security.

There have been a couple of whistle-blowers in the tobacco industry. I admire them without having met them. One, Merrill Williams, was a consultant with Brown and Williamson Tobacco Corporation. He copied 4,000 pages of Brown and Williamson documents that showed that company officers were all lying when they said they had no reason to believe that their product was carcinogenic or addictive or that they were selling it to minors. It was very clear that they knew perfectly well. He copied those documents and gave them to the *New York Times*. He did exactly what I did. And he may have saved an immense number of lives—more than one can save in a war. Four hundred fifty thousand Americans die each year directly from tobacco. And another 50,000 die from the indirect effects of secondary smoke. Five hundred thousand. Which is more than all Americans who have died in wars except for the Civil War. If you add up all the other wars together—Vietnam, World War I, World War II, the Revolutionary War, the War of 1812—it still doesn't add up to 500,000.

But the main question that occurs to me is what about all the other people in the tobacco industry who have known that and keep silent? Who go along with this holocaust? Or the pharmaceutical industry? Look at what we are hearing about Vioxx. Merck knew about the dangers. They had experiments and hid those results. They buried the results when they were bad.

To a large extent that silence is dictated by conscience. It's wrongful silence. But people say, "I signed an agreement." Merrill Williams had signed a nondisclosure agreement with Brown and Williamson. They tried to sue him, to enjoin him from putting anything out. In his case, he had given information to some people who put it on the Internet and made it possible to get it out. Something I could not do thirty years ago.

But people really feel they are doing the right thing when they keep their mouths shut even when they see these things going on. They think that it would be bad for their company, or the president, if they exposed any of that. They are *not* lying with a guilty conscience to protect these people. They are doing it because they feel it is the right thing to do. So conscience isn't a totally reliable guide either. Where do you turn then? For example, Bush said, "God told me to strike the Taliban. And I did. God told me to attack Iraq and I did." My opinion on that is, "That wasn't God. It was a wrong connection." When you hear the voice of God telling you to do something—in Bush's case, an unprovoked attack on another country—get a second opinion. Look skeptically. Paradoxical as it may seem, even your conscience is not the last word, especially when it tells you to be obedient to leadership that is leading you astray or to keep their secrets.

Frankly, we've reached the point where it would be very hard to change under this current administration, though we need to get Bush out of office before 2008. That is too long. Impeachment is well deserved but not possible under a Republican Congress. I was not exactly surprised by the government response to Hurricane Katrina. Its performance shows the same priorities that underlie Bush's policies start to finish—which include a great disdain for the poor of the world. He initially referred to people in the Gulf coast region as "people in this part of the world" as if he were speaking of a Third World country. He didn't seem to feel any identity with them, even if they lived in his own country. In his presidential campaign, John Edwards spoke of two Americas. He made a good point that there's this general feeling that the poor deserve what they get. After all, as one of Bush's officials pointed out, these people had chosen to stay. Apparently, 50,000 people didn't have cars in New Orleans, which is a fraction of the people who didn't have health or flood insurance.

Clearly, the country as a whole goes pretty much along with the theory "what's good for the U.S. is good for the world." Not just Bush. He is really an extremist for "what's good for the rich is good for the country." It's the whole market theory. Whatever inequality results from the operation of the market is the result of free contracts between equals. The inequality is necessary for development because it concentrates assets in the hands of some who then invest it wisely and the economy as a whole develops and grows so that we all eventually benefit not only from the wealth of the rich but from increasing the proportionate wealth of the rich, in effect, forsaking the rest of the population. That's the theory. Of course, Reagan enshrined this theory in direct opposition to the New Deal attitude which involved a greater role for government.

Anyway, this is just my own reflection as a former economist as to what economics has been up to for a long time and, really, since its birth in the nineteenth century, while Adam Smith goes back to the late eighteenth century. It has evolved into an ideology opposing government regulation and opposing the welfare state to a large extent. It benefits the people who start richer and stronger. And you know? It increases their own advantage. Bush also believes that what is good for the rich is good for *everyone*. It's good for the Third World.

It's good for the Empire of Free Trade. But it really isn't that good. It takes a long time to have an effect. Well, he doesn't care that much. So he acts out this unconcern which is sustained by the ideology.

Lately, I have been doing a lot of thinking about how wars are so much a part of human experience. As a species, we are given to mass violence and war and empire. How easy it is for our species to be fooled, and to fool each other. There are two primates which regularly kill their own species. While ants have wars actually, as for primates, it is chimpanzees and humans. If a group of chimpanzees catches a single, isolated male of a different tribe in its territory, it will kill him by beating him. Everyone beats him. Or it will even raid into a neighboring territory. Apparently, its evolutionary function is by reducing the number of males in a neighboring tribe, it restricts the feeding area of the neighboring tribe and enlarges its own. What about the other 4 percent genetic inheritance that we don't share with the chimpanzees? There's our speech and walking upright. Specifically we are the only animals that use weapons. Tools to kill with, thanks to our opposed thumb. We are the only ones that throw rocks. Chimps do a little throwing, but not accurate or strong enough to kill.

We are the only animals that kill at a distance beyond our own arm length. And to kill, we need weapons. Not 100 percent of the time, as chimpanzees show. But we can kill at a distance. Our ability to be concerned about the harmful effects of our actions on other humans especially falls off very quickly with physical and social distance and visibility. With the rock and spear and club and knife, we are still pretty close in. With the bow and arrow you definitely get a lot of distance. When you are talking about the longbow, you are killing people you can barely see. That's the start, of course. With bombing and missiles, you're harming people you don't see—and that is very easy for humans.

I'm not aware of any bomb crews in the Second World War having a problem with bombing through clouds when they got to radar bombing. In fact, the people who had the most problems were those flying low over Tokyo. They could see the fires. The updraft from the smell of burning human flesh below hit their nostrils and made them throw up. It smells like roast pork.

Unlike other animals, we have the capability of foreseeing long-term consequences, and even being concerned about them. We have the ability to act on them, and God knows, we have a unique ability to cause long-term consequences. The chimpanzees don't do that, let alone any other primate. They don't threaten themselves and they don't threaten other species the way we do. And so, we have this ability to cause harm in the long run and at a distance, and this ability—if we used it—to foresee that harm. Yet we don't worry that much about the long run or distant victims. So if the victims in wartime are foreigners, we talk about collateral damage as if we were not sure what would happen. That it's just an accident.

And here, I think, other things come into play for people in power. The first is their tendency not to look beyond the next election or to look beyond to the long run. Another thing is their willingness and determination to keep their jobs. Men in power are willing to gamble with any number of human lives in order to keep power. There is virtually no limit to the number of people they will risk killing in the future in order to keep their jobs. There is no real limit to it.

When I say there is no limit, I am ultimately referring to nuclear war. The willingness to contemplate the use of nuclear weapons is the willingness to contemplate something that goes beyond what any earlier humans or any earlier species had any reason to contemplate. There would have been a genuinely inadvertent and unforeseen effect if the U.S. government had carried out its plan for general nuclear war while I was in the government, say, during the Cuban Missile Crisis. There would have been nuclear winter. Bombs would have hit every city in Russia and China. They would have caused so much smoke to rise that all highly complex life on Earth would have been wiped out.

Well, I hope to live another ten to twenty years—I could die anytime—but my father lived to be ninety-six, and I'll be very surprised if there are not some more Hiroshimas during that time. Really surprised. In fact, I would say within ten years. The promise made to the dead of Hiroshima—"Let all the souls here rest in peace, for we shall not repeat the evil"—is not going to be kept. At this moment, I think that it will probably be a terrorist weapon. Katrina is a pretty good taste for what will happen when we lose a city. Of course, the death rate will be much bigger.

Let's say a small terrorist weapon goes off, and because Bush has done his best to cut funds for safeguarding Russian nuclear materials, that action is exactly comparable in its irresponsibility to flood control in New Orleans although the effects will be much greater. After all, if a hole occurs in that dike around Russian nuclear materials, there's really no limit to what can come out of it in the way of plutonium and uranium. Which takes us back to the market theory. If terrorist organizations can't use Saudi money and drug money to buy a Russian nuclear warhead, then Adam Smith's theory of markets can be almost discarded. If you can't buy warheads that are guarded by people who are raising vegetables in their back gardens for the nourishment of their families, then the notion that everything has a price can be decisively refuted. I think they are going to get that material. And who knows how long it will be before Pakistan or North Korea will sell full warheads?

Practically speaking, can it be said that this country is likely to prevent these things? No. That can be said very quickly. Is it impossible that we will? No. Nothing's impossible. Can other countries prevent proliferation? Can they hold the tide back entirely? You see, I am plagued with the kind of knowledge that almost nobody has. I've read some secret documents. Almost nobody else has actually seen these actual plans and the calculations that go with them. When I say that our plans called for killing 500 to 600 million people, nobody knows that. Nobody has seen such calculations. But I held that piece of paper in my hand. They all called for simultaneous attacks on China and Russia. So take the notion of attacking North Korea, which I am sure the current administration is still entertaining, though they may have rejected it for the moment. It quickly involves possible nuclear weapons. Here's my guess. If they decide for whatever reason to attack North Korea, it will be proposed to the president and he could well accept it that he must use airburst tactical weapons in rather large numbers against their artillery that threatens Seoul, that nothing else will prevent the embedded artillery pieces in their concrete emplacements from coming out. They are arranged so that they can pop out and fire. To destroy them, you need nuclear weapons. And if you can't get rid of that artillery, you can't attack—because you will lose Seoul. Now could the president take that gamble? And perhaps lose Seoul? Well, yes. That's what humans do, in power, under various circumstances. And we have made gambles like that in the past.

North Korea is one case. What if Saddam had WMDs? I am sure the White House did believe he had them. And what if he'd used them? There would have been a good chance we would've replied with nuclear weapons. Not against Baghdad probably. Unless it was the Israelis replying. But against their supposed underground sites. Of which, we found that they didn't have any. But we believed we knew where they were and that they were underground and we needed nuclear weapons to attack them. A former CIA agent, Philip Giraldi, has said that there are plans to hit underground sites for nuclear materials in Iran with our tactical nuclear weapons. Under what event? The next 9/11? Well, our response will be, among other things, to attack Iran even if it wasn't responsible just as our response after 9/11 was to attack Iraq, which had nothing to do with 9/11. But that is where the White House wanted to attack.

India and Pakistan remain a serious threat, and it hasn't gone away although it goes up and down in terms of intensity. They have been close to using nuclear weapons several times. In 1992, CIA Director Robert Gates was sent over there to twist arms on both sides and say, "Don't do that. You must try to engineer a compromise. Pull back forces. We'll give you this and give you that." And so, American intervention may have had a very critical role. Pakistan is a terrible danger. Here we are worrying about North Korea and Iran. Or earlier, Iraq. None of those three represented an imminent, terrible danger compared to Pakistan with not only its confrontation with India but the possibility of nuclear materials getting into the hands of the old Taliban regime, since Pakistan's ISI intelligence service did after all create the Taliban. So they are totally sympathetic to the Taliban and, for that matter, to Osama bin Laden. If I were in the U.S. government, I surely would be anguished by the task of what to do if there's a coup in Pakistan. That's a genuinely hard problem. There's no good answer to that one.

Most of my civil disobedience arrests have been in connection with nuclear weapons demonstrations of various kinds. Except for the Pentagon Papers during the Vietnam War, my first act of civil disobedience was in 1976, just after the war. It was at the Pentagon at the end of the Continental Walk for Peace and Social Justice, which was really an anti-nuclear weapons walk across the country. I've been arrested at various nuclear test sites and laboratories. My oldest son was arrested with me at Rocky Flats outside Denver. That was very nice. To feel it's a family business, you know. It was very bonding. My younger son was arrested with me outside the U.S. Mission to the United Nations before we invaded Iraq.

I continue to do civil disobedience against the Iraq War. The latest was in Crawford, Texas, where Cindy Sheehan took her stand. I like to take part and encourage other people as well. Each person has the ability, though they may not know it, to encourage others to speak out or to take a stand or to go beyond what they've done before. So there is a kind of chain reaction here. That's essential.

Katrina reminds us that large dangers are not just hypothetical. They are not all in the distant future. They are not to be shunted aside simply because they are uncertain and we don't know exactly when they are going to happen. There is a great gap between what we are capable of and what we actually do to avert dangers and to help other people.

We are in a crisis in this country, and the world is in a crisis right now, in large part because of our country. It calls for fast change in many respects. To a large extent we as a people do share the responsibility, though we are not all equally responsible. But President Bush is very responsible. I would despair of changing Bush's behavior very much in itself. To think that our Democratic leadership right now would do an adequate job of dealing with these problems is absurd. Reid, Hillary, Lieberman, and Biden are all calling for more troops in

Iraq and a more muscular reaction to North Korea and Iran. That's predictable and outrageous, and we Democrats cannot allow that. It is up to us to get different leadership in there.

While I am going to continue working against the war in Iraq, it is not with the hope or belief that it will change quickly. But we do need to see how all the global issues go together. We need to look at the world as a whole, rather than disclaiming our miserable commitment to 0.7 percent of our GNP for developing countries. That's not acceptable. That's not tolerable. We need to address the issues of poverty, the issues of empire, the issues of nuclear weapons, the issues of health and of education—which, of course, means sex education and health education and AIDS education. It is not acceptable that we should be coercing countries like Uganda to turn away from the free distribution of condoms in order to pander to a crazy fundamentalist Christian sect here in America.

Now, is anything going to change right away? No. Actually it isn't. We're dealing with powerful institutions. But that's why we've got to be trying to change. And not just the Iraq War. I'm going to do whatever I can. My wife says, "You're not up to that." There's the lectures, meetings, and rallies. It's too much traveling. Jet lag is hard on me. I don't sleep well. But at this moment I have to do whatever I can—which virtually requires getting a Democratic majority in the House in 2006. There would have seemed no chance of that earlier. But look at Katrina and the indifference of the president's initial reactions. Think what Chernobyl did to Gorbachev's policies. I believe it had a very major effect. Now, Bush is no Gorbachev. Still, in '85, Gorbachev was going full blast in Afghanistan. He was trying to win. He was not pulling back. He changed a lot of policies after Chernobyl, including his attitude toward nuclear energy and weapons and the war in Afghanistan and the need to change budget priorities. So Katrina may be our Chernobyl when it comes to getting a Democratic House or Senate and getting Democrats to act like an opposition.

ACKNOWLEDGMENTS

The 2004 presidential election was thankfully over. I woke up late the next morning with a political hangover. I felt exhausted by all the tumult, innuendo, and mudslinging that left the country even more divided than it was four years earlier. I sensed the initial stirrings of post-partisan depression. Twenty-four hours after Ohio guaranteed that Bush would remain in the White House, I received an e-mail from Lyons Press executive editor Tom McCarthy: "Don't have a title yet, but how about an oral history of what it was like to live under an increasingly restrictive U.S. government, for example, the McCarthy Era in the '50s? You could speak to blacklisted people, people who were thrown in jail for political reasons, atheists who were chastised and challenged, politicians who were ostracized, etc. We use it as a cautionary tale, lessons learned for people to use over the next four years." McCarthy (no relation to *that* Wisconsin senator) had been my editor for *Embedded: The Media at War in Iraq*. The guy moves fast. His suggestion energized me, and I e-mailed back that I was interested. By the following week, we had cobbled together a game plan. But about a month into the project, I decided to shift the book's focus and concentrate on today's political climate.

Timothy Carlson helped me in innumerable ways with the book's structure and content. He provided wise counsel and offered unflagging support during all stages of the yearlong project. I owe him big time; in this life, and perhaps in the next. Marty Higgins performed yeoman's work as a whip-smart reader and wonderful raconteur; and a special thanks to Laura Higgins. Kristie Nova has always been there in the clutch; her good cheer and brio brightened my days and nights in front of my iMac. Long-time dear friends David Farber, Mitch Thrower, Mike Sitrin, and Kat Guevara assisted by being there. I am grateful for their place in my life. John d'Arbeloff has been a steady presence. John Duke, for well, being a James Carville-like rascal. And my kind of adventurers: Scott Tinley, Ian Adamson, and Roman Urbina.

Tracking down many of the interview subjects for *Patriots Act* involved some sleuthing, lots of Googling, and the generous assistance from these helpful individuals: Beth Daley, director of communication of the nonprofit Project on Government Oversight (POGO), which investigates and exposes corruption in order to achieve a more accountable federal government. I highly recommend POGO's Report on Homeland and National Security Whistleblower Protections (www.pogo.org/p/government/go-050402-whistleblower.html); Sibel Edmonds; Barton Gellman; Laura Blumenfeld; Stephen Leeds; Rita Zawaideh; Bernice Funk; Max Bailey/Farber; Irv Arthur; Terry Barr; Andrew Schneider; and Scott Gold.

And thanks to everyone at The Lyons Press for their steadfast belief in this book. Production editor Jessie Shiers helped make *my* train run on time. For transcription of interview tapes, Diane Micheli was superb.

Finally, as an oral history, *Patriots Act* represents a collaboration between listener and talker. The format required me to depend on the kindness of strangers who graciously gave me their time. I would like to offer my gratitude once again for their participation.

INDEX